Socratic Questioning for Therapists and Counselors

This book presents a framework for the use of Socratic strategies in psychotherapy and counseling.

The framework has been fine-tuned in multiple large-scale cognitive behavior therapy (CBT) training initiatives and is presented and demonstrated with applied case examples. The text is rich with case examples, tips, tricks, strategies, and methods for dealing with the most entrenched of beliefs. The authors draw from diverse therapies and theoretical orientation to present a framework that is flexible and broadly applicable. The book also contains extensive guidance on troubleshooting the Socratic process. Readers will learn how to apply this framework to specialty populations such as patients with borderline personality disorder who are receiving dialectical behavior therapy. Additional chapters contain explicit guidance on how to layer intervention to bring about change in core belief and schema.

This book is a must read for therapists in training, early career professionals, supervisors, trainers, and any clinician looking to refine and enhance their ability to use Socratic strategies to bring about lasting change.

Scott H. Waltman, PsyD, ABPP, is a clinician and an international CBT trainer specializing in case-conceptualization-driven approaches to psychotherapy.

R. Trent Codd, III, EdS, is a clinician and trainer.

Lynn M. McFarr, PhD, is President of the Academy of Cognitive and Behavioral Therapies, a fellow of the Association of Behavioral and Cognitive Therapies, and President-Elect of the International Association for Cognitive Therapy.

Bret A. Moore, PsyD, ABPP, is a prescribing psychologist and the author and editor of 22 books in the area of psychological trauma, military psychology, and psychopharmacology.

Clinical Topics in Psychology and Psychiatry

Much of the available information relevant to mental health clinicians is buried in large and disjointed academic textbooks and expensive and obscure scientific journals. Consequently, it can be challenging for the clinician and student to access the most useful information related to practice. **Clinical Topics in Psychology and Psychiatry** includes authored and edited books that identify and distill the most relevant information for practitioners and presents the material in an easily accessible format that appeals to the psychology and psychiatry student, intern or resident, early career psychologist or psychiatrist, and the busy clinician.

Series Editor: Bret A. Moore, PsyD, Boulder Crest Retreat, Virginia, USA

Treating Disruptive Disorders
A Guide to Psychological, Pharmacological, and Combined Therapies
Edited by George M. Kapalka

Women's Mental Health Across the Lifespan
Challenges, Vulnerabilities, and Strengths
Edited by Kathleen A. Kendall-Tackett and Lesia M. Ruglass

Practical Psychopharmacology
Basic to Advanced Principles
Thomas L. Schwartz

Integrating Psychological and Pharmacological Treatments for Addictive Disorders
An Evidence-Based Guide
Edited by James Mackillop, George A. Kenna, Lorenzo Leggio, and Lara Ray

Neurodevelopmental Disorders in Children and Adolescents
A Guide to Evaluation and Treatment
Christopher J. Nicholls

Cognitive Behavioral Therapy for Beginners
An Experiential Learning Approach
Amy Wenzel

Handbook of Psychosocial Interventions for Chronic Pain
An Evidence-Based Guide
Edited by Andrea Kohn Maikovich-Fong

Socratic Questioning for Therapists and Counselors
Learn How to Think and Intervene Like a Cognitive Behavior Therapist
Scott H. Waltman, R. Trent Codd, III, Lynn M. McFarr, and Bret A. Moore

For more information about this series, please visit: www.routledge.com/Clinical-Topics-in-Psychology-and-Psychiatry/book-series/TFSE00310

Socratic Questioning for Therapists and Counselors

Learn How to Think and Intervene Like a Cognitive Behavior Therapist

Scott H. Waltman, R. Trent Codd, III,
Lynn M. McFarr, and Bret A. Moore

Routledge
Taylor & Francis Group
NEW YORK AND LONDON

First published 2021
by Routledge
52 Vanderbilt Avenue, New York, NY 10017

and by Routledge
2 Park Square, Milton Park, Abingdon, Oxon, OX14 4RN

Routledge is an imprint of the Taylor & Francis Group, an informa business

Library of Congress Cataloging-in-Publication Data
A catalog record for this title has been requested

ISBN: 978-0-367-33527-4 (hbk)
ISBN: 978-0-367-33519-9 (pbk)
ISBN: 978-0-429-32039-2 (ebk)

Typeset in Baskerville
by Newgen Publishing UK

Contents

Figures, Tables, and Worksheets

Figures

Tables

Worksheets

Series Editor's Foreword

Socratic Questioning for Therapists and Counselors: Learn How to Think and Intervene Like a Cognitive Behavior Therapist is the latest volume in one of Routledge's most popular series, Clinical Topics in Psychology and Psychiatry (CTPP). The overarching goal of CTPP is to provide mental health practitioners with practical information on psychological and psychopharmacological topics. Each volume is comprehensive but easy to digest and integrate into day-to-day clinical practice. It is multidisciplinary, covering topics relevant to the fields of psychology and psychiatry, and appeals to the student, novice, and senior clinician. Books chosen for the series are authored or edited by national and international experts in their respective areas, and contributors are also highly respected clinicians. The current volume exemplifies the intent, scope, and aims of the CTPP series.

In *Socratic Questioning for Therapists and Counselors,* Scott H. Waltman, R. Trent Codd, Lynn McFarr, and Bret A. Moore provide a superb review of one of the most important aspects of cognitive-behavioral therapy—Socratic Questioning. Socratic Questioning, also referred to as guided discovery, has been noted to be one of the most difficult skills to learn for therapists new to the field of cognitive-behavioral therapy. Recognizing the importance of developing proficiency in this skill, and the challenges inherent in learning the technique, the authors of this volume teach a four-step model for mastering the art of Socratic Questioning. The model includes: (1) focusing on key content; (2) developing a phenomenological understanding of the cognition; (3) fostering a collaborative curiosity; and (4) creating a summary and synthesis. Throughout the book the authors illustrate how this four-step model applies to a variety of conditions, treatment approaches, and clinician styles. For example, the content is delivered in a way that will be appealing to general practitioners, eclectic therapists, and so-called "third-wave" clinicians. The material is presented in a straightforward, easy-to-understand manner. The authors do a nice job of minimizing psychological jargon, and when specific terms are referenced that may be familiar to seasoned therapists, but not new or early career practitioners, the terms are expertly explained.

I am convinced that *Socratic Questioning for Therapists and Counselors* will become one of the lead textbooks in training clinicians in the effective application of Socratic Questioning, but more broadly, in training clinicians to become expert therapists. Moreover, it will help already practicing clinicians hone their skills and become more effective and efficient therapists. I anticipate that *Socratic Questioning for Therapists and Counselors* will become a required reading in graduate psychotherapy training programs of all sizes, shapes, and theoretical orientations.

Bret A. Moore, PsyD, ABPP
Series Editor
Clinical Topics in Psychology and Psychiatry

Foreword

When I first learned how to do therapy it was all psychodynamic. The therapist maintained distance and neutrality, refrained from giving direction, interpreted the motives and unconscious thoughts, and pointed to analogies and parallels with earlier childhood experiences. It all seemed rather deep, complicated, and—in fact—it put the power of interpretation in the hands of the therapist. And, most importantly, it didn't seem to work very well.

Beck's model broke me out of my pessimistic view of psychotherapy and appealed to my inquisitive, sometimes logical, and even disputatious mind. As I learned cognitive therapy from the founder, I realized that I needed to step back from a professorial and didactic stance to enter into a dialogue with the patient. Watching Beck, I realized that effective cognitive therapy was not like a prosecutor cross-examining a patient. It was a gentler, more inquiring, more respectful examination of the beliefs and experiences that the patient reported. Indeed, watching Beck do therapy often made you feel that he wasn't using the techniques that he wrote about. But, then, on careful reflection, you realized that he seamlessly wove into his dialogues examination of the consequences of thoughts, evidence of their validity, and alternative ways of looking at things. Beck wasn't "talking at" the patient. He was sharing perspectives and examining how the patient thought about things. He was trying to make sense of what often seems senseless.

I recalled courses in philosophy that I had taken in college. One in particular was taught by Paul Weiss, an eminent philosopher of that time. Weiss was a cantankerous, charismatic, and spontaneous lecturer who refused to lecture. He had about 100 Yale students waiting for each of his questions, which—when one of us was brave or impulsive enough to answer—led to another Weiss question. His was the true Socratic dialogue—question after question, pointing out the implications and contradictions of our answers. What Weiss did—and what Socrates did—was not teach us the facts. No, they did something much more important. They taught us how to think. That is what good therapy does.

So, is Socratic questioning didactic and power-driven? Or, is it a way of empowering, by teaching the patient how to think, how to reflect, and how to see another point of view? I suggest it is the empowerment of the patient who now is asked to reflect. The goal is to think about thinking, reflect about feeling, stand back and examine why your thoughts lead you to feel and act in ways that—on reflection—seem self-defeating. I suggest we call this "insight." In fact, the Socratic method is the tool to engage insight, develop it, and use it to construct new realities and opportunities.

The cognitive therapy approach owes a great deal to philosophy. Indeed, I think that some of the best preparation for the Socratic method is to read Plato's *Republic*.

And the best background for understanding Ellis is to read Epictetus. And, of course, as in most other things that matter in life, the best description of the cognitive model is to be found in Shakespeare (*Hamlet* Act 2, Scene 2) where our despondent, ambivalent, self-reflective Hamlet observes:

> Why, then, 'tis none to you, for there is nothing either good or bad, but thinking makes it so. To me it is a prison. Well, then it isn't one to you, since nothing is really good or bad in itself—it's all what a person thinks about it. And to me, Denmark is a prison.

But how do we escape the prison that our thoughts may serve as confining barriers? How do we break free?

Therapists often like to divide themselves into camps—much as religious acolytes who believe that they hoard the truth. But this book, written by four sophisticated, thoughtful psychologists, will help liberate those readers whose minds seek to open up to new ways of thinking, new curiosities, and new challenges.

Indeed, this book is a tour de force. It is an intellectual jaunt across the landscape of a range of cognitive behavioral therapies, breaking new ground, and climbing new heights. When I first began thinking of reading this book, my first thought was "Is there anything new under the sun?" in understanding Socratic dialogues? And, the answer, is "Yes!" The answers are here, in this book.

This is a book that anyone interested in serious reflection about psychological inquiry in psychotherapy should read. Yes, not only should they read this book, but they should reflect on it. Even our Third Wave approaches have Socratic elements, even behavioral approaches ask us to think and observe and extract ideas, and even in prescribing medications we need to consider how the patient is thinking about it.

We don't just hand patients a solution. We don't say to the patient suffering from anorexia, "Here's a bagel. Eat it." We need to make sense of where the patient is coming from, how resistance, non-compliance, even suicidal gestures make sense. And we need to help them reflect on their thinking, emotions, and behavior. As Socrates implied in his inquiry, the answer lies within. It is there to be elicited and elucidated. Indeed, the Socratic method reflects the Latin derivation of the word "education" which is "to lead out." The goal is to lead the suffering out of their habits of thinking and acting. It is to make clear what was automatic and often self-defeating and to make clear that there are different ways of thinking, feeling, and acting. Similar to the flexibility concept in ACT, this book reveals the need for flexibility on the part of both patients and therapists. By helping patients think in new ways, and by demonstrating that questioning one's ideas one can access new tools, the examples in this thoughtful book will help therapists from any school of CBT find new ways to help patients become their own therapists. I found this book encouraging, given the past turf-wars of the various waves that seemed to drown us at times.

There is a lot of wisdom to be gained in reading this book. It is there if you are curious enough to find it.

Robert L. Leahy, PhD
New York City, NY
Director, American Institute for Cognitive Therapy
Past-President, Association for Behavioral and Cognitive Therapies
Past-President, International Association for Cognitive Psychotherapy

Past-President, Academy of Cognitive Therapy
Associate Editor, International Journal of Cognitive Therapy
Honorary Life-time President, New York City Cognitive Behavioral Therapy Association
Clinical Professor of Psychology, Department of Psychiatry, Weill-Cornell University Medical College, New York Presbyterian Hospital

About the Authors

Scott H. Waltman, PsyD, ABPP, is a clinician, international trainer, and practice-based researcher. His interests include evidence-based psychotherapy practice, training, and implementation in systems that provide care to underserved populations. He is certified as a qualified cognitive therapist and trainer/consultant by the Academy of Cognitive & Behavioral Therapies. He also is board certified in behavioral and cognitive psychology from the American Board of Professional Psychology. More recently, Dr Waltman, worked as a CBT trainer for one of Dr Aaron Beck's CBT implementation teams in the Philadelphia public mental health system. Currently, he works as a clinical psychologist in private practice and a managed care system, where he is a frontline clinician and practice-based researcher. Clinically, Dr Waltman strives to flexibly and compassionately apply cognitive and behavioral interventions to help people overcome the barriers in their lives, to facilitate building meaningful lives that are guided by passion and values.

R. Trent Codd, III, EdS is vice president of clinical operations in North Carolina for Refresh Mental Health. In addition to delivering clinical services, he is active in training and supervision, including delivering training in the largest United States-based training initiative. He is a diplomate, fellow, and certified trainer and consultant of the Academy of Cognitive & Behavioral Therapies, and a former Academy of Cognitive Therapy board member at large.

Lynn M. McFarr, PhD, is a professor of health sciences for the UCLA David Geffen School of Medicine at Harbor-UCLA Medical Center and the founder and executive director of CBT California. She is the president of the Academy of Cognitive & Behavioral Therapies, a fellow of the Association of Behavioral and Cognitive Therapies, and the president-elect of The International Association for Cognitive Therapy. Dr McFarr serves as the practice lead for CBT and DBT for the Los Angeles County Department of Mental Health where she initiated the Los Angeles County Roll Out of CBT (LACROCBT) training over 1,500 front-line clinicians to competency in CBT. Dr McFarr was the senior editor of *Cognitive Therapy* for eight years and founded the first DBT dedicated publication DBT Bulletin in 2018. Dr McFarr conducts research and publishes on all aspects of training, supervision, dissemination and implementation of CBT and DBT. She is a member of the Dialectical Behavior Therapy Strategic Planning Meeting, a consortium of international DBT researchers, and served as program chair for the International Society for the Improvement and Teaching of Dialectical Behavior Therapy (ISITDBT) for 2014–2015.

Bret A. Moore, PsyD, ABPP, is a prescribing psychologist and board-certified clinical psychologist in San Antonio, Texas. He is vice chair of Boulder Crest Institute and a former active duty Army psychologist and two-tour veteran of Iraq. He is the author and editor of 22 books and dozens of book chapters and scientific articles in the area of psychological trauma, military psychology, and psychopharmacology.

Chapter 1

Introduction

Why Use Socratic Questioning?

Scott H. Waltman

❖ CONTENTS

The notion that corrective learning is essential to psychological healing and growth stems back to the origins of psychotherapy (Alexander & French, 1946; Yalom, 1995), this phenomenon is commonly called the corrective emotional experience (Alexander & French, 1946; Yalom, 1995). From an integrative perspective, the nonbiological elements of a psychiatric disorder are often rooted in a pathogenic underlying belief (see Silberschatz, 2013; Weiss, 1993), and bringing about a change to that belief can alleviate suffering, leading to healthy changes in affect, thinking, and behavior. There are different routes to changing underlying beliefs, such as: interpersonal learning in a group setting (Yalom, 1995), the therapist providing a corrective experience that is counter to early learning (Alexander & French, 1946; Silberschatz, 2013; Weiss, 1993), use of questioning and Socratic Dialogue to help a client see things from a different perspective (Padesky, 1993), or using Socratic questioning to channel inborn knowledge, perhaps from a collective unconscious or spiritual realm (Peoples & Drozdek, 2017). This book focuses on using Socratic questioning to directly bring about change and using Socratic strategies to enhance experiential/interpersonal methods of change.

Of course, Socrates was not a therapist and a pure application of the Socratic method with a perfect fidelity would not be therapeutic (Kazantzis, Fairburn, Padesky, Reinecke, & Teesson, 2014). This book presents a more empathic and collaborative approach to using Socratic strategies in a clinical context; Socratic strategies are integrated with good clinical practices in a manner that is consistent with the evidence-base of what constitutes effective therapy. *Collaborative empiricism* appropriately describes this process of using collaborative strategies to join with the client in applying scientific curiosity to their thought processes (Tee & Kazantzis, 2011). *Beckian Socratic Dialogue* or *Beckian Dialogue* are also accurate descriptions of the process (see Kazantzis et al., 2018).

A wealth of proven cognitive change strategies can be found in the cognitive therapies. The basic principle underlying cognitive therapy and the broader cognitive and behavioral therapies is that the way people think and make meaning of their lives and situations affects what they do and in turn how they feel (Beck, 1979; Waltman & Sokol, 2017). Therefore, bringing about change in a person's life is accomplished through bringing about changes in the way that they think. This process is called cognitive restructuring and it is typically more complicated than simply providing a reframe or alternate explanation. Socratic methods lead to a deeper, more lasting cognitive change and have been found to be predictive of symptom change (Braun, Strunk, Sasso, & Cooper, 2015)—this relationship remains significant even after controlling for the therapeutic alliance.

How Does a Therapist Become Good at Socratic Questioning?

If you are browsing or perusing this book, you likely have an interest in using Socratic strategies in clinical settings. You may be seeking to improve your own practice, or you may be seeking to find tools to help your students learn this valuable (yet complicated) skillset. This book is an excellent resource for either situation. Collectively, we have trained several thousand therapists in how to effectively utilize Socratic questioning in therapy to bring about lasting cognitive change that translates to emotional and behavioral changes. We have improved and refined our methods along the way, and this book represents a collection of the strategies we have found to be most effective in our own work and in the clinical practice of the clinicians we have trained.

So, how does a therapist become proficient at Socratic questioning? People learn well through experiential methods—learning through doing (Wenzel, 2019). In Chapter 3, "Getting Started," we will review Kolb's (1984) four phases of experiential learning: concrete experience, reflective observation, abstract conceptualization, and active experimentation. Like anything else, you must be able to persist at initially not being as good as you want to be, take risks, reflect, and get better.

It can be helpful to remember that Aaron Beck did not start out as Aaron Beck and Socrates did not start out as Socrates. You could be the next Aaron Beck or Socrates, or really your name could stand on its own, as you are the first you. As we learn from our predecessors, we learn about the value of curiosity and having an empirical mindset. Curiosity will take you quite far in this practice (Kazantzis et al., 2014), and cultivating a collaborative curiosity will help you and your client get further.

A common question from the therapists who are learning how to use Socratic strategies is what questions will be most effective for changing their clients' minds. We will get there, but the first questions on which to focus are identifying what to evaluate, what the emotional meaning of the cognitive target is, and how the client sees it from their perspective. The best questions are based on having a thorough understanding of the client and the situation. If you can come to see the situation from their point of view, you can work to expand that viewpoint together.

Pragmaticism is another key attribute to cultivate. I have very fond memories of talking about this practice with Aaron Beck, when I used to worked for him. He was remarkably pragmatic in his views of Socratic methods and cognitive modification. In discussing cases, he had an uncanny ability to quickly grasp the essence of the situation and form a hypothesis of what he thought was the key cognitive content on which to focus. Depending on the complexity of the case, great creativity was often required. Consistent with research findings of how experts conduct psychotherapy (Solomonov, Kuprian, Zilcha-Mano, Gorman, & Barber, 2016), Beck was apt to integrate strategies that may have seemed to the observer to be beyond the bounds of traditional cognitive therapy—such as interpersonal, emotion-focused, mindfulness-based, and insight-focused strategies. Whenever this was pointed out, he would often smile and say, "If it works, it's cognitive therapy."

Similarly, this book represents an inclusive approach to Socratic strategies, with a focus on what works. Traditional cognitive strategies are enhanced with elements pulled from emotion-focused therapy, acceptance and commitment therapy, dialectical behavior therapy, functional analytic psychotherapy, schema therapy, and the existential and humanistic psychotherapy traditions. Additionally, strategies are pulled from philosophical, epistemological, formal logic, mathematical logic, business management, and legal realms to build a robust framework for using Socratic strategies to bring about lasting cognitive change.

Promoting Change

People typically have good reasons for believing what they believe—they have come by it honestly. Our tasks as therapists are to align with our clients, foster a relationship of trust, slow down and clarify cognitive and behavioral processes, and then jointly work to bring about change together. This can be more easily said than done. Over the past several decades, a wealth of effective strategies has been developed to help bring about cognitive and behavioral change. This book serves to present a framework for using Socratic strategies to bring about cognitive and behavioral change.

So how does a therapist go about promoting cognitive change? The trouble is that you cannot just tell someone how to think about a situation. I am sure we have all been there, and we can all remember a time that we have been trying to help someone see things from a different perspective by sharing the perspective that we thought was more accurate—typically our own perspective. Only what happens is that we have the same conversation week after week, and although we give people what we think may be the right answer, it does not seem to stick. So, the goal of Socratic questioning is to help people learn to see situations in a different way on their own. The thought being that if they can come to these new conclusions on their own, that the new perspective will be more impactful in their lives. In cognitive therapy, there is also a focus on helping clients learn to come to these new conclusions on their own; so that they can continue this process without us. Ultimately, we want them to learn to be their own therapist (Beck, 2011).

Brief Example

Sometimes, a single well-placed question can do a world of good and other times it is a much lengthier process. Consider the example of a young therapist who sought his own therapy after experiencing emotional burnout secondary to his experience of doing trauma work with adolescents in the foster care system. This therapist had an early experience of parentification and felt immense sadness at not being able to save the youth with whom he was working. His therapist saw a parallel between his early experiences and his current difficulties and wondered what beliefs or attitudes had been developed early on that might be exacerbating his current situation. The therapist's therapist drew out a cognition related to having a responsibility for taking care of other people and used Socratic strategies to evaluate this cognition. A few targeted questions about why as a child his job had been to take care of the family and why the adult members of the family had not stepped up were enough to help the young therapist ask the questions he had never asked. This led to more reasonable attitudes about responsibility for others, decreased emotional burnout, and improved clinical effectiveness for the therapist.

Longer Example

Of course, it is not always that easy. Sometimes an exceptionally painful or unhelpful underlying belief can be like a great brick wall that was built brick-by-brick, that is, experience-by-experience; in these cases, disassembling the belief and building up a new belief can be an incremental and ongoing process. Consider the following example of a client with posttraumatic stress disorder (PTSD). This client grew up in an emotionally unpredictable environment. His mother had issues with alcohol and emotional dysregulation, and his father had been abusive. He reported that academically he did well in school, but he struggled socially. His life became significantly more difficult as a young teenager, when he decided to come out to his very religious family regarding his being gay. His father held some leadership role in the Christian church that they attended, and the client experienced several invalidations where several members of the congregation tried to preach and minister to him to "correct" him. These early efforts at a conversion therapy obviously did not change his sexual orientation, but they did cause him much distress and led to internalized heterosexism that he spent years working through. Soon after, his father became physically and emotionally abusive towards him, and the abuse went on for years.

He went on to get a degree in marketing and started a very successful company. He met a man with whom he fell in love and they were married. Approximately a year prior to my meeting with him, his partner experienced his first manic episode. During that time, his partner became increasingly paranoid and erratic; this culminated in his partner holding him captive and killing their beloved only child in front of him with a kitchen knife. His partner was later arrested and committed to a state-run psychiatric facility after being found not guilty by reason of insanity to charges related to the traumatic event. Undoubtedly, the killing of his daughter was extremely distressing to him, and he ultimately blamed himself for the occurrence. This horrific trauma was assimilated into his previous belief that the world was dangerous. He blamed himself for not being able to anticipate that this would happen, and for not being able to stop it.

He told himself that he knew that the world was unsafe and that he had been a fool for letting his guard down. Further, he saw this as a moral failure. He told himself that if he had been a better person, then he would have been able to stop this from happening; in other words, "My dad was right, and I really am bad."

The most distressing of his trauma-related beliefs were related to the notion that he should have been able to anticipate what happened and that he should have been able to stop it. Through the use of thought logs and Socratic questioning, we relentlessly worked on these beliefs. The notion that he should have been able to anticipate the trauma was relatively easy for him to re-evaluate. His guilt and anxiety came down slightly afterward. The belief that he should have been able to do something to save his daughter was much more insidious. Consistent with the recent emphasis in the literature on attentional focus (Beck & Haigh, 2014), we used visual aids to facilitate guided discovery. He reported that the most impactful intervention that we used was the white board to map out the house and what he thought he would do differently. As he explained his hypothetical alternative courses of action, we looked at what his partner would have done differently. So, as he second-guessed himself and presented what, after months of rumination, emotionally felt like it would have been the "right answer," we played through the revised scenarios to demonstrate that there had not been a realistic option that would have saved his daughter. He reported that this helped him to see that there was literally nothing he could have done in the situation and that in reality he was lucky to have escaped with his life. Following a dose of cognitive therapy, his symptoms decreased, he no longer met diagnostic criteria for PTSD, and his real-world functioning improved. This work of using Socratic strategies to bring about cognitive change can be challenging, but the potential rewards are great.

What to Expect in the Rest of the Book

The first few chapters of this book will focus on why Socratic strategies are needed and what you as a therapist can do in-session to create the necessary conditions where you will have an increased likelihood of being able to use Socratic strategies effectively in your sessions. Afterwards, a four-step framework for Beckian Socratic Dialogue is presented. Each step of the framework will have a devoted chapter and will be reviewed in detail and with ample case examples. Subsequent chapters will focus on advanced topics such as troubleshooting, specific cognitive and behavioral strategies, and working with core beliefs. Specialty topics on the frontier of practice, for example, using Socratic strategies with the contextual behavioral therapies, such as acceptance and commitment therapy and dialectical behavior therapy, are presented. Additionally, special considerations are given to chapters on Socratic strategies for prescribing clinicians and training strategies for supervisors and clinical trainers. This book is intended to be read in order, but you can also jump around depending on your needs and preferences.

References

Alexander, F., & French, T. M. (1946). *The corrective emotional experience. Psychoanalytic therapy: Principles and application.* New York: Ronald Press.

Beck, A. T. (1979). *Cognitive therapy and the emotional disorders.* New York: Meridian.

Beck, A. T., & Haigh, E. A. P. (2014). Advances in cognitive theory and therapy: The Generic Cognitive Model. *Annual Review of Clinical Psychology, 10,* 1–24. doi:10.1146/annurev-clinpsy-032813-153734

Beck, J. S. (2011). *Cognitive behavior therapy: Basics and beyond* (2nd ed.). New York: Guilford Press.

Braun, J. D., Strunk, D. R., Sasso, K. E., & Cooper, A. A. (2015). Therapist use of Socratic questioning predicts session-to-session symptom change in cognitive therapy for depression. *Behaviour Research and Therapy, 70*, 32–37.

Kazantzis, N., Beck, J. S., Clark, D. A., Dobson, K. S., Hofmann, S. G., Leahy, R. L., & Wong, C. W. (2018). Socratic dialogue and guided discovery in cognitive behavioral therapy: A modified Delphi panel. *International Journal of Cognitive Therapy, 11*(2), 140–157.

Kazantzis, N., Fairburn, C. G., Padesky, C. A., Reinecke, M., & Teesson, M. (2014). Unresolved issues regarding the research and practice of cognitive behavior therapy: The case of guided discovery using Socratic questioning. *Behaviour Change, 31*(01), 1–17. doi:10.1017/bec.2013.29

Kolb, D. A. (1984). *Experiential learning: Experience as the source of learning and development.* Englewood Cliffs, NJ: Prentice-Hall.

Padesky, C. A. (1993). Socratic questioning: Changing minds or guiding discovery. Paper presented at the A keynote address delivered at the European Congress of Behavioural and Cognitive Therapies, London. Retrieved from: http://padesky.com/newpad/wpcontent/uploads/2012/11/socquest.pdf

Peoples, K., & Drozdek, A. (2017). *Using the Socratic method in counseling: A guide to channeling inborn knowledge.* New York: Routledge.

Silberschatz, G. (2013). *Transformative relationships: The control mastery theory of psychotherapy.* New York: Routledge.

Solomonov, N., Kuprian, N., Zilcha-Mano, S., Gorman, B. S., & Barber, J. P. (2016). What do psychotherapy experts actually do in their sessions? An analysis of psychotherapy integration in prototypical demonstrations. *Journal of Psychotherapy Integration, 26*(2), 202–216.

Tee, J., & Kazantzis, N. (2011). Collaborative empiricism in cognitive therapy: A definition and theory for the relationship construct. *Clinical Psychology: Science and Practice, 18*(1), 47–61.

Waltman, S., & Sokol, L. (2017). The Generic Cognitive Model of cognitive behavioral therapy: A case conceptualization-driven approach. In S. Hofmann & G. Asmundson (Eds.), *The science of cognitive behavioral therapy* (pp. 3–18). London: Academic Press.

Weiss, J. (1993). *How psychotherapy works: Process and technique.* New York: Guilford Press.

Wenzel, A. (2019). *Cognitive behavioral therapy for beginners: An experiential learning approach.* New York: Routledge.

Yalom, I. D. (1995). *The theory and practice of group psychotherapy.* New York: Basic Books.

Chapter 2

Why Doesn't Corrective Learning Happen Automatically?

Scott H. Waltman

❖ CONTENTS

Pertinent to a discussion about using Socratic strategies to bring about cognitive change is a review of why this corrective learning does not always happen automatically. Why does a person with family members who love them, persist in the belief that they are unlovable? Why does a young professional, who started a new job that they worked hard to get, have thoughts of being an imposter or incompetent? Why does the over-achieving perfectionist, with a string of successes, have thoughts of being a failure? The answer is that our expectations tend to guide what we think, how we feel, what we do, and even how we perceive reality—everything is cognitively mediated (see Lorenzo-Luaces, German, & DeRubeis, 2015).

This principle was humorously demonstrated in popular media on a television show that featured a taste test between organically grown and non-organically grown fruit (Jillette et al., 2009). Participants were given two pieces of fruit and told which piece was organically grown. Consequently, the participants described the quality, taste, and texture of the two pieces of fruit to be substantially different. The host would then show them that the two pieces had been cut from the same whole piece of fruit; for example, a single banana, cut in half, and presented as being parts of two separate bananas. The participants were unable to explain why the two halves of the same fruit had tasted different to them, but they maintained that their sensory experiences had been distinct. There are a number of principles from social psychology that help explain these findings. This chapter will provide a quick review of relevant concepts from social psychology, an overview of the updated cognitive model, a description of cognitive case conceptualization, quick tips for clinicians, an extended cognitive case conceptualization example, and an in-session collaborative case conceptualization example.

Cognitive Biases from Social Psychology

These mental processes include: selective perception, confirmation bias, memory biases, and self-fulfilling prophecies (Plous, 1993). Selective perception is our tendency to see what we expect to see and to miss what we do not expect to see. This construct overlaps with the confirmation bias (Nickerson, 1998), where people (intentionally or unintentionally) selectively attend to evidence that confirms their expectations, provide inordinate weight to such evidence, and can even misconstrue the evidence to confirm their biases (Nickerson, 1998).

These cognitive processes are illustrated by a quotation from the influential book *Public Opinion* by Walter Lippman (2017): "For the most part we do not first see, and then define, we define first and then see." He went on to say: "[People] live in the same world, but they think and feel in different ones." A number of social psychology experiments have demonstrated this principle (Plous, 1993), and, to the objective party, it is also readily observable in the current geopolitical environment. If you reflect on the latest political controversy (whatever it might be), with confidence it can be suggested that there was markedly different coverage and interpretation of the situation. A person reading various media accounts might find themselves wondering if the reporters are covering the same event. It is hard to find common ground when cognitive biases lead to different consensus realities.

Other complicating factors include the unreliability of human memory. In the past, people have compared our memory to being like a computer, where a file is encoded, stored, and retrieved. This is an overly generous comparison for the human mind, as what is retrieved is often not what was initially stored (Plous, 1993). A newer model compares human memory to being more like a compost heap (Randall, 2007), where memories will layer, degrade, and intermingle. Though a perfect metaphor for human memory is still being sought, the finding that memories are not always reliable is well established (Foley, 2015; Plous, 1993). This is perhaps best demonstrated in the phenomenon of impossible memories, where people form memories based on events that could not have happened (Foley, 2015). Further, belief in false memories can persist even in the face of contradictory evidence (Foley, 2015).

Another social psychology concept that is important to review is something called a self-fulfilling prophecy. The idea is that expectations shape behavior, which in turn can shape the outcome, possibly causing the expectation to happen (Plous, 1993). This is well demonstrated by a seminal study where teachers were led to believe that a random sampling of their students were in fact gifted or had a higher level of potential than their peers. At an eight-month follow-up, those identified students had improved at a rate greater than their peers. This finding was explained by the teacher's expectations of the students leading to increased attention, praise, and encouragement for the randomly selected students (Rosenthal & Jacobson, 1968). Thus the "prophecy" was self-fulfilled, and we can see that our expectations impact not just how we perceive, but also what we do, and both of these can lead to a shaping of actual and perceived reality to confirm the pre-existing expectations. These social psychology findings are consistent with the cognitive behavioral model, also called the Generic Cognitive Model (Beck & Haigh, 2014; Waltman & Sokol, 2017).

The Generic Cognitive Model of CBT

The basic tenet of the Generic Cognitive Model is that the perception of a situation directly influences emotion, physiology, and behavior (Beck, 1963, 1964). This idea is not unique to cognitive behavior therapy (CBT), Ellis was quick to point out that the Stoic philosopher Epictetus wrote, "People are disturbed not by things, but by the views which they take of them" (Epictetus, 125, as cited in Ellis & Harper, 1961). This is supported by basic science and clinical outcomes research (see Lorenzo-Luaces, German, & DeRubeis, 2015).

The Generic Cognitive Model holds that situation-specific thoughts or automatic thoughts typically arise spontaneously, are often brief and fleeting, take the form of a thought or image, and are regarded as true without reflection or evaluation. These automatic thoughts stem from an underlying belief system and influence how we feel and what we do. While CBT therapists can directly target changing behaviors (Barlow et al., 2010; Meichenbaum & Goodman, 1971) and use emotion-focused strategies (Leahy, 2018), cognitive change strategies represent a wealth of clinical tools that can change belief systems and the corresponding beliefs and emotional responses (Waltman & Sokol, 2017). As CBT holds a robust tradition of research and scientific inquiry, the Generic Cognitive Model of CBT has been revised and refined over the years (Beck &

Haigh, 2014). An advance in the cognitive model is the inclusion of something called modes (Beck & Haigh, 2014). Modes can be understood to be the activation of schema (a pattern of thought) and the associated coping/compensatory strategies. Modal activation describes a person's current emotional-cognitive-behavioral state (Fassbinder, Schweiger, Martius, Brand-de Wilde, & Arntz, 2016).

The concept of modes was first introduced in the schema therapy literature to account for rapid changes in the presentation of clients with borderline personality disorder. Schema therapists noted that when these patients would get dysregulated, they would have extreme thinking patterns, high emotional activation, and engage in impulsive behaviors (see Fassbinder et al., 2016). Alternatively, when these people were regulated, their thinking would not be extreme, their emotions were not elevated, and their behavior was not impulsive. These different presentations represented different modal states (Fassbinder et al., 2016). As the Generic Cognitive Model has been revised over the years, other modes have been identified (e.g., depressive mode; Beck & Haigh, 2014). Clinically, this concept is quite useful when your client has large variability in their presentations. When a clinical presentation includes modes at relative extremes (e.g., over-control and under-control), the goal of treatment might be to foster a more balanced mode.

Another advance in the Generic Cognitive Model is the continuity of adaptive and maladaptive function (Beck & Haigh, 2014); that is to say, people do not have only negative or maladaptive core beliefs, but they also have positive and adaptive beliefs. Therefore, clinically we strive not only to target the beliefs that are associated with distress and dysfunction, but we also want to build up previously existing healthy beliefs. This practice is well demonstrated through strengths-based CBT, where there is both an assessment and targeting of the traditional treatment targets (i.e., maladaptive beliefs and behaviors) and a fostering of strengths and adaptive beliefs (Padesky & Mooney, 2012).

Conceptualizing a Belief

Core Beliefs

CBT is a learning theory, and core beliefs are the ideas we formulate about others, the world, and ourselves over the course of time, through our experiences and our perceptions of our experiences. These ideas can be positive and negative and typically are accepted as absolute truths regardless of their validity. Often negative core beliefs are overgeneralizations of partial truths, and sometimes they are a reflection of the complete opposite of the actual truth. While automatic thoughts reflect the view of a given situation, core beliefs are more global ideas that exist independently of any given situation.

Negative core beliefs about one's self often fall into two major themes, that is, competency or desirability (Dozois & Beck, 2008). A person may have beliefs in both domains or may more strongly endorse negative views about themselves in only one domain. Examples of core belief labels reflective of incompetence are as follows: I am incompetent; I am a failure; I am weak; I am not good enough; I am inferior; and I am dumb. Examples of core belief labels reflective of undesirability are as follows: I am undesirable; I am unattractive; I am unlovable; I am unlikable; I am bad; and I am worthless. It is possible to embrace one global negative belief about oneself or many. These core beliefs may always prevail, biasing every situation the person faces, or only rule when the person is facing a difficult or challenging situation or struggling with a psychological disorder such as depression or anxiety. The Generic Cognitive Model accounts for this, by holding that certain beliefs or schema may at times be inactive, but can be triggered or energized under certain stressors (Beck & Haigh, 2014); for example, the sudden end of a romantic relationship could activate previously dormant beliefs of being unlovable or defective.

Compensatory Strategies

Behaviors are another important component in the conceptualization. In keeping with the concept of a self-fulfilling prophecy (Rosenthal & Jacobson, 1968), behaviors that are associated with core beliefs can lead to outcomes that reinforce that belief. For example, consider a man with the belief that he is weak and vulnerable and an assumption that the world is a dangerous place. If he responds by being quick to detect a slight, quick to get angry, and quick to fight, he will likely receive aggression in return. This would only reinforce his assumptions. Compensatory strategies can either be belief consistent (i.e., acting as if the belief were true), over-compensatory (i.e., heavy-handed attempts to prove the belief wrong), or belief avoidant (i.e., attempting to avoid the belief by avoiding situations where the belief might be activated) (Young, 1999).

Rules and Assumptions

In between situation-specific automatic thoughts and more pervasive core beliefs are what are referred to as rules or assumptions. Rules are universal ideas that people believe about themselves, others, or the world, such as the following: things will never work out for me; everyone else is capable; or, the world is a dangerous place. Assumptions are conditional statements that link behavioral strategies with core beliefs. These are framed in an "if-behavior, then-outcome" format, and are typically a way of connecting what a person is afraid of happening and what they are doing to avoid that perceived injury.

- For example, a person with beliefs about incompetence might be wary of taking risks for fear that failing will prove they are incompetent. They likely would learn to avoid trying difficult things at which they might fail or quitting at the first sign of failure—because quitting is less painful than failing for these individuals. Such a person would likely develop the conditional assumption that, "If I try, then I'll fail; but, if I don't try, then I can't fail."
- Alternatively, a person with a similar core belief, but an overcompensating behavioral response, might have the idea that they must accomplish big things and take risks, as otherwise people will see them as incompetent. This person might develop the conditional assumption, "If I don't achieve, then people will see how

incompetent I am; but, if I try extra hard, and push as hard I can, then maybe I can keep people from noticing that I am completely incompetent."

Other examples of conditional assumptions include the following:

- "If I tell other people what I want, then I'll be vulnerable to injury; but, if I keep it to myself, then maybe I'll be OK"
- "If I let myself feel sad, then I'm weak; but, if I avoid my feelings, then I won't have to feel weak"
- "If I let people really get to know me, then they'll see how terrible I am and leave me; but, if I keep my relationships really superficial/ focus on taking care of other people then maybe no one will notice how bad I am"
- "If I say no, they won't like me; but, if I always acquiesce and say yes, then people will like me"

Conditional assumptions represent a strategic intervention point, as they demonstrate how the beliefs and behaviors fit together. Targeting both the belief and the corresponding behavior can be especially important when the behavior is an avoidance strategy. Take the example of the person who is afraid of failing and so they do not take risks or try difficult things. If you were to weigh the evidence of their perceived incompetence with them, there would not be many useful experiences from which to draw in order to demonstrate their competence. Similarly, take the example of the person who is afraid people will not like her if she declines their requests. If she never says "no," then there is a limited pool of experience from which to draw.

Cognitive Filters

The updated Generic Cognitive Model places an emphasis on the role of attentional processes and mental filters in maintaining a belief set (Beck & Haigh, 2014), though seminal texts on the topic often address this as well (Beck, 2011; Padesky, 1994). Judy Beck (2011) refers to this mental process as the information-processing model in which people selectively attend to negative information that confirms their core beliefs and either ignore or misconstrue positive information that would be disconfirming to their belief set. Others use the metaphor of a "mental crusher" that sits outside of our awareness and "crushes" or shapes discrepant experiences to be consistent with pre-existing beliefs (Butler, Fennell, & Hackmann, 2010). Consider the example of a man with a belief that he was a bad person, who at the start of the session shared about how terrible he felt for having had the veterinarian put down his dog earlier that day. For this man, that was further evidence of what a wretched man he was; however, there was much context that he was missing. In discussing the situation with him, the therapist learned that this dog had been a rescue dog and that this client had a penchant for taking in rescue dogs, typically focusing on dogs that no one else would take in. This dog had a degenerative neurological condition that made it violent and unpredictable. This man had exhausted all medical options and was no longer able to house the dog safely at his home. He contacted various dog rescues to see if anyone would take this dog and was unsuccessful. The decision to have the dog euthanized was his last option and one that the veterinarian strongly recommended. To the objective observer, this was not an example of the client being a completely bad person, so why did he think this situation was simply more evidence that he was bad? This is because he was selectively attending only to the elements of the story that were consistent with his previous belief, and he was twisting information to fit his assumption.

There is a popular euphemism about seeing the world through rose-colored glasses, meaning that one has an overly positive view of the situation. From the perspective of CBT, people view the world through a schematic lens that filters information in a way that confirms their biases (see Nickerson, 1998).

Forming and Using the CBT Conceptualization to Inform Treatment

A number of different methods to form case conceptualization have been developed. Judy Beck's Cognitive Conceptualization Diagram (CCD) is among the most popular (see Beck, 2011). Other commonly used methods include one developed by Persons (2012) that is similar to the CCD. Padesky and Mooney (2012) have modified the collaborative case conceptualization form to incorporate strength and resiliency factors, and Moorey (2010) developed a "vicious flower" conceptualization format that is used to draw out the cycle of thoughts, beliefs, behavior, and compounding factors involved in maintaining a client's difficulties. Notably, even the best case conceptualizations are hypotheses (informed guesses), and therapists are prone to all the same judgement and perceptual errors as everyone else (see Ruscio, 2007). Therefore, it is important to treat your case conceptualization as a working hypothesis where you are looking for confirmatory and disconfirmatory information to help refine your formulation over time.

Regardless of the specific format used to help construct a cognitive case conceptualization, there are a number of common elements which comprise the individual's current problematic situations, their corresponding thoughts, feelings, and behaviors, and the underlying beliefs that are driving these current thoughts, feelings, and behaviors. The CBT therapist employs a strategic approach and is most interested in what is maintaining these belief sets; therefore, a main objective of the case conceptualization is to draw out how the underlying beliefs are impacting current thoughts and behaviors and how current cognitive styles and behaviors strengthen and reaffirm strongly held core beliefs and underlying assumptions. For example, consider the assumption listed above, "If I try then I'll fail, but if I don't try then I can't fail." This type of assumption would likely correspond to core beliefs of incompetence and behavioral strategies of avoiding difficult tasks and bailing out at the first sign of failure. This type of pattern tends to get stronger and stronger over time. This individual likely feels shame and sadness when having thoughts about their inadequacy. "I'm such a failure." "I can't do anything right." "I have nothing to show for my life." Consequently, they do not take a lot of risks in their life—why try if you're sure you'll fail? Therefore, they have a low level of accomplishment in their life, which they construe as evidence

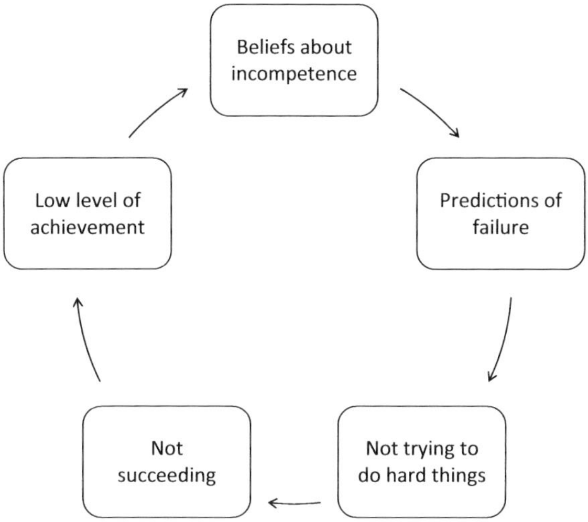

Figure 2.1 Compensatory Strategies often Prevent New Learning and Maintain a Belief Set

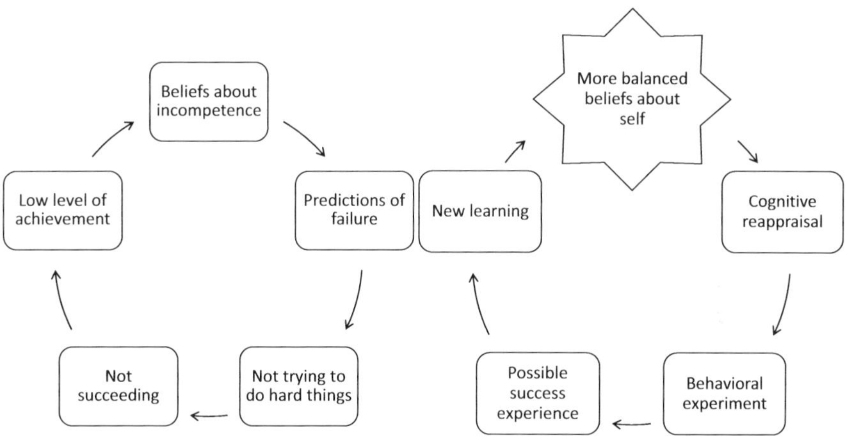

Figure 2.2 Changing Strategies to Promote New Learning

that they are incompetent. "Of course, I'm a failure; I have accomplished nothing with my life." This leads to more thoughts about their inadequacy and further behavioral avoidance.

Thus, it is a cycle and a cognitive therapist would seek to break up this pattern by using cognitive strategies and behavioral experiments. Correspondingly, there are a number of potential intervention targets and opportunities for Socratic strategies.

Sometimes the pattern is less obvious. Consider the high-achieving professional with a constant fear of failure. She has accomplished much in her personal and professional life and yet why is she plagued with thoughts and predictions of failure? It is because her information-processing style does not allow her to form more balanced beliefs about her competency or successfulness. While she was growing up, high expectations were placed upon her and she learned that even small mistakes could be met with criticism, which led to the development of a rigid assumption that "If I make a mistake, then others will see how incompetent I am, but if I work as hard as I can, harder than anyone else, maybe people won't notice that I'm incompetent and they'll keep me around for now." This thought process led to great productivity and accomplishments, none of which she was able to enjoy, as she was constantly worried about being found out as the failure that she was sure she was. This attentional bias led to her fixating on minute missteps, causing her to miss the big picture. An unsophisticated cognitive therapist may try to address her beliefs about incompetency by focusing on her accomplishments. A more nuanced approach would be to ask: "Why does she still have thoughts of being a failure given her success?" In other words, "Why hasn't this problem resolved on its own?" This is the key treatment target. In this case, the key cognitive structure to target is her all-or-nothing thinking related to how she defines success, and how human she is allowed to be before she becomes a failure.

Functional Belief Conceptualization Diagram

In the discussion above, we reviewed how a person's beliefs influence how they think and what they do, which, in turn, influence what happens, and how they perceive what happens. All these factors can create a feedback loop that ultimately strengthens the pre-existing belief. Drawing out this cycle can help the clinician understand how the belief is being maintained and identify strategic intervention points. If this cycle is completed collaboratively (and flexibly), it can also serve as in-session intervention that helps the client mentally take a step back in order to see the cycle on which they have been stuck and build motivation for doing something new. A number of high-quality case conceptualization diagrams and formats already exist (e.g., Beck, 2011; Moorey, 2010; Padesky & Mooney, 2012; Persons, 2012), all of which are recognized to be of high quality and to have high clinical utility. We present a new format that is informed by the extant diagrams and the literature reviewed above.

The specific purpose of the new case conceptualization diagram is to draw out the pattern that leads to the reinforcement of the pre-existing belief—what is maintaining the problem? This is a simplified format and not meant to be a replacement for more extensive conceptualization diagrams. The tradeoff is that the Simplified Functional Belief Conceptualization Diagram we present is one that can be used collaboratively in session. Historically, there have been cautions about using the alternate, more complicated, case conceptualization forms in session, as the client might feel that you are trying to fit them into a box (Beck, 2011); conversely, this new simplified form is a functional analysis of the belief and the impact of that belief. This makes for a smaller (and less overwhelming) task than trying to fit the totality of a person into a single form during the session. We also present an elaborated form to help the clinician think through a case outside of session.

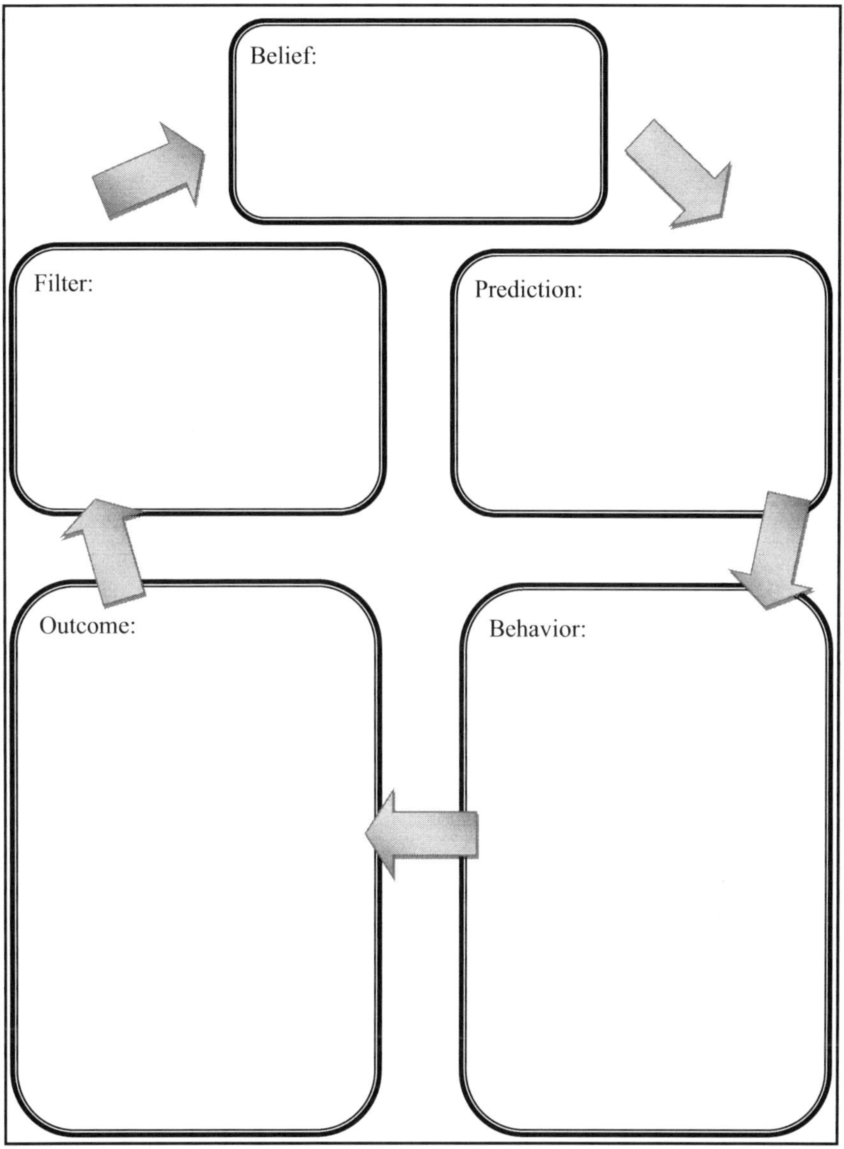

Worksheet 2.1 Simplified Functional Belief Conceptualization Diagram

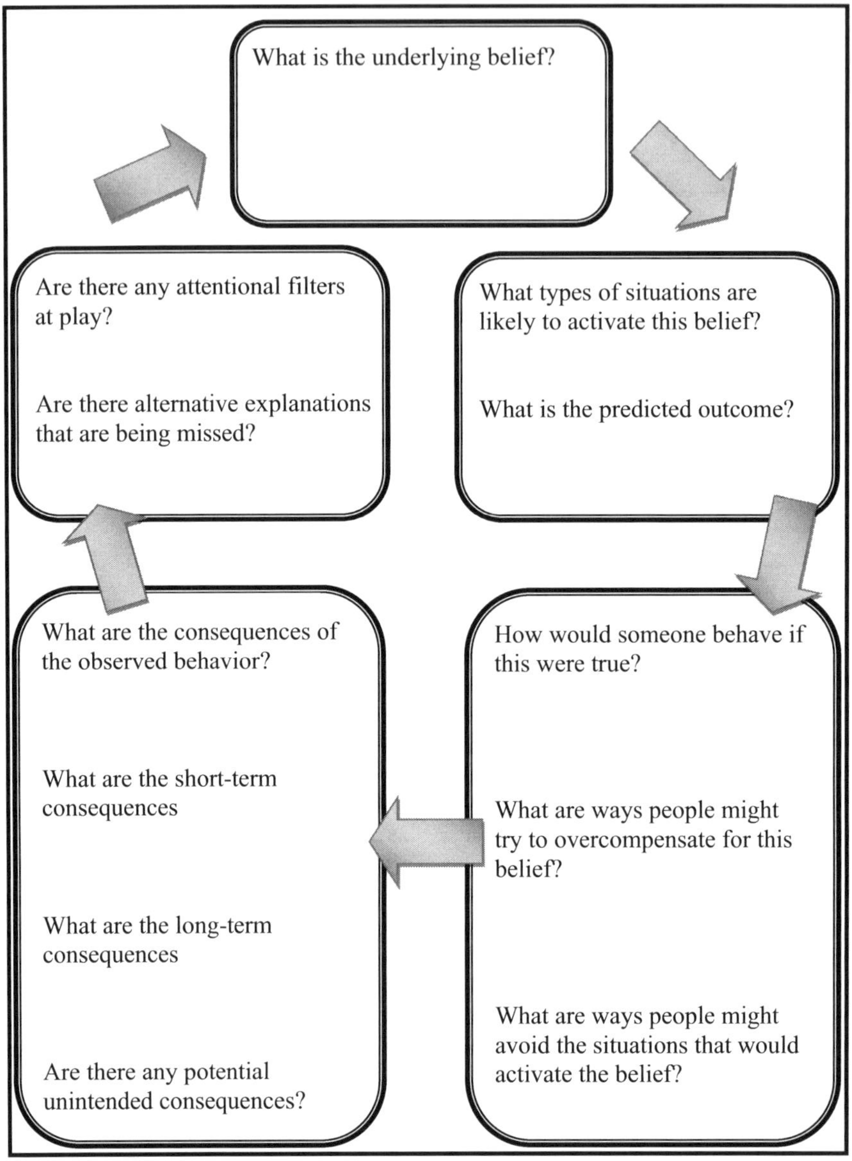

Worksheet 2.2 Elaborate Functional Belief Conceptualization Diagram

Tools and In-Session Strategies

There are a number of questions therapists can ask themselves to guide this process including:

- What is the underlying belief?
- What types of situations are likely to activate this belief?
- What is the predicted outcome? / If that belief was true what would the client predict would happen in these situations?
- How would someone behave is these predications were true?
- What are ways people might try to overcompensate for this belief?
- What are ways people might avoid the situations that would activate the belief?
- What are the consequences of the observed behavior?
- What are the short-term consequences?
- What are the long-term consequences?
- Are there any potential unintended consequences?
- Are there any attentional filters at play?
- Is there evidence of a confirmation bias, selective filter, or self-fulfilling prophecy?
- Are there alternate explanations that are being missed?
- Is there missing context to the evidence?
- Are there factors we have yet to identify?
- What factors are leading to the maintenance of this belief?
- How does this all fit together?
- Objectively, how can we map this out?

Here is an example of what this looks like in practice.

Case Example: Trisha

Trisha (pseudonym) was a 50-year-old, cisgender, heterosexual, Latina woman. She presented to therapy with complaints of symptoms of depression and anxiety. She had a history of attention-deficit/hyperactivity disorder (ADHD), had intermittently been in talk therapy, and had been "on-and-off" with her medication. Her chief concern was "I just cannot seem to get it together. I've been a mess since my father died about a decade ago, and I just don't know what's wrong with me." She reported that her upbringing had been unremarkable, saying she grew up without problems and having her life together. It was observed in session that she would apologize and appear embarrassed whenever displaying negative emotions, like the sadness she had about her father's passing. This led to a discussion about how emotions like sadness were handled when she was younger and she shared the view that no one was ever sad when she was younger. After some further curious questioning, she clarified, "growing up it was not OK to be not OK," highlighting some unspoken family rules about emotions.

Her current difficulties were typified by her morning routine. She would wake up, notice she felt anxious and depressed and then feel demoralized for the day. Her thought processes were clarified to be a series of self-judgements and pessimistic predictions. She would castigate herself for being so weak and emotional, and "just know" it was going to be a terrible day where she would not be able to get anything done. These thoughts led to secondary symptoms of depression, anxiety, and guilt—being depressed about being depressed (see Ellis & Harper, 1961). Consequently, she would have an unproductive day where she would mostly ruminate about how terrible she was and how she could not do anything right. At the end of the day, she would reflect on how "awful" she had been that day, tell herself she should be doing more than she was, and try to use harsh self-talk to force herself out of her rut. She was so exhausted by this cycle that she withdrew from previously enjoyed activities and her depression only worsened. This went on for a number of years.

The therapist asked himself these questions to help develop a conceptualization of her presentation and beliefs:

- What is the underlying belief? *This early on, we're still sorting out the precise belief, but beliefs about incompetence are pronounced. She also seems to have a rule or assumption about emotions in general.*
- What types of situations are likely to activate this belief? *This thought is activated for her in the morning when she thinks about her day and at the end of her day when she reflects on everything that she didn't get accomplished. This pattern has been going on for years and there might be other avoided situations that have yet to be identified.*
- What is the predicted outcome? / If that belief were true, what would the client predict would happen in these situations? *In the morning she predicts she will have a terrible day and not accomplish anything.*
- How would someone behave if these predictions were true? *Just like she is. They would assume failure and incompetence and as a result have poor productivity. She also spends hours ruminating about this belief.*
- What are the ways people might try to overcompensate for this belief? *People might overdo it and work at unsustainable paces or set unobtainable goals. Earlier in her life she did some of this, but after the death of her father there had been less overcompensating.*
- What are the ways people might avoid the situations that would activate the belief? *Avoiding situations where she might fail or prove herself incompetent.*
- What are the consequences of the observed behavior? *She's distracted and exhausted from rumination, which makes her less productive and less effective.*
- What are the short-term consequences? *Exhaustion, demoralization, increased distress, some avoidance of difficult tasks*
- What are the long-term consequences? *Low level of achievement, chronic depression, engrained beliefs about self*
- Are there any potential unintended consequences? *She's so tired from ruminating about being incompetent that she hardly has any energy to get anything done. At times she is able to chide herself into getting something done, but the cumulative effects of her self-denigration are that her thinking about herself gets more and more extreme.*
- Are there any attentional filters at play? *Yes, she completely misses all the things she is actually doing right!*
- Is there evidence of a confirmation bias, selective filter, or self-fulfilling prophecy? *I think each of these might be at play and are exemplified by her prediction in the morning that it would be a terrible day and her conclusion at the end of the day that she was right.*
- Are there alternate explanations that are being missed? *Unresolved grief issues? She behaves as if she is incompetent and therefore believes she is.*

- Is there any missing context for the evidence? *Yes, her relationships with her emotions appears to be important. If she thinks it is not OK to feel sad, this is only going to lead to more distressing emotions. Essentially, it appears to be a setup.*
- Are there factors we have yet to identify? *I'm sure there are. Given her emotion avoidance, I'm sure there are factors we're both missing, which hopefully will emerge as treatment progresses.*
- What factors are leading to the maintenance of this belief? *Rumination behavior and beliefs about emotions.*
- How does this all fit together? *It seems like there is a natural sadness about the death of her father and difficulty expressing and tolerating those emotions. She is afraid of and embarrassed about her feelings, which ultimately makes for more distress and a compounding unhappiness. She internalized early messages about it "not being OK to not be OK" and correspondingly is given to excessive rumination about how unacceptable she is and how incompetent she is for not being able to just "snap out of it." All of this reinforces beliefs about incompetence.*
- Objectively, how can we map this out? *It helps me to visually map it out, and later check it out with the client.*

Here is how a therapist might present and test out the formulation:

Therapist: Trisha, we've been spending some time talking about thoughts you have about being incompetent and weak and lazy, and I was wondering if we could spend some time seeing how it all fits together

Client: Um, yeah, I guess (sounding a little puzzled)

Therapist: I just want to talk through with you, what I'm hearing and understanding from what you've already shared with me. I want to make sure I'm understanding you correctly and I want to see if we can learn anything that might help you from this pattern you seem to be stuck in. Is that OK with you?

Client: If you think it will help, I feel like I'm just a big mess.

Therapist: I know you have a lot of thoughts about what a mess you think you are.

Client: (nodding)

Therapist: From what you shared with me, it sounds like there's a common pattern that happens for you. Mornings sound like an especially difficult time for you.

Client: They are! I hate mornings, I feel terrible, and I just know the day is going to be terrible, and there isn't anything I can do about it.

Therapist: And it sounds like you spend a lot of time thinking about how terrible the day is going to be as well.

Client: Yes. I know it's going to be just another terrible day. I think about how much I have to do and how I know I won't do any of it, because I'm just such a weak mess who can't do anything right.

Therapist: There's a lot to unpack there. First, that sounds like a miserable way to start your day. You wake up feeling depressed, have thoughts about what a terrible day it is going to be. Then you start having thoughts about yourself?

Client: Yeah, I think about how it's my fault that it's going to be a terrible day, that if I could just get myself together, then it wouldn't be so bad. But, I'm just too much of a screw up to even do anything.

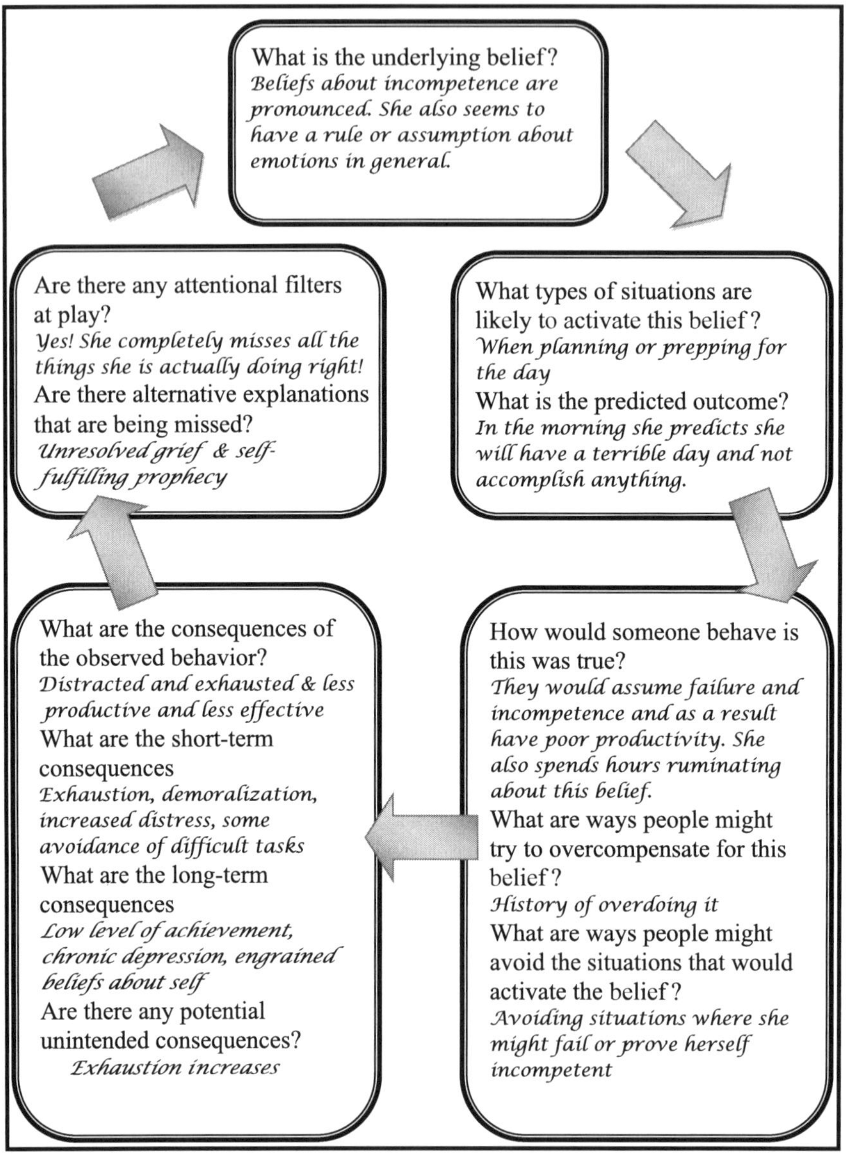

Worksheet 2.3 Example of an Elaborated Case Conceptualization Diagram: Trisha

Therapist: Even now, I can see how harsh these thoughts you have about yourself are. When you have these types of thoughts about yourself in the morning, how does it make you feel?

Client: Angry … sad … like I'm a lost cause.

Therapist: So, you start thinking about you being a lost cause. You feel sad and angry. And the anger is directed at?

Client: Me, I'm so mad at myself.

Therapist: What did you do to warrant this anger?

Client: Nothing, that's the problem, I don't do anything, and I should know better. I was raised better.

Therapist: You're mad that you aren't better than you are. You aren't the person you were raised to be.

Client: Yes

Therapist: How much time do you spend thinking about this in the morning?

Client: Hours, maybe more, I'm sort of always thinking about how terrible I am and how I should do better.

Therapist: That's a lot of time, and I would presume energy.

Client: Yeah, it's a lot, but I have to be hard on myself or I won't get anything done.

Therapist: So, you sort of whip yourself into shape.

Client: Yes

Therapist: Everyday

Client: Yeah

Therapist: How is that for you?

Client: It's really tiring, I'm just too much of a mess to do it any other way.

Therapist: So, let's start fitting this together. You wake up in the morning feeling down. You have thoughts that it will be a bad day, that you won't be able to do anything right, and that you're weak for being down and for not getting anything done.

Client: Sounds like a typical morning.

Therapist: This leaves you feeling, sad, angry, and exhausted.

Client: Yes

Therapist: You'll often respond to this by spending hours ruminating about how terrible you are and trying to figuratively whip yourself into doing something.

Client: (nodding)

Therapist: Sometimes this works and you do get something done and other times it doesn't, but it is always exhausting.

Client: So exhausting

Therapist: What are the short- and long-term effects of this pattern of behavior?

Client: Well, I'm tired and my life's a mess.

Therapist: This sounds exhausting, let's try and parse this out a little bit more. The immediate short-term effect of the harshness you have on yourself is?

Client: Sometimes, I get stuff done.

Therapist: Yes, and?

Client: I feel terrible and exhausted.

Therapist: You have all the weight of the depression you normally have and then on top of that you put this weight of being mad at yourself for being depressed.

Client: Why am I doing this to myself?

Therapist: I'm sure you came by this behavior honestly. It sounds like there might have been some messages you received early on about whether it was OK to feel sad or down.

Client: Definitely. That was not OK.

Therapist: So, you tell yourself now that it's not OK to feel down?

Client: I guess so, I don't like it, in fact I hate it.

Therapist: I definitely want to get you some relief. I just worry that making yourself feel bad about feeling bad isn't going to make you not feel bad

Client: (slight exhale and an almost chuckle)

Therapist: We can't solve the problem with more of the problem.

Client: Right

Therapist: So, let's keep looking at this, short-term effect of being harsh on yourself is you might get something done and you feel exhausted, what are the long-term effects?

Client: At some point, I started believing all the terrible things I tell myself about myself.

Therapist: That's a heavy price, anything else?

Client: I don't think so.

Therapist: So, I wonder about a possible unintended consequence of this behavior. Can I walk you through it?

Client: That would be fine.

Therapist: So, you wake up in the morning feeling down and then are really harsh on yourself for feeling so down and for the assumption that you won't get anything done.

Client: Yeah

Therapist: Then you feel miserable and it is very exhausting.

Client: Yes

Therapist: Then day in and day out this takes a big toll on you. You start believing more and more these things you're saying to yourself, and you feel more tired and more run down.

Client: So tired, from all of this.

Therapist: It sounds so exhausting. Here's the part, I'm wondering about. Isn't this exhaustion part of why it is hard for you to do things?

Client: Yes, I'm so tired all the time.

Therapist: You tire yourself out by telling yourself you're terrible for not getting anything done and then you're too tired to get anything done.

Client: Huh?

Therapist: I just wonder if part of the reason you're so tired and can't get anything done is because of this self-harshness behavior you engage in.

Client: I guess I never realized this.

Therapist: Right, the mind has these filters that sit just outside our awareness and make us more likely to see things in a way that would strengthen our preexisting belief. So, if you had a belief that you were incompetent, it would make perfect sense that you would interpret this course of events as evidence that you're incompetent.

Client: Doesn't this just mean that I'm really screwed up.

Therapist: I'm not sure I arrive at the same conclusion. Let me draw out on the board how I'm understanding this. You have a belief that you can't do anything right, that you're incompetent. You make a prediction (based on this belief), that you aren't going to be able to get anything done today because of how incompetent you are. You respond to this prediction with a behavior of very harsh self-talk. The outcome (or effect) from this harsh self-talk behavior is you preoccupy and exhaust yourself. From a resource perspective, there is then just less energy and attention to get things done. This leads to less things getting done, which you then interpret through your mental filters as further evidence that you are incompetent. And around and around the cycle goes until you are so tired and exhausted and have learned to really believe this belief about being incompetent.

Client: Yes, wow, OK, uh, yeah that's what happens for me.

Therapist: OK, so if this feels reasonably accurate, the good news is we have a lot of intervention points. We can target this belief about being incompetent. We can target these predictions you make that you're going to have a terrible day and these thoughts that you are weak. We can target this harsh ruminative self-talk that is so corrosive to you. In addressing those elements, we can change the outcome and help you start having some more productive days. And, we also want to look at your filtering process, how you're taking all this complex information and collapsing it down to being just more about how bad you are. How does that sound?

Client: I think that's what I need.

Therapist: Great, let's pick a target and see what strategies we can start plugging in today to start disassembling the belief and behavior pattern.

In going over this with Trisha, I learned something about the pattern that I previously had not known, and that was about how harsh her rumination was. Going over the cycle together helped us both attend to information we had been missing, and it helped us create a shared understanding of the problem so we can collaboratively work together on her problems and towards her goals.

Summary

In this chapter, we have focused on reviewing why corrective learning might not happen implicitly. This has included a brief review of relevant items from the field of social psychology, an overview of the Generic Cognitive Model, an introduction to case conceptualization, and an extended case example that demonstrated both the above elements and how to address the concepts in session. We have included a simplified and elaborated Functional Belief Conceptualization Diagram in the worksheet for your use in clinical practice.

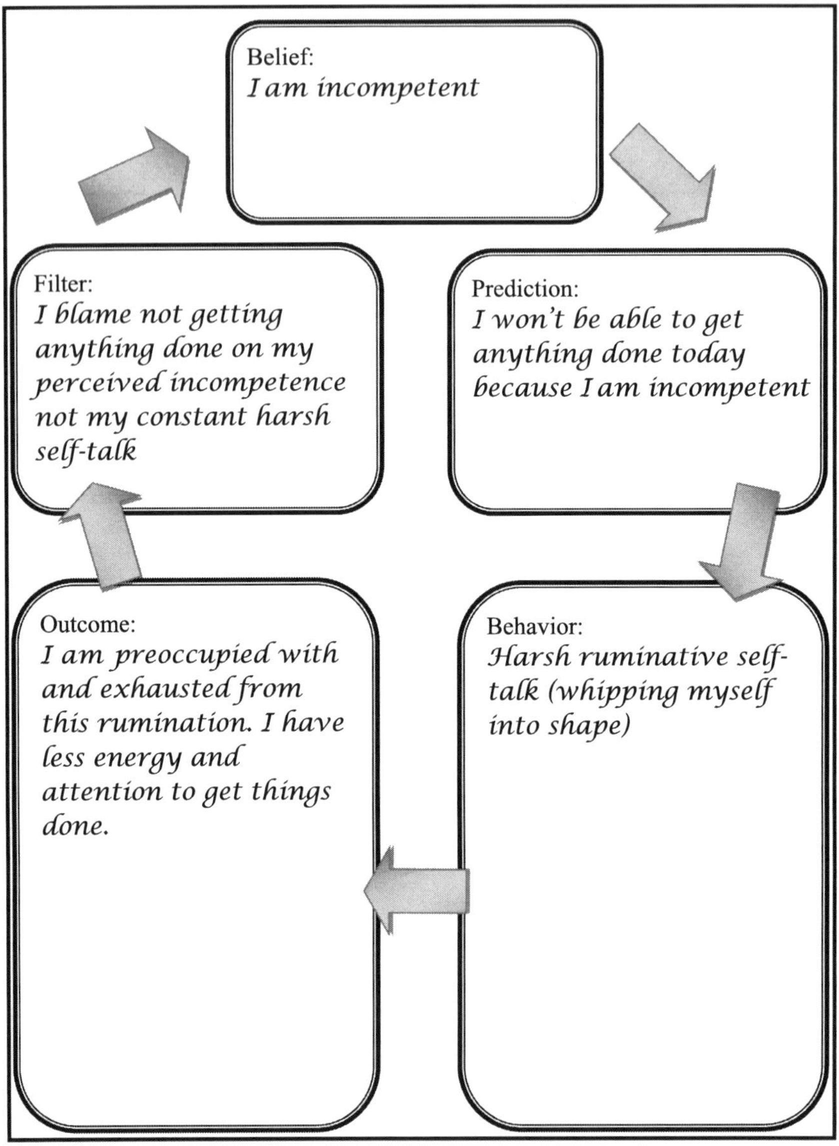

Worksheet 2.4 Example of a Simple Case Conceptualization Diagram: Trisha

References

Barlow, D. H., Farchione, T. J., Fairholme, C. P., Ellard, K. K., Boisseau, C. L., Allen, L. B., & May, J. T. E. (2010). *Unified protocol for transdiagnostic treatment of emotional disorders: Therapist guide.* New York: Oxford University Press.

Beck, A. T. (1963). Thinking and depression I. Idiosyncratic content and cognitive distortions. *Archives of General Psychiatry, 9*, 324–333. doi:10.1001/archpsyc.1963.01720160014002

Beck, A. T. (1964). Thinking and depression II. Theory and therapy. *Archives of General Psychiatry, 10*(6), 561–571. doi:10.1001/archpsyc.1964.01720240015003

Beck, A. T., & Haigh, E. A. P. (2014). Advances in cognitive theory and therapy: The Generic Cognitive Model. *Annual Review of Clinical Psychology, 10*, 1–24. doi:10.1146/annurev-clinpsy-032813-153734

Beck, J. S. (2011). *Cognitive behavior therapy: Basics and beyond* (2nd ed.). New York: Guilford Press.

Butler, G., Fennell, M., & Hackmann, A. (2010). *Cognitive-behavioral therapy for anxiety disorders: Mastering clinical challenges.* New York: Guilford Press.

Dozois, D. J., & Beck, A. T. (2008). Cognitive schema, beliefs, and assumptions. In K. S. Dobson & D. J. Dozois (Eds.), *Risk factors in depression* (pp. 122–144). Amsterdam: Elsevier/Academic.

Ellis, A., & Harper, R. A. (1961). *A guide to rational living.* Englewood Cliffs, NJ: Prentice-Hall.

Fassbinder, E., Schweiger, U., Martius, D., Brand-de Wilde, O., & Arntz, A. (2016). Emotion regulation in schema therapy and dialectical behavior therapy. *Frontiers in Psychology, 7*, 1–19.

Foley, M. A. (2015). Setting the records straight: Impossible memories and the persistence of their phenomenological qualities. *Review of General Psychology, 19*(3), 230–248.

Jillette, P., Penn, Price, S., Melcher, S., Goudeau, S., Wechter, D. (Writers), Price, S., Rogan, T., Selby, C., Uhlenberg, S., & Wechter, D. (Directors). (2009). Organic Foods [Television series episode]. In S. Adagio (Supervising Producer), *Penn & Teller: Bullshit!* Las Vegas, NV: Showtime.

Leahy, R. L. (2018). *Emotional schema therapy: Distinctive features.* New York: Routledge.

Lippmann, W. (2017). *Public opinion.* New York: Routledge.

Lorenzo-Luaces, L., German, R. E., & DeRubeis, R. J. (2015). It's complicated: The relation between cognitive change procedures, cognitive change, and symptom change in cognitive therapy for depression. *Clinical Psychology Review, 41*, 3–15.

Meichenbaum, D. H., & Goodman, J. (1971). Training impulsive children to talk to themselves: A means of developing self-control. *Journal of Abnormal Psychology, 77*(2), 115.

Moorey, S. (2010). The six cycles maintenance model: Growing a "vicious flower" for depression. *Behavioural and Cognitive Psychotherapy, 38*(2), 173–184.

Nickerson, R. S. (1998). Confirmation bias: A ubiquitous phenomenon in many guises. *Review of General Psychology, 2*(2), 175–220.

Padesky, C. A. (1994). Schema change processes in cognitive therapy. *Clinical Psychology & Psychotherapy, 1*(5), 267–278.

Padesky, C. A., & Mooney, K. A. (2012). Strengths-based cognitive-behavioural therapy: A four-step model to build resilience. *Clinical Psychology & Psychotherapy, 19*(4), 283–290.

Persons, J. B. (2012). *The case formulation approach to cognitive-behavior therapy.* New York: Guilford Press.

Plous, S. (1993). *The psychology of judgment and decision making.* New York: McGraw-Hill.

Randall, W. L. (2007). From computer to compost: Rethinking our metaphors for memory. *Theory & Psychology, 17*(5), 611–633.

Rosenthal, R., & Jacobson, L. (1968). Pygmalion in the classroom. *The Urban Review, 3*(1), 16–20.

Ruscio, J. (2007). The clinician as subject: Practitioners are prone to the same judgment errors as everyone else. In S. O. Lilienfeld & W. T. O'Donohue (Eds.), *Great ideas of clinical science: 17 principles that every mental health professional should understand* (pp. 29–47). New York: Routledge.

Waltman, S., & Sokol, L. (2017). The Generic Cognitive Model of cognitive behavioral therapy: A case conceptualization-driven approach. In S. Hofmann & G. Asmundson (Eds.), *The Science of Cognitive Behavioral Therapy* (pp. 3–18). London: Academic Press.

Young, J. E. (1999). *Cognitive therapy for personality disorders: A schema-focused approach.* Sarasota, FL: Professional Resource Press.

Chapter 3

Getting Started

Scott H. Waltman

CONTENTS

Introduction

There are a number of things a therapist can do to make it more likely that effective Socratic strategies can be used. You may have noticed that some clients appear to be more readily amenable to cognitive change strategies. With these clients, you can often easily fold into the session some well-placed questions that lead to a very insightful discussion. Alternatively, there are some clients who seem to not even notice your brilliant questions or even situations where your questions appear to fall flat. There are some general strategies that are facilitative of this process, which will be reviewed in this chapter. The strategies can be used in a manner where they build on the skills covered in the previous chapter.

As cognitive behavior therapy (CBT) trainers, we often review audio samples of trainees and clinicians who are seeking to be certified as qualified therapists in CBT. We notice a large difference between the clinicians who use these strategies and those who do not. Some clinicians appear to be like parents who try to sneak vegetables into the food of their young children. Often the scene is a very pleasant supportive therapy session, where the therapist shifts their behavior and starts asking questions about weighing evidence or cognitive distortions and the client is not exactly sure what to make of it. The client might engage in the practice for a few moments, but invariably they end up continuing their story or telling a different story. From the perspective of a rater, it appears as though the client and therapist might not have been on the same page. In general, there are four treatment elements that help facilitate effective Socratic strategies and productive therapy sessions: therapeutic alliance, session structure, skills training approach, and self-monitoring.

Therapeutic Alliance

Therapeutic alliance refers to the working relationship that exists between the therapist and the client (Creed & Waltman, 2017; Okamoto, Dattilio, Dobson, & Kazantzis, 2019). It can be described as having three interdependent components: goals, tasks, and bonds (see Creed & Waltman, 2017; Gilbert & Leahy, 2007). Goals refer to whether there is agreement on the goals of treatment, tasks refer to whether there is agreement on how those goals will be achieved (the process of therapy), and bonds refer to the affective bond between the clinician and client (Creed & Waltman, 2017).

The term therapeutic alliance is often used interchangeably with terms like therapeutic relationship, working relationship, and working alliance. The therapeutic alliance is among the most studied factors in psychotherapy research. Poor ratings of alliance at the start of treatment have been shown to be consistent predictors of treatment dropout. Alternatively, a moderate and robust positive relationship has been found between the strength of the alliance and treatment outcomes. However, the direction of the association between alliance and treatment outcome remains unclear (see Creed & Waltman, 2017). Although some evidence suggests that as the therapeutic alliance improves, the client's functioning also improves, some contradicting evidence suggests that as clients improve, their relationship with the therapist improves. Although the direction of the effect remains unclear, the association between the therapeutic alliance and treatment outcome indicates that the therapeutic alliance merits careful clinical attention (Gilbert & Leahy, 2007).

All well-established therapies emphasize the importance of the therapeutic alliance; therefore, it is referred to as a common factor, as it is a treatment factor commonly observed across the therapies (Wampold, 2001). There are also factors that are unique or specific to individual therapies—these are called specific factors (Wampold, 2001). Effective use of Socratic strategies in therapy is dependent on the successful implementation of both common and specific factors, which is illustrated by the concept of collaborative empiricism.

Collaborative empiricism is a parallel term to Socratic dialogue. These terms are overlapping, yet distinct, concepts. Collaborative empiricism is a core component of CBT and it speaks to how well the therapist and client are jointly engaged in the discovery and change process (Beck, Rush, Shaw, & Emery, 1979). Collaborative empiricism is also thought to be a core element to forming a strong relationship in CBT (Kazantzis, Beck, Dattilio, Dobson, & Rapee, 2013). In practical terms, effective collaborative empiricism relies on the ability of the therapy dyad to collaborate and the application of an empirical mindset to a situation or belief (Tee & Kazantzis, 2011). In order to have collaborative empiricism, you need to have both components (i.e., collaboration and empiricism; Tee & Kazantzis, 2011). A therapist could have a good application of an empirical mindset, but a lack of collaboration, this might look like a therapist quickly pointing out that a client's thoughts are distorted (see Tee & Kazantzis, 2011) or a therapist jumping ahead and engaging in the process of "provided discovery," where they give the client the answer instead of helping them arrive at a new conclusion on their own (Waltman, Hall, McFarr, Beck, & Creed, 2017). Alternatively, a session could have good use of collaboration, but lack an empirical mindset; these sessions are often pleasant but have a risk of being underpowered.

Goals

A first step in establishing a therapeutic alliance is to arrive at an agreed-upon goal of treatment. If your goal is to restructure or challenge your client's beliefs and their goal is to feel better, you might run into trouble if they do not see the cognitive restructuring as being part of feeling better. A general good practice is to define from the outset, in practical terms, what we are trying to accomplish here. This is often achieved through making a problem list and a goal list. Some clients will be more focused on problems like symptoms or practical problems and others will be more focused on goals or ambitions. With the more problem-oriented clients, you might need to spend some time developing the goal portion. Commonly this process is done by asking some variation of the ubiquitous miracle question (M. Stith, Miller, Boyle, Swinton, Ratcliffe, & McCollum, 2012). There are different ways of doing this, but it typically involves asking the client to imagine that a miracle has occurred, and that their problem was now resolved. The therapist then asks how things are different and this can inform goal setting. So, what would the client be doing if this problem was not a problem? And, is that a possible goal on which to focus during treatment?

Another way to address this issue is through the contextual behavioral and positive psychology principle of goals for living people (see David, 2016). The idea is that when clients come in saying that their goal is an absence of bad, perhaps something like, "I want to eliminate anxiety from my life," this is a place to talk about goals for living people versus goals for dead people. The absence of bad is not necessarily good, or life enhancing. Dead people are very good at not having anxiety or panic attacks; conversely, there are a lot of costs that go with being dead, like missing out on life. Also, anxiety is a fundamental part of being alive—as are all the emotions (David, 2016). We want goals that are stated in positive terms. What do you want? Not, what do you not want? As the Cheshire Cat says in *Alice's Adventures in Wonderland*, "If you don't know where you want to go, then it doesn't matter which path you take" (Carroll, 2011). So, we need to find a shared direction or heading, by asking the following questions: "What do you want instead?" "How would you rather spend your time and energy instead of being unhappy about being anxious?" "What do you think you could do if you weren't anxious, and why does that matter to you?" This process can be enhanced by values-based strategies (Hayes & Smith, 2005). At some point in therapy, we are going to ask them to do something difficult, and we need to know beforehand why it is worthwhile for the client to tolerate distress in the service of pursuing their goals and values.

CBT is inherently a goal-directed or goal-oriented process (Beck, 2011). The client's individual goals can sometimes be lost when there is rigid adherence to a treatment manual; however, collaborative empiricism, guided discovery, and the Socratic method can be used in a manner whereby they "Help therapy move beyond the rote application of a treatment manual" (Overhosler, 2011, p. 62). This can and should include making collaborative treatment goals.

Tasks

When we know what the client wants, we can try collaboratively to figure out what obstacles stand in the way and what it will take to overcome them. This is how we create a collaborative treatment plan to target clinical problems (barriers) and mechanisms maintaining those problems, while also fostering the factors that will help them get what they want. A good way to do this is to base it on the conceptualization. If you refer to the conceptualization diagram in the previous chapter, you will see a way to draw out the cycle of an underlying belief leading to cognitive predictions (i.e., automatic thoughts), leading to behavioral responses (probably some form of avoidance), leading to short-term, long-term, and unintended consequences, all of which is filtered through our cognitive biases to reinforce the pre-existing belief.

Drawing out the pattern can be a rationale for doing something different to change up the pattern (i.e., creating a shared understanding of the tasks it will take to accomplish their goals). In session it might sound like this:

> If the problem is you have these pre-existing beliefs about yourself that make you feel awful, then we're going to use cognitive strategies to target these negative predictions you are making. We are also going to use behavior change strategies (skills training, behavioral experiments, behavioral activation, exposure, etc.) to change how you respond to these predictions. This will help us get some new and discrepant experiences, and we're going to focus on your cognitive filters, so you do not miss all this new information that is incompatible with your underlying belief. This overall process will help us build a life that is more in-line with the life you want to

> have, and this will help us build up new beliefs and new patterns of behavior that will persist after we stop meeting. How does that sound to you?

Another method for fostering agreement that the tasks/strategies of therapy will help the client meet their treatment goals is through an initial phase of treatment process called self-monitoring. These tasks will be discussed in greater detail later in this chapter. The flow of this process will comprise orienting the client to the cognitive behavioral model and then applying the model to their life and distressing situations to demonstrate the fit between the model and their situation. As your client sees in real-life that how they are thinking and what they are doing is affecting how they are feeling, they will be more willing to focus on cognitive and behavioral strategies. Spending time targeting this understanding is often an initial focus of treatment that will pay off in later sessions.

Bonds

There are a number of things a therapist can do to facilitate a strong bond, and these strategies are not unique to CBT. Basic counseling skills like empathy, warmth, validation, and reflective listening are also important components of CBT (Gilbert & Leahy, 2007). Theodore Roosevelt is attributed with having said, "Nobody cares how much you know, until they know how much you care." In our experience, clinicians who are new to CBT but not new to therapy, often have little difficulty with the bonds-element of the therapeutic alliance (see Waltman et al., 2017). They may at times become so focused on what is new that they forget to keep practicing the rapport-focused strategies of therapy (Waltman et al., 2017); typically, a simple reminder to keep using all of their wonderful empathic and validation strategies is enough to correct this. The therapeutic relationship is among the most researched topic in the psychotherapy literature (see Creed & Waltman, 2017; Gilbert & Leahy, 2007; Wampold, 2001); therefore, interested readers are referred to Gilbert and Leahy's (2007) excellent edited book on the topic for a more thorough review and instruction.

The core OARS skills from motivational interviewing (open-ended questions, affirmation, reflective-listening, and summarize; see Miller & Rollnick, 2012) are a good framework for bonds-consistent approaches that will line up well with the principle of collaborative empiricism (Westra & Dozois, 2006). As you ask open-ended questions that are guided by your curiosity, provide accurate and authentic affirmations, engage in reflective listening that demonstrates you are really listening and trying to understand your clients, and tie it all together with periodic summaries, you will find that you develop a strong bond with your client. You will also gain much information that can be used to inform your overall conceptualization and later Socratic interventions.

Session Structure

People are often attracted to CBT by the interventions; whereas, the structural aspects often seems less exciting. You may even have thought about skipping this section when you read the heading. The semi-structured approach of CBT is something that can

Table 3.1 CBT Session Structure

At Start of Session	Mood Check Bridge Action Plan Review Generating Agenda Items Finalizing Agenda Plan
Bulk of Session Time	Working the Agenda Plan
At the End of the Session	Summarizing the Session Seeking Feedback Setting New Action Plan

be new for clinicians (Waltman et al., 2017). The value of the session structure is that it helps facilitate interventions like Socratic questioning. What follows will be a brief overview of and practical guide to CBT session structure. At the start of the session, a CBT therapist will collaboratively plan with the client how to spend their time together and at the end of the session there will be a debrief on how it went and whether modifications are needed to help personalize treatment. Typically, the session follows a structure of starting with a mood rating, followed by a bridge, an action plan (homework) review, agenda setting, and agenda finalizing. Then the dyad works the agenda. They later summarize the session, seek feedback, and make a new action plan (homework). There is some variation in how this goes, but these are the common steps.

Basic Session Structure

The mood check is a quick way to find out how the client is feeling. It is not intended to be a lengthy update, where you hear about everything that happened in the week. Instead, it is intended to be a quick way to gauge how the client is doing in order to inform the focus of the session. Typically, a therapist will have the client rate their overall mood on a scale of 1 to 10 or 1 to 100. Sometimes therapists track specific moods (e.g., depression 1 to 10) and other times they will track the client's mood in general, where a higher number might be a more positive mood and a lower number will be a more negative mood. You are free to choose how you want to do it; it is recommended that you are consistent with the scale as you are teaching the client how to monitor their mood through this process.

The bridge is intended to be a figurative bridge between sessions in order to help you pick up where you left off. If you think about watching a television show before the age of streaming, people used to have to wait a week to see what happened, and if the plotline was important there would be a quick recap that covered what had happened in last week's show, so they could pick up where they left off in the previous episode. This is similar to what a bridge is. It is not intended to be a memory test. You can ask the client to provide the bridge or you can provide it yourself, both are acceptable. A review of the previous session summary can be a good bridge.

As the action plan (homework) is ideally an extension of what happened in session, reviewing the previous session's main points is a good way to transition into reviewing the previous action plan or homework for the previous week. Notably, the term homework can have negative connotations or be paired with previous negative experiences; therefore, people often use alternative terms, such as action plan, commitment, skill practice, goal, or out-of-session tasks (see Cohen, Edmunds, Brodman, Benjamin, & Kendall, 2013). In reviewing the previous week's action plan, we want to ask "How did it go?" and "What did they learn?" If they had a success or new type of experience, we might want to put that on the agenda and spend more time unpacking and synthesizing the new information. If they ran into trouble, we want to reinforce their efforts and engage in problem solving to see what went wrong and how we can adjust the practice for next time. If the client did not complete the homework, then it is important to nonjudgmentally assess what happened: "What got in the way?" In this assessment, it is important to identify if this was a problem related to the assignment being too difficult, unclear, or not being perceived as helpful. We want to try to problem-solve the barrier so they will be more likely to be successful in the future; for example, if the client "forgot" and still thinks it would be useful to do this practice, then troubleshooting ways to remember future homework is indicated. We might also choose to do the task together in session.

It can help to think about setting the agenda as two distinct tasks of generating possible agenda items and finalizing the plan. When setting an agenda, it is important to be realistic (try to keep it to one or two items) and collaborative (balancing the client's suggestions and the treatment goals). Before a client is fully oriented to CBT, it is quite common for them just to start talking about whatever is on their mind before the agenda has been set or finalized. In these cases, it is important to gently interrupt the client to set and finalize the agenda before starting the session (Beck, 2011)—just because something comes up in the check-in doesn't mean it is the most pressing/distressing issue. The next thing to work towards will be putting specific questions or problems on the agenda. General items (or topics) like "my mother is visiting" tend to lend themselves to a less-focused session of updates and stories, while specific problems like "handling stress related to my mother's upcoming visit" or "planning for a successful visit with my mother" lend themselves to a more active session. In setting the agenda, you want to ask yourself if there is a clear objective for the session: "What are we hoping to accomplish today?" Another strategy for making an agenda more specific is to ask for specific examples of when the problem occurred. For example, if when setting an agenda, the client states that they want to talk about their emotional eating, then you can ask: "Was there a time this week that was particularly bad?" "Should we put talking about that on the agenda?" When we have some ideas of how we might spend our time, then we want to finalize the agenda. This includes prioritizing the agenda items. A good habit to get into is reading back the plan you have written down to make sure there is agreement and mutual understanding of the plan.

If the client is not sure what they want to talk about, then you still have some good options. You can read back your goal and problem list and ask them to pick one to work on—working on something is better than spending large amounts of time trying to figure out what to work on. You can talk about what a natural next step would be, given the bridge (or how the action plan went). You can suggest practicing skills or learning new skills. These strategies will address most of the problems that come up.

After you have finalized an agenda, you then work with the plan you have. Ideally, you want to save 5–10 minutes at the end of the session for the close-out. A good way to start transitioning to the close-of-session structure is to start summarizing the session. Ideally, periodic summaries are provided or gathered after each learning experience and intervention, and then feedback is elicited. Broadly, we are interested in feedback related to their reaction/satisfaction with the session and their learning/understanding of what we are doing and why we are doing it. This information can help us tailor the treatment to our clients. The question "How was the session?" can be followed up with inquiring about specific areas of strengths and areas to change: "What did you like about the session?" "What would you change next time?" Also, it is important to elicit encapsulating summaries: "What did you learn today?" "What's the takeaway message from today's session?" These questions can be informative even if the client does not exactly know how to answer them. If your client is not quite tracking what you are saying in the session, this will be a good indicator of that. You can then use that information to modify your approach, perhaps by slowing down, drawing things out on a white board, or asking your client to restate ideas in their own words throughout the session.

Finally, we want to design a new action plan. Ideally, we want this to be a collaborative process; though, notably, collaborative is not the same thing as going with whatever your client suggests. Often, especially early in treatment, you'll need to shape their suggestions and provide your own suggestions. If you happen to get a good take-away message when you are seeking feedback, you can use that as an anchor for the action plan: "How can you apply that to your coming week?" or "I like that idea. Can I suggest a small modification that I think will make it more impactful?" or "That sounds like general good self-care that I would be in support of, can I suggest something else you might do that would help you practice the skills we're learning here, to help you get the most out of therapy?" It is wise to avoid assigning something you would not do yourself. Regarding the amount and difficulty of assignments, too easy is much better than too hard, especially when you are still building momentum. We want to meet them at where they are, and so introducing new skills/worksheets as homework is not optimal. The idea of homework is that we want clients to practice applying these skills in their lives. Ideally, we would practice the assigned skills together in session first and then assign it as homework if they find it to be helpful. Often clients, with the best of intentions, let the week get away from them and forget to do the homework. So, we want to help them to plan when they will do it and how they will remember to do it. We will also address and troubleshoot other anticipatable barriers that might come up.

Problems with Structure

When clients are reluctant to join in the structural aspects of session (e.g., hesitancy to set or follow a session agenda) we might encourage them to treat it as an experiment (Beck, 2011). Such a proposal might sound like this:

> So, I gather you're not sold on this idea of structuring our sessions. You seem unsure about picking a specific goal to work towards each session and then focusing solely on that objective with the hope that it will help us make as much progress as possible in our sessions. Can I suggest that we might treat this as an experiment? What if we were to set aside our next four sessions to use this structure, and then we'll see if it actually makes a difference. What are your thoughts on that?

Similarly, if you are not sure about the whole notion of a structure, you might consider using it as an experiment. Some of the most common feedback we get as CBT trainers is how surprised people are by how much they like the session structure. Often people will report using it across the board, even with their clients who are not receiving CBT. You can think about the agenda as being a time budget. If you meet with your clients for one hour weekly, then they are spending less than 1% of their time with you, and so we need to make that clinical hour go as far as it can, by budgeting our time to prioritize the most important items—similarly to how, if one does not have much money, it is important to have a specific budget to prioritize what needs to be paid.

Another strategy to address clients who are harder to contain, or who are less willing to follow a set agenda, is to propose splitting the agenda between time for support and time for the more active work (Beck, 2011). Such an arrangement might be suggested by saying:

> I can see there is a lot going on for you, and I know you don't have a lot of places to talk about this. So, I want to find a way to make sure you're getting the support you need, and at the same time, I don't want to just talk about how bad things are, I want to work to make things better. I'd suggest that we try splitting our session time. Let's set aside and protect 10 minutes every session, just for support and stories, and then we'll use the remainder of the time to work on problem solving, skills training, and working on some of these very painful beliefs that you have. How would you feel about that?

When you decide to implement CBT session structure, having a structure cheat sheet such as that found in the table or the worksheet in this chapter is an easy way to get used to following the session structure.

In essence, this treat-it-as-an-experiment approach is a way to side-step potential power struggles and demonstrate the principles of collaborative empiricism. If the structure makes your sessions more productive (and by extension improves your likelihood of being able to employ effective Socratic strategies), then it will be easy to talk about continuing to use it. If it seems not to make any real difference, then you might not need to worry about the structure so much—though, first you might want to reassess your diagnosis, formulation, and treatment plan, as a general course correction might be indicated.

Skills Training Approach

The thing about using Socratic strategies to bring about cognitive and behavioral change is that it is not magic—we can teach our clients how to do this for themselves. In this way, a primary aim of therapy is skills training, and we are teaching the client to be their own therapist (Beck, 2011). We are just as interested in them learning how to evaluate their thoughts as we are with them arriving at new beliefs (Overholser, 2011). If you employ a skills training approach to therapy, it makes it easier use and teach skills in session. However, the success of this approach is likely to be dependent on the items above. You need a strong therapeutic alliance where there is a consensus

Name:	Date:
Diagnosis:	Current Treatment Goal:
Cognitive, Behavioral, & Affective Treatment Targets:	
Today's Session	
Mood Check:	
Bridge:	
Action Plan Review: *What was the plan?* *How did it go?* *What did we learn from this?* *What would be the next natural step?* *Are there barriers to overcome to increase future success?*	
Potential Agenda Topics: *Are these related to our treatment goals? What skills can we practice? What's the most pressing issue?*	
Finalized Agenda Plan:	
Assessment of Agenda Item: *Why does this seem to be happening? What are the most upsetting elements? What elements are under the client's control? What relevant thoughts and behaviors can we target? Is this related to the overall conceptualization?*	
Interventions: *Focusing on Key Cognitions:* *Understanding why the thought makes sense:* *Collaborative Curiosity:* *Summary and Synthesis:*	
How did the interventions go? What was the impact? What's the next step?	
Session Summary:	
Feedback (Client Learning/Understanding)	
Feedback (Client Satisfaction/Reaction to Session)	
New Action Plan *How can we extend the session by practicing the skill we used or applying the conclusion we came to?*	

Worksheet 3.1 Session Structure and Plan Handout

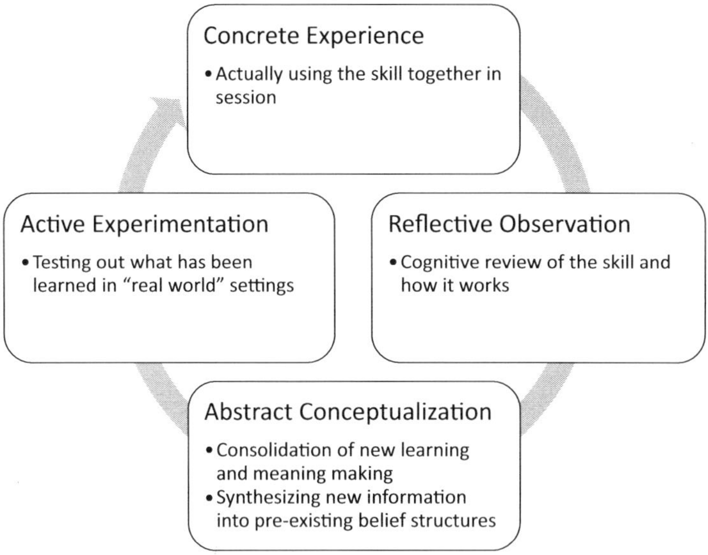

Figure 3.1 Kolb's Model of Experiential Learning

that learning new skills will help the client get what they want. You also need to use CBT session structure to maximize the time available for skills training and skill use.

In general, skills training is accomplished in the following way: first, introducing a skill and explaining how it works; second, demonstrating the skill and then using the skill together; third, debriefing the skill and how it works; fourth, capitalizing on new learning and discrepant experiences to facilitate overall learning and cognitive change; and, finally, practicing the skill in real-world and in-the-moment settings. People learn well through experiential methods—learning through doing (Wenzel, 2019). These elements of skills training can be fit into Kolb's (1984) four phases of experiential learning, namely, concrete experience, reflective observation, abstract conceptualization, and active experimentation (see Edmunds et al., 2013), which will be discussed below.

Concrete Experience

The first step in skills training is getting concrete experience with the skill. Psychological strategies can be abstract or full of jargon, so we do not want to leave the skills training up to something like assigning the client to read a handout as homework to figure out a skill on their own. We want to first explain what the skill is and why we are using it. As CBT is a strategic approach (Waltman et al., 2017), the skill you select to teach or use should be rooted in the client's individual conceptualization or the problem formulation (Wenzel, 2019). You should explain how the skill is going to address the problem, how the skill works, and perhaps quickly demonstrate the skill so the client knows what they are getting into. For example, when teaching cognitive skills, you might point out the connection between a thought and their distress or problematic behavior, you might introduce something like a thought record and give an overview of what it is and how it work, and then you could walk them through the thought record by using an example that you have already discussed or that you think you can move through quickly. Here is what that might look like:

> OK, Francine, we've spent a few sessions talking about how unhappy you are how terribly you feel about the death of your brother. We've also touched on some thoughts that perhaps it was your fault and perhaps there was more that you could do than you did. I want to move into evaluating these thoughts with you. Let me explain a little bit about what that is going to look like and how it works. The basic strategy is that we want to shift our focus onto some of the more distressing thoughts you have, and we want to break those thoughts down and see if we can't find a more balanced and less painful way of looking at things. First, we'll talk about the situation to try and pick which thought we think is the most upsetting. Then, we'll start looking at that specific thought by trying to understand why it might make sense that you came to think that way, and after we have a good idea of why it makes sense, we're going to look together at what you might be missing or if there are any indications that initial perspective isn't true. Finally, we'll mentally take a step back and see how it all fits together and then we'll have a better idea of the big picture and we'll be able to come up with a new thought that is believable. How does that sound to you?
>
> Francine, I can draw out a quick example, to give you a better idea of what this skill is. Once you get a hang of it, it's not complicated and ultimately, I want to help you learn to do this all on your own, so you can get some relief outside of session as well. I remember during our first session; you spoke about how growing up it was not OK to be emotional and so you developed the idea that being sad was weakness. So, there's a thought, "being sad is weak." It makes sense you previously had this thought because it is something you were told by people in authority. Also, there were some things you were missing, you talked about how a previous therapist helped you understand that feelings are natural and not shameful. So, pulling it together, you previously had the idea that being sad was weakness, this was based on lessons you learned growing up, you learned new lessons as an adult that suggest that maybe it is OK to be sad and you fit these together previously to come to the conclusion that your parents might have been uncomfortable with your feelings, but that doesn't make them wrong. Granted, I think there might still be some work to do there, but this is how the process of cognitive change works—change can be gradual. Can we focus in on your feelings of guilt and thoughts of responsibility with similar strategies in today's session?

If the client says, "No," they were not going to go along with it anyway, and you can check in with them to see what they think would be helpful and come up with a collaborative plan of attack. If they say, "Yes," then you are both on the same page and it will be a lot easier to use effective Socratic strategies in session. Also, as you are being transparent with what the skill is and how it works, you are starting to teach the client how to do this on their own—though it is typically a while before they master the skill.

After demonstrating the skill, you will want to do it together in session. Later chapters in the book will focus more on the particulars of general and specific Socratic questioning-based interventions to target cognitive and behavior change. If you are new to a particular skill, you will probably want to practice it a few times on your own. This will help you to have a better understanding of how the skill works through your own experiential learning (Wenzel, 2019). It also gives you the benefit of being able to vouch for the skill and present it as something with broad utility—rather like the old Hair Club for Men commercials: "I'm not just the president, I'm also a client." So, really you and your clients will both need to gain much hands-on experience with the skills you are teaching.

Reflective Observation

Many clinicians skip this step. They practice the skill and then trust that the client has understood everything as well as they did. The thing to keep in mind is that the content of what we are discussing is likely to be more emotionally laden for the client than for the therapist. They could be emotionally flooded, mesmerized by the process, unsure of the process, or distracted through thinking about details for the story you had discussed. So, it is important to pause and check how they are doing and what their impression of the skill is. Here is an example of how that might look:

> "We just did a lot and I want to check in with you Francine to see how you are doing and what you make of this whole evaluating your thoughts strategy we are using."
> "How are you feeling after the exercise we did together?"
> "What are your views on this exercise?"
> "Does this seem like it will be helpful to you?"
> "Is this something you want to spend some more time practicing and learning how to do?"
> "Do you have any questions about the process?"

You will want to take the time to clarify any misconceptions and answer questions they might have. You will want to lead with providing positive feedback (Bellack, Mueser, Gingerich, & Agresta, 2013). Reinforce what they did well and reinforce their willingness to engage in the process. You will want to provide constructive feedback as well (Bellack et al., 2013). You might need to revisit the skills training in the next session. Typically, there is some tweaking to do after they start using the skills as homework; normalizing this beforehand can make it easier to do later: "OK, it sounds like we have a general idea how the skill works. The next step is to put it into practice, so you can bring back your experiences. We can talk about how it went and smooth out the skill for you."

Abstract Conceptualization

This is the consolidation of the learning step. Here is where want to help clients make sense of what they learned from the skill practice. There are two main levels on which we can focus: (1) their self-efficacy and (2) their schema.

Even if you are not directly targeting their belief system, you can still connect what you are doing back to their beliefs about themselves. Clients often view themselves as being incapable in a number of ways. We should capitalize on any chance we get to highlight and draw attention to competency moments. If they were able to use progressive muscle relaxation to decrease their overall distress, there is a lesson here about their having some control over how they are feeling. If they practiced a skill that they really dislike, but did it anyway because they wanted to give it a shot, there is a lesson here about their ability to persist in doing things that are not fun, but they have the ability to choose to do it anyway. If they tried a skill and it did not work as intended, there is a lesson here about their willingness to try and having an open mind. Reinforce the skills and attributes that will be life-enhancing and treatment facilitating.

When you target cognitive change, either directly through Socratic strategies or indirectly through changing behavior patterns, there will be new experiences and new information to draw out and reinforce. We should try to integrate this new information into their overall belief system. Key questions to ask include asking how this new experience or information fits with their previous assumptions, and if necessary, how do they explain the discrepancy. "So, we just broke the situation down and came to a new conclusion that there are some people in your life who seem to really care about you, how do you reconcile that with your belief that you are unlovable?" "So, you had a prediction that you wouldn't be able to do it. This is actually a theme for you, predicting and assuming that you are incapable, and in the situation we just looked at, you concluded that this skill helped you succeed, what does that mean about you and your ability to do things?" A later chapter (Chapter 8) will focus on summary and synthesis skills. These are an essential part of the skills training process, as they help you get the most out of the new experience.

Active Experimentation

Experiential learning is an ongoing process, the fourth link in Kolb's experiential learning cycle (1984) is active experimentation; this is where the client practices the skills in the world outside the therapy room. This can be framed as a way to validate the in-session findings. "Let's see if this skill works in the real world." Although, it can be good to temper expectations. What frequently happens is that a client will wait to practice a skill until they are in crisis and at that point, they are not exactly proficient at the skill; consequently, it does not produce the desired result. They, in turn, come in to tell you that the skill does not work. The trouble with this conclusion is that the skill has not had a fair trial. The behavioral principle to employ is overlearning (see Bellack et al., 2013): "You have to overlearn something for it to become automatic." In helping the client set appropriate expectations, you want to talk with them about how to practice and when to practice. Just like how we first learn to drive in a parking lot and not on the freeway, we want them to practice their skills often and initially in low-demand situations. You do not want them to wait till they are in crisis and tell them to use it then: "When you first start using this skill it won't work as well as we need it to, you need to keep practicing it, so you can build up this skill, so it will work when you need it to."

"Real world" skill practice is ideally done as homework (or outside skills practice). However, you are really missing out if you treat the skills as things that the client is only supposed to use outside of session—you also will not really know about their mastery or fluidity with the skill. In-the-moment skills practice can be very valuable. If you taught your client grounding skills, you will want to coach them to use them if they are dissociating in-session with you. If you taught your client emotion regulation skills and they are emotionally dysregulated, you might want to coach them to use their regulation skills—assuming that would not be counter to an exposure activity. As your client gets more proficient with Socratic change strategies, you can have them start taking more of a lead when you evaluate thoughts together in a session.

Self-Monitoring

Beck (1979) noted in his observations that people needed to be trained to focus on certain types of thoughts. His initial strategy was to use shifts to unpleasant affect as a signal and would teach people to look at what they were thinking about just prior to the shift. This initial phase of treatment is called self-monitoring. This is where we teach people how to have greater self-awareness to facilitate their noticing and labeling their thoughts and feelings (Foster, Laverty-Finch, Gizzo, & Osantowski, 1999; Korotitsch & Nelson-Gray, 1999). We then use those skills to gather data that can be used to inform our conceptualization and later interventions (Cohen, Edmunds, Brodman, Benjamin, & Kendall, 2013). We are interested in tracking the frequency, intensity, and duration of the self-monitoring target (Cohen et al., 2013). We also want to learn about the context within which the thought, behavior, or emotion occurs. What is the function of the behavior? What are the antecedents? What are the consequences? This will help to clarify why the behavior is occurring and whether there is a short-term payoff (Cohen et al., 2013; Rizvi & Ritschel, 2014; Waltman, 2015). Functional analysis or behavioral chain analysis (see Rizvi & Ritschel, 2014) will be covered extensively in the later chapter (Chapter 12) on incorporating Socratic strategies into dialectical behavior therapy.

Gathering New Information via Self-Monitoring

In the previous chapter, we reviewed cognitive processes and biases that impact a person's perceptions. When we pair those biases with a possible low self-awareness, it can be clear that we might be missing some important pieces of the puzzle if we were to base our conceptualization and treatment plan only on information obtained in early sessions. While you might have heard about something called *depressive realism* in an undergraduate psychology course (see Ackerman & DeRubeis, 1991), much of that research was done on nonclinical samples and the idea that people with clinical levels of depression have a more realistic view of the world is not exactly accurate (Ackerman & DeRubeis, 1991). They are perhaps less prone to the error of overconfidence or errors of making overly optimistic predictions, but their view of the past is often distorted (Ackerman & DeRubeis, 1991).

People with depression are often overgeneralizers. That is to say, they have a harder time remembering specifically what happened, and they tend to remember what they think happened based on overgeneralized ruminative processes (Brittlebank, Scott, Mark, & Williams, 1993; Kuyken & Dalgleigh, 1995). Further, there might be especial difficulty in their remembering positive experiences or memories (Brittlebank

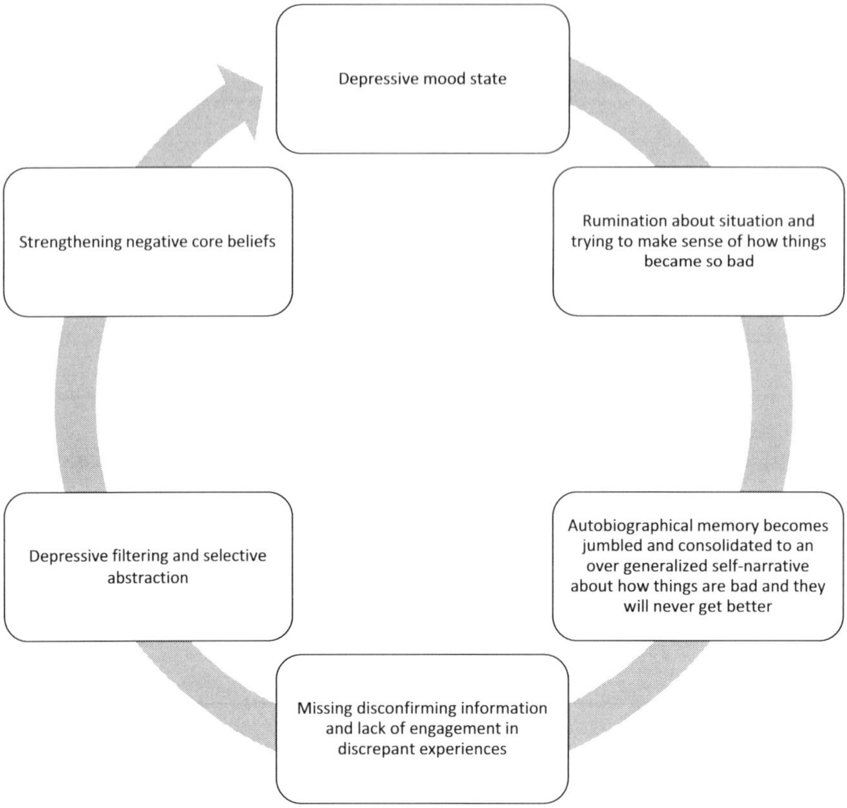

Figure 3.2 Rumination-Overgeneralization Cycle

et al., 1993; Williams & Scott, 1988). It is thought that this is due to their ruminative thought processes (Watkins & Teasdale, 2001), as they churn through their memories of the past (see Randall, 2007), there is a re-storying and consolidating of memories in a way that produces overgeneralized memories—ones that tend to fit with their depressive core beliefs and assumptions (Watkins & Teasdale, 2001). Similar cognitive processes and problems with autobiographical memories are also observed in other psychiatric disorders (see McNally, Lasko, Macklin, & Pitman, 1995).

Increasing Self-Awareness of Thoughts

An automatic thought by definition is a rapid evaluative thought that occurs just outside of our awareness (Beck, 1963, 1964). People need to be taught to notice and recognize their thoughts, especially the ones that are impacting their mood (Beck, 1979). Some clients will take to this more naturally than others. People typically accept and state their thoughts as facts. Our job is to help them take the first step of pausing and catching their thoughts. There is a simplified CBT skilled called the 3 Cs (Catch it, Check it, Change it; see Creed, Waltman, Frankel, & Williston, 2016);

this is actually three distinct skills that need to be taught separately. Before you can move into checking and changing thoughts, you need to teach your client how to "catch" a thought.

We want to catch thoughts that we are interested in working with. A later chapter (Chapter 5) on focusing on the key cognitions will go into more detail on how to find the most strategic thoughts to evaluate. When we are initially teaching the client to notice their automatic thoughts, we often use a strong emotional reaction as the clue.

- "What was going through your mind right before you got really upset?"
- "What were you telling yourself?"
- "What were you thinking was going to happen?"
- "How were you making sense of what happening?"

Some clients will easily be able to tell you what they were thinking, but others will need some help. Often people might share a thought that is really a situation or emotion and you will need to help them identify the actual thought, as in the following example:

Therapist: OK, so your shift was over, your supervisor was trying to talk to you about something that maybe wasn't too urgent, and you found yourself getting really angry. What were you thinking that was getting you so angry?

Client: I was thinking it was time to go home.

Therapist: Right, your shift was over, and it was your planned time to go home. But what was actually going through your mind, what were you telling yourself in the moment?

Client: I was just thinking about how mad I was and how much I hate him.

Therapist: So, you were really angry. You had the emotion of anger. Behaviorally, it sounds like you fell into a little rumination about work. And also, the later behavior of snapping at your boss. But what was the initial thought that lead to this?

Client: I'm not sure what you mean.

Therapist: OK, this can actually be a good thing, we might be able to identify the thought that led to this whole chain of events, and all that misery you had. Let's dig in a little bit. I want you to close your eyes and picture that day, well, that afternoon. What does your work look like? What are people wearing? What does it sound and smell like? You're watching the clock and it is time to leave and your boss comes over and starts talking to about something that does not seem urgent. What's going through your mind?

Client: He's a complete jerk for waiting till the end of the day to come and talk to me. It's just so inconsiderate!

Therapist: Excellent job! We identified some potential thoughts that came up for you. You had the thought that your boss was a jerk for waiting till the end of the day. You also had the thought that he was being inconsiderate. These thoughts made you emotionally angry, and this led to the behavior of ruminating about your anger, emotionally feeling angrier, and then verbally blowing up on your boss.

Client: Yeah, that sounds about right, you summarized it well.

Therapist: Well, you're doing a great job with this. These are exactly the kind of thoughts we want to learn to catch. These are the thoughts that are making a bad situation worse for you.

Client: If it helps me not explode at work, I really can't afford to lose my job.

Step one is listening for thoughts and labeling thoughts as thoughts. In fact, labeling situations as situations, thoughts as thoughts, emotions as emotions, and behaviors as behaviors will get you pretty far in this practice. Some clients will have more difficulty with this and there can be a temptation to skip past this step.

This self-awareness and self-monitoring skill is foundational and it will be really hard to implement that later step if the client is not able to take a step back mentally and notice what they are thinking. Imagery strategies such as those illustrated above can be helpful. Drawing out a timeline can be helpful. Asking for an interpretation of the situation will give you an approximation of their automatic thought which is something you can work with. Ideally, we are not providing the client with guesses of what we think they were thinking. Judy Beck (2011) presents the brilliant strategy of guessing the opposite of what you think they might be thinking. This is actually quite useful. So, for the scenario, the therapist might have guessed, "So, you were thinking your boss was being really considerate by waiting until it was time to go to talk with you about this?" While we want to avoid telling clients what we think they were thinking, we can label their thoughts as thoughts when we hear them. The earliest phases of treatment are often focused on rapport building, and you can fold labeling thoughts as thoughts into your reflective listening. This is illustrated in the example above.

Increasing Self-Awareness of Emotions

Clients will present to treatment with a broad variability in their emotional awareness, emotional tolerance, and beliefs about emotion (Leahy, 2018). Therefore, the amount of work that needs to be done on this item will depend on your client's presentation. In some cases, basic emotional education is an important part of treatment, and perhaps a pretreatment of sorts. In other cases, you can fold it in as you go. At the very least your client should be able to name a few of the basic emotions (anger, disgust, fear, happiness, sadness, and surprise; see Ekman, 1992). See Persons (2012) for a more thorough review of theories of emotion as they relate to CBT and Leahy (2018) for a more thorough guide of working with emotions in CBT.

Therapist: So, you are going through your boyfriend's phone and you find some text messages from his ex. How were you feeling at the time?

Client: Bad … really bad.

Therapist: You felt bad, and what emotions were you feeling?

Client: (*looking confused*)

Therapist: Angry, disgusted, afraid, happy, sad, or surprised?

Client: Oh, a bunch of those. Angry for sure.

Therapist: So, you were feeling angry, any other emotions come up for you?

Client: I guess I was also feeling a little afraid and a sad, but mostly anger, lots of anger.

Therapist: You were mostly feeling angry, but there was also some sadness and worry, do I have that right?

Client: Yes

Therapist: Good job identifying all the different feelings, it sounds like it was a very intense situation and you were feeling a lot of anger, but also some sadness and fear. As we identify these strong emotional reactions, we can use those to clue us into the most important areas to work on. Do you find that you are often feeling angry, sad, and afraid lately?

Client: All the time

Therapist: That can be a lot to manage and it feels complicated with all the layers of the situation. I think it might make sense to spend some time untangling the situation, identifying all the different thoughts and corresponding feelings. It seems like it might make sense to start tracking your moods. Let me show you a form that might be helpful to you.

As the client gets more able to identify their emotions, you can move into self-monitoring strategies like the CBT triangle or three-column thought record which will be discussed below. If your client has continued trouble identifying their feelings, you might have them track upsetting situations and you can help them unpack the situations and label their emotions in session.

Increasing Self-Awareness of Behaviors

We can use self-monitoring to target behaviors we are trying to increase or decrease (Korotitsch & Nelson-Gray, 1999). The first question to ask yourself is whether the client is aware of the behavior when they are doing it. If not, you might need to first track the occurrence of the consequences of the behavior. As they start tracking a behavior, there can be a reactive effect, where we see a decrease in an undesired effect as a byproduct of their being more aware that they are doing it (see Korotitsch & Nelson-Gray, 1999). If there are specific behaviors that are you are wanting to target, you will want to track what is happening before and after the behavior to help clarify potential treatment targets. Tracking an individual's overall behaviors in a day can be a helpful way to better understand their situation and functioning. You will typically find something unexpected or something you would have missed if you simply relied on retrospective remembering a week later in your therapy session (Brittlebank et al., 1993; Williams & Scott, 1988). Behaviors can be logged in a number of ways (Cohen et al., 2013). Typical elements are behavior or occurrence logs that track when a behavior happened, the context, and the co-occurring mood and thoughts.

Demonstrating the CBT Model with Self-Monitoring

Orienting to the CBT Model

Orienting your client to the CBT model is really a multistep process. You first will explain the model and then later you need to show them the model with the content from their own life. There are a lot of ways to explain the CBT model the most

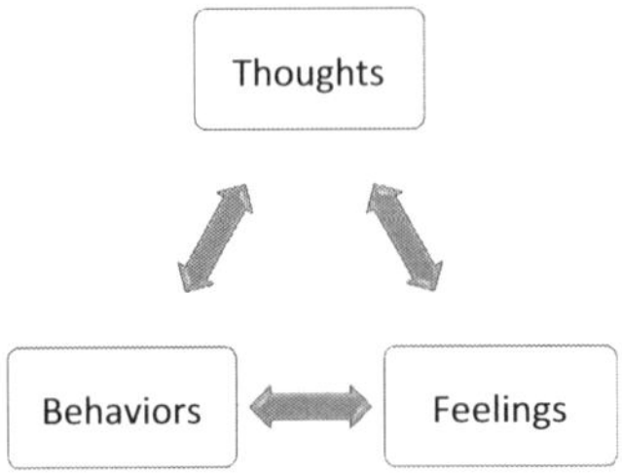

Figure 3.3 CBT Triangle

common are either with an ambiguous hypothetical situation to demonstrate that different people could have different reactions to the same situation. The other is to use a triangle (or rhombus; see Greenberger & Padesky, 2015). Below is an example that blends this together.

Therapist: I wanted to talk with you a little bit about how I work and why I do what I do. Different therapists do things differently, and I wanted to introduce one of the main ideas for this treatment. First, I want you to imagine a scenario with me. Imagine you post a picture onto social media and no likes it and no one comments on it. How might you feel in such a situation?

Client: I think I'd be mad. I wouldn't like that at all.

Therapist: So, in this situation you'd be mad. Do you know anyone who might have a different reaction?

Client: Yeah, my sister would get really sad and I don't even know if my dad would notice.

Therapist: So, different people in similar situations who have different reactions, why do you think that is?

Client: I think it would mean more to me than my dad, but my sister would also be upset.

Therapist: In this hypothetical scenario, what would you be telling yourself to make yourself so angry?

Client: I would be mad at my friends. I like all their stuff even if it isn't great, so why would they be so rude to me?

Therapist: So, you have the thought your friends are being rude and you feel angry. What might your sister being thinking to make her sad?

Client: She might be thinking that no one likes her.

Therapist: That is a sad thought, I can see how she'd feel so sad. What about your dad?

Client: He's funny, he might just be thinking that he likes the picture and not be worried about it like I am.

Therapist: What do you make of these three situations?

Client: I just need to be less negative.

Therapist: It sounds like you even have thoughts about your thoughts. So, the idea is that the three of you had three different thoughts and three different emotional reactions. So, it is not just what happens that affects how we feel, but it is also how we interpret or make sense of what happens. The type of therapy I use is focused on not just trying to improve the overall situation, but also looking at your meaning making system, your thought and beliefs, so we can maximize the benefit you get.

Client: That makes sense.

Therapist: Here's another way of thinking about it (*drawing out a triangle with thoughts, feelings, and behaviors at the different corners*).

Have you ever found that it is hard to just not be angry or not be sad?

Client: Uh, like is it hard to not always be happy?

Therapist: Yeah, like have you ever tried to just not be angry or sad, and only be happy?

Client: Story of my life!

Therapist: And people probably tell you things like "don't be so angry" or "don't be sad," maybe "don't worry." How easy is that?

Client: It's hard.

Therapist: Yes, it is really hard, and I think if it was easy no one would ever come to see me. The thing is while we don't have a lot of direct control over how we are feeling, we do have some control over our thinking and even more control over what we are doing. If you look at this diagram, what we've found is that our thoughts, feelings, and behaviors are connected. So, by making adjustments to what you are doing and how you are thinking, we can bring change to how you are feeling. How does that sound?

Client: It makes sense.

Therapist: I know it can be a little abstract, so the first thing I want to do is spend some time over the next few weeks talking more about your concerns and seeing how well this model applies to you. I want to test out with you if your thoughts, feelings, and behaviors are connected, because if they are this model should be a good fit for what is going on with you. Would that be alright?

Client: Yes. I like the idea of first testing out to make sure it's a good fit.

The next step is to talk with the client about their concerns and recent upsetting situations and then fold those situations into the model to test whether CBT will be a good fit for them. After you have done this a few times, you will then want to start asking questions to help them start seeing the connection between thoughts, feelings, and behaviors. Their seeing this connection will make it much easier to advance cognitive and behavior change strategies.

Example with a Behavior: Behavioral Activation

This "getting started" phase is called self-monitoring in the literature, and it accomplishes two objectives: helping to further orient the client to the model and helping to uncover strategic targets. There can be a big pull to jump right into trying to change thoughts or change behaviors and these attempts can fall flat if we do not yet know where to intervene or if the client does not see the connection between how they think and act and how they feel. Take, for example, behavioral activation (Martell, Dimidjian, & Herman-Dunn, 2013). It is commonly understood that the goal of behavioral activation is to get the client more active to help them feel less depressed. The commonsense approach is just to tell your client directly to get more active and that it will help them feel better. The problem is that if you have clinical depression, you have very low energy and often have thoughts that you will not enjoy anything, that you will not have the energy to do anything, and that you're too depressed to do anything. So, when your therapist tells you to get more active, you say to yourself: "Yeah, but I'm depressed. I don't have the energy. I can't do it." You might even say to yourself: "When I start feeling better, then I'll do more." This is, of course, a trap, because you will likely not feel better before you start changing your behavior.

So, what is a therapist to do? The early goal is to resist the pull to jump into giving the client advice that they likely will not follow and instead align with them to help them see for themselves that what they are doing is affecting how they are feeling. Ideally, this is a joint discovery (collaborative empiricism) that is called activity monitoring. The idea is simple—use details from the client's life to prove the cognitive behavioral model and look for strategic points to intervene. Activity monitoring involves looking at the client's week as it is, and then framing it as a way to learn more about them. Consider the example that follows.

Chad was a young man stuck in a job he did not like, and struggling to pay for a child he and his wife had not planned on having. He had been depressed for a number of months and presented in session as emotionally flat and exceedingly apathetic. Often when symptoms are severe, behavior change is the first target and as symptoms improve, cognitive strategies are used for further gains (Beck et al., 1979). I explained to Chad the model of how his feelings and behaviors were connected. I had some initial ideas about things he might do differently to feel better, but resisted the pull to tell him what I thought the answers were and instead suggested we study his depression together. I asked him to track his depression for a week. This entailed tracking what he was doing and how he was feeling. I asked him to look for subtle variance in his depression—the times he felt more depressed and the times he felt slightly less depressed. The following week we reviewed his log together. He was quite unhappy at work and had a high frequency of "depression naps" that often left him feeling worse. I noticed he had a slight "bump" in the early evening, and so I focused on being curious about this. He explained that he actually rather enjoyed himself when he was cooking dinner. "Great!" I internally exclaimed. I showed more curiosity about this, what was it about cooking dinner that was enjoyable to him? He explained that he felt like he was not really good at his job, or at being a dad, or at many other things, but that he knew quite well how to cook. And, when he was cooking, he felt (thought) he was finally doing something right.

This was hugely important. We had identified an activity that helped to alleviate his depressive symptoms. From looking at overall log, I asked him if he saw any connections between what he was doing and how he was feeling. He could see the connection. I asked him what he wanted to do about this connection, and he said that he thought he might want to make some changes to his schedule to see if it helped him feel better. We talked about other ways to feel more of a sense of mastery, and as we increased his mastery experiences his depression lifted. He became a more engaged father and spouse, and he found a more fulfilling career. The takeaway for myself was clear. If I had just told him to do the first thing that I had thought of, then I would have completely missed this great intervention, and by guiding him to discover this for himself, it increased his buy-in and motivation for the activity.

Example with a Thought: Cognitive Therapy

The basic flow of this process is straightforward layering. First, we teach the client how to notice their thoughts and feelings. As they learn how to do this, we build on it by drawing a connection between their thoughts and feelings. As they come to see a connection between how they are thinking and feeling, we use that to build a rationale for learning cognitive change strategies. Below is an example of that rationale being built, with a continuance of the case example from above.

Therapist: Jasmine, we've been talking for a little while about the situation with your recent breakup. It's clear this has been very hard on you.

Client: It's been hell, I just feel so bad.

Therapist: It feels really bad, and the emotion?

Client: Sad, really sad.

Therapist: So, you're feeling really sad and we've been looking at some of the thoughts behind this sadness. Which ones stand out to you?

Client: That thought that, "I'll always be alone, and no one will ever love me," is a big one.

Therapist: You have these very painful thoughts that you'll always be alone and that no one will ever love you and you end up feeling profoundly sad.

Client: Ain't that the truth.

Therapist: Do you see a connection between these thoughts of being alone forever and being unlovable and your feelings of sadness?

Client: Yes, I think so. I think they are connected. I certainly feel worse when I spend more time thinking about that.

Therapist: So, what do you want to do about that?

Client: Maybe, I just need to distract myself from those thoughts. I just need to stay busy, so I don't have time to be sad.

Therapist: Have you tried that already?

Client: I did and I ended up crying at work and then picking a fight with someone who didn't do anything wrong.

Therapist: If distraction isn't going to solve the problem, what else might we try?

Client: I don't know, that's why I'm here.

Therapist: And we have gathered some good data to inform our plan. You found that these thoughts of being unlovable tend to make you sadder.

Client: That's true.

Therapist: So, what do you want to do about that?

Client: I guess find some new thoughts that are less depressing.

Therapist: Hold on. Slow down, this sounds important, let me write this down. You are suggesting that if your thoughts are part of what is making so sad that coming up with new thoughts might help you feel better?

Client: That makes sense.

Therapist: I like it, and in fact I have a lot of useful skills and strategies I can teach you to help us find some new thoughts that are balanced and believable. How does that sound to you?
Client: That sounds like just what I need.

Summary

There are a number of techniques that a therapist can use to increase the likelihood that they will be able to use effective Socratic strategies in-session. Having a strong therapeutic alliance is important across therapies, and a strong alliance would suggest an agreement on treatment goals and the method to accomplish these goals. CBT session structure helps maximize session efficiency and facilitates productive sessions. CBT is inherently a skills training therapy and we are just as interested in you teaching your clients how to apply Socratic strategies to their own thought processes as we are in bringing about cognitive change. Self-monitoring is a crucial first step in treatment, whereby we teach clients to notice and track their thoughts, feelings, and behaviors. As they come to see a connection between thoughts, feelings, and behaviors, we use that to build a rationale for using cognitive and behavioral change strategies such as Socratic questioning. Developing mastery in these areas will make it easier for you and your clients to use Socratic strategies to help overcome the barriers in their life.

References

Ackermann, R., & DeRubeis, R. J. (1991). Is depressive realism real? *Clinical Psychology Review, 11*(5), 565–584.
Beck, A. T. (1964). Thinking and depression II. Theory and therapy. *Archives of General Psychiatry, 10*(6), 561–571. doi:10.1001/archpsyc.1964.01720240015003
Beck, A. T. (1963). Thinking and depression I. Idiosyncratic content and cognitive distortions. *Archives of General Psychiatry, 9*, 324–333. doi:10.1001/archpsyc.1963.01720160014002
Beck, A. T. (1979). *Cognitive therapy and the emotional disorders.* New York: Meridian.
Beck, A. T., Rush, A. J., Shaw, B. F., & Emery, G. (1979). *Cognitive therapy of depression.* New York: Guilford Press.
Beck, J. S. (2011). *Cognitive behavior therapy: Basics and beyond* (2nd ed.). New York: Guilford Press.
Bellack, A. S., Mueser, K. T., Gingerich, S., & Agresta, J. (2013). *Social skills training for schizophrenia: A step-by-step guide.* New York: Guilford Press.
Brittlebank, A. D., Scott, J., Mark, J., Williams, G., & Ferrier, I. N. (1993). Autobiographical memory in depression: State or trait marker?. *The British Journal of Psychiatry, 162*(1), 118–121.
Carroll, L. (2011). *Alice's adventures in wonderland.* Ontario, Canada: Broadview Press.
Cohen, J. S., Edmunds, J. M., Brodman, D. M., Benjamin, C. L., & Kendall, P. C. (2013). Using self-monitoring: Implementation of collaborative empiricism in cognitive-behavioral therapy. *Cognitive and Behavioral Practice, 20*(4), 419–428.
Creed, T. A. & Waltman, S. H. (2017). Therapeutic alliance. In A. Wenzel. (Ed.), *The SAGE encyclopedia of abnormal and clinical psychology* (pp. 3511). Thousand Oaks, CA: SAGE.

Creed, T. A., Waltman, S. H., Frankel, S. A., & Williston, M. A. (2016). School-based cognitive behavioral therapy: Current status and alternative approaches. *Current Psychiatry Reviews, 12*(1), 53–64.
David, S. (2016). *Emotional agility: Get unstuck, embrace change, and thrive in work and life.* New York: Penguin.
Edmunds, J. M., Beidas, R. S., & Kendall, P. C. (2013). Dissemination and implementation of evidence-based practices: Training and consultation as implementation strategies. *Clinical Psychology: Science and Practice, 20*(2), 152–165.
Ekman, P. (1992). An argument for basic emotions. *Cognition & Emotion, 6*(3–4), 169–200.
Foster, S. L., Laverty-Finch, C., Gizzo, D. P., & Osantowski, J. (1999). Practical issues in self-observation. *Psychological Assessment, 11*(4), 426.
Gilbert, P., & Leahy, R. L. (Eds.). (2007). *The therapeutic relationship in the cognitive behavioral psychotherapies.* London: Routledge.
Greenberger, D., & Padesky, C. A. (2015). *Mind over mood: Change how you feel by changing the way you think.* New York: Guilford Press.
Hayes, S. C., & Smith, S. (2005). *Get out of your mind and into your life: The new acceptance and commitment therapy* (2nd ed.). Oakland, CA: New Harbinger Publications.
Kazantzis, N., Beck, J. S., Dattilio, F. M., Dobson, K. S., & Rapee, R. M. (2013). Collaborative empiricism as the central therapeutic relationship element in CBT: An expert panel discussion at the 7th international congress of cognitive psychotherapy. *International Journal of Cognitive Therapy, 6*(4), 386–400.
Kolb, D. A. (1984). *Experiential learning: Experience as the source of learning and development.* Englewood Cliffs, NJ: Prentice-Hall.
Korotitsch, W. J., & Nelson-Gray, R. O. (1999). An overview of self-monitoring research in assessment and treatment. *Psychological Assessment, 11*(4), 415.
Kuyken, W., & Dalgleish, T. (1995). Autobiographical memory and depression. *British Journal of Clinical Psychology, 34*(1), 89–92.
Leahy, R. L. (2018). *Emotional schema therapy: Distinctive features.* New York: Routledge.
M. Stith, S., Miller, M. S., Boyle, J., Swinton, J., Ratcliffe, G., & McCollum, E. (2012). Making a difference in making miracles: Common roadblocks to miracle question effectiveness. *Journal of Marital and Family Therapy, 38*(2), 380–393.
Martell, C. R., Dimidjian, S., & Herman-Dunn, R. (2013). *Behavioral activation for depression: A clinician's guide.* New York: Guilford Press.
McNally, R. J., Lasko, N. B., Macklin, M. L., & Pitman, R. K. (1995). Autobiographical memory disturbance in combat-related posttraumatic stress disorder. *Behaviour Research and Therapy,* 33(6), 619–630.
Miller, W. R., & Rollnick, S. (2012). *Motivational interviewing: Helping people change.* New York: Guilford Press.
Okamoto, A., Dattilio, F. M., Dobson, K. S., & Kazantzis, N. (2019). The therapeutic relationship in cognitive-behavioral therapy: Essential features and common challenges. *Practice Innovations, 4*(2), 112–123.
Overholser, J. C. (2011). Collaborative empiricism, guided discovery, and the Socratic method: Core processes for effective cognitive therapy. *Clinical Psychology: Science and Practice, 18*(1), 62–66.
Persons, J. B. (2013). *The case formulation approach to cognitive-behavior therapy.* New York: Guilford Press.

Randall, W. L. (2007). From computer to compost: Rethinking our metaphors for memory. *Theory & Psychology, 17*(5), 611–633.
Rizvi, S. L., & Ritschel, L. A. (2014). Mastering the art of chain analysis in dialectical behavior therapy. *Cognitive and Behavioral Practice, 21*(3), 335–349.
Tee, J., & Kazantzis, N. (2011). Collaborative empiricism in cognitive therapy: A definition and theory for the relationship construct. *Clinical Psychology: Science and Practice, 18*(1), 47–61.
Waltman, S. H. (2015). Functional analysis in differential diagnosis: Using cognitive processing therapy to treat PTSD. *Clinical Case Studies, 14*(6), 422–433.
Waltman, S. H., Hall, B. C., McFarr, L. M., Beck, A. T., & Creed, T. A. (2017). In-session stuck points and pitfalls of community clinicians learning CBT: Qualitative investigation. *Cognitive and Behavioral Practice, 24*, 256–267. doi:10.1016/j.cbpra.2016.04.002
Wampold, B. E. (2001). *The great psychotherapy debate models, methods, and findings.* Mahwah, NJ: Lawrence Erlbaum.
Watkins, E. D., & Teasdale, J. D. (2001). Rumination and overgeneral memory in depression: Effects of self-focus and analytic thinking. *Journal of Abnormal Psychology, 110*(2), 353.
Wenzel, A. (2019). *Cognitive behavioral therapy for beginners: An experiential learning approach.* New York: Routledge.
Westra, H. A., & Dozois, D. J. (2006). Preparing clients for cognitive behavioral therapy: A randomized pilot study of motivational interviewing for anxiety. *Cognitive Therapy and Research, 30*(4), 481–498.
Williams, J. M. G., & Scott, J. (1988). Autobiographical memory in depression. *Psychological Medicine, 18*(3), 689–695.

Chapter 4

A Framework for Socratic Questioning

Beckian Socratic Dialogue

Scott H. Waltman and R. Trent Codd, III

❖ CONTENTS

Socrates used questioning and confrontation to help people arrive at what he regarded as universal truths. His method consisted of dismantling the learner's argument and then constructing a new point of view that was typically consistent with his own (Peoples & Drozdek, 2017). He accomplished this by asking a sequence of questions based on the anticipated responses of the respondent (Hintikka, 2007). Philosophy and therapy have different goals, however. In philosophy, the use of Socratic methods can be called the *elenchus*. Socrates and other philosophers would have considered themselves to be midwives for thoughts, beliefs, and ideas (Grimes & Uliana, 1998; Overholser, 2018). Socrates focused on questions relating to ethics or morality (Peoples & Drozdek, 2017). Alternatively, the focus in therapy is helping clients find their own truth that is informed by their experiences, the evidence, and their values; therefore, Socratic questioning in psychotherapy differs from what Socrates would actually do with someone whose mind he was trying to change. To account for this, Leahy suggested that perhaps the terms *Beckian Socratic Dialogue* or *Beckian Dialogue* are more accurate descriptions of the process (see Kazantzis et al., 2018). The overarching principle that directs a Beckian Socratic Dialogue is called *guided discovery* or *collaborative empiricism*, which denotes that in the therapy dyad there is a partnership, and that therapists need to embody principles such as openness and willingness (see Hayes, 2005) as well.

There is some evidence that Socratic strategies are among the hardest skills to learn how to perform competently. For example, in a qualitative and quantitative study of the common pitfalls associated with learning cognitive behavior therapy (CBT), problems with guided discovery were the most frequently observed difficulty (Waltman, Hall, McFarr, Beck, & Creed, 2017). Further, it was also observed that even with ongoing support this skillset can be difficult to learn (Waltman et al., 2017). One of the trainers from this study described the common trap well: "Therapists have a propensity to engage in 'provided discovery' instead of guided discovery" (p. 263). This means trying to give clients the answers instead of helping them find them on their own. Padesky (1993) noted this difficulty in her seminal talk on the topic of Socratic Dialogue. She detailed how therapists would have difficulty knowing which questions to ask and would fall into the trap of trying to convince the client or trying to get them to arrive at a specific conclusion.

Padesky's 1993 Model of Socratic Dialogue

Padesky (1993) developed a four-step model of Socratic Dialogue that included: (1) asking informational questions, (2) active listening, (3) summarizing, and (4) asking synthesizing or analytical questions. This model served as the foundation of training in Socratic strategies for decades. It demonstrated that this process does not involve a confrontational process in which the goal is to eviscerate the individual's argument. Rather, it illustrated the importance of the clinician first learning from their client, followed by their jointly applying that learning to the client's situation to aid in the formation of a new perspective in the context of their collaborative line of inquiry.

We were interested in how senior CBT therapists applied this framework while applying change strategies such as cognitive restructuring or behavior modification, so we conducted a survey of expert therapists and trainers with robust Socratic

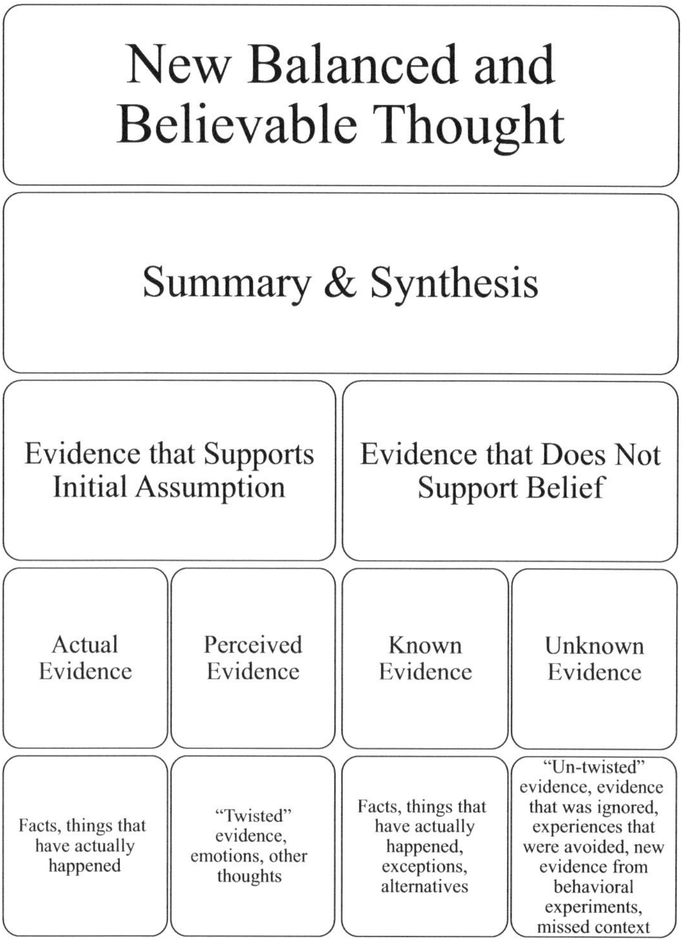

Figure 4.1 Overview of Beckian Socratic Dialogue

questioning skills. While we found some variability, the majority of CBT therapists surveyed used Padesky's framework or a model similar to the Padesky model. We also asked these respondents how they applied this model, how they moved from step to step within this approach, and what their internal mental processes were as they traveled through these four steps. A few themes emerged from our analysis. These included: relational factors, attending to client feedback, cognitive and behavioral conceptualization, and task orientation.

Revised Framework for Socratic Questioning

Based on these results and feedback from experiences as CBT trainers, we made some revisions to Padesky's (1993) original framework. We have found this to be helpful for

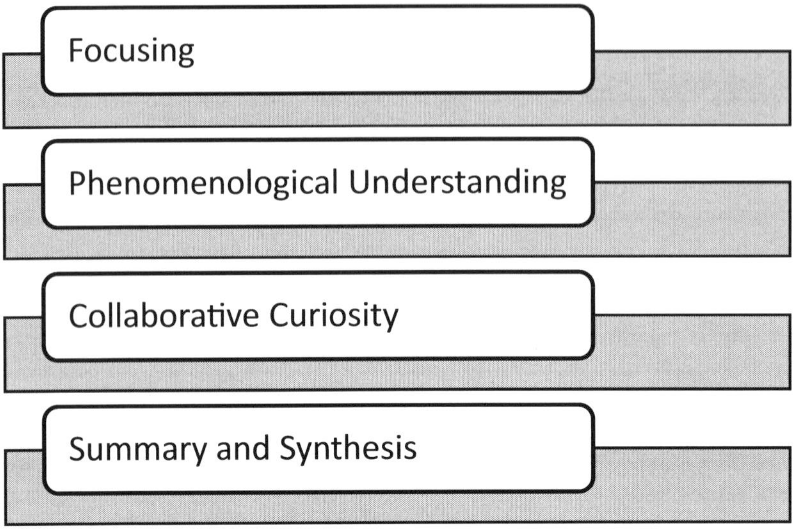

Figure 4.2 Revised Framework for Socratic Questioning

the frontline therapists and graduate students that we teach, and it fits with our inductive study of how expert therapists actually conduct Socratic questioning.

The revised model consists of first *focusing* on the key cognitions to target. After a suitable or strategic target is identified, the therapist works to develop a *phenomenological understanding* of the thought. That is, to understand how it makes perfect sense that the client came to think in this way. Once seen from their point of view, we work to expand that view together through the process of *collaborative curiosity*. The capstone to this process is a *summary and synthesis*, where the therapist helps the client make sense of the big picture and tries to reconcile their initial assumptions with their newly developed, more balanced perspective. What follows is a quick summary of this process. A more fine-grained presentation is given throughout the remainder of the book where we break these steps down into component skills and competencies that are addressed in applied case examples and cheat sheets.

Case Example: Fiona

Fiona (pseudonym) was a 34-year-old African American heterosexual cisgender married woman. She grew up in an emotionally invalidating environment, where emotionality was shamed, and achievement was emphasized. Consequently, normative human emotion was interpreted as being dangerous, confusing, and shameful. Though Fiona was much achieved in relation to academics and sports, she often felt like something was wrong with her, and she developed the belief that she was not good enough and that she was defective. These feelings and beliefs were very shameful to her, which only compounded her feelings of depression. Over time, Fiona developed the compensatory strategies of constantly reinventing herself, hoping that if she could just learn to be like the people that she admired that she would finally be good enough. An unintended consequence of these behaviors was that her sense of self remained undeveloped and her relationships tended to be shallow.

Step 1: Focusing

The first step in applying Socratic strategies is to identify the targets for these strategies. In a practical sense, we simply do not have time to address every thought that we think might be distorted. We want to target the thoughts that are central to their problems and related to their core difficulties and underlying beliefs. These are often called the *hot thought* (Greenberger & Padesky, 2015), so therapists are taught to follow the affect or, "find the heat." There are a number of questions therapists can ask themselves and the client to facilitate this step, including the following:

- What is so upsetting or difficult about the situation for the client?
- What is the most upsetting part?
- How are they making sense of it?
- How does this relate back to their underlying beliefs?
- What is the most distressing thought?
- Can we break that thought down into different components?
- What does that thought mean to them?
- How are we defining the target cognition?
- How can we frame this thought to facilitate collaborative empiricism?
- Are they on board to evaluate the thought?

Here is an example of what this looks like in practice.

Therapist: So, Fiona, you mentioned you've been having a really rough time and yet it was *really* hard for you to decide to come give therapy a try.

Fiona: Yes, I've been stuck for a really long time but the thought of coming into therapy was always so scary … so … not OK.

Therapist: I gather you would have rather worked this out on your own.

Fiona: Yes!

Therapist: So, it's difficult for you to be here and it probably took some courage to come in. Let's take a moment and just honor the effort it took to get here.
(pausing for a moment)
Can I ask what it is about coming in for therapy that felt so dangerous to you?

Fiona: Growing up I was taught that therapy is for weak people.

Therapist: Coming into therapy means you're weak?

Fiona: Look, I just … I … you don't even know how hard it is for me to sit here and admit that … that I'm depressed.

Therapist: For you, what's worse, being depressed? Or admitting that you're depressed?

Fiona: (tearing) I think I've been depressed for a while, but this, being here is pretty hard

Therapist: What does it mean that you're here in my office admitting to someone else, and yourself, that you've been feeling depressed?

Fiona: It means that there's something wrong with me.

Therapist: Help me understand this, is it more that this means that there's something wrong with you and it's not OK to have something wrong with you or that there's something wrong with you and you're the only one with something wrong with them?

Fiona: Both.

Therapist: OK, so this is really intense for you just being here in my office. Which of these thoughts is more upsetting to you, the thought that there's something wrong with you or that you're the only one with something wrong with them?

Fiona: I feel like I'm the only one who feels this way and that's why I don't like talking about it.

Therapist: So, it's sort of a secret that there's something wrong with you, that you feel depressed.

Fiona: My biggest secret.

Therapist: How does that secret make you feel?

Fiona: Bad, dirty, like I'm broken.

Therapist: Ashamed?

Fiona: Yes!

Therapist: So, you have the thought that you're the only one with this particular problem and that makes you feel ashamed and so you keep your problems to yourself, like a dirty secret. And, this secret is so shameful that it's hard to tell me, your therapist, that you feel depressed?

Fiona: So hard. I really wish I could have figured this out on my own.

Therapist: I think I'm getting some ideas about what we might target. You have these longstanding feelings of depression, and then you have these thoughts and feelings about your depression that create like an extra layer of suffering. Can we spend some time over the next few weeks evaluating these ideas that there's something wrong with you and you're the only one who has this dirty secret?

Fiona: If you think it will help, I'm so tired of feeling this way.

With Fiona, specific cognitions to target included: "There's something wrong with me." "I'm the only one who feels this way." "If my family knew how I was feeling they would reject me." "If people got to know the real me, they wouldn't like me." The beauty of collaborative empiricism is that it allows us to be transparent with our clients. As her therapist, we talked openly with her about these thoughts and assessed whether she was interested in evaluating them and their corresponding behaviors.

There is a well-known saying among those who teach calculus about their students: "At the end of the course they may not know calculus, but they will surely know their algebra." This sentiment reflects the importance of algebra mastery for doing successful calculus. Often, when students struggle to learn calculus, they mistakenly blame calculus. However, the difficulty is often with algebra skills that were not fully developed. Similarly, students of Socratic questioning who experience difficulties in learning this process often fail to identify procedures that occur at the beginning of the chain. That is, executing step 1 of the Socratic process effectively is crucial to the success of Socratic interventions. Therefore, in Chapter 3, "Getting Started," we emphasize the foundational procedures a therapist can execute in the early sessions to set the stage for effective Socratic questioning.

Step 2: Phenomenological Understanding

This step can be thought of as a practice of validation. In Dialectical Behavior Therapy (DBT) terms this is an opportunity for levels 4, 5, and 6 validation (see Linehan, 1997). We provide specific recommendations for integration, which are discussed later in this book. The task of this step is to understand the client and the target cognition. The guiding principle is that people come by their beliefs honestly and we want to come to understand how it makes complete sense that they came to think in that way. This early emphasis on validation is also strategic in that it is relationship enhancing and can be regulating for the client. In our experience, people are more willing to have an open mind to alternatives when they feel that you have truly and sincerely listened to them. There are several questions therapists can ask themselves to guide this process:

- What experiences are this thought based on?
- What are the facts that support this?
- If this was true, what do you think would be the strongest evidence to support it?
- What are the reasons they think this is true?
- Is this something people have directly said to them in the past?
- How much do they believe this?
- How long have they believed this?
- When do they tend to believe this more and less?
- What do they typically do when thoughts like this come up for them?

Here is an example of what this looks like in practice.

Therapist: OK, so we want to start out looking at why it makes sense that you developed the beliefs that there's something wrong with you and that you're the only one. This will help me understand you better. Where do you think you learned this from?

Fiona: I grew up in a very strict home, where everyone was very high achieving, and it wasn't OK to not excel.

Therapist: There were high expectations and not doing well was a problem.

Fiona: Yes, my dad made it like a competition between us, he was always telling me how well my brother was doing and how I needed to do better if I didn't want to get left behind.

Therapist: As a child how was that for you?

Fiona: It was really really hard, like as a mom now, I realize that was a terrible way to raise your kids, making them feel like they're not good enough when they're doing the best they could.

Therapist: (*making notes for later that she has acknowledged that some of the rules she grew up with are not ones that she would want to use with her own children*)
So, one of the places you learned that it wasn't OK to have problems was from your dad and the things that he would say when you were growing up?

Fiona: Yes, he would get so mad when I would cry, I learned really fast how to turn it off and put on a straight face.

Therapist: (*noting for later that for some reason it was OK for dad to be angry but not for Fiona to be sad*)

So, you learned how to not have feelings or how to hide that you had feelings?

Fiona: To hide them, I still had them, but I hid them because they got me in trouble and no one else seemed to have the problems I did.

Therapist: And, how did you come by the idea that you're the only one with these problems?

Fiona: I don't know, I think I just always knew.

Therapist: OK, I think I missed something, how did you know that you were the only one?

Fiona: Um … I guess I just never saw anyone else cry the way I did or explode like I did.

Therapist: So, growing up you never saw another kid cry?

Fiona: No, I mean, kids cry, I never saw people cry as much as I did, and I never saw my brother cry.

Therapist: You thought you had more feelings than other people.

Fiona: Yes.

Therapist: Now, when these other kids would cry what would happen?

Fiona: Well, their parents would pick them up and sooth them and they wouldn't cry that long.

Therapist: So, it seemed like you would cry more than these other kids, and also, they seemed to live in a different system than you did, where their parents had a different response to their crying than your parents did.

Fiona: I guess so, I never really thought about that or talked about that with them.

Therapist: It seems like you never really talked about this with anyone.

Fiona: No, I learned to keep a lid on it.

Therapist: Let me try and fit this all together and see if I'm understanding this right, growing up achievement was praised, and emotionality was punished. You learned at an early age to hide your feelings. You developed the idea that you were the only one with emotions as intense as yours, and there is some evidence that there may have been some sort of double standard where your father was more strict with you than your peers' parents were with them. Is that right?

Fiona: Yeah, that sounds about right, I haven't thought about all of that for a while.

Therapist: Looking at your background, it makes total sense that you would grow up with feelings of shame about your feelings and that you'd think there was something wrong with you for having your feelings.

Fiona: I can see that, but this is still intense.

For Fiona, her target cognitions developed in response to messages she directly heard from her father and the resulting behaviors created a self-sustaining system—a vicious cycle. She had a shameful secret—she had feelings—and the fact that she thought these feelings were shameful caused to her to have suffering and shame. She believed that she was the only one who felt this way and that people would reject her if they really had the chance to get to know her, but that was a risk she never took. As we mapped this process out on the board, it helped us to better understand the context that these thoughts developed in and to have some ideas about what was maintaining them.

Step 3: Collaborative Curiosity

While this is functionally the disconfirming evidence step, curiosity is key to this process. In the seminal mathematical logic book, *How to Solve It*, Polya (1973) describes a key step to problem solving as being determining the unknown. Now that we see it from their point of view, we can work to expand that view together. We ask ourselves: "What are they missing?" Functionally, there are two kinds of blind spots: things you don't see and things you don't know. We need to figure out what are they not attending to due to attentional filters as well as the gaps in their experiences that developed as a result of their avoidance pattern.

Many great questions and lines of inquiry can often be found from evaluating elements from the previous steps. People tend to twist information to fit into their preexisting assumptions and beliefs. So, we want to help them mentally take a step back and look at both context and the big picture. We ask ourselves: "If the thought wasn't true, what would be the indicators of that, and can we look for that evidence?" We may need to draw on time orientation: "Has it always been this way?" "Does it always have to be this way?"

There are a number of questions that therapists can ask themselves to guide this process, including the following:

- Can we add context to the supporting evidence to mitigate its effect or that would lead to a new conclusion?
- If we had been in that situation what would we have expected to happen?
- Are there exceptions or discrepancies that we can help them remember?
- What are the facts?
- What would they tell a friend?
- Has it always been this way?
- How has believing this thought affected their behavior and the available evidence to draw from?
- Can we go and gather new evidence?

Here is an example of what this looks like in practice.

Therapist: Alright, so we have some ideas about how it makes sense that you developed the belief that there was something wrong with you and that you were the only one who had these problems. Can we take a look at the other side of the coin, and try and figure out if there's anything we're missing?

Fiona: Yeah, I think that's fair, it's been a while since I've really thought about this stuff.

Therapist: I made a note that you said that you wouldn't want to raise your children the way your father raised you. Can you tell me more about what you don't agree with?

Fiona: He was always so angry, and nothing was ever good enough for him. I try to always tell my kids that I love them and build them up instead of tearing them down.

Therapist: So, his system wasn't perfect.

Fiona: (*chuckling*) Yeah, you could definitely say that.

Therapist: And the rule that it is not OK to be sad or have feelings came from him?

Fiona: Yes, he would tell my brother that boys don't cry and me that my brother didn't cry.

Therapist: If some of his approach to parenting was flawed, how does that apply to his rules about feelings?

Fiona: Hmm, I guess, maybe that was a bad rule, or a rule that was bad for us.

Therapist: It seems like it had a real toll on you over the years.

Fiona: You have no idea.

Therapist: And, you mentioned that your dad was angry a lot of the time?

Fiona: He wasn't always angry, but if things didn't go the way he wanted, he would get really angry, like scary angry!

Therapist: And anger is a feeling?

Fiona: Uh, yeah, I guess it is.

Therapist: So different rules for you and him?

Fiona: … It's total BS and classic my dad.

Therapist: So, what do you think about this rule of your dad's, that it's not OK to have feelings?

Fiona: I never questioned it growing up, but I think it's not right.

Therapist: And, there's this piece about you being the only one.

Fiona: Yeah?

Therapist: Let me draw this out to see if I'm understanding the cycle right. You had the thought that you were the only one who felt this way. This made you have feelings of shame. Shame lead to avoidance and secret keeping, so you never talked about this with anyone. And, you kept thinking you were the only one because you never talked about this with anyone.

Fiona: That's how I got stuck, I just kept going around that circle.

Therapist: Right, in a sense, we don't know if you're the only one because you've never really checked it out.

Fiona: But it's scary to check it out, like what if someone tells me I'm weird and I'm the only one who feels that way?

Therapist: Do you want to ask me if I feel the same feelings you do?

Fiona: (*taking a deep breath*) I guess.

Therapist: So, ask me.

Fiona: Do you have feelings like I do?

Therapist: Yes, I feel all the feelings. I have times where I feel happy and other times where I'm sad, or scared, or embarrassed. Sometimes, I get jealous or nervous. I tend to feel them all.

Fiona: You do?

Therapist: Yeah, but I'm just one person, I could be crazy. How would you like to see if more than just you, me, and your dad have these feelings?

Fiona: I want to know.

Therapist: Let me open up my internet browser and let's do some searching.
Fiona: I've never thought to do this.

For Fiona this process involved helping her understand the context in which her assumptions developed, questioning her early assumptions, and engaging in experiments to gather new experiences and new evidence. An early experiment to test out her assumption that she was the only one who felt this way was to do some internet searches in session, where we looked up both prevalence data and firsthand accounts of other people who had difficulty with feelings of depression and anxiety. This helped her to see that this was much more common than she thought it was, and led to a decrease in shame, which helped her engage in more active experimentation. To test out the assumption that her family would reject her if they learned about her depression, she talked with her sister about her mental health. From that experiment she learned that her sister had a history of depressions and that her father had been in therapy for years himself. New experiences lead to new context and allowed for a re-examination of previous evidence.

Step 4: Summary and Synthesis

The summary and synthesis steps are important and easy for novice therapists to skip. This is where we work to make new learning explicit. Because we typically do not have the same schema and belief structures as our clients it is often easier for us to see a new perspective before clients do. There can also be a pull for the therapist to try to pick a purely positive thought because they might feel better. The trouble with purely positive thoughts or thoughts that are only based on the disconfirming evidence is that they can be brittle if they do not fit the reality of the client's life. Therefore, we are looking to develop new thoughts that are balanced and adaptive. This process involves summarizing both sides of the story, and helping the client to develop a new more balanced thought that captures both sides. The question we should ask is whether the new thought is believable. Once we have a summary statement, we should then help them synthesize that with their previous statements and assumptions. How does the new conclusion compare to the initial assumption? And their underlying beliefs? How do they reconcile their previous assumptions and this new evidence? We also want to help solidify these gains by helping the client translate the cognitive shift into behavior change. So, we ask them how they want to put the new thought into practice in the coming week or how they want to test it out in the coming week.

There are a number of questions that therapists can ask themselves to help with this question:

- So how does this all fit together?
- Can we summarize all the facts?
- What is a summary statement that captures both sides?
- How much do they believe that?
- Do we need to shape this to make it more believable?
- How do they reconcile our new statement with the thought we were evaluating? With the core belief we are targeting?

- How should we apply our new statement to their upcoming week? How can we test this out?
- If this was true, what would that mean about (the client, the world, the future, the target core belief, target problem, goals, etc.)?
- What did we learn about their thought processes from this exercise?

Here is an example of what this looks like in practice.

Therapist: OK, so, we gathered a lot of data and talked about a lot of things. Can you help me summarize what we talked about?

Fiona: We talked about a lot stuff, I don't think I can say it all.

Therapist: Let's start with why it makes sense that you came to think that there was something wrong with you and that you were the only one.

Fiona: Growing up with my dad … being my dad … I got in trouble for having feelings and learned to hide my feelings and not talk about them, so I thought I was the only person who felt this way.

Therapist: What did we talk about today that we can add to those facts?

Fiona: My dad had some of his own issues and so his rules for feelings were maybe not exactly right, and also he had like major emotional issues.

Therapist: And what else?

Fiona: And then we looked stuff up.

Therapist: Good, we'll get to that, you did something brave and asked me if I had feelings and what did I say?

Fiona: You said you felt all the feelings.

Therapist: And are we the only ones who have these?

Fiona: No, we looked online and there were millions of results for the searches we did, and we read people's stories.

Therapist: So, what does that mean?

Fiona: It means I'm not the only one … I'm not alone.

Therapist: So, on the one hand, you were raised to believe that feelings aren't OK, and you kept them a secret thinking you were the only one, and on the other hand, there's some indication that there are lots of people, millions, maybe billions who have feelings and sometimes trouble with their feelings.

Fiona: (*tearing*) yeah.

Therapist: So how can we summarize this whole conversation into a statement you can take with you?

Fiona: My dad didn't like feelings, but everyone has them, and maybe that's OK.

Therapist: Hold on, say that one more time while I write it down.
(*writing it down and then reading it back to her*)
Do you believe that?

Fiona: I do, kind of.

Therapist: This is new stuff we're getting into, exciting, and maybe a little scary. What's the part you believe? Or should we restate it in more believable terms?

Fiona: I guess, I believe that you have feelings and that internet people have feelings, but I don't really know about the real people in my life.

Therapist: That's a good point, what do you want to do about it?

Fiona: I know what I need to do, but I'm scared and embarrassed.

Therapist: Fear and shame have kept you from taking these steps for a while, what do you want to do about it?

Fiona: I don't want to keep doing what I've been doing.

Therapist: That's a lot of courage you've shown today. The courage to come into therapy, to tell me you're depressed, to talk about your feelings with me, and to ask me about my feelings.

Fiona: This is hard.

Therapist: This is the complete opposite of your training. The easiest thing to do would be to keep doing what you've always done.

Fiona: I can't do that anymore.

Therapist: OK, so let's make a goal for this week. Something doable, but a step in the direction of not letting shame and fear run your life.

Fiona: I think I need to talk with my sister about my feelings and our childhood.

Therapist: I love it! Let's talk logistics and help set you up and plan for a successful interaction.

As Fiona learned to fit it all together, she was able to see that although she was shamed at an early age for her emotionality, the way she was treated was more about her father's discomfort with his own feelings rather than a sign that she was fundamentally flawed. As she was asked to reconcile this with her earlier statements, she was able to gain the following insights: (1) there was nothing wrong with her; (2) emotions were a natural part of her life; (3) some people might be uncomfortable with her feelings; and (4) she didn't want to live the small life that came with being chiefly worried about what other people will think. These gains were used to facilitate increases in value-directed behavior and assertive behavior, which helped reshape her environment to reinforce her new beliefs.

Summary

In this chapter, we introduced a framework for applying Socratic questioning to clinical practice based on the reported behavior of a sample of expert CBT clinicians. This framework was illustrated with a case example that included transcripts of key dialogue. Socratic procedures include both within- and across-session strategies to help enhance rapport, teach skills, and bring about large-scale lasting change. The ensuing chapters will further break down and clarify the steps of the Socratic questioning framework. Readers are encouraged to practice this material shortly after reading each segment, so that they may instill these procedures into their clinical repertoire. We have included a thought record based on this model in the worksheet for this chapter for you to use in clinical practice.

Focusing: What are we targeting?
What are the different parts of the problem?
Which part is most upsetting?
What's the meaning I'm attributing to this situation? What am I telling myself?
How are we defining our target?

Understanding: How does it make sense that I think this?
Where did I learn this?
Is this something people have told me before?
What are the facts that tell me this is true?
How does this thought make me behave?

Curiosity: What are we missing?
Is there important context missing from the above statements?
Do my behaviors influence my experiences?
What do we not know?
What are the facts that tell me this might not be true?
Are there any exceptions we're forgetting about?

Summary: How can we summarize the whole story?

Synthesis: How does this summary fit with my original statement?
How does it fit with what I typically tell myself?
Take-Away Message: What's a more balanced and believable statement?

How can I apply that statement to my upcoming week?

Worksheet 4.1 Socratic Thought Record

References

Greenberger, D., & Padesky, C. A. (2015). *Mind over mood: Change how you feel by changing the way you think.* New York: Guilford Press.

Grimes, P., & Uliana, R. L. (1998). *Philosophical midwifery: A new paradigm for understanding human problems with its validation.* Costa Mesa, CA: Hyparxis Press.

Hayes, S. C. (2005). *Get out of your mind and into your life: The new acceptance and commitment therapy.* Oakland, CA: New Harbinger Publications.

Hintikka, J. (2007). *Socratic epistemology: Explorations of knowledge-seeking by questioning.* Cambridge: Cambridge University Press.

Kazantzis, N., Beck, J. S., Clark, D. A., Dobson, K. S., Hofmann, S. G., Leahy, R. L., & Wong, C. W. (2018). Socratic dialogue and guided discovery in cognitive behavioral therapy: A modified Delphi panel. *International Journal of Cognitive Therapy, 11*(2), 140–157.

Linehan, M. M. (1997). Validation and psychotherapy. Empathy reconsidered: New directions in psychotherapy. In A. C. Bohart & L. S. Greenberg (Eds.), *Empathy reconsidered: New directions in psychotherapy* (pp. 353–392). Washington, DC: American Psychological Association.

Overholser, J. C. (2018). *The Socratic method of psychotherapy.* New York: Columbia University Press.

Padesky, C. A. (1993). Socratic questioning: Changing minds or guiding discovery. Paper presented at the A keynote address delivered at the European Congress of Behavioural and Cognitive Therapies, London. Retrieved from: http://padesky.com/newpad/wpcontent/uploads/2012/11/socquest.pdf

Peoples, K., & Drozdek, A. (2017). *Using the Socratic method in counseling: A guide to channeling inborn knowledge.* Routledge.

Polya, G. (1973). *How to solve it* (2nd ed.). Princeton NJ: Princeton University Press.

Waltman, S. H., Hall, B. C., McFarr, L. M., Beck, A. T., & Creed, T. A. (2017). In-session stuck points and pitfalls of community clinicians learning CBT: Qualitative investigation. *Cognitive and Behavioral Practice, 24*, 256–267. doi:10.1016/j.cbpra.2016.04.002

Chapter 5

Focusing on Key Content

Scott H. Waltman

❖ CONTENTS

Overview

In any given therapy session, a therapist using Socratic cognitive change strategies has a choice. You can either spend a little bit of time on many different items, or you can spend a good amount of time on the key items. You can either jump on every possibly distorted thought you hear, or you can delve into a problem area to find the strategic target. In a recent study on the common stuck points of clinicians learning cognitive behavior therapy (CBT), it was found that identifying optimal cognitive targets was a common difficulty (Waltman, Hall, McFarr, Beck, & Creed, 2017). Trainers reported as follows:

> While it is easy to pick a thought to be challenged, it takes more experience to pick a thought that is central the presenting problem (Trainer 19)
>
> Not targeting central cognitions, but "jumping" from thought to thought throughout a session ... it's unclear what they are trying to accomplish at times and often feels they are looking for any thought that appears as though it may be distorted. (Trainer 8)
>
> The most common difficulty is focus on the most relevant cognitions or behaviors. Sometimes clinicians will go with the first thing the client says rather than probing for the most relevant. (Trainer 2)

By pulling these ideas together, it is clear that not every distorted thought is connected to a person's conceptualization or presenting problem. As Hank Robb pointed out at the 2014 SMART Recovery Annual Conference, in Washington, DC, "It's A-B-C not A-T-C." This clever statement highlights that we are more interested in targeting the cognitions that the client actually believes, and we do not need to target every distorted thought we come across. The optimal target is probably not the first thing the client says, and if we jump from target to target, we will have a batch of half-baked interventions. Sometimes the best strategy for a peripheral automatic thought is to simply notice it (and perhaps label it as being a thought). A few minutes spent assessing a situation and the corresponding thoughts can be invaluable. Spending some time fleshing out the situation can help to identify the most relevant thoughts to target. This is what Beck (1979) referred to as finding the hidden message in his first book, and this chapter will focus on teaching you how to identify and target the key cognitions.

A key reason why focusing on the key cognitions is important is because CBT is a relatively time-limited treatment, which calls for adjustments in the treatment approach. If you were going to visit a new area for a weekend, you would approach the weekend much differently than if you were there for an extended period of time. You might consult with reliable sources such as the concierge or people you meet about what the "must do" activities are. Spending some time planning your visit would increase the likelihood that you would not miss anything important. Similarly, if you were eating lunch in a food court, you probably would not order the first adequate food option you saw. If you were looking to order the optimal dish, you would look around a little bit first. Sometimes, you find something you have been seeking for a while and go for it, but if you are only having one lunch, some assessment can help you make the best choice and get the most of out the hour.

Clinical Example: Pamela, the Anxious College Student

Just as important as knowing which questions to ask, and how to ask them, is identifying an optimal target for your questions. Very rarely is the first thing that comes up the best thing to go after. A savvy therapist needs to be able to unpack a situation, feel around for affect, delve, and collaborate to identify strategic intervention points. Consider the following example.

Pamela is a second-career college student who presents to treatment with complaints of excessive anxiety and worry. At the start of your session, she reports increased anxiety that she attributes to needing to select her classes for the upcoming semester. In these situations, there can be a pull to jump right into problem-solving, counseling, or soothing, but all of these strategies miss the mechanism that is maintaining Pamela's anxiety, her underlying thoughts—of course, all of those strategies could be useful treatment components for later in the session. Leading with empathy and validation, you first seek to understand more about the situation. This can involve classic prompts, such as "Can you tell me more about the situation?" Pamela shares with you the logistics of selecting her schedule and gets into some of the complaints about the school. Often everything is connected and it is very easy to jump from one topic to another; so, you ask some focusing questions bring her back to the topic and to obtain some more information.

"How is needing to select your schedule affecting you?" Pamela talks about how she is not sleeping, is distracted, and is spending much time worrying about the situation. At this point, you are still unpacking the situation, and you want to wrap that in empathy and validation to increase engagement. "Selecting a schedule can be a really big deal; it makes sense that you are feeling this way. It sounds like this whole situation is really stressful for you and your anxiety is way up from last week. What are some of the worries you're having?" Pamela worries a lot and has many worries to share. As she is sharing these worries, you are listening for subtle changes in affect. Many of the worries she shares relating to choosing a good professor or time of day do not seem to be emotionally laden to her, so you form a hypothesis that it is not really about the schedule, or at least it is not a logistical concern. At this point, you shift gears to start delving into underlying thoughts and fears: "So, you are worried about selecting your schedule, what is the outcome you are afraid of happening?" Pamela instantly looks anxious and says that she is just worried she will make the wrong decision. This seems to be where the affect is, and so you look further in this direction: "Alright, you make the wrong decision, and then what happens?"

With a look of defeat, Pamela says that what would happen next is that she would be a failure. At this point, you think you have found it, but you want to make sure and you also want to see if it needs to be fleshed out. Leaning in and with increased warmth in your voice, you say, "That sounds like a really painful thought. So, let me see if I have this right. You currently need to pick your class schedule, but you're worried you might make the wrong decision. And, if you make the wrong decision, that means you failed. Well, actually, you are saying that you would then be a failure. Does that sound accurate?" Meekly, Pamela says this sounds about right. Again, leading with validation, "I can see why you are so anxious; this is a high-stakes decision." At this point, there a few different directions in which you can go. The unsophisticated therapist might jump on evaluating the likelihood or evidence that Pamela will make the wrong decision. While she reports being worried about making the wrong decision, there is a larger issue in play. Here we have a chance to uncover some of her life rules (intermediate beliefs; see Chapter 2) that are at play.

"It sounds like the prospect of making a wrong decision feels dangerous to you. Can you help me understand what makes this so awful?" Pamela talks about how she does not like to make mistakes. "Right, I think most people prefer to not make mistakes, but it sounds like it is more than that in this instance. Is it Okay if you make a mistake? Like, if you made a mistake and picked the wrong schedule, how terrible would that be?" Pamela affirms that it would be really bad if she made a mistake. "It sounds like you have an idea that it is not okay to make mistakes, and this thought cause you a lot of anxiety, can we spend some time and take a closer look at that thought?" Pamela agrees this is a good idea and you could move onto the next step in the framework with a good cognitive target.

Differential Diagnosis of Thought

This whole chapter could have been called, differential diagnosis of thought. The skills involved include analysis and synthesis; that is to say: breaking a situation down into its parts, focusing in on the key elements, and then developing that content. You might consider the example of a physician treating a sports injury. Before jumping in with interventions, the physician will likely ask questions to find out what the problem area is, focus on that area and probably move things around a little bit, develop some hypotheses about possible diagnoses and then go about verifying or excluding those diagnoses to inform the overall treatment plan. Lawyers might call this narrowing the content and developing the claim (see Trachtman, 2013); whereas, a clinician might call this the "is-it-this-or-is-it-that" phase of assessment. The notion of identifying where the distressing domain is, focusing in and delving into the topic, moving the content around to figure out where exactly the hurt is, and using that to inform what you target can be a useful strategy.

Hot Thoughts

There are at least two different targets for Socratic questioning: *hot thoughts* (Greenberger & Padesky, 2015) and the emotional meaning of the hot thought (Beck, 1979). Later chapters will address other targets such as behaviors. The idea of the hot thought is that people often have a number of different thoughts about an upsetting situation and we want to focus on the one that is most likely to have the largest impact. Hot thoughts can be good initial treatment targets. They are important thoughts that are connected to distress and patterns of avoidance, but they are not as deeply rooted or entrenched as the emotional meaning of the hot thought, which is connected to the core belief (Beck, 2011). Clinicians might first target a hot thought to help teach cognitive skills and get some symptom relief, and then move into the more underlying meaning of the hot thought as the treatment progresses. Targeting the meaning of the hot thought can be an especially useful strategy if the hot thought seems as if it might be true or difficult to assess.

Identifying the Hot Thought

In many parts of the world, there are variations to a game called hotter/colder or warmer/cooler, in which participants will guide a person to find a hidden object by saying "hotter" or "colder" as the person gets respectively closer or further from the hidden treasure. Finding the hot thought can be a similar process, only you are jointly discovering the hot thought together and instead of following obvious prompts you are following the affect. Trained therapists learn to listen for changes in someone's voice as a means of identifying when the content is more emotionally laden (Wenzel, 2019). While you are still learning how to do this (and to double-check your assumptions), you can simply ask the client which of the thoughts that you have already identified is most upsetting, painful, anxiety-provoking, depressing, shame-inducing, aggravating, and so forth. If you did a good job of analyzing the situation and drawing out their various thoughts, then identifying which of those thoughts is associated with the most distress will produce a thought that has a good likelihood of being the hot thought.

A first step in identifying a hot thought is determining where to look for one. Often, you may first need to break a situation down. Consider talking with a client who has ongoing feelings of depression and shame associated with a history of miscarriages and problems with infertility. There likely is much to work on here. There is her current difficulty in getting pregnant. There is the future she envisions. There is a history of miscarriages. There is loss. There is some background information related to why this is especially distressing to her. There is the interaction between her and her partner. There is the interaction between her and her family, and her and herself. There are probably other areas that have yet to be identified. A competent and compassionate therapist will need to empathically unpack these components and their corresponding emotion. We cannot work on everything at once and so we need to figure out where we should start. It is easier to do this if you do it in a transparent manner. There is a good opportunity for validation here as you talk about all the different pieces to the story and all that she has been through. After mapping it out and providing empathy and validation, we can move into collaboratively deciding on where we want to start. Often, starting with the most upsetting element is recommended, but the decision should be collaborative.

Table 5.1 Breaking Down the Story

What are the different parts of the story?
What's the most upsetting part?

Table 5.2 Identify the Hot Thought

What are the different thoughts about the most upsetting situation?
Which is the most upsetting thought?

After we have identified the different components of the situation and decided where to start or focus, we want to start unpacking that situation to process their emotions, identify their thoughts, and see how it all fits together. After we have a good sense of the situation, we then ascertain which thought is the most upsetting or distressing (i.e., has the most heat), and we treat that as a hot thought.

Identifying the Emotional Meaning of the Hot Thought

The emotional meaning (see Beck, 2011), or hidden meaning (see Beck, 1979), of the hot thought is typically connected to the core belief or schema system. Targeting the emotional meaning of the hot thought allows you to work on a deeper level. It is fitting that a classic strategy for uncovering the meaning of the hot thought is called the downward arrow (Beck, 2011).

This strategy is rather straightforward and involves following a thought to find the underlying vulnerability. Once you have identified the hot thought, you simply ask the client what it would mean if the hot thought were true. There are few variations to this process. Some therapists try to anchor it back to the client, by asking the client: "If this thought was true, what would it mean about you?" Other therapists, might turn it into a sideways arrow of sorts to find the feared outcome when evaluating anxious thinking, by asking: "So, if the that happened, what are you worried would happen next?" or "If that happened, why would that be so bad?"

Typically, there is a brief series of items that you work your way through till you get to the underlying meaning, which is probably a core belief, or closely connected to a core belief. Therapists will often ask: "How far down do I need to or how many times do I need to ask the question before I find the core belief?" There is no set amount. You keep going until you hit a noticeable change in affect, or you hit a loop. This skill (and identifying the hot thought) is demonstrated below. In this example, a client who is a young adult is talking about how upset she has been in reaction to her closest friend not responding to her text messages.

Therapist: Geraldine, I wanted to work with you on some of this distress you have related to this situation with your friend is that OK?

Client: Please, I've been miserable about it.

Therapist: So, paint a picture for me, as I understand it, you had a really tough day and then messaged your friend about it, and she didn't respond.

Client: Yes!

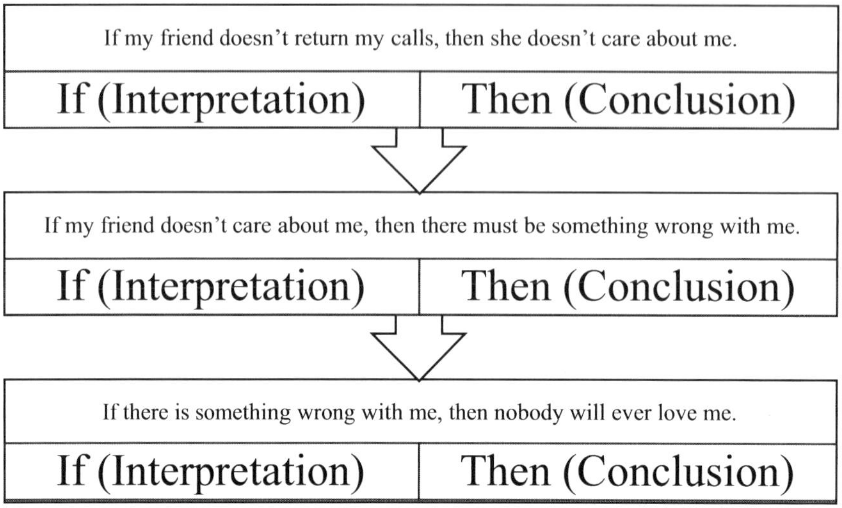

Figure 5.1 Downward Arrow

Therapist: How were you feeling at that time?

Client: Angry! But, also, sad … and worried

Therapist: A lot of feelings were going on for you. Let's try and pick out and line up the thoughts that went with the different feelings. What were you thinking when she didn't respond that made you so angry?

Client: I was thinking about all the times I had dropped everything to be there for her.

Therapist: And, what were you telling yourself?

Client: That she was selfish. That she's not as good as a friend as I am.

Therapist: So, your anger was pointed at her?

Client: Yes

Therapist: No anger at yourself or other directions?

Client: Nope, I was just really mad at her.

Therapist: Any, other thoughts going on that made you angry?

Client: Mostly, I was just thinking about how she was abandoning me.

Therapist: So, you had thoughts that she was abandoning you, thoughts that she was being selfish, and thoughts that she is not as good of a friend as you are, and you felt angry at her.

Client: Yes

Therapist: What about the sadness? What sad thoughts were you having?

Client: Um … I guess that she didn't like me or was sick of me.

Therapist: You had thoughts that she didn't like you or was sick of you and felt sad. Those sound like very sad thoughts, I can see how you ended up feeling sad. Any other sad thoughts?

Client: I guess I was thinking about how I might have lost another friend.

Therapist: You were thinking about how this friendship might be over and you were also thinking about other friendships you've lost over the years. It sounds

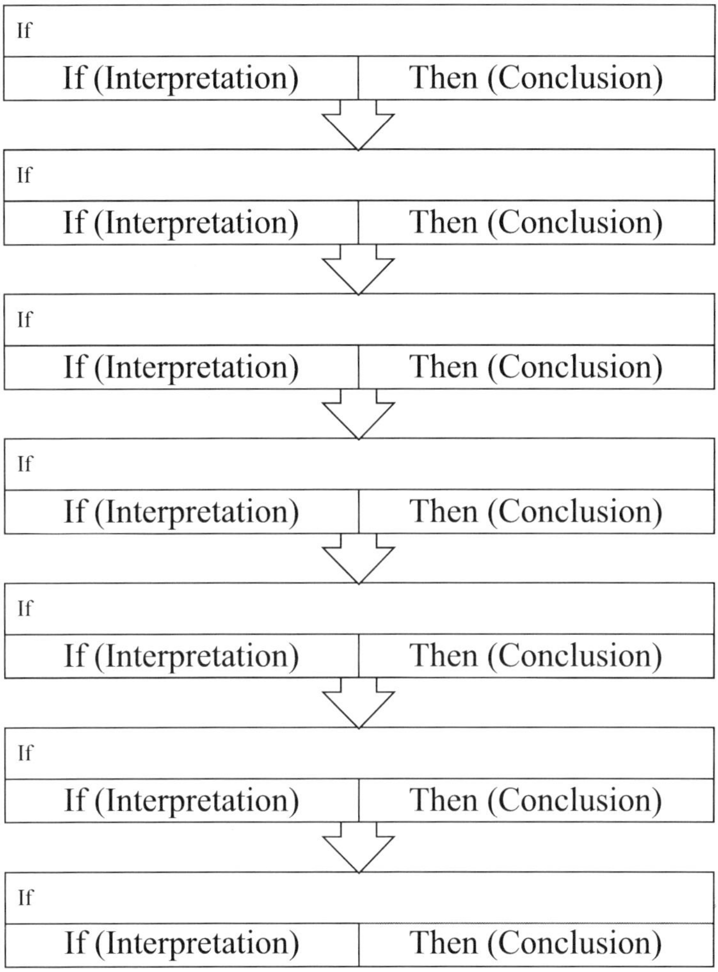

Figure 5.2 Blank Downward Arrow

like you had a lot of time to think and ended up thinking a lot about friendships ending. And, what were you telling yourself?

Client: Huh?

Therapist: When you were thinking about this theme of relationships ending in the past and maybe in the present, how were you making sense of that?

Client: I guess I was telling myself that maybe I'm just really messed up and I drive people away.

Therapist: So, another pretty heavy thought. I see how you had a lot of sadness, and then might have been even more mad about not being able to get a hold of her or to get support or reassurance from her.

Client: It was pretty bad.

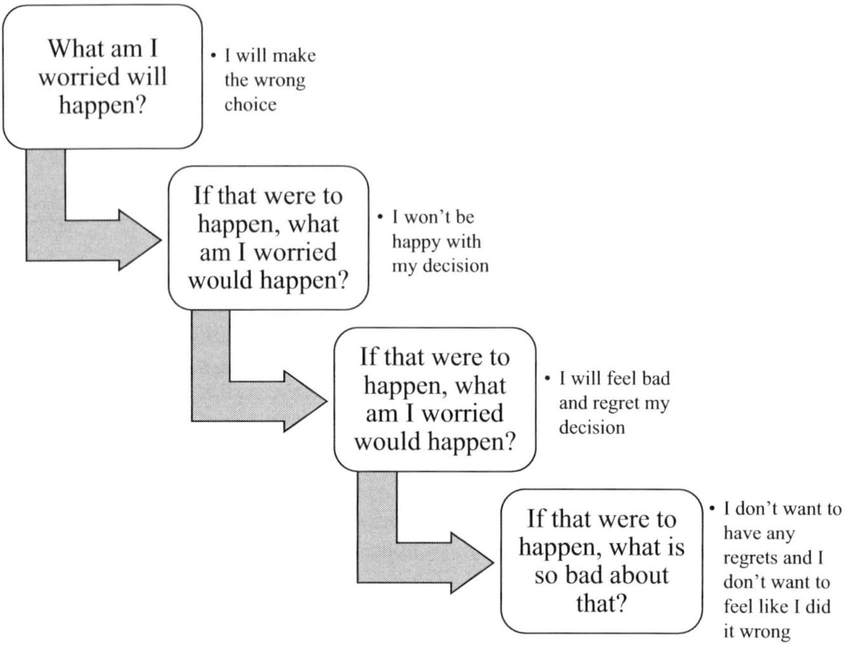

Figure 5.3 Sideways Arrow

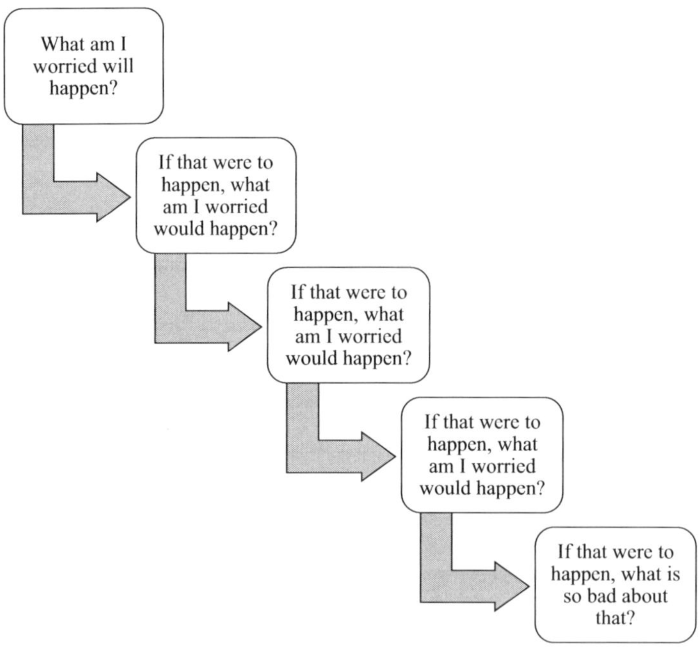

Figure 5.4 Blank Sideways Arrow

Therapist: Sounds like it. How about the anxiety? What anxious thoughts were you having?

Client: Mostly, similar to the driving people away thought. I was just thinking about how bad I am at making friends and I was afraid of having to meet new people.

Therapist: Pulling it all together, you had a really intense day and then tried to call your best friend and could not get a hold of her and then had a lot of thoughts and feelings. (*writing out the content white board*) You had thoughts that she was abandoning you, was being selfish, and not as good of a friend as you are, and you felt angry. You had thoughts that you drive people away and that maybe you lost another friend and you felt sad. You had worries about needing to find new friends and felt anxious. This is a lot for anyone to deal with and then add in the fact that you had a really tough day before this, and this sounds like a really intense day. Let's figure out what we want to focus on. Of, all the thoughts I've written out here, which one is the most painful to you?

Client: That's a tough call, they're all pretty bad.

Therapist: I agree that there is a lot for us to work on, let's pick one to work on first. Which one do you think is keeping you the most stuck?

Client: This thought that I drive other people away.

Therapist: That sounds like an important thought to go after.

[*This is the hot thought*]

How much do you believe this thought that you push other people away?

Client: It varies. Sometimes all the way, other times not as much.

Therapist: What about that night?

Client: I was worried it was true.

Therapist: It sounds like it was an emotional night for you. Now, we've never evaluated that thought, so I don't know if it is true at all, but clearly, it's a scary thought. A painful thought. Let's see if we can figure out why this thought is so emotionally threatening. If we were to imagine that this thought was true, that you were driving other people away, what would that mean about you?

Client: It would mean I suck at relationships and I'll probably die alone.

Therapist: OK, let's stay with that, if that was true, that you sucked at relationships and would probably die alone, what would that mean about you?

Client: Maybe there is something wrong with me deep down, like I'm broken.

Therapist: That sounds like a really painful thought too. If you were broken what would that mean about you?

Client: That my life is hopeless, I'm never going to get it figured out. Everyone is going to leave me eventually.

Therapist: So, is this thought about driving everyone away, more about you or them? Like, it feels like there is something wrong with you? Or, it feels like there is something wrong with them?

Client: Maybe both, but mostly me.

Therapist: We followed that thought down to ideas of being broken and that everyone will leave you eventually, if those thoughts were true, what would that mean about you?

Client: Just more about being broken.

Therapist: In this scenario, is it broken but repairable? or broken beyond repair?
Client: Forever broken, I never worked right, and I never will.
Therapist: So, defective?
Client: Exactly
Therapist: So, you had the thought that you drive people away and the emotional meaning of that thought is that you are defective. I can see why you felt some sad, and these are exactly the types of thoughts and beliefs about yourself that we want to target. These underlying beliefs about ourselves tend to be more entrenched and it can be a process to work on them, but we can get the process started today. How does that sound to you?
Client: If it helps me feel better, I'll gladly give it a shot

After identifying the hot thought and the meaning of the hot thought, we have a good idea of what to target to bring about meaningful change in the client's life. Additionally, because these elements were identified in a collaborative manner, the client is on board to evaluate these items, which means that the thought and meaning of the thought can be targeted open and directly.

Other Important Considerations

Finding the ideal target for Socratic questioning strategies can be more complicated than simply finding the hot thought or the meaning of the hot thought. Sometimes there isn't a clear hot thought and not all thoughts are connected to core beliefs. Below we will review some other considerations to aid in the strategizing of what to target in session.

If-Then Rules

An initial goal of knowledge seeking and Socratic questioning is to uncover the "tacit premises" upon which a subjective reality is built (Hintikka, 2007). A conclusion or interpretation is typically based upon an assumption that may or may not have been met. Formal and informal logic frame this as an if-then condition (Hintikka, 2007; Priest, 2017; Trachtman, 2013). From earlier chapters, we can add that this if-then process can be quite subjective (Beck & Haigh, 2014). The 'if' is a premise that must be met for a conclusion ('then') to be true. In a previous chapter, we discussed the if-thens of the intermediate beliefs in a cognitive case conceptualization (see Beck, 2011). An if-then statement can be embedded in the conceptualization or it can just be a deduction the client makes—though it is probably influenced by schema. Consider the earlier example, in which there are probably a number of if-then assumptions being made: "If my friend does not respond in a timeframe that I deem reasonable, then they are ignoring me." "If my friend is ignoring me, then they are being selfish." "If someone is being selfish, then they do not care about you." Cognitively, we can target the if, the then, or the link between the if and the then—asking whether the if necessitates the then. We can call these if-then statements, which people make, rules or attitudes. Often, they are more about the expectations, processes, or implications than the content.

Situation Description:
What are the different upsetting things that happened?
1.
2.
3.
4.
5.
6.
7.
What was the most upsetting part?

What thoughts were going through your mind?	What was the corresponding feeling?

Which thought was the most upsetting?
What's the emotional meaning of that thought?

Worksheet 5.1 Focusing Worksheet

Folding in the Conceptualization

In a panel discussion at the International Congress of Cognitive Psychotherapy, which was held in Hong Kong in 2014, Bob Leahy explained why the conceptualization matters for deciding what to target cognitively:

> The question as the therapist is, "Which thought is the most important to discover?" If the client has the thought of, "Other people don't like me." I think that's universal. Everybody is disliked by a lot of people. So, looking at the evidence where "people don't like you" might not actually be worth discovering. But the question is, "What is the underlying assumptions, or rule books, or schema, or behaviors that follow from that thought that need to be discovered?" That's where the therapist can own up to his or her sense of power or insight into where the problem is for the client. The client thinks, "Other people don't like me, and that's the problem." That's not the problem, the problem is the underlying assumptions or schemas.
>
> (Kazantzis et al., 2018, p. 9)

Judy Beck added:

> And something I think we haven't quite made explicit is how important the case conceptualization is to decide whether or not to focus on a particular cognition. When there is an upsetting situation, are we going to focus on cognitions at all? If we are, are we going to focus on the automatic thought level, are we going to do guided discovery to figure out the meaning to the client? Are we going to work on clients' underlying assumptions, rules, or their basic core beliefs? The conceptualization helps therapists determine how to guide the session: How are they conceptualizing the problem? and How will they best help this client?
>
> (Kazantzis et al., 2018, p. 10)

If you reflect on the previous chapter that explained how to draw out the cycle to identify the maintaining factors, those are the types of cognitions we want to prioritize targeting. Key questions to ask yourself include the following:

- "Given my understanding of the client, how are they making sense of the situation?"
- "What is the emotional meaning for them?"
- "What perceptual biases are they likely to be vulnerable to?"
- "Why is the situation particularly upsetting for my client?"
- "How does this fit with my understanding of their underlying beliefs?"
- "Which thoughts are the ones that are keeping the client stuck?"
- "How are the behaving in response to these thoughts?"
- "What is the outcome from their perception-dependent behaviors?"

The cognitive case conceptualization can influence what you choose to focus on in two ways. You can either use it to inform the focus of specific events or problems that come up, or you can target the key elements of the case conceptualization directly when you are setting the session agenda. If you are taking the latter approach, it can be useful to keep in mind that change in strongly held beliefs is often incremental. In addition, if you are working with a client who is given to overgeneralizing (Brittlebank et al., 1993; Williams & Scott, 1988), it will be easier to find exceptions to their assumptions if you work with specific situations and events instead of seeking to evaluate the overgeneralized belief directly. After you have drawn out some inconsistencies, it will be easier to target the larger belief. A later chapter will focus on working with core beliefs and schema.

Thinking Traps

There are a number of different lists of cognitive distortions, thinking errors, thinking traps, and so forth (Beck, 1979; Beck, 2011; Beck et al., 1979; Burns, 1989). Overtime the thinking about cognitive distortions has changed (Gellatly & Beck, 2016) and a consensus list does not exist—possibly due to copyright reasons, new lists are always being generated. At the focusing stage, you do not need to have a comprehensive list of distortions, and you definitely should not be trying to dispute and correct every distortion you hear. But, it can be helpful to have an idea of what types of thoughts to look out for. Keep an eye out for thinking in all-or-nothing or black-or-white terms. Watch for unrealistic predictions of the future or what other people are thinking. Look for selective filtering of information or overgeneralizing of events. You also want to be aware of absolutist beliefs, but those are well addressed by having a basic understanding of irrational beliefs.

Irrational Beliefs

In rational emotive behavior therapy (REBT), there are four irrational beliefs that can be commonly targeted (Dryden, 2013): demandingness, frustration intolerance, person rating, and awfulizing. A distinction between Rational Emotive Behavior Therapy (REBT) and Beckian CBT is the emphasis on *musts* in REBT. Ellis (2003) postulated that all of CBT's cognitive distortions were predicated on absolutistic musts (i.e., demandingness), which is also seen as the central irrational belief in REBT. We can consider demandingness as being the opposite of willfulness or acceptance (Ciarrochi & Robb, 2005; Ciarrochi, Robb, & Godsell, 2005; Ellis, 2005). Whereas Beckian CBT practitioners tend to place an initial emphasis on automatic thoughts, REBT therapists directly focus on irrational beliefs (Ellis, 2003). It has been suggested that the two concepts are highly similar; both have been found to predict emotional distress (Szentagotai & Freeman, 2007).

A meta-analysis was performed to better understand the relation between automatic thoughts and irrational beliefs (Şoflău & David, 2017). The researchers noted the conceptual overlap of irrational beliefs and automatic thoughts, stating that irrational beliefs could be viewed as being core beliefs or automatic thoughts, whereas automatic thoughts can compromise both evaluations and inferences (Şoflău & David, 2017). Modeling studies have found that automatic thoughts partially mediate the effect of irrational beliefs on depressive symptoms (Szentagotai & Freeman, 2007); however, the effect of the irrational beliefs on distress was only partially accounted for by automatic thoughts—meaning there was some unique variance that was not accounted for by automatic thoughts. This lends support to the notion that irrational beliefs have a unique effect of emotional distress that is not fully accounted for by automatic thoughts.

Szentagotai and Freeman's (2007) study was replicated with the use of more sophisticated instruments and design, and comparable results were found (see Buschmann et al., 2018); this lent further support to the *sui generis* (i.e., uniqueness) of irrational beliefs. Statistical modeling supported the primacy of demandingness as a central irrational belief and other irrational beliefs such as self-downing and low frustration tolerance also emerged as nodes in the model (Buschmann et al., 2018).

The clinical implications for the therapist using Socratic strategies is that there are additional places you can target. If we take the if-then conditional statement of if-prediction then-conclusion, you can look for absolutistic irrational beliefs associated with the assertion. You can watch for and target underlying demandingness (i.e., musts), frustration intolerance, awfulizing, and person rating. For example, Jonathan presents to treatment with problems with anger and depressive symptoms. He is working in a job he does not like and where he seems to not be treated well. In discussing a target situation, you identify the hot thought, "They don't care about me," and the emotional meaning of the automatic thought is that he is being treated unfairly. Both thoughts seem to be at least partially true to the therapist and so the therapist might go for the underlying awfulizing (e.g., "Being treated unfairly is terrible"; see Waltman & Palermo, 2019), demandingness (e.g., "People must always treat me with respect"; see Ellis, 2003), frustration intolerance (e.g., "I can't stand being treated unfairly"; see Dryden, 2013), or person rating (e.g., "People who treat me unfairly at work are fundamentally bad people"; see Dryden, 2013). The late George Carlin is attributed with having said, "Scratch any cynic and you will find a disappointed idealist." If you can identify the disappointed ideal, you can look for absolutist musts that correspond to the ideal to target.

Collaboratively Defining the Target

This is a crucial step that is often skipped. If you have ever felt like you were chasing a client in session and trying to evaluate something, but they kept moving on, a good question to ask yourself is whether they understood what you were trying to do. This can be done as an overt act; it will make the rest of the process much easier. Once you have identified your preferred cognitive target, you should talk about it with the client, so they understand that you are shifting the focus of the session onto this one cognition, as opposed to hearing more stories. This can be done fairly quickly, and it typically pays off with easier sessions. It is also a crucial step if you are taking a skills-training approach to treatment.

> Okay, John, we've been talking about this situation with your boss and how you have thoughts that he doesn't care about you, this meaning that you're being treated unfairly, and this idea that you can't stand being treated unfairly. I want to shift focus and really take a look at this last idea. Would it be alright with you if we were to spend some time focusing on evaluating this idea that you can't stand being treated unfairly?

If they say "no," then you were not going to have a successful evaluation anyway, but if they say "yes," then you are both oriented to what you are doing. This way if he gets off topic you can bring it back to the agreement: "So, I noticed we've moved onto a different topic and we didn't finish evaluating whether you could stand being treated unfairly at work. Would it be Okay if we got back to evaluating that central idea we identified?"

Creating a Shared Definition

Often, the cognitive target initially can be vague. What does it mean to be a good person? How do we define being a loser? What is a good mother? What does it mean to be successful? Typically, our clients' definitions are skewed in a way that a way that is consistent with their underlying beliefs. Evaluating a thought using a skewed definition is working harder than you need to. Once we know what we want to evaluate, it can be helpful to create a shared or universal definition (see Overholser, 1994, 2010, 2018).

It is important to note that creating a universal definition is not a discovery task. The goal is not to get their definition and see how well they measure up against their definition, because their definition is skewed. The goal is to jointly create a fair definition so the thought can have a fair evaluation (Overholser, 2010). Below is a more straightforward example.

Therapist: Freddie, we've been talking for a while about these fears you have that people will judge and reject you for being weird, and I wanted to take a closer at look at this belief you have about being weird, but first I wanted to just make a shared definition of weird to make sure we're on the same page. So, when you say weird, what does that mean?

Client: Different

Therapist: So, weird is different, not the same.

Client: Yes

Therapist: Different from what?

Client: Everyone else. Like everyone is the same, but some people are different and that is weird.

Therapist: So weird would be deviating from the norm. I'm curious, is weird bad?

Client: Huh ... um ... to some people.

Therapist: So, some people don't like weird, but does that make it bad to be weird?

Client: If you want people to like you, it is bad to be weird

Therapist: So, weird and likeability are related?

Client: I guess so

Therapist: Is it a perfect correlation, like no one likes you if you are weird and everyone likes you if you are not weird?

Client: It can feel like it

Therapist: What about you, do you like people who are weird?

Client: All the very few friends I have are so weird!

Therapist: And, you don't like that about them?

Client: No, I really enjoy them, they are weird as can be, but I like it.

Therapist: So maybe not everyone dislikes weird, let's look it up and see how they define weird. Will you do me a favor and search in your web browser on your phone a definition of the word weird.

Client: Uh, yeah, I'll look in my "web browser."

Therapist: (*slight chuckle*) Thanks

Client: It says, of strange or extraordinary character: odd, fantastic

Therapist: It's a good thing we looked it up, I would have missed some of that. What do we learn from the dictionary definition?

Client: Well it says odd and then it says fantastic

Therapist: What do you make of that?

Client: Maybe, weird makes you different, but being different is what makes you interesting.

Therapist: And fantastic.

Client: Ha, yeah, I guess

Therapist: So, there's a few places we can go from here, we can look at whether being interesting and fantastic is worth being judged by some people, we can look at you to see how weird you are, or we can evaluate our definition we came up with and see if the people you know who are weird are interesting and fantastic, but also maybe not appreciated by everyone. Which do you think would be most useful for you?

Client: I guess looking at being afraid of being judged for being weird, but maybe being weird isn't necessarily bad.

Therapist: This sounds like it is going to be really interesting to take a look at. So, we're going to look at what you gain and what you lose by being weird, to see if it is worth it. Does that sound like a plan?

Client: Yes, I really want to know if it is worth it, I've been scared of it for a long time, but even just talking about it now I do like the idea of being interesting and fantastic.

Often, when you start creating a shared definition, the client will start listing the reasons that they think they do or do not fit their own criteria. You will need to interrupt them, highlight what they are doing, and redirect them into making a universal definition. You can draw from dictionaries, encyclopedias, or other established sources to help create a fair definition. As illustrated above, when you are setting the definition you can construct it in a way that will make it easier to evaluate the target cognition and influence the types of generalizations that are made (Overholser, 1994). Consider the example below of a client named Zora. Zora was working to become sober and get her children back, after they were removed from her by Child Protective Services. Zora, and her therapist identified a belief that she was a bad mother. Prior to evaluating this thought, the therapist suggested they make a universal definition of a bad mother to help them have a fair evaluation.

Therapist: Zora, we identified this very painful thought of being a bad mother, before we get into evaluating it, I want to first make a shared definition of what is a bad mother that we both agree on. Is that alright with you?

Client: Yeah, I guess so.

Therapist: So, how should we define this concept of being a bad mother?

Client: Well, a bad mother doesn't do drugs. She doesn't get her children taken away. She isn't a junkie (*starting to tear up*)

Therapist: Zora, I want to pause for a second. Clearly, this is a difficult topic and I think it's important that we honor that. What I hear you doing is listing out all the reasons you think you are a bad mother. I don't want to do that. I don't think that will be helpful. I think you already do that a lot when I'm not around. I want to make a general definition, a universal definition of bad mother so we can look at this belief you have. Maybe it will be easier to define the two extreme definitions of perfectly good mom and completely bad mom. Does that sound OK?

Client: (*taking a resolute breath*) Yes, I can do that.

Therapist: Good, we are already doing a good job with this. Let define the perfect mother then.

Client: She cooks, she cleans, she irons, her kids have food.

Therapist: Probably, like really good food like organic and healthy and carb balanced and naturally sourced, and that whole GMO thing

Client: (slight chuckle) Yeah, and everything is neat and clean.

Therapist: How about the kids' emotional needs?

Client: Oh, right, they love their children and let them know they love them.

Therapist: They make their children important.

Client: Yes, your children have to be the most important thing.

Therapist: So, there's a practical needs item, emotional needs item, prioritizing item; what else?

Client: Being a mom, you just have to do your best and they always need you.

Therapist: So, being a good mom is long-run issue. You don't hit a point where you do enough and don't have to try anymore?

Client: Nope, it's a forever job.

Therapist: So, all things we talked about with an across time perspective.

Client: Yes, it's exhausting.

Therapist: Sounds like it. What about on the other extreme. How do we define the completely bad mom?

Client: The completely bad mom doesn't care about her kids. She puts herself first.

Therapist: Is it just about caring? Are there actual bad things a mom can do to harm her children?

Client: Like not being for them because they were taken away because the mom is a user.

Therapist: Maybe that's one example, but I'm sure you've heard or could think of other examples.

Client: Yeah, one of the women I bunk with was saying her mom would pimp her out for money, so her mom could get high.

Therapist: That sounds like it belongs on our list. What else would be bad mom behavior?

Client: I guess abusing your kids.

Therapist: Maybe, also abandoning your kids. Deliberately harming your kids?

Client: Yeah, there are some really disturbing stories out there.

Therapist: So, we have content for our definition. It sounds like the all good mom does all good things all the time, and the bad mom puts herself first and hurts her children. We need to set the criteria. How good do you have to be to be good? How many mistakes can you make before you are bad? Once you're bad are forever bad, or is there a path for redemption?

Client: I don't know.

Therapist: These are big questions. How many mom's do you know are all-good moms? Like, all the way all the time?

Client: Uh … like that I actually know, or just think are good?

Therapist: Yeah, how many confirmed cases of perfect moms are there?

Client: Probably none. Kids are so hard. And things that work with one kid, might not work with the next.

Therapist: So, let's define the good enough mom.

Client: The good enough mom is someone who works hard to make sure her kids have what they need.

Therapist: She loves them and works to put them first.

Client: She doesn't deliberately hurt her kids.

Therapist: And, she never gives up. How does that sound?

Client: That sounds like a good mom, but a realistic good mom.

Therapist: What about the question about redemption? Can a mom make mistakes, and get back on track and be good enough again?

Client: I think so … I hope so.

Therapist: What is going to make it easier to focusing on what you have to do to get your kids back?

Client: Having a path to redemption, getting back to being good enough

Therapist: OK, so we have a shared definition that we both agree on, and I've written down. Let's look at where you've been in past, where you are now, and where you are trying to get at

This principle step of creating a shared universal definition for the cognitive target is consistent with the origins of the Socratic method, where the goal was to first define the virtue being discussed (see Hintikka, 2007).

Tools and In-Session Strategies

There are a number of questions that therapists can ask themselves to guide this process, including the following:

- What are the different components of the story that could be upsetting to my client?
- What is the most upsetting part? / Where is the heat?
- How do they feel about the situation?
- What are the client's different thoughts about the situation?
- Do their thoughts and feelings line up?
- Am I missing anything?
- How does what I am hearing fit with my case conceptualization of the client?

- Am I hearing any cognitive distortions or irrational beliefs?
- Which thought do I want to target?
- Which thought is most connected to the behaviors that are keeping them stuck?
- Which thought is most distressing?
- What is the emotional meaning of this thought?
- Does the client appear to have a fair definition of this term, or should we create a shared definition?
- Is the client on board to evaluate the thought?

Here is an example of what this looks like in practice.

Case Example: Harold

Harold (pseudonym) was a heterosexual African American man, in his late thirties, who had spent over a decade in law enforcement. He had recently undergone a divorce after learning that his wife of almost 20 years had been cheating on him. He subsequently experienced symptoms of depression, anger, anxiety, and insomnia. Cognitively, he tends to become stuck in thinking about how he did not deserve what happened to him and about how his future is hopeless. In this session, he reported an increase in symptoms after finally selling his house and needing to give his wife most of the equity, as this was a stipulation in the divorce agreement. The following is an example of how his therapist worked with him to identify a suitable and productive target for Socratic questioning.

Therapist: Harold, from what you're telling me it sounds like you had an incredibly difficult week. You talked about feeling angry and sad and you even almost didn't come in today because you were feeling pretty down.

Client: Yeah, it's been really bad lately.

Therapist: I'm sorry that you've been feeling down and before we move on, I just want to say that I think anyone going through a divorce after decades of being married would have an especially hard time with it. And, then we add in the other items like having to move and sell your old house and it adds up. It's a lot to go through.

Client: (*sighing*) Yeah, it really is

Therapist: So, I want to talk about what happened, and I want to try and focus on the hardest parts to make sure we cover the most important stuff. So, first let's just try and list out all the different parts of the story so we can make a menu of areas to focus on. Does that sound OK?

Client: Yeah, it all seems to go together, but I guess tackling it piece by piece might be easier than doing it all at once.

Therapist: What are the different pieces of this story? I already wrote down the stress of moving because you mentioned that in the check-in. What else?

Client: The money, I had to sell this house, my house, and then give her all the equity that I spent decades of my life building.

Therapist: That's a big piece. Let me definitely write that down. What else?

Client: I'm not sure

Therapist: You've also talked about the stress of having to start over in a new neighborhood, you've mentioned missing your kids, and just missing the house. Any of these items could be a lot to deal with, and we've made a good-sized list already. Any other potential areas for the situation that we might need to focus on?

Client: I think we have a pretty big list already. I don't know how I can get through it.

Therapist: Well, let's pick one item and see what we can get done, which area have you found yourself thinking about the most lately?

Client: Kind of, all of them.

Therapist: I know you have a very active mind. We've been trying to prioritize improving your sleep, so which are you thinking about when you could be sleeping?

Client: The part about giving her all the money. I'm just so mad about it. My lawyer said it was a good idea in the long-run, but I don't think she should get anything.

Therapist: I can see this is really upsetting to you. What are the different feelings you have about the situation?

Client: Anger

Therapist: Anything else?

Client: Some sadness, but mostly anger

Therapist: So, a lot of anger and some sadness. What are the angry thoughts you are having?

Client: I call her an expletive a lot in my head.

Therapist: I imagine you do, and what is it about this situation where you sold the house and gave her most the equity that has you so mad?

Client: I was a good guy and I don't deserve this.

Therapist: You have the thought that you were a good guy and you don't deserve this and that makes you angry? What other angry thoughts are you having?

Client: She got away with it.

Therapist: You have the thought that she got away with it, and that makes you angry too. What other thoughts are you having that are making you so angry?

Client: I think about how my kids don't really know what happened and everything they know, they hear from her.

Therapist: Yeah, we've talked about that before too. That thought seems to get you stuck sometimes. Any other thoughts that make you angry?

Client: Those are the main ones.

Therapist: What about the sadness, what thoughts are making you sad?

Client: I think that I'm all alone and I'll never have the kind of life I want to have again.

Therapist: That's a very sad thought, you have thoughts that you are all alone and thoughts that you'll never have the kind of life you want to.

Client: And it is her fault!

Therapist: There's that anger popping up as we touch on the more vulnerable content

[*Conceptually, the therapist has noted that the client tends to use his anger as a way to avoid his sadness. He has a lot of thoughts about the unfairness of the situation, and he, like many clients, would spent most the session time talking about his ex if the therapist didn't intervene.*]

Client: Yeah, I guess you're right.

Therapist: So, let's pick a thought to focus on. Which of these thoughts is the most distressing to you?

Client: The fact that she got away with it. I'll always be so mad about that.

Therapist: The thought that she got away with it is a real hot button issue for you. I sort of also want to touch on the sadness piece too. We've talked before about how you tend to use anger to cover up some of your sadness [*gesturing laying one hand on top of another*]

Client: I know, you keep bringing it up

Therapist: I won't force you to work on it. How willing are you to work on your sadness?

Client: I don't want to feel sad

Therapist: Not a lot of people want to feel sad, how *willing* are you to work on your sadness?

Client: I think it is time, I've been putting it off long enough

Therapist: OK, first let me just reinforce your willingness. This emotional vulnerability work can be really tough. It is a different kind of bravery than you typically exhibit in your everyday life with your badge.

Client: Yeah, I'm good at that kind

Therapist: I know, we've talked a lot about that. So, if we're going to work on your sadness, let's use this thought that you're all alone and will never have the life you want to have again as a starting point. If this thought was true, what would that mean about you?

Client: My life will be pointless

Therapist: There appears to be a lot of hurt under this for us to work on. So, if we treat this assumption as being true, that your life would be pointless, what would that mean about you?

Client: I just can't have the kind of life I want.

Therapist: And, if you can't have the kind of life you want, what would that mean about you?

Client: I'll never be happy.

Therapist: And, if you were never happy again, what would that mean about you?

Client: That my life wasn't the way I wanted it to be.

Therapist: [*Seeing that a loop has been hit, hypothesizes this is the emotional meaning of the hot thought*] So, you have the thought that you're all alone and will never have the life you want to have again, and the emotional meaning of this thought seems to be you'll never be happy.

Client: And it is all her fault!

Therapist: So, the sadness lies in this idea that you'll never be happy again and then you add on this angry piece about it being her fault. Does that sound about right?

Client: Yeah, that's the theme of what I think about all the time.

Therapist: We probably want to target both of these, but we can only look at one at a time. Can we start with this idea that you'll never be happy again?

Client: Yeah, I just feel like I'll never be happy again.

Therapist: That is a very sad belief to have. Before we get into looking at whether this belief is true or not, can we define what a happy life would look like?

Client: A happy life is you have a loving wife and family to come home to after work.

Therapist: Maybe, that's a part of it, what is it about having a loving wife or family to come home to after work that makes people happy?

Client: It's important to have people in your life who care about you and that make a bad day worth it.

Therapist: That sounds really important, let me write this down. So, our definition of a happy life includes having people in your life who care about you and make a bad day worth it. What else makes people happy?

Client: They say money can't buy happiness, but you need to have enough to live and be comfortable.

Therapist: I'm writing down adequate material resources. This is good. What else?

Client: You need a purpose.

Therapist: That's also a good point, let me add that to our list. Anything else?

Client: I'm not sure.

Therapist: What do you think makes other people happy?

Client: My brother lives for golf and my sister could live in a library.

Therapist: So, hobbies are going on the list. Anything else?

Client: I can't think of anything.

Therapist: Is there anything you wanted to do with your life that you haven't been able to do?

Client: I always wanted to get a camper and drive around and see everything.

Therapist: So, traveling? New experiences?

Client: Yes, to both.

Therapist: Let's add them to the list, and I know your job is hard but meaningful to you.

Client: Yeah, service is important.

Therapist: We got a pretty good list here. A happy life includes having people you love who make bad days better, adequate material resources, purpose, hobbies, travel, new experiences, and service. Do you want to add anything else?

Client: No, it actually sounds really nice.

Therapist: Yeah, it does. I think we have a good list. OK, so the next step to evaluate this belief that you'll never be happy is to use this list we made to evaluate where you are at and what the future could hold for you. Does that sound alright?

Client: Yes, this interesting to me. Maybe, things aren't as hopeless as they feel.

In this session, the therapist worked to help Harold focus on the most upsetting element of a large story and in doing so they homed in on some key content directly related to his feelings of sadness. Harold at first wanted to talk about his anger and his ex-wife, but the therapist knew that in this way the client avoided both his sadness and working to improve his situation. They collaboratively discussed this and found a good hot thought related to his sadness. They delved in, using the downward arrow strategy, and found a belief that he would never be happy again. Before moving on to evaluate that belief, they created a shared definition of a happy life to aid in the evaluation.

Situation Description: *Recently sold house and had to give most the equity to ex-wife*
What are the different upsetting things that happened?
1. *Giving ex-wife the money*
2. *Stress of moving*
3. *Missing children*
4. *Having to start over somewhere new*
5. *Missing the house*
6.
7.
What was the most upsetting part? *Giving the ex-wife the money*

What thoughts were going through your mind?	What was the corresponding feeling?
She is getting away with this	*Anger*
I'm a good guy, I don't deserve this	*Anger*
My children think I'm the bad guy	*Anger*
I can't have the kind of life I want to have	*Sadness*

Which thought was the most upsetting? *I can't have the kind of life I want to have*
What's the emotional meaning of that thought? *I'll never be happy (and it is her fault)*

Worksheet 5.2 Focusing Worksheet: Example of Harold

This proved helpful, as it was quickly apparent the client had a skewed definition of a happy life that was mostly focused on what he thought he was missing. The focusing worksheet is filled out with his information to demonstrate the flow.

Summary

In this chapter, we have concentrated on reviewing how to focus on the key content. We discussed breaking a situation down into its components, identifying the various thoughts and feelings about the most upsetting part of the situation, identifying the hot thought from among those thoughts, and delving into finding the emotional meaning of the hot thought. We also discussed other important elements such as identifying if-then assumptions, linking back to the conceptualization, watching for cognitive distortions and irrational beliefs, collaboratively defining the cognitive target, and creating a shared universal definition for the target when necessary. Spending time on these tasks can take up valuable session time, but the payoff is that you can have a more strategic intervention. Focusing on the key cognitions allows you to get more done in less time. In addition, it is easier to have good Socratic strategies when we pick a good meaty thought to work on. The dilemma is whether to spend a little bit of time evaluating every surface-level distortion you come across or to take the time to focus on and delve down to the key content, so that you can spend more time on the more important content. This chapter advocates the latter strategy. A focusing worksheet is provided to aid in this process.

References

Beck, A. T. (1979). *Cognitive therapy and the emotional disorders.* New York: Meridian.

Beck, A. T., & Haigh, E. A. P. (2014). Advances in cognitive theory and therapy: The Generic Cognitive Model. *Annual Review of Clinical Psychology, 10,* 1–24. doi:10.1146/annurev-clinpsy-032813-153734

Beck, A. T., Rush, A. J., Shaw, B. F., & Emery, G. (1979). *Cognitive therapy of depression.* New York: Guilford.

Beck, J. S. (2011). *Cognitive behavior therapy: Basics and beyond* (2nd ed.). New York: Guilford Press.

Brittlebank, A. D., Scott, J., Mark, J., Williams, G., & Ferrier, I. N. (1993). Autobiographical memory in depression: State or trait marker? *The British Journal of Psychiatry, 162*(1), 118–121.

Burns, D. D. (1989). *The feeling good handbook.* New York: William Morrow.

Buschmann, T., Horn, R. A., Blankenship, V. R., Garcia, Y. E., & Bohan, K. B. (2018). The relationship between automatic thoughts and irrational beliefs predicting anxiety and depression. *Journal of Rational-Emotive and Cognitive-Behavior Therapy, 36*(2), 137–162.

Ciarrochi, J., & Robb, H. (2005). Letting a little nonverbal air into the room: Insights from acceptance and commitment therapy. Part 2: Applications. *Journal of Rational-Emotive and Cognitive-Behavior Therapy, 23*(2), 107–130.

Ciarrochi, J., Robb, H., & Godsell, C. (2005). Letting a little nonverbal air into the room: Insights from acceptance and commitment therapy. Part 1: Philosophical and theoretical underpinnings. *Journal of Rational-Emotive and Cognitive-Behavior Therapy, 23*(2), 79–106.

Dryden, W. (2013). On rational beliefs in rational emotive behavior therapy: A theoretical perspective. *Journal of Rational-Emotive and Cognitive-Behavior Therapy, 31*(1), 39–48.

Ellis, A. (2003). Similarities and differences between rational emotive behavior therapy and cognitive therapy. *Journal of Cognitive Psychotherapy, 17*(3), 225–240.

Ellis, A. (2005). Can rational-emotive behavior therapy (REBT) and acceptance and commitment therapy (ACT) resolve their differences and be integrated? *Journal of Rational-Emotive and Cognitive-Behavior Therapy, 23*(2), 153–168.

Gellatly, R., & Beck, A. T. (2016). Catastrophic thinking: A transdiagnostic process across psychiatric disorders. *Cognitive Therapy and Research, 40*(4), 441–452.

Greenberger, D., & Padesky, C. A. (2015). *Mind over mood: Change how you feel by changing the way you think.* New York: Guilford Press.

Hintikka, J. (2007). *Socratic epistemology: Explorations of knowledge-seeking by questioning.* Cambridge: Cambridge University Press.

Kazantzis, N., Beck, J. S., Clark, D. A., Dobson, K. S., Hofmann, S. G., Leahy, R. L., & Wong, C. W. (2018). Socratic dialogue and guided discovery in cognitive behavioral therapy: A modified Delphi panel. *International Journal of Cognitive Therapy, 11*(2), 140–157.

Overholser, J. C. (1994). Elements of the Socratic method: III. Universal definitions. *Psychotherapy: Theory, Research, Practice, Training, 31*(2), 286.

Overholser, J. C. (2010). Psychotherapy according to the Socratic method: Integrating ancient philosophy with contemporary cognitive therapy. *Journal of Cognitive Psychotherapy, 24*(4), 354–363.

Overholser, J. C. (2018). *The Socratic method of psychotherapy.* New York: Columbia University Press.

Priest, G. (2017). *Logic: A very short introduction* (Vol. 29). Oxford: Oxford University Press.

Şoflău, R., & David, D. O. (2017). A meta-analytical approach of the relationships between the irrationality of beliefs and the functionality of automatic thoughts. *Cognitive Therapy and Research, 41*(2), 178–192.

Szentagotai, A., & Freeman, A. (2007). An analysis of the relationship between irrational beliefs and automatic thoughts in predicting distress. *Journal of Cognitive and Behavioral Psychotherapies, 7*(1), 1–9.

Trachtman, J. P. (2013). *The tools of argument: How the best lawyers think, argue, and win.* Lexington, KY: Trachtman.

Waltman, S. H., Hall, B. C., McFarr, L. M., Beck, A. T., & Creed, T. A. (2017). In-session stuck points and pitfalls of community clinicians learning CBT: Qualitative investigation. *Cognitive and Behavioral Practice, 24*, 256–267. doi:10.1016/j.cbpra.2016.04.002

Waltman, S. H., & Palermo, A. (2019). Theoretical overlap and distinction between rational emotive behavior therapy's awfulizing and cognitive therapy's catastrophizing. *Mental Health Review Journal, 24*(1), 44–50.

Wenzel, A. (2019). *Cognitive behavioral therapy for beginners: An experiential learning approach.* New York: Routledge.

Williams, J. M. G., & Scott, J. (1988). Autobiographical memory in depression. *Psychological Medicine, 18*(3), 689–695.

Chapter 6

Phenomenological Understanding

Scott H. Waltman

❖ CONTENTS

In Polya's (1973) classic mathematical logic book, he states, "It is foolish to answer a question that you do not understand" (p. 6). To answer a mathematical problem, you first need to define the question and then identify what is known, what is unknown, and how it all fits together (Polya, 1973). Hintikka (2007), the famed philosopher and principal architect of game-theoretical semantics, stated, "As every puzzle fan knows, often a key to the clever reasoning needed to solve a puzzle lies precisely in being able to imagine the circumstances in which the normal expectations evoked by the specification of the puzzle are not realized" (p. 20). Additionally, any litigator understands that sometimes the best arguments is pulling at the loose threads of the opposing argument (Trachtman, 2013). Of course, the role of the therapist is not to solve the client like a puzzle, with clever reasoning or confrontative, purely logical arguments (Wenzel, 2019).

Notably, although we call it Socratic questioning or Socratic dialogue, Socrates himself was not a therapist, and actually would not have been a good therapist: "Socrates certainly did not engage in what we refer to as Socratic questioning. He would not identify with what we talk about. He was apparently famously ruthless with his questioning and would pin people to the ground almost with his questioning" (Kazantzis, Fairburn, Padesky, Reinecke, & Teesson, 2014; p. 6). Arguably, the first job of a therapist is to work to understand your client (Kazantzis et al., 2018). The perfect contrast to Socrates' true approach would have been Carl Rogers of client-centered therapy, who stated: "It is my purpose to understand the way he feels in his own inner world, to accept him as he is, to create an atmosphere of freedom in which he can move in his thinking and feeling and being, in any direction he desires" (Rogers, 1995; p. 108). Rogers famous paradox was that acceptance was a precursor to change (Rogers, 1995).

The principle of collaborative empiricism bridges this gap and combines these elements in a powerful way (Wenzel, 2019).

> Again, in the spirit of collaborative empiricism—you as the therapist and your client being co-detectives examining the evidence before drawing a conclusion—we do not presuppose that a client's thinking needs challenging, but instead, we take a more neutral, curious evaluative stance, and we only decide that thinking is not adaptive or helpful if the results from our evaluation support that.
>
> (Wenzel, 2019, p. 191)

Phenomenological Understanding

If we conceptualize the steps of Socratic dialogue as lining up with the elements of the seven-column thought record (see Kazantzis et al., 2014), this next step is functionally where you seek to identify the supporting evidence. We want to understand the client's case for the thought or belief being true. Although, as previously covered, an individual's perceptions are filtered through their expectations and biases (Beck & Haigh, 2014; Lippman, 2017). Therefore, if you only evaluate the belief based on factual evidence, you can end up with people intellectually knowing something, but emotionally not believing it. A clinical situation with which we are all familiar. While we ultimately want to evaluate the belief on empirical terms, we first need to understand

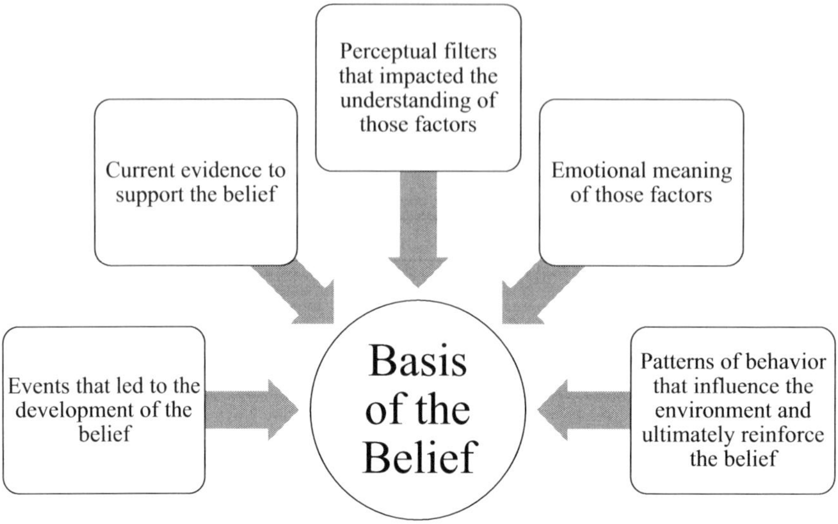

Figure 6.1 Understanding of the Believing of the Belief

the totality of the belief. For now, we are gathering all the potential evidence. Later, we will evaluate the evidence. Some evidence that is not objective will still have important emotional significance and will need to be attended to.

Collaborative Phenomenology

Phenomenology is born out of philosophy and built on the introspective nature of psychology. Phenomenology can be understood to be the study of the essence of consciousness (Grossman, 2013). A phenomenologist is interested in both the study of an individual's subjective and objective reality to get to the essence (i.e., gestalt) of the issue (Davidsen, 2013; Mishara, 1995). This involves suspending judgments and preconceived notions and bringing a mindset that is consistent with the mindful notions of a beginner's mind (Kabat-Zinn, 2006).

> So phenomenology may be thought of as a style of thinking that suspends traditional scientific explanation and attempts to get in touch with the primordial experiences underlying all our more mature constructions of the world ... Remember that the aim of phenomenological study is to rediscover the whole living person and how being in the world is experienced by that person and those around that person.
>
> (Chessick, 1995, p. 161)

This suspending of prior assumptions is called *bracketing* in the phenomenological tradition (Chessick, 1995), and it requires the therapist to tolerate a number of elements including uncertainty of outcome, vulnerability of not being the omnipotent expert, and openness to the emotional experience of the client (Kazantzis et al., 2014).

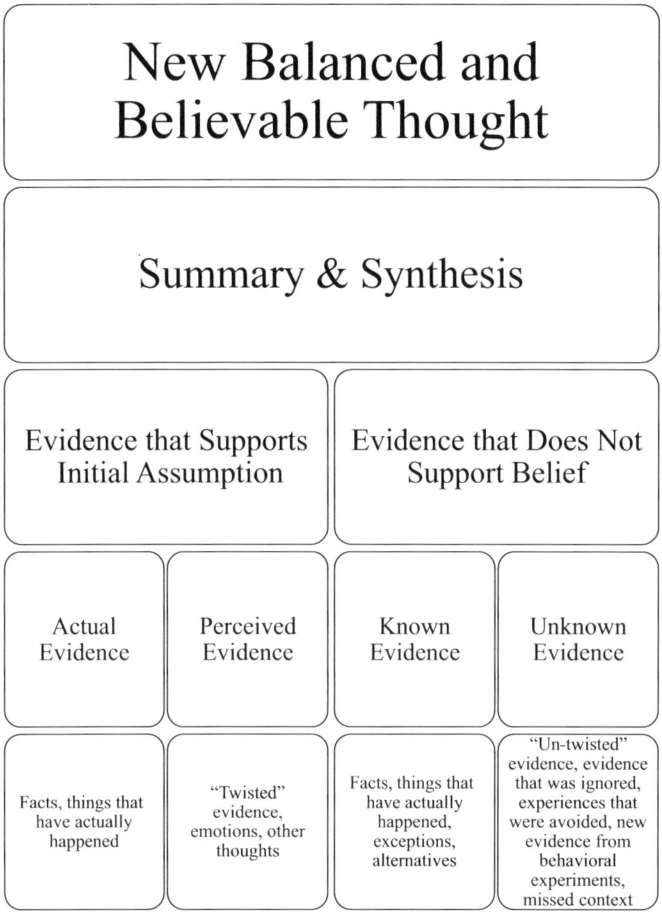

Figure 6.2 Conceptual Overview of Socratic Questioning Mode

Figuratively, we are trying to see what it is like to be the client. We don't just want to know how they justify the belief we are targeting; we want to know what it is like have the belief. Why does it make sense that they developed this belief? What would it be like to live with that belief system? How did it feel to develop that belief? How does that belief currently affect the way they view the world (i.e., filtering)? What impulses and behavior accompany that belief? What is the risk of letting go of that belief?

In keeping with the spirit of collaborative empiricism, the application of phenomenology to Socratic questioning would suggest the need for a *collaborative phenomenology*. Just as we are trying to understand the subjective and objective underpinnings of the belief, we are trying to help the client join with us in our inquiry. This can and should be an emotionally informed process for the therapy dyad and there will be a discussion below of how to address, encourage, process, and use emotion in this process.

Conceptualization-Informed Phenomenological Perspective

A case conceptualization-driven approach to treatment is inherently consistent with the phenomenological movement in that it is idiographic, or person specific. There are a number of items to make a note of mentally during this process. As Judy Beck (2011) explains with her information processing model, people have a tendency to completely take in information that fits with their assumption, and then ignore information that does not fit with their biases. Information can also be twisted and construed to a forced fit with their assumptions; such that, elements that are not actually evidence for a belief can be presented as evidence, because the person has twisted them to be so in their mind.

Take the example of Mary, a young working mother who was referred to a therapist after being hospitalized for a suicide attempt. In assessing the situation, she ascribes the attempt to mounting pressure that she must do everything for everyone. In the phenomenological understanding phase of evaluating this belief, one learns that she actually receives very little help around the house, which on the surface would seem to support this idea that she has to do everything. As the therapist and Mary dig deeper to understand the situation, further context is jointly discovered. Mary's spouse used to do more around the house and to help out, but Mary was not satisfied with how the tasks were performed and she took back for herself those tasks, because she did not want them done incorrectly. So, in a way, her receiving little help is evidence that she has to do everything herself, and in another way, there is more context with which to work.

Considering the influence of belief-dependent perceptual filters (e.g., confirmation bias) and schematic-related behavioral responses can help you better understand the situation. For example, if your client has a pre-existing belief that the world is dangerous, tends to have a heightened threat perception, and responds to perceived slights by becoming angry and hostile, this is important context for better understanding the situation. Sometimes, it is less obvious. The thing to keep in mind is that your client will state many things as if they were true and we want to demonstrate empathy and curiosity while maintaining the empirical metacognitive awareness of how the evidence fits with conceptualized beliefs, behaviors, affect, and perceptual filters.

Attending to Emotions and Emotional Processing

The great lesson from the advent of emotion-focused therapy (EFT) is the importance of attending to emotions when promoting change (Johnson, 2009; Greenberg, 2004). Cognitive behavior therapy (CBT) has always held that processing and not avoiding emotions are an important part of treatment (Beck, 1979); however, following the broadly successful dissemination of CBT (Beck, 2011; Beck & Haigh, 2014; Wenzel, 2019), there had been various oversimplifications to the model which may have resulted in misconceptions about CBT (Waltman, Creed, & Beck, 2016; Wenzel, 2019). These included erroneous notions such as emphasizing purely positive thinking or logical analysis being all that mattered. Recently, there has been a groundswell of renewed focus on the essential role of attending to emotions in CBT (see Thoma & McKay, 2014).

From the perspective of EFT, the goal of therapy is to change a person's emotional experience and the corresponding narrative (i.e., schema) where that emotion is embedded (Greenberg, 2004). From a CBT perspective, various emotional experiences are connected to schematic activation; this (and the corresponding behavioral response) is called a mode or modal activation (Beck & Haigh, 2014). To best bring about change in those emotionally laden schemas, we need to activate the associated emotion to work directly on the schema. Ideally, we want to have a moderate level of emotional activation.

If your client is under-emotionally involved, we want to get them more in touch with their feelings; this can be done with various CBT, EFT, or general counseling skills. If your client is overly emotionally activated, you might need to help them become regulated by providing validation, teaching and coaching them to use emotional regulation skills, or helping them sit with the emotion until it lessens on its own.

Table 6.1 Strategies for Under- and Over-Emotional Expression

Strategies to Increase Contact with Emotions	**Strategies to Regulate Emotion**
In-the-moment emotional identification	Providing validation
Increasing focusing by attending the body sensations of emotional experience	Teach emotional regulation skills (e.g., diaphragmatic breathing)
Use of imagery to increase salience of emotionally laden material	Coach to use emotion regulation skills in session
	Coaching willingness or acceptance of emotional experience
	Sitting with the emotion
	Grounding

Table 6.2 Steps of Emotional Processing

From the perspective of Emotion Focused Therapy (Greenberg, 2004)	From the Perspective of Cognitive Behavior Therapy
Foster Emotional Awareness	Initial focus is on increasing emotional awareness (and perhaps tolerance). Therapists expresses empathy and validation as emotion is used to help the therapist identify strategic intervention points. Therapist assesses client's willingness and tolerance of emotional experience. Relation to emotional experience may become an initial treatment goal.
Regulation of Emotion	Cognitive restructuring will result in emotion regulation if the client is well engaged in the process.
	Attending to the more emotionally laden items of evidence or subjective evidence can improve emotional engagement in session. May need to coach increased emotional engagement or emotion down-regulation strategies.
Emotion Transformation	As the underlying belief is modified emotional experience can be softened and more adaptive emotional experiences can be fostered. New beliefs and emotions are reinforced by planning changes in behaviors based on new perspective.

In cases where you are working with a client whose core difficulty is emotional regulation (e.g., a person with borderline personality disorder), this process can be more involved, and a later chapter (Chapter 12) will focus on incorporating Socratic strategies within a dialectical behavior therapy (DBT) framework. If avoidance of emotions is a pronounced part of the clinical presentation, you may need to target beliefs about emotions directly (see Leahy, 2018).

Attending to and processing the emotional experience of the client are an important part of the cognitive change process. While feelings are not facts, they can certainly feel like it, and we need to honor and spend time speaking to our client's pains. The goal of this step is to create a holistic understanding of our client and the belief we are targeting, and to do this we need to understand the emotional experience of that belief.

Consider the example of John, a middle-aged man who presented to therapy with a chronic history of anger and depression. At the start of the session, he reported increased suicidal ideation secondary to thoughts that his family would be better off without him. The therapist can see that factually this appears inaccurate, but this is something that the client feels strongly about. The therapist knows he needs to process and attend to this feeling because it will persist after the session as well. The therapist attends to the associated emotional experience to help him understand the thought that the family would be better off without him, in order to help inform cognitive restructuring to target the identified reason for the client being suicidal.

Therapist: OK, John, let's talk about this thought you just told me that you think your family will better off without you.

Client: Yeah, I think we probably should, I haven't had this kind of thoughts for a while.

Therapist: What is the emotion that goes with these thoughts?

Client: Well, some relief, like maybe it would be better without me.

Therapist: Let's take one step earlier in the timeline, can you tell me about the build up to your ideation?

Client: I'm just worried I'm turning into my dad.

Therapist: I know you have very strong feelings about him.

Client: I HATE him so much! I'm just so glad he's dead.

Therapist: And, so, if you were your dad, then your kids would be happy you're dead?

Client: I guess so

Therapist: Let's focus on this I'm worried I'm turning into my dad piece. Emotionally, what is that like for you?

Client: Scary, like it really just freaked me out.

Therapist: So, it's a scary thought. Let's pause for a moment and just honor how scary this thought is.

[*pausing*]

Can you tell me more about this fear?

Client: I'm just afraid of turning into my dad.

Therapist: It's certainly a scary thought, especially given what you've told me about him. Tell me more about the emotional experience of your fear. Where are you feeling this fear in your body?

Client: It's like a sinking feeling, but also like all my hairs are standing on end.

Therapist: That's a very good description. Where is the sinking?

Client: [*motioning to his chest*] It's like my heart is sinking.

Therapist: So, you have this feeling that your heart is sinking and at the same time you are so alert you said it is like all your hairs are standing on end.

Client: Exactly.

Therapist: OK, so there is a thought that you are turning into your dad and then a big emotional and physical reaction where you feel scared and it feels like your heart is dropping and all your hairs are standing on end. This sounds like something we want to take a good look at. To you what are the indicators that you are turning into your dad?

Client: I don't know. I just feel like I am.

Therapist: Let's access that feeling and see if we can identify what is leading you to think you are turning into your dad. Would that be OK?

Client: I'm kind of nervous.

Therapist: This can be intense, I understand. I also don't want to avoid talking about something that is connected to something as important as keeping you alive. What if we plan to use some of those breathing exercises together afterwards to help you get good and grounded?

Client: Yeah, that would probably be smart.

Therapist: So, we're going to access those feelings to see if we can identify some of your reasons for thinking you are turning into your dad?

Client: Yes

Therapist: Alright, so, let's use some imagery. I want you to close your eyes and think about your dad. Picture his face, imagine his voice. Think about how he used to walk and what he used to say and do.

[*pausing*]

Are you getting an image of him?

Client: [*appearing a little flustered*] yeah

Therapist: OK, you are doing a good job. Now that you have an image in your mind of your father what is it about him that you feel like you are taking on?

Client: His face!

Therapist: His face, like you are looking more like him as the years go on?

Client: Yes, but not that, his face, like [*gesturing at his jawline*] his face always looked so angry and I feel like I'm doing that.

Therapist: Good job, we have something to look at. So, what is making you think you are having facial expressions like your dad?

Client: I guess I'm remembering. The other night I caught a glimpse of my face in the mirror and I looked so angry, just like him. It scared me so much.

Therapist: I can see how that would be a scary thought to have after seeing yourself like that. Was there any context to you being angry?

Client: Yeah, I rounded out a bolt in my engine, and I was just mad that I did something so stupid.

Therapist: So, you got mad and your dad also got mad, what else did you do that he did?

Client: I raised my voice and told my family to leave me alone.

Therapist: From what I remember, your dad would also raise his voice a lot too.

Client: All the time.

Therapist: He did other stuff too; like, was the reason you hated him because he was loud?

Client: No, I hated him because he beat my mom and us kids.

Therapist: So, we see why it is so scary to think about turning into your dad.

Client: It messed me up all weekend.

Therapist: You were afraid all weekend that you were turning into your dad. You hated him and your life has been better without him. You have thoughts that your family would be better off without you too.

Client: Exactly.

Therapist: But we skipped a step, did you put your hands on your wife or kids this weekend?

Client: No, I would never do that. I would kill myself before I ever hurt them.

Therapist: How does that statement compare to what your father did?

Client: He would have killed me before he ever thought about hurting himself at all.

Therapist: So, are you your dad?

Client: No, I guess not.

Therapist: Why not, sell me on the idea that you are not your dad.

Client: Oh, that's tough.

Therapist: I just really want to help your uptake with this new idea to help keep you safe. So, if you aren't your dad, why not?

Client: I'm not my dad because he was mean and abusive and out of control.

Therapist: So, what's the implications for you not being your dad on your family being better off without you?

Client: I guess, it's a different situation, and I wouldn't want my kids to grow up without their father. The absence of an abusive father would have been nice for me, but I don't want them to feel alone.

Therapist: What does it say about you, that you want those things for your kids?

Client: Well, I love them.

Therapist: You love your kids. Let's pause and stay with this feeling for a moment. [*tearing up a little*]

Client: [*sigh of relief*]

Therapist: Emotionally, how does it feel to recognize that you are not your father and your family would not be better off without you?

Client: Much better

Therapist: What about the sinking feeling you had before where it felt like your heart was dropping?

Client: Actually, I feel lighter and relaxed.

Therapist: OK, let's talk about ways to remember these thoughts and feelings in the coming week.

It could have been easier just to tell the client that he was engaging in emotional reasoning and there really wasn't any evidence that he was turning into his father, but those feelings would have lingered. In the case above, attending to, focusing on, and accessing his emotions both allowed the therapist to identify the unspoken case for why he was turning into father, and it also made for a more impactful intervention. As our first goal is to understand the client and their subjective experience, we need to recognize that collaborative empiricism does not mean strict empiricism. Later, there will be a place where we evaluate the data we have gathered, but first we need to capture a good understanding of the situation.

Validation

This understanding step is a great opportunity to provide validation. People have an innate need to be heard and understood (Kazantzis et al., 2018). Validation takes this a step further as it provides evidence to the client that you heard them, you understand what they are saying, and the elements you are validating (i.e., acknowledging) are well-grounded or justifiable (Linehan, 1997). Of course, in this process we are seeking to understand how they came to believe this thought and what lends support to it's being possibly true; we are not tacitly agreeing with everything they say—you can't validate the invalid (Linehan, 1997). From the perspective of DBT, there are six levels of validation. An in-depth review and analysis of these six levels are beyond the scope of this current chapter. A later chapter will focus more on Socratic strategies and DBT. Instead, we will focus here on the elements of the six levels.

There are things you can do that are generally validating to the client as a person. These include paying attention, actively listening, accurately reflecting what was said (to demonstrate you are listening to what is being said and the meaning of what is being said), and being genuine with your client (Linehan, 1997). These elements are broadly consistent with Padesky's (1993) famous recommendation that *listening* is a key step in the Socratic process. A by-product of listening is that you will understand the client's perspective better. This will allow you to provide other elements of validation that pertain to demonstrating how the element in question (e.g., thought, feeling, or behavior) makes perfect sense in light of early learning, environmental cues, or how they were interpreting the situation (Linehan, 1997).

The behavioral perspective is that all behaviors are learned and that all behaviors make sense. Similarly, our clients tend to come by their beliefs honestly. Life teaches them various lessons and they live their life in a way that minimizes pain and meets their needs; however, these lessons are often based on overgeneralizations, overcorrections, skewed interpretations, skewed data, or limited data. In the next step, we will attempt to expand the picture to help them see what they have been missing, but first we need to come to see it as they see it. Validation is the perfect vehicle for doing

Table 6.3 Element of Validation

Paying attention
Active listening
Accurate reflections
Articulating the unspoken
Making sense of belief, behavior, or emotion based on history
Making sense of belief, behavior, or emotion based on environmental cues
Making sense of belief, behavior, or emotion based on internal cues
Making sense of belief, behavior, or emotion based on interpretation of the situation
Radical genuineness

this. It is relationship enhancing, emotion regulating, and tends to decrease defensiveness (Linehan, 1997). A skilled CBT practitioner will weave validation into the discovery process.

Chance for Course Correction

Ideally, you would have found a suitable or optimal cognitive target in the focusing stage. There may be times during the understanding phase when you choose to make a course correction or identify an alternative thought to target. The two extremes for this situation include instances where there really isn't much to the thought being targeted. It might be that you selected a thought that was distressing but not central—not all thoughts are connected to core beliefs or the identified problem. Alternatively, sometimes when you are working through the understanding phase it will seem like the target belief seems to be obviously true (of course it might not be). In these cases, it can be helpful to make a course correction. We can treat debatably true thoughts as situations and target the meaning of the belief. For example, if when evaluating a thought that your client's family hates them, and in the understanding phase they tell you that their family has often and repeatedly told your client that they hate them, you might consider shifting to the meaning or implications of their family's hating them (i.e., "Does this mean no one will ever love them?"). If (and when) you decide to shift targets, you should make it an overt (out loud) decision, so you both continue to be on the same page.

Questions for Understanding

There are a number of questions that can help you gain an understanding of your client and their belief. Of course, the existence of a list of questions does not mean you have to ask every (or any) question on the list. You could ask variations of these questions. Or other questions that naturally stem from the content you have been discussing. These questions will be demonstrated as follows with an example of Nicole, a young mother who is in dual recovery from posttraumatic stress disorder and amphetamine use disorder. She entered treatment a few months ago after her children were removed from her home by Child Protective Services. She is currently in a diversion program and mandated to treatment. She has large amounts of shame relating to her situation. She has been doing fairly well in treatment. She has recurrent ruminative thoughts about what a terrible mother, in her opinion, she is and how she has ruined everything. In the previous session, you focused on the hot thought that she is a bad mother. Below is how a therapist might seek to develop a phenomenological understanding of her belief. Later steps would include evaluating the elements she is missing, but first the therapist needs to understand and honor "kernels of truth" (Linehan, 1997) in her belief.

There are several questions that therapists can ask themselves to guide this process:

- What experiences are this thought based on?
- What are the facts that support this?

- If this was true, what do you think would be the strongest evidence to support it?
- Is this something people have directly said to them in the past?
- What is it like to believe this thought?
- How long have they believed this?
- When do they tend to believe this more and less?
- What do they typically do when thoughts like this come up for them?

What Experiences Are This Thought Based On?

To better understand the cognition that you are evaluating, we want to find out what events led to the development of this belief. If your client believes they are unlovable, were there instances where someone who would have been expected to love them did not? If your client believes they are a failure, have they failed? If your client believes the world is dangerous, have they been injured or been in danger of being injured in their past? Understanding the experiential basis of the development of the belief will give you a better understanding of what you are working with.

Therapist: Nicole, we decided to evaluate this belief that you are bad mother. I know from previous sessions that this is something you think about often and it really weighs on you, and you feel a lot of shame with this thought

Client: I just feel terrible.

Therapist: So, in evaluating this thought, I first just want to better understand where you are coming from. What are the events in your life that have led to you developing this belief that you are a bad mother?

Client: Well, the judge took my kids away because I was an unfit mother.

Therapist: So, the court found you to be an unfit mother at the time of their evaluation.

Client: Yeah, so, legally I'm a bad mom

Therapist: That's a heavy piece of evidence. So, it makes sense you went on to develop this belief about yourself being a bad mother. Are there other major instances that come up?

Client: Well, there is the time I was arrested.

Sometimes, I left the kids alone when I was out using or scoring.

Therapist: There are a few more instances, let me make sure I'm taking good notes on all this. Any other instances?

Client: I think the fact that I have to be here with you is evidence that I screwed up.

Therapist: You are mandated to be here, so it makes sense that you have to do something to get mandated. But also, you're saying that getting treatment *feels* like evidence that you are a bad mom.

Client: Or, at least that I was really messed up.

Therapist: [*noting the term was reflects a change from how she was*]

You're doing a great job. Help me understand, a little bit more. Which of these events holds the most weight in your mind?

Client: Being declared unfit. I've never felt so bad in my life

Therapist: So, the absolute worst part was when you were declared an unfit mother.

[*mentally noting that if the event of being declared unfit was the heaviest piece of evidence, that perhaps exploring the path towards becoming fit again might be fruitful in the next step*]
What made that so particularly painful for you?

Client: I guess, I just hadn't realized until then what a mess my life was. I was in just such a fog trying to deal with my PTSD, that I hadn't realized it had gotten so bad.

Therapist: [*mentally noting some other mitigating factors to explore later on*]
So, it was a particularly painful experience because of what happened—being declared unfit. But, also, it was sort of shocking in a way, like getting a rug pulled out from underneath you.

Client: More like a gut punch.

Therapist: That's powerful imagery, and I guess it sort of knocked the wind out of you then?

Client: Exactly

In this example, we see how the therapist attends to the emotional experience, validates where appropriate, and is initially focused on understanding where the client is coming from. As you explore an issue, you will naturally come across important pieces of information that can be used in the next step when you go to help her expand her point of view in order to attend to the evidence that she is missing and the missing context from the evidence that you have discussed.

What Are the Facts that Support This?

This can be a fairly similar question to the one on experiences above. Something to watch for is facts that are not objective facts. From the perspective of gaining a phenomenological understanding of the client, we do not want to reject or only attend to facts that are objective facts—at least initially. Later in the process we will evaluate these facts to see if they are really facts. Commonly, people will build a mental house of cards, where a thought is based upon another thought and interpretation. Ultimately, from the perspective of collaborative empiricism we will want to evaluate the belief based on solid evidence; however, if we ignore the emotional elements of the case, we risk changes in perspective of logic but not the corresponding emotion.

One way to handle this is to have an informal *voir dire* of sorts. *Voir dire* is French for "to speak the truth," and it is a legal term that speaks to a preliminary examination of evidence, jurors, or witnesses. Such strategies need to be approached from an empathic place such as collaborative empiricism. Below are examples of how this may be handled in session.

Therapist: Nicole, we've decided to evaluate this hot thought you are a bad mother. What evidence do you have that you are a bad mother?

Client: Well, I'm just terrible at it and I failed at being a mom.

Therapist: Those are two large statements that sound upsetting.

Client: Yeah, I feel really bad.

Therapist: And, you said some of the evidence that you are a bad mother is because you have thoughts that you are terrible as a mother and thoughts that you failed as a mother.

Client: Correct.

Therapist: I don't know that we've evaluated these two statements yet. This idea that you are terrible as a mother and that you failed as a mother.

Client: What do you mean?

Therapist: Well, it sounds like some of the evidence for your thought that you are a bad mother is more thoughts that about you as a mother.

Client: But, I am terrible as a mom and I did fail at it.

Therapist: It feels like you are terrible and like you failed at it, this sounds like another set of thoughts to evaluate. I'm happy to look at these two questions with you, I just don't want to treat these painful thoughts as facts if they are not.

Client: I guess that makes sense.

Therapist: So, in my log I'm going to write down that you have thoughts about being a bad mother and feels like they are true. Those thoughts and feelings are certainly real, and we want to factor them in to our analysis. For now, let's focus on the facts that we know and later we'll circle back and evaluate these two very painful thoughts that you are terrible as a mother and that you failed as a mother. Is that OK?

Client: That's OK, I guess I tend to sort of spin myself up sometimes.

Therapist: I know you've had a lot of down time lately and that can be the perfect place to overthink. I want to honor this emotional experience that you are having. It is important that we acknowledge these thoughts and feelings, and I also want to help you take an objective and balanced look at the situation. So, what are the facts that support you being a bad mother?

Client: My children were removed from my home because I was using meth.

Therapist: That sounds like a fact, let me write this down. What other facts support this idea that you are a bad mother?

Client: I just felt like I never knew what I was doing.

Therapist: What emotion goes with that?

Client: Uncertainty, anxiety

Therapist: So, you had thoughts that you didn't know what you were doing, and you felt anxious and uncertain. Factually, what were the conditions that these thoughts and feelings happened in?

Client: Well, no one ever taught me how to be a parent. I just sort of tried to figure it out as best I could, and most the time I didn't know what to do.

Therapist: And, how did you handle that?

Client: I did the best I could I guess

Therapist: Pulling it together, the fact for our list is that you had to figure out how to be a parent on your own, and you did the best you could, and you still often felt like you didn't know what you were doing and you felt a lot of anxiety and uncertainty.

Client: Yeah

Attending to the subjective elements of the case allows you to incorporate and address emotional elements of the schema, which will help you ultimately to achieve a deeper level of change. It can also be validating to the client when you treat their thoughts and feelings as important. Their thoughts might be true, and the feelings might be connected to important context or information. The pitfall to avoid in this process is becoming stuck in a lengthy evaluation of a piece of evidence; this can lead to several strings of partially evaluated thoughts and no clear outcome from the session. Similar to the above, sometimes the best strategy is to acknowledge one of the submitted pieces of evidence as emotionally important, but a thought that has not yet been evaluated. We can evaluate it together, but first we want to stick with the target we worked so hard to identify.

If This Was True, What Do You Think Would Be the Strongest Evidence to Support It?

Sometimes it can be pragmatic to focus on the weightiest evidence (the crux of the case). There can be much emotional importance attached to items that are subjectively held as being the most important. Sometimes, these items not what you expect and can inform the focus of the evaluation.

Therapist: So, Nicole, you have this idea that you are a bad mother. We decided to evaluate this thought together to see if it was true and if it was true what to do about it. First, we want to see if it actually true. So, if this thought you are a bad mother was true what would be the strongest evidence to support it?

Client: I think the strongest evidence is how unhappy my kids are. I've put them through a lot with them being put in the foster system. It wasn't their fault, but they are the ones who are suffering.

Therapist: For you, the strongest evidence for this idea that you are a bad mother, is how unhappy your kids have seemed in the foster system. In your mind they are being punished for your mistakes.

Client: Yes

Therapist: I can see how that would be really upsetting to you. So, let's take a closer look at this, it sounds is the idea that if your children are unhappy you are a bad mother?

Client: No, you can't keep kids forever happy, it's the fact that it is my fault, that's the biggest piece of evidence.

Therapist: Alright, so the biggest piece of evidence for this idea that you are a bad mom is that your kids are unhappy, and it is your fault.
[*noting that the idea of fault may be useful in the next phase*]
So, help me understand why this is the biggest piece of evidence for you.

Client: I know how terrible the foster system can be and I never wanted to put them through that.

Therapist: You've been in the foster system yourself?

Client: Yeah, I grew up all over and I hated the foster system. I know some people have good experiences, but I had terrible experiences. And, my kids are so young.

Therapist: So, you have a real-life idea of what they are going through right now.

Client: Yeah, I just keep picturing them crying in a locked room, all alone and not knowing why.

Therapist: That's a haunting image.

[*mentally noting that imagery may be an important part of the case and imagery might need to be folded into the summary and synthesis part*]

Client: It is, I just can't sleep, I can't focus, I just keep picturing it

Therapist: Of course, you feel terrible, that's a really painful image to have. Let's keep talking about this, but I also want to make a note to coordinate with your caseworker to see if we can get some general details about your children's living conditions.

Client: That would be great, I just can't stop thinking and worrying about them.

Therapist: So, pulling it together, the main case for you being a bad mom is tied to this idea that your children are unhappy, and it is your fault because they were put into the foster system due to your meth use. And you have this mental image of your innocent children, locked up, alone, and crying, and it is really upsetting.

[*noting that the remorse she has might be a potential piece of evidence to counter being a completely bad mother*]

Do I have that right?

Client: Yeah, that sounds about right.

Therapist: OK, let's get into evaluating the biggest piece of evidence then.

By examining the strongest piece of evidence, you can focus on the more emotionally laden elements of the case. By exploring that content, you can develop a better understanding of the belief and why the client believes the belief. This strategic knowledge will help you know where to focus in the next steps.

Is This Something People Have Directly Said to You in the Past?

Sometimes a painful thought or belief is based on something the client has been directly told. In these cases, we want to learn more about the context in which it was said and the credibility of who said it.

Therapist: Nicole, I'm curious, with this belief that you are a bad mother, has anyone ever actually ever told you that you are a bad mother?

Client: Yeah, a few people.

Therapist: Let's talk about that. What were the circumstances where this was said?

Client: Well, when my caseworker was going over my case with me, she talked about how I screwed up.

Therapist: And, she told you that you were a bad mother?

Client: Well, not directly, but she was talking about how I messed up.

Therapist: So, she didn't tell you that she thought you were a bad mother, but you sort of inferred it from what was being said.

Client: Yeah, I guess, I just felt really bad.

Therapist: You were feeling really bad and having thoughts that you were a bad mother. Were there any instances where someone actually told you that you were a bad mother?

Client: When I was first pregnant my ex told me that I should have gotten an abortion because I was going to be a bad mom.

Therapist: That's sort of like be told you're a bad mom, did your ex ever see you in action as a mother?

Client: Well, no, but that's for the best, he was bad news.

Therapist: So, one time you inferred but it was sort of just a thought you were having, another time someone predicted it, though it sounds like maybe he wasn't the best judge. Any other times?

Client: One of the correction officers told me I needed to get my stuff together and stop being a bad mom and junkie.

Therapist: That's some blunt feedback. And, did this person know what was going on with you?

Client: Well, he knew what I had been arrested for and that I was a mom, because I was asking about how to call my kids.

Therapist: So, he knew you were a mom, and you were arrested on drug-related charges, did he know how you were as a mom? Like, could he make an overall judgment about you as a mom?

Client: I guess not, but maybe he's like seen my type before and he was right, I do need to get my stuff together.

Therapist: OK, pulling it together, there are times you've gotten the message that you are a bad mom. Once it was a message you inferred when you were talking with your case worker and she was talking about how you screwed up, another time it was predicted by your ex, but it sounds like he never saw you as a mom and we also don't know how good his judgment was. Then there was this correction officer who gave you the tough love advice that you need to get your stuff together and that your drug-related charges are getting in the way of you being a mom.

Client: That sounds about right.

Therapist: Let's take a look at the context in which this was and the reliability of the source.

Typically, it is important to find out what really happened. The emotionality of a situation can color the messages a person takes away from a situation. Drawing out the context of the situation can help you to better understand the client's and the other people's state of mind in order to better understand what transpired.

What Is It Like to Believe This Thought?

This is an important question for the emotional processing of the belief and associated affect. Accessing those feelings in conjunction with the belief is important for bringing about cognitive and affective change; in addition, this can help identify other pieces of evidence you might have missed that held emotional significance.

Therapist: Nicole, when you say that you are bad mother, what is it like to believe that you are a bad mother?

Client: It's heart-breaking, like I feel frantic like I need to fix it, but also, I just feel so bad, and really it just makes me want to use.

Therapist: So, there's this big emotional experience, an urge to change the situation, but also an urge to escape how you are feeling?
Client: Yeah, this would be a lot easier if I was using, but I won't get my kids back if I go there.
Therapist: I imagine this is may be doubly hard for you.

In this case, exploring the effects of believing the thought clarified the situation and helped the client access their feelings. This also helped the therapist learn about the corresponding emotional and behavioral responses to target.

How Long Have You Believed This?

If a belief developed, then logically there was a time when this belief did not exist and, by extension, it may not have to be true in the future. Additionally, the belief may have formed in reaction to a major stressor or trauma, identifying this will change how you decide to go after the belief. If the client endorsed believing something as far back as they can remember, then you might be looking at what made it true then and now.

Therapist: Nicole, how love have you believed that you are a bad mother?
Client: I guess I always felt like I wasn't great.
Therapist: OK, but was there a time that "not great" flipped to "bad?"
Client: Definitely, when my kids were taken away from me. I guess that's when I realized I was actually a bad mother.
Therapist: To help me better understand this, let's make a timeline of you as a mom and then map out how you think you were doing at the various points.

The therapist is focusing on how the client is making a global judgment based on a discrete interval of time. Drawing out a timeline will help the therapist later examine any discrepancies or instances (past or future) where the belief might not have been true.

When Do You Tend to Believe This More and Less?

This is a very useful question. If we can identify when the client believes the target belief the most and the least, we can get a good idea of what types of evidence are most salient to her belief system.

Therapist: Nicole, how constant is this belief that you are a bad mother?
Client: Hm?
Therapist: When do you believe it the most? And are there times you believe it slightly less?
Client: I believe it the most when I think about my kids being taken away.
Therapist: We talked about that being an especially painful memory, and are there times you believe it slightly less than that?
Client: I guess when I reflect on how hard I've been working. This is the longest I've been clean in as long as I can remember.
Therapist: You have been working really hard. It has been very apparent to me that you care a lot about this.

From this question, the therapist learns what types of evidence to focus on in trying to understand the target belief. Also, good information is gathered about future areas to both look at to help the client attend to some salient areas she is missing and to work on for continued behavior change in the direction of her goals and values.

What Do You Typically Do When Thoughts Like This Come Up for You?

This question can help you understand the influence of the belief on the client's behavior, and in turn how that affects the environment and possibly the information the client takes back in. For example, if your client often thinks that people will not love them and responds by pushing people away, this will affect whether people stick around and influence their perceptions of whether people love them.

Therapist: Nicole, I want to learn more about this belief that you are a bad mother. When these thoughts come up for you, how do you tend to emotionally feel?

Client: Bad, really bad.

Therapist: What emotion do you feel?

Client: Shame, sadness, and anger.

Therapist: You have thoughts that you are a bad mother, and you feel ashamed, sad, and angry. What do you tend to do when you think this way and feel this way?

Client: Well, before, I would have gotten high. These feelings are so intense I'm really feeling it, the urge to escape.

Therapist: I see how you get there, and what about now?

Client: I cry a lot and then I sleep a lot. Sleep is one of the only escapes I have left.

Therapist: So, you have thoughts of being a bad mother, you feel intense shame, guilt, and anger, and then you escape or want to escape?

Client: Yeah

Therapist: How does your sleeping to escape or history of using to escape affect your belief about being a bad mother?

Client: Well, it helps me not think about it.

Therapist: Does it make you believe it less?

Client: Well, no, I usually feel worse afterwards.

Therapist: Oh?

Client: I then have thoughts about what a coward I am and then I think, what's the use, and I think I won't be able to get my kids back anyway.

Therapist: This sounds like a rollercoaster of sorts. You have high shame, anger, and anxiety. You escape those feelings with some avoidance behavior, but your relief ends up being spoiled by thoughts that you are coward and you won't get your kids back anyway.

Client: It is the worst rollercoaster in the world.

Therapist: Sounds like it is not a fun rollercoaster. How does the emotional fall-out from this affect your belief that you are a bad mother?

Client: Well, I feel worse and then I really feel like a bad mother. Like, I should be facing this head on. This is important.

Therapist: So, the emotions get stronger and you believe the belief that you are a bad mother more?

Client: Absolutely

Therapist: And it sounds like your avoidance behaviors are further evidence to you that you are a bad mother?

Client: I guess so. I feel like a better mother would be handling this better than I am.

Therapist: Well, let's talk about this idea that your avoidance behaviors are further evidence that you are a bad mother.

As we discussed in the previous chapter, behaviors that are associated with our underlying beliefs can be avoidance behaviors, overcompensating behaviors, or behaviors that are consistent with those beliefs (Young, 1999). Learning more about the behaviors is important to understanding the situation. Further, we are interested in learning about the client's perceptions of their behavior and the outcome of their behavior. A client can think that their behavior is further evidence of the belief, or they could think that their compensatory strategy failing to fix the problem is evidence of that belief. They could fail to see the impact of their avoidance behavior on themselves, others, and the overall situation.

Summary

After we have identified a suitable target for Socratic questioning. We next want to focus on trying to understand how the thought or belief makes sense. Ideally, we want to understand the client's case for believing the cognition. We want to attend to both the subjective and objective elements of the basis for the belief to help us gain an overall feel for the essence of the belief. Attending to and incorporating emotion is an important part of this process. This process can be framed as an exercise in validation and application of collaborative empiricism. Leading with understanding before using change strategies helps the client feel understood, decreases dysregulation of emotion, reduces defensiveness, and helps the therapist understand where promising prospects for expanding the client's perspective may be found. Later steps will include evaluating the subjective elements of evidence that were gathered in the understanding phase.

References

Beck, A. T. (1979). *Cognitive therapy and the emotional disorders.* New York: Meridian.

Beck, A. T., & Haigh, E. A. P. (2014). Advances in cognitive theory and therapy: The Generic Cognitive Model. *Annual Review of Clinical Psychology, 10,* 1–24. doi:10.1146/annurev-clinpsy-032813-153734

Beck, J. S. (2011). *Cognitive behavior therapy: Basics and beyond* (2nd ed.). New York: Guilford Press.

Chessick, R. D. (1995). The application of phenomenology to psychiatry and psychotherapy. *American Journal of Psychotherapy, 49*(2), 159–162.

Davidsen, A. S. (2013). Phenomenological approaches in psychology and health sciences. *Qualitative Research in Psychology, 10*(3), 318–339.

Greenberg, L. S. (2004). Emotion-focused therapy. *Clinical Psychology & Psychotherapy: An International Journal of Theory & Practice, 11*(1), 3–16.
Grossman, R. (2013). *Phenomenology and existentialism: An introduction.* London: Routledge.
Johnson, S. M. (2009). Attachment theory and emotionally focused therapy for individuals and couples. In J. H. Obegi & E. Berant (Eds.), *Attachment theory and research in clinical work with adults* (pp. 410–433). New York: Guilford Press.
Hintikka, J. (2007). *Socratic epistemology: Explorations of knowledge-seeking by questioning.* New York: Cambridge University Press.
Kabat-Zinn, J. (2006). *Mindfulness for beginners.* Louisville, CO: Sounds True.
Kazantzis, N., Beck, J. S., Clark, D. A., Dobson, K. S., Hofmann, S. G., Leahy, R. L., & Wong, C. W. (2018). Socratic dialogue and guided discovery in cognitive behavioral therapy: A modified Delphi panel. *International Journal of Cognitive Therapy, 11*(2), 140–157.
Kazantzis, N., Fairburn, C. G., Padesky, C. A., Reinecke, M., & Teesson, M. (2014). Unresolved issues regarding the research and practice of cognitive behavior therapy: The case of guided discovery using Socratic questioning. *Behaviour Change, 31*(01), 1–17. doi:10.1017/bec.2013.29
Leahy, R. L. (2018). *Emotional schema therapy: Distinctive features.* New York: Routledge.
Linehan, M. M. (1997). Validation and psychotherapy. Empathy reconsidered: New directions in psychotherapy. In A. C. Bohart & L. S. Greenberg (Eds.), *Empathy reconsidered: New directions in psychotherapy* (pp. 353–392). Washington, DC: American Psychological Association.
Lippmann, W. (2017). *Public opinion.* New York: Routledge.
Mishara, A. L. (1995). Narrative and psychotherapy—the phenomenology of healing. *American Journal of Psychotherapy, 49*(2), 180–195.
Padesky, C. A. (1993). Socratic questioning: Changing minds or guiding discovery. Paper presented at the keynote address delivered at the European Congress of Behavioural and Cognitive Therapies, London. Retrieved from: http://padesky.com/newpad/wpcontent/uploads/2012/11/socquest.pdf
Polya, G. (1973). *How to solve it* (2nd ed.). Princeton, NJ: Princeton University Press.
Rogers, C. R. (1995). *On becoming a person: A therapist's view of psychotherapy.* New York: Houghton Mifflin Harcourt.
Thoma, N. C., & McKay, D. (2014). *Working with emotion in cognitive-behavioral therapy: Techniques for clinical practice.* New York: Guilford Press.
Trachtman, J. P. (2013). *The tools of argument: How the best lawyers think, argue, and win.* Lexington, KY: Trachtman.
Waltman, S. H., Creed, T. A., & Beck, A. T. (2016). Are the effects of cognitive behavior therapy for depression falling? Review and critique of the evidence. *Clinical Psychology: Science and Practice, 23*(2), 113–122.
Wenzel, A. (2019). *Cognitive behavioral therapy for beginners: An experiential learning approach.* New York: Routledge.
Young, J. E. (1999). *Cognitive therapy for personality disorders: A schema-focused approach.* Sarasota, FL: Professional Resource Press.

Chapter 7

Collaborative Curiosity

Scott H. Waltman

❖ CONTENTS

It is important to understand the goal of this step. This is not an interrogation where we are trying to get a person to admit we are right or a sales presentation where we are focused on closing a deal. Similarly, we are not trying to get the client to arrive at a predetermined correct answer. In the previous step, we focused on coming to see things as our clients see them. In the current step, we are focused on expanding that viewpoint together. We will jointly discover the truth and we will focus on teaching the client how to mentally take a step back and do this on their own (Overholser, 2011, 2018).

Collaboration and Curiosity

Socratic ignorance is a term that denotes a disavowal of knowledge (Overholser, 2010, 2011, 2018). Of course, Socrates was not truly ignorant (Hintikka, 2007) and had an idea in his mind what the truth was and an intended destination to direct the client towards (Kazantzis et al., 2018). Socratic ignorance is different from the *Columbo approach* sometimes used in motivational interviewing. The literary figure Columbo was a brilliant detective who would play dumb so that people would lower their defenses and reveal more than they meant to. In this collaborative empiricism process, we have a goal of true and authentic curiosity (Schein, 2013). Beckian Socratic Dialogue is different from a purely Socratic approach in that the therapist has an openness to jointly discovering with the client, and it is different from the Columbo approach in that this curiosity is authentic.

Christine Padesky illustrated this point well in a previous panel discussion on Socratic questioning:

> When I'm advising people about how to get better at using Socratic dialogue and guided discovery in therapy, one of the things that I emphasis the most is having a genuine curiosity, because I think curiosity—genuine curiosity on the part of the therapist—is often the best predictor of how good a therapist is going to be at using Socratic processes. I would disagree with one aspect of what you said ... because you said, 'We know where we're going'. And I think that sometimes we do have a sense of where we are going but I think that it's a dangerous trap if, as therapists, if we have too much in our minds, in the sense that we know where we're going.
>
> (Kazantzis, Fairburn, Padesky, Reinecke, & Teesson, 2014, p. 7)

Table 7.1 Collaborative Empiricism Matrix

	Low Collaboration	**High Collaboration**
Low Empiricism	Low Collaborative Empiricism	Supportive Therapy
High Empiricism	Provided Discovery Disputing by labeling thinking as distorted or irrational	Collaborative Empiricism Jointly Discovering Fosters client motivation Brings about change

Based on Tee & Kazantzis (2011)

Tee and Kazantzis (2011) previously created a matrix to demonstrate the intersection of collaboration and empiricism. They connected their model to factors related to self-determination and motivation, with it being thought that high collaboration and high empiricism led to high motivation, self-determination, and change.

Restating Their Case: If and Then

The first step in this process is finding your bearings and restating the client's case. This will help you consolidate the information and understand what you are working with. In this step, you are summarizing their case, or the reasons why they believe the cognition you are evaluating. As, ultimately, the client will be their own arbiter of truth, we are paying attention to which items they lend the most weight to. We are seeking to frame their case in an if-then framework. The "if" portion is their interpretation of events and the "then" is the conclusion they are reaching. We want to make sure we have a good understanding of their interpretation, which is really two separate components: their interpretation of what happened and their subjective understanding that this meets the criteria for their conclusion, both are potential intervention points. We have already taken a head start on this process by creating a shared or universal definition (see Overholser, 1994, 2010, 2018) in the focusing step of the framework.

In the legal realm, the analogue for this concept is that there are legal or statutory definitions of a crime or civil liability, and in order to establish a conclusion of criminal or civil liability, a litigator may need prove intent, causation, injury, and lack of mitigating factors (Trachtman, 2013). We don't necessarily need to evaluate all of these, but these certainly are factors to consider when evaluating the case that the client has made for the belief you are evaluating. You want to ask yourself: "What exactly are we evaluating here?" and "What would have needed to happen for that to be true?"

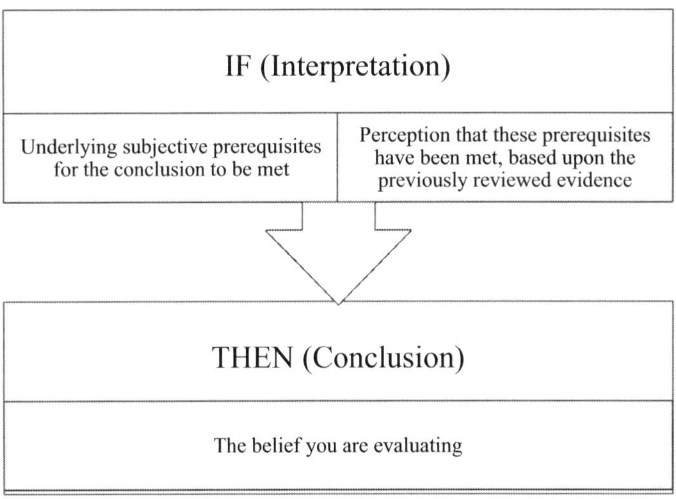

Figure 7.1 Clarifying Their Perspective

Consider the example of a mother who is frustrated with her teenage daughter not heeding her counsel. The mother concludes that "She doesn't respect me." We want to understand and evaluate the interpretation (if) that leads to this conclusion (then), because that is how we get a different conclusion. We want to understand her interpretation of what happened and her interpretation of how the criteria of not "respecting me" is met. So, we will have mapped out with her what exactly happened, including what was our client doing before, during, and after this event. We also want to talk broadly with her about the abstract rules of respect and disrespect, and we would want to narrow that abstract conversation to specific observable behaviors. We would also probably seek to evaluate the reasonableness of her assumptions about respect and how absolute those assumptions are.

Clinically, we can progress by either expanding her interpretation of what happened or by evaluating the assumptions that underlie her reaction to the situation.

Therapist: OK, so, the thought we have been evaluating is that your daughter doesn't respect you and in taking about it, the main evidence for this thought is that she treats you disrespectfully. Do I have that right?

Client: Yes, that sounds about right.

Therapist: To better understand this, I want to break it down a little bit, if that is alright.

Client: That's fine.

Therapist: So, we have two pieces to look at: what your daughter does that seems disrespectful and then your own personal rules of what you think is respectful and not respectful. Let's start with what actually happened. What are the specific behaviors she does that seem disrespectful?

Client: Where do I begin? She doesn't listen to anything I say. She has a real attitude towards me. She's always on her phone when I'm talking to her.

Therapist: Those all sound like they could be annoying. I'm sure the list could go on, are those the main ones?

Client: Yes, those are the ones that bug me the most.

Therapist: Of the three which is the worst one to you, which one seems most disrespectful?

Client: It's the phone, she's always on it, her face is glued to it, it's so rude.

Therapist: So, she's on her phone almost all the time.

Client: If she's awake, she's on her phone.

Therapist: And is it that you don't like her being on her phone? or there is something about being on her phone that is disrespectful?

Client: It's the fact that she's on her phone when I'm talking to her.

Therapist: She doesn't put the phone down when you talk to her and that's the part that feels disrespectful.

Client: Exactly!

Therapist: And is it only you she does this with?

Client: You mean like, does she put the phone down for everyone else, but not me?

Therapist: Yeah, does she put her phone down for your partner?

Client: No, she doesn't put that phone down for anyone.

Therapist: Have you ever seen her interact with her friends in real life?

Client: They come over sometimes, they are so loud, but they never leave the house, I guess they don't want to leave the safety of the Wi-Fi.

Therapist: So, she's on her phone when her friends are over too?

Client: She doesn't put it down for anyone. Sometimes, I think they're talking to each other through their phones, even though they are in the same room!

Therapist: Maybe, I wouldn't be surprised.

So, what does it mean about respect, if she does this phone-related behavior with other people like your partner, and her friends, and maybe everyone?

Client: I guess, maybe, for her it's not about respect it is just normal.

Therapist: It also sounds like maybe you and your daughter have different assumptions or rules about respect and what behaviors are respectful.

Client: I definitely would believe that!

Therapist: In your mind, what's the line between respect and disrespect?

Client: I'm not sure. I think it has to do with being rude.

Therapist: So, if you are being rude, then you are being disrespectful

Client: Yes.

Therapist: Whose standard are we using to determine if something is rude? If we were questioning whether I was being rude with you, would we judge me by my standard of rudeness or yours?

Client: I'd probably use my own, but you seem like you would have high standards for yourself.

Therapist: So, with your standards of rudeness, there are probably things people can do overtly that are rude, sins of commission. And, there are respectful things that people fail to do, sins of omission. What's the cutoff for being rude? How many bad things does someone have to do, or good things do they have to fail to do before we decide they are rude?

Client: I don't know, I mean sometimes, something is obviously disrespectful.

Therapist: I'll concede that. But what about cases that are greyer, like your daughter?

Client: ??

Therapist: If she does disrespect you at times, is that enough to conclude that on the whole she is rude towards you and therefore does not respect you?

Client: I wouldn't say that she is wholly rude to me.

Therapist: She is a pain sometimes.

Client: Yes, but I don't think it is personal.

Therapist: So, how are we pulling this all together?

Client: I do think it is disrespectful to not look someone in the face when they are talking to you, but I don't think it is personal, I'm not happy she does it, but I don't think she means to be rude to me.

Therapist: That sounds like something we can work with; how does that affect your overall feelings about the situation?

Client: I'm not happy, but I'm a lot less mad.

Another example of this is someone with social anxiety who has perceptions that people at school are judging them. The conclusion they are reaching is that people are judging them, and we want to understand the interpretations that are leading to

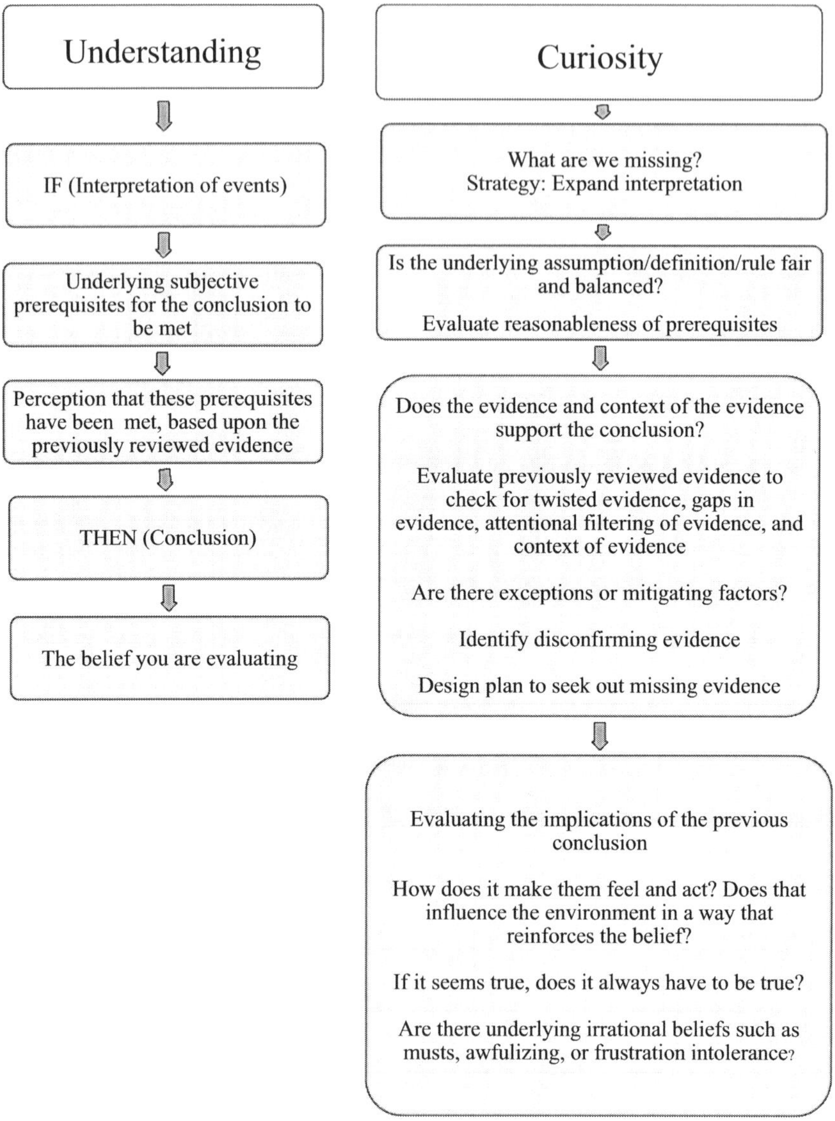

Figure 7.2 Expanding Their Perspective

this. There are interpretations grounded in what is happening, which might include people looking at them, people laughing, or overhearing gossip. There are also underlying assumptions about what constitutes being judged (and also of the perceived terribleness of being judged). So, we could look to see if things actually happened the way they think they did; we can also look to see if it means what they think it does. Additionally, we can target the implications of the conclusion by the evaluating the perceived terribleness of the conclusion, their resulting behavior, or the pervasiveness/permanence of the conclusion.

Evaluating Their Case

Teaching Scientific Reasoning

Aaron Beck initially described cognitive therapy as the application of the experimental method to thought (Beck, 1979). A goal of CBT is to teach clients how to identify, evaluate, and modify their thoughts (Beck, 2011). This process invariably includes skills related to meta-cognition and scientific reasoning, which are thought to be associated with learning CBT skills (Garber, Frankel, & Herrington, 2016). Scientific reasoning refers a hypothesis-testing mindset that involves gathering and examining evidence to test hypotheses (Kuhn 2002, Sandberg & McCullough, 2010). If you are a trained researcher, you can apply those scientific reasoning skills to this process to help evaluate your client's conclusions. In research, we are seeking to find out whether the method and results support the conclusion.

If you remember what we covered in Chapter 5, "Focusing on Key Content," logical arguments are typically based on if-then statements; if-perception then-conclusion. We are interested in evaluating the validity of the conclusions (i.e., whether the "if" necessitates the "then") and the validity of the generalizations made from those conclusions (i.e., whether global conclusions are supported by the scope of the available data). There are a number of threats to validity that we can account for (see Codd, 2018 for a review of research methods). These are all potential areas to explore in our collaborative curiosity.

Loose Thread Strategy

Lawyers have something they might call the *loose thread strategy* (Trachtman, 2013). The idea is that there can be gaps in evidence that can be like a loose thread of a knit sweater, and as we pull on those loose threads their case or conclusion can unravel. A key question in this process is "How do you know?" and it is imperative that it is paired with genuine empathy and curiosity. Sometimes, they will have really strong reasons and that is good to know. At other times, you can find something useful to evaluate.

This is a useful strategy for when there are leaps in logic or a thought is being used as evidence for another thought. Consider the example below: Tony has a belief that he is unlovable, mostly supported by a belief that his mother never loved him. Clinically, the therapist will target how Tony knew that his mother never loved him.

Therapist: So, Tony, we're looking at the evidence for your thought that you are unlovable, and you said one of the main reasons you believe you are unlovable is because your mother never loved you.

Client: Yeah, I mean, if she couldn't love me, how could anyone love me?

Table 7.2 Threats to Validity

Sampling Bias	The basic concept here is does the data source reflect the target for the conclusion; is the sample representative of the overall population? For example: Does your client think no one will ever love them because everyone from their high school class seemed to not like them? Can we help them explore how well the individuals we are discussing represent the larger population? We can also look at how well the situation or interval of time generalizes to the bigger picture. Are they seeking to make broad conclusions about their life, themselves, or other people based a non-representative sample?
Confounding Variables or Third Variables	Life is multi-variate and complex. The basic idea behind a confounding variable or a third variable is that there can be items we are not measuring that are impacting our findings. Are there factors we are not considering that could be influencing the situation? For example: An abuse survivor might be wondering what they did to deserve the abuse and there are likely confounding variables related to the abuser and the abuser's history that had a major impact on what happened.
Data Collection Variables/ Method Variables	There are a whole host of other methodological variables that could influence our ability to have complete confidence in the initial assumption we are evaluating. Is the information from a reliable source? Are we relying too much on retrospective data? Are we trying to predict a low base rate event? There is a lot to think about and we do not need to make a formal audit of their thought process, but we do want to try and map out what happened, how they made sense of it, and if there are any concerns about how the conclusion was made that might decrease our confidence in the validity of those conclusions.
Historical Factors	Context is important, and the idea behind the history bias is that research does not occur in a vacuum. Here, we are looking to see if there are any situational factors, historical factors, or contextual factors that may have had an influence on what happened or on the perception of what happened. For example: If you client has thoughts about being a failure for not being able to find a job, is it possible that a global economic downturn impacted the situation? A good example of historical factors is the impact of the 24-hour ratings-based news platforms on the vicarious exposure to violence and tragedy. This cultural shift could have an impact on your client's views that the world is becoming more dangerous.
Maturation	Maturation refer to normative development as a confounding variable. It is not uncommon for an adult client to wonder why they as a child did not know or understand then what they know now.
Expectancy Effects	The basic idea here is that someone's expectations can influence an interaction. If you expect someone will treat you terribly, that can influence your thoughts, feelings, and behaviors in such a way that can impact how they respond to you. If you suspect expectancy effects, you'll want to map out with your client what they were thinking, feeling, doing, right before the event in question.

(continued)

Table 7.2 continued

Observer and rater bias	This can be similar to expectancy effect, except the emphasis is on the impact of expectations on perception.
Regression to the mean	On average, life is very average. While things might be extremely good or bad at times; in general, more extreme happenings tend to be less extreme over time. We can see this come up in two places. Where there is a catastrophizing or magnifying process where the absolute worst moments are treated as typical. On the other hand, sometimes a client may be apt to prematurely think a problem is resolved, this can be observed often in cases where someone is the victim of domestic violence or early in their recovery from chemical dependency.

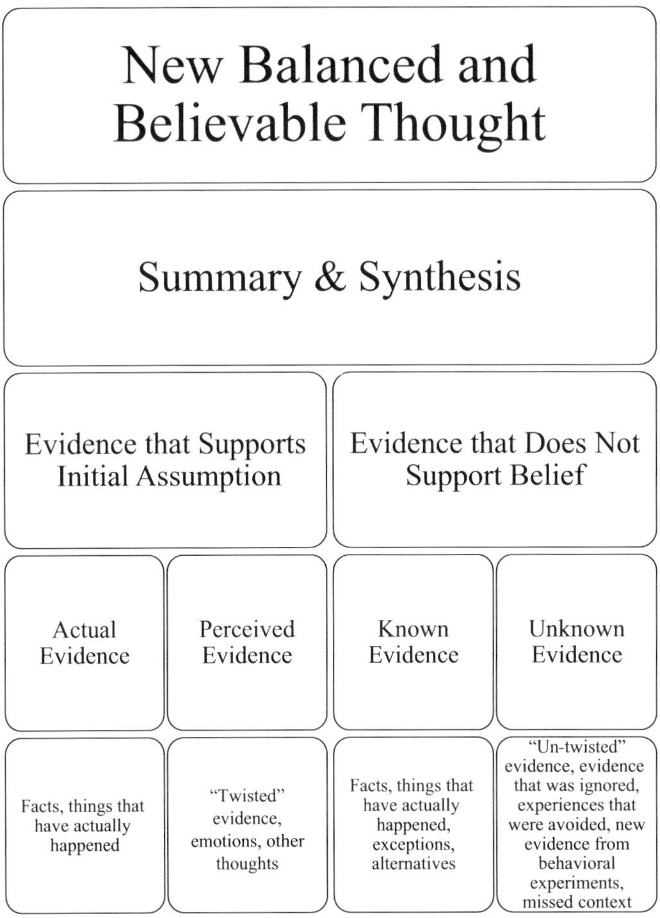

Figure 7.3 Conceptual Overview of Socratic Questioning Model

Therapist: This is a really heavy piece of evidence that is associated with a lot of suffering on your part. Would it be OK if we took a closer look at that piece of evidence?

Client: Uh, yeah, if you think it would help.

Therapist: I'm curious, how do you know that your mother didn't love you?

Client: Well, she wasn't really there for me and she was always out getting high instead of being home with me.

Therapist: And you were quite young at the time, that had to be really hard for you.

Client: It was, I didn't understand why she was always gone, and I would wonder if I did anything to make her mad.

Therapist: On, some level you thought it was your fault that she was out getting high and not at home. Do you still think that?

Client: No, I know she was an addict and she never really cared about me.

Therapist: I'm glad you are not blaming yourself anymore, but I'm not sure I quite get the she never loved you part.

Client: Huh?

Therapist: So, the evidence that she never loved you is that she was gone a lot, and not there when you needed her, also there is some context about her addiction. How does that mean she doesn't love you?

Client: She loved getting high and herself more than me.

Therapist: That's a painful thought, "She loved getting high and herself more than me." Or it at least *felt* that way.

Client: Yeah.

Therapist: So, it *felt* like she loved her addiction more than she loved you, and somehow this gets you to thinking that she never loved you. Personally, I never knew her, so I can't speak to her affection for you. I'm just trying to understand how this equals her never loving you.

Client: I guess … maybe, she did love me …

Therapist: But?

Client: She was never there for me!

Therapist: That's real, that's real that you spent a lot of time alone, not knowing what was going on, feeling sad and scared, and wondering if it was your fault. I don't want to lose sight of the reality of your experience. And, I'm just not sure we've established that she never loved you.

Client: I think maybe she did love me, in her own way, it just wasn't enough to keep her around. I wasn't enough to keep her around.

Therapist: So, there are actually two different pieces to this puzzle. One is the question of whether your mother loved you, and, two, whether your intrinsic lovability could be enough to keep someone who has a chemical dependency from their addiction. Does that sound like I understand what's going on well enough?

Client: Yeah, that sounds right.

Therapist: So, first question first, do you believe it, when you said you think she loved you in her own way?

Client: I do, and I do have some memories of things not always being terrible and of her being excited to see me sometimes. But …

Therapist: Hold on to that second thought, we'll get there. So, yes, your mother did love you. Let me write that down, and while I'm writing this down, I want you to tell me that your mother loved you, like you believe it.

Client: My mother loved me.

Therapist: Can you close your eyes and picture her face and imagine her telling you that she loves you?

Client: [*pausing and tearing a little*]

Therapist: Did you do it?

Client: Yeah

Therapist: Did you believe it?

Client: I do, I lose sight of it sometimes, but she did love me, I know it.

Therapist: I think it makes sense that you lose sight of sometimes, given the context of all the hurt that happened. Now, how about that thought that you should have been able to keep her from using drugs with her love for you.

Client: That's a big piece of it.

Therapist: I know this is a historical soft spot for you. How much do you know about the science of addiction or recovery from addiction?

Client: Well, I know a lot about addiction from watching my mom ruin her life with her addiction.

Therapist: I'm sorry you had to go through that. Along the way, did she ever try to quit or get clean?

Client: Dozens of times, in the end, after I was taken from her custody, she was always telling me she was going to quit, she just couldn't stay quit.

Therapist: So, quitting is really hard.

Client: Yes

Therapist: We see this on a brain chemistry level, where people keep using despite catastrophic problems in their life.

Client: There were definitely catastrophic problems in her life.

Therapist: I know; we've talked about how she died.

The idea that seems to come up in your mind is that if she would have really loved you, she would have quit.

Client: I thought about that a lot over the years.

Therapist: Yes, but how did you know that it was true that if she would have loved you enough, she would have quit?

Client: I know people who make big changes for their kids.

Therapist: If you had kids, you would do anything for your kids?

Client: Definitely.

Therapist: So, how strong did her addiction have to be to override that?

Client: I guess, I never thought of that.

Therapist: Well, you were only a kid at the time, so it makes sense that you saw things the way you did. How are you seeing things now?

Client: I do believe that she loved me, I wish she would have loved me enough to quit, but maybe it's more complicated than that, and maybe opiate addiction overrode the love she had for me.

Therapist: It's a real tragedy, what happened to her and how it affected you. When you look at everything you said about her loving you and her addiction, what does this mean about your overall lovability?

Untwisting Evidence

In a previous chapter, we reviewed the case of Benjamin, a man with a belief that he was a bad person, who at the start of the session shared about how terrible he felt for having had the veterinarian put down his dog earlier that day. For this man, that was further evidence of how wretched he was; however, there was much context that he was missing. In discussing the situation with him, the therapist learned that this dog had been a rescue dog and that this client had a penchant for taking in rescue dogs, typically focusing on dogs that no one else would take in. This dog had a degenerative neurological condition that made it violent and unpredictable. This man had exhausted all medical options and was no longer able to safely house the dog at his home. He contacted various dog rescues to see if anyone would take this dog and was unsuccessful. The decision to have the dog euthanized was his last option and one that the veterinarian strongly recommended. To the objective observer, this was not an example of the client being a completely bad person, so why did the he think this situation was simply more evidence that he was bad? Because, he was selectively attending only to the elements of the story that were consistent with his previous belief, and he was twisting information to fit his assumption. Below is a how a therapist would work to untwist this evidence in session.

Therapist: Benjamin, we've been working on this belief you have that you are a bad person, and one of the reasons you came up for being a bad person is the fact that you recently had your dog put down. Is it OK with you if we take a closer look at that?

Client: I guess so.

Therapist: I'm just not sure that I see it the way you see it. For you, this story is evidence of you being a bad person, but it feels more complicated to me. I want to break the story down and plug the different pieces into this strategy we call "Hypothesis A/ Hypothesis B." Which, basically means, I'm going to draw out two columns and we are going to sort the different pieces into either being evidence that you are a bad person, our hypothesis A, or evidence of you being a compassionate person, our hypothesis B. How does that sound to you?

Client: I'm willing to look at it.

Therapist: OK, so let me draw this out on the board. We have two columns to sort the items into being either evidence that you are a bad person or evidence you are a compassionate person
[see Figure 7.4, Hypothesis A/Hypothesis B]
Any questions so far?

Client: No, this seems to make sense.

Therapist: Let's start at the beginning then, so this dog was a rescue dog, right? Which column should we put that into?

Client: I mean, I don't feel bad about rescuing him, I feel bad for putting him down.

Therapist: We'll get there, but first recuing him from the shelter, which column does that fit into?

Client: Well, it's more compassionate than bad, but I never rescued him to be one of those people who always talk about their rescue dogs. He just needed a home and I was happy to do what I could.

Therapist: I remember you saying they were having trouble placing him before you took him in.

Client: Yeah, he had all sorts of medical problems and was kind of wild and no one would take him.

Therapist: So, you adopted the dog no one else would take. Which column does that go in?

Client: I guess compassionate. He was a good dog and I could tell he had a lot of love to give and he just needed a chance.

Therapist: He did have some pretty major medical problems.

Client: Yeah, we had to take him to all sorts of veterinary specialists.

Therapist: Which column should we put that into?

Client: The "it was expensive" category.

Therapist: I'm sure it was very expensive, was your willingness to take him to those specialists and pay for those specialists more evidence of you being a bad person or evidence of you being a compassionate person?

Client: Probably compassionate.

Therapist: And, his situation deteriorated, right?

Client: Yeah, he got violent, the vets said it was a brain problem that would only get worse.

Therapist: He was a big dog, I'm sure that was pretty scary. How did you deal with that?

Client: Well, at first, I tried to separate him from the other dogs, because I worried about him hurting one of them. He went after them a few times.

Therapist: So, you were trying to protect your other dogs. Is that a sign of being a bad person or a compassionate person?

Client: I guess compassionate.

Therapist: And, what did you do next?

Client: Well, I tried to find someone else to take him in.

Therapist: Like who?

Client: Well, I tried calling the rescue we got him from, and they wouldn't take him. I tried calling other sanctuaries or dog rescues and no one would take him.

Therapist: So, you actually called a few places then.

Client: Yeah, I just couldn't find anyone, and I felt awful about it.

Therapist: Why were you calling so many places?

Client: I just wanted this poor dog to be taken care of. The whole thing was breaking my heart.

Therapist: You really wanted a good outcome for this dog. Which column should that go in?

Client: I guess compassionate as well.

Therapist: What happened next?

Client: Well, I couldn't find anyone to take him in and he was getting worse and my vet kept telling me I needed to put him down.

Therapist: Oh, the vet was recommending that the dog be put down?

Client: Yeah, he said basically we can't do anything for him and the most humane thing to do would be to have him gently put down.

Therapist: That had to be hard to hear, after all you did for the dog.

Client: It was. It broke my heart. I really wished I could have found a way around this.

Therapist: What happened next?

Client: Well, I had the vet come over and we made my dog comfortable and then put him down. It was a relief, but it was also terrible.

Therapist: I can see how it would be a relief but also just feel terrible.

So, before you were saying that the evidence for you being a bad person was the fact that you had your dog put down, but there was some missing context. If we put followed your veterinarians' medical advice and had your dog put down, which category does that go in?

Client: I felt like a bad person.

Therapist: I can see that; I can see you emotionally felt bad and had thoughts you were a bad person. Was the decision you made from a bad place or a compassionate place?

Client: Compassionate … I thought it was the compassionate thing to do.

Therapist: There's also this thing where you feel really bad about what happened. You seem to be telling yourself that you feel bad because of how bad you are, but I think maybe you feel bad because you are a compassionate person who really cared about this dog. My sense is that if there was another viable option, you would have taken it, and how bad you feel is sort of evidence to me of that. How does that sound to you?

Client: I guess, that sounds right, I guess a bad person wouldn't feel bad for putting their dog down.

Therapist: True, your compassion for your dog is evidence of your being a compassionate person. So, when we look at these two lists, what do you see?

Client: I guess when we break the situation down, this thing that I thought was evidence of my being a bad person is actually evidence of the opposite.

A useful strategy for untwisting a piece of evidence is to break it down into its components and then rate each element as either fitting with the target cognition or an alternate explanation. In the above example, the therapist broke down the situation of the client's having put their dog down into its components and then collaboratively sorted the components as either evidence the client was a bad person or that the client was a compassionate person (a suitable alternative belief). This approach is consistent with a popular method for treating heath anxiety called Hypothesis A/Hypothesis B (Salkovskis & Bass, 1997).

Sort the evidence according to the hypothesis it supports	
Hypothesis A	Hypothesis B
What belief are we evaluating?	What alternative belief are we considering?
Evidence that supports Hypothesis A	Evidence that supports Hypothesis B
Summary of Hypothesis A Evidence	Summary of Hypothesis B Evidence
Overall Summary	

Figure 7.4 Hypothesis A/Hypothesis B

Many great questions and lines of inquiry can often be found from evaluating elements from the understanding step of the framework. People tend to twist information to fit into their pre-existing assumptions and beliefs. So, we want to help them mentally take a step back and look at both context and the big picture. We ask ourselves, "If the thought wasn't true, what would be the indicators of that, and can we look for that evidence?"

Consider another example. Pam was a young mother with a series of late-term miscarriages. Pam, understandably, is extremely distraught by the circumstances and has been to countless doctors trying to understand why this is happening and what she did wrong. Her case for this situation being her fault is because she has not been able to fix it yet; however, this is twisted evidence as she is missing the fact that she has been diligently and tirelessly trying to get the situation resolved. To untwist the evidence, we would first lead with emotional validation and then work to help her see that actually the tireless work she has been doing to resolve the situation is evidence that it is not her fault. Additionally, there is an opportunity to use her emotion as evidence. If we can demonstrate a link between how bad she feels and how hard she has been trying to resolve the situation, we can extrapolate that if there had been anything else she could have done, then she would have done it; this can be an effective counterpoint to the nagging feeling of wishing that she had done more. To do this, we need to hold onto the notion that people are generally doing the best they can with what they have available.

Time-Orientation and Permanence of Their Conclusions

When evaluating the case for their belief, it can be helpful to look at whether they are generalizing to the rest of their life based on their current circumstances. Often, clients come into therapy at a low-point or soon after a low-point in their lives and it can be hard for them to see that things can get better. Sometimes a thought can be true (or debatably true in the moment), but it doesn't have to stay true. Consider the example, of a jilted lover—someone who was suddenly abandoned by a partner who goes on to conclude that because their beloved no longer loves them, that no one will ever love them. This person is failing to recognize that just as they once had attributes to attract a potential mate, they will likely once again be able to attract a new mate. The key questions for a therapist to ask themselves are "Has it always been this way?" and "Does it always have to be this way?"

Contextualizing the Evidence

Sometimes a useful strategy can be to contextualize the evidence which supports their case. In a previous chapter, we discussed Fiona, who grew up with a belief that it was not acceptable to have or show emotions. The evidence she had for this was that she had been directly told this by her father. The context we were able to add to this was that her father had actually had posttraumatic stress disorder and his rules about emotions were really more about him being uncomfortable with emotions. Adding this context helped her to reinterpret her history and re-evaluate her attitudes about emotions.

The question a therapist might want to ask themselves is "How well does the environment that this belief developed in match the bigger picture?" If there is some discrepancy, you might explore how the context might have influenced the development of the belief.

Distortions and Irrational Beliefs

There are two different ways to approach cognitive distortions and irrational beliefs when using Socratic strategies. The first is to disqualify a cognition as distorted if it appears to represent a thinking style on your list of distortions. The other is to have an understanding of what the various distortions are and evaluate those elements of the belief. Notably, a disputatious approach to cognitive restructuring can lead to a negative reaction from the client (Kazantzis et al., 2014). There is a sharp distinction between the evaluation of thoughts based on the therapist pointing out the cognitive

Table 7.3 Commonalities Across Distortions and Irrational Beliefs

Thought Processes	Descriptions
Errors in Prediction	Examples: Catastrophizing, Fortunetelling or Impact Bias Description: Errors in prediction of outcomes that cannot be known or of an unlikelihood negative valence. Alternatively, this can manifest as seeing potential event as having an unrealistically large impact on one's life or the situation (i.e., seeing something as the solution all your problems or seeing something as the absolute worst thing that could happen)
Errors in Overgeneralizing	Examples: All-or-Nothing Thinking, Overgeneralizing, and Magnification (Minimizing) Description: Creating a false dichotomy and failing to attend to dimensional (continuum) elements of the appraisal. This can also be an error of permanence where something is seen as permanent or unchangeable when it is not.
Errors in Perceptions	Examples: Selective Abstraction, Negative Filter, Mind Reading, Emotional Reasoning, and Personalizing Description: Attentional filtering errors where people tend to emphasize or solely attend to information that is consistent with their expectations.
Illusions of Control	Examples: Magical Thinking, Illusion of Control, and Hindsight Bias Description: Illusions where an individual sees themselves as having power over things they do not, as having known things they could not have known, or other superstitious thinking.
Core Irrational Beliefs	Demandingness: Absolutistic musts; Demands of the universe and other people Awfulizing: Judging something as absolutely terrible or worse than bad. Frustration Intolerance: Refusal to tolerate distress and seeing self as being unable to tolerate distress Person Rating: Judging or labeling yourself or someone else in absolute terms

distortions and a therapist joining with a client in collaborative empiricism to evaluate the thought (see Tee & Kazantzis, 2011). A number of different lists of cognitive distortions exists, and there is no single agreed-upon list—probably due to copyright reasons. The common types of cognitive distortions are presented in Table 7.3. It is recommended that you be aware of the distortions and evaluate those elements. If a thought is actually distorted, then it will come out in the evaluation. If over time you see someone has a "go to" distortion, you might talk with them about that specific distortion, but in general a more inductive approach is recommended, as it does not involve your discounting your client's view without first evaluating it with them.

Having a working understanding of the irrational beliefs found in rational emotive behavior therapy (REBT) can be helpful, as it provides an alternative strategy in case you need it. The idea is we can intervene on a few different levels. We can evaluate the content of the belief; we also can look at the underlying demandingness and frustration intolerance associated with the belief. Windy Dryden's pantomime horse strategy (Dryden, 2013; Waltman & Palermo, 2019) can be a good way to include REBT strategies in your Socratic strategies. The idea of a pantomime horse calls back to an era of simpler entertainment. A storyteller might have a horse marionette that was split into front and back halves to simulate the movement of a horse. The pantomime horse cognitive strategy was devised to target awfulizing and was used to demonstrate that something bad could happen and it could be not terrible. This strategy can be expanded where we consider the front end of the horse and evaluation of truthfulness of the belief and the back half of the horse is an evaluation of whether there are any underlying irrational beliefs/assumptions to be addressed—both are potential intervention points.

What Are We Missing?

While this is functionally the disconfirming evidence step, curiosity is key to this process. In the seminal math logic book, *How to Solve It*, Polya (1973) describes a key step to problem solving being determining the unknown. We ask ourselves: "What are they missing?" Functionally, there are two kinds of blind spots: things you don't see and things you don't know. We need to figure out what are they not attending to due to attentional filters as well as the gaps in their experiences that developed as a result of their avoidance pattern.

Disconfirming Evidence

This step is rather straightforward, but it is important. Clients are typically more willing to look at the evidence that does not support their belief after we have honestly sought to understand why it makes sense that they came to see things as they do. We want to directly ask about evidence that the target belief is not true. We also want to ask about evidence that might support an alternate plausible conclusion. Sometimes, your client will be directly aware of this evidence, and at other times you will need to help them remember things they have previously said or dig for disconfirmatory evidence in places where we think it might be found.

"Is there any evidence that this belief might not be true?"

Typically, a client is already aware of some evidence that the belief you are looking at is not true. If they are not sure, then you might soften the question by asking, "Is there any evidence that this belief might not be true?" You can also look at fluctuations in how much they believe the belief and target the low points: "Are there times you believe this thought more than others?" and "When you tend to believe it a little bit less than usual, what are some of the reasons you have for believing it a little bit less?" Exceptions to an overgeneralized belief are excellent strategies and will be reviewed below.

"I remember you saying ..."

As we previously reviewed, mood can determine what you are able to remember, and therefore it can be hard for a client who feels angry or depressed to remember things that happened when they were not angry or depressed. This is a place where we can remind them of discrepant events or evidence that they have previously mentioned but are currently not attending to. There are no tricks to this strategy—you just need to have a good understanding of their cognitive conceptualization and be paying attention when you are talking with them. Although jotting down a little note here or there when something unexpected happens, or when they discuss something that would be inconsistent with a negative core belief, can be helpful.

"I wonder ..."

This approach can be a little bit of a gamble. The idea is that you imagine the belief you are targeting not being true and then ask yourself what evidence would exist to support that. You then wonder aloud about the possible existence of such a situation. For example, consider you are treating a client with social anxiety and you are evaluating a thought that people will not like your client if they really get to know her. You know your client has a small group of friends and has had close friends in the past. You might wonder aloud if her friends (that probably know her better than most people) like her or if her close friends from the past liked her. This could result in your client acknowledging that while her group of friends is small, they do seem to like her as a person, which would be helpful to creating cognitive change. Alternatively, she might say that her friends are actually quite mean to her and are often telling her there is something wrong with her. We would certainly want to work with that situation and learning that might help us better address the overall situation; however, this is not going to be direct evidence that the target belief is not true.

Exceptions

When our clients have made global and universal statements, we can look for exceptions to demonstrate that, although they are treating something as being always true, there are some instances where it has been different. We can ask the following questions:

> "Are there any times that hasn't happened?"
> "Has there ever been a time where something different happened?"
> "Have you ever been surprised by this not happening?"

People can be apt to discard these exceptions as flukes or luck. We want to increase the salience of these exceptions by using imagery strategies. We want to have them describe in detail what happened. You might consider having them picture the event in their mind and walk you through what happened. This can be a way to induce a different mood, which might make it easier to access other disconfirmatory evidence.

The Impact of the Belief

A guiding principle in the evaluation of a thought is "Is it true and is it helpful?" Evaluating the impact of a belief is a way of evaluating the helpfulness of the thought. We can ask the following questions:

"How does believing this thought make you feel?"
"What does that make you do?"
"Will believing this thought make it easier to accomplish your goal?"
"What are the short-term and long-term consequences of believing this thought?"

The basic idea here is that you are asking the client what belief would help them have the type of reaction they want to have. If you consider the A-B-C model of Antecedent-Belief-Consequence. The antecedent of the situation has already been determined and so we ask the client these questions: "What type of emotional and behavioral consequence do you want to have?" "And, what plausible belief would you need to help you get there?"

Is Their Belief-Dependent Behavior Shaping the Environment to Make the Belief Seem True?

A similar, but slightly different strategy is to help the client draw out the vicious cycle of how their belief impacts what they think and do, and how that affects what happens, possibly reinforcing their belief. If your client has a belief that if they ask for help no one will care or help them, and so in turn they never ask for help, then when you try to evaluate the evidence that people are willing to help, there will not be many instances of their receiving help from other people. This is not necessarily evidence of their belief being true, but rather is evidence of their behavior. Similarly, for a client who has a belief of being incompetent and consequently they avoid difficult tasks and quit at the first sign of failure, there will not be much evidence of accomplishments to counter the idea of incompetence. Not because of the person's supposed incompetence, but because of their fear of being incompetent. Trying to draw out the cycle can help contextualize the evidence or lack of evidence that they have. This can also create a rationale for going out and gathering new evidence with behavioral experiments.

Unknown Evidence

As we reviewed before, there are two types of blind spots: things people don't see, and things people don't know. Going out and gathering new evidence is an important part of the Socratic process and collaborative empiricism. Behavioral experiments

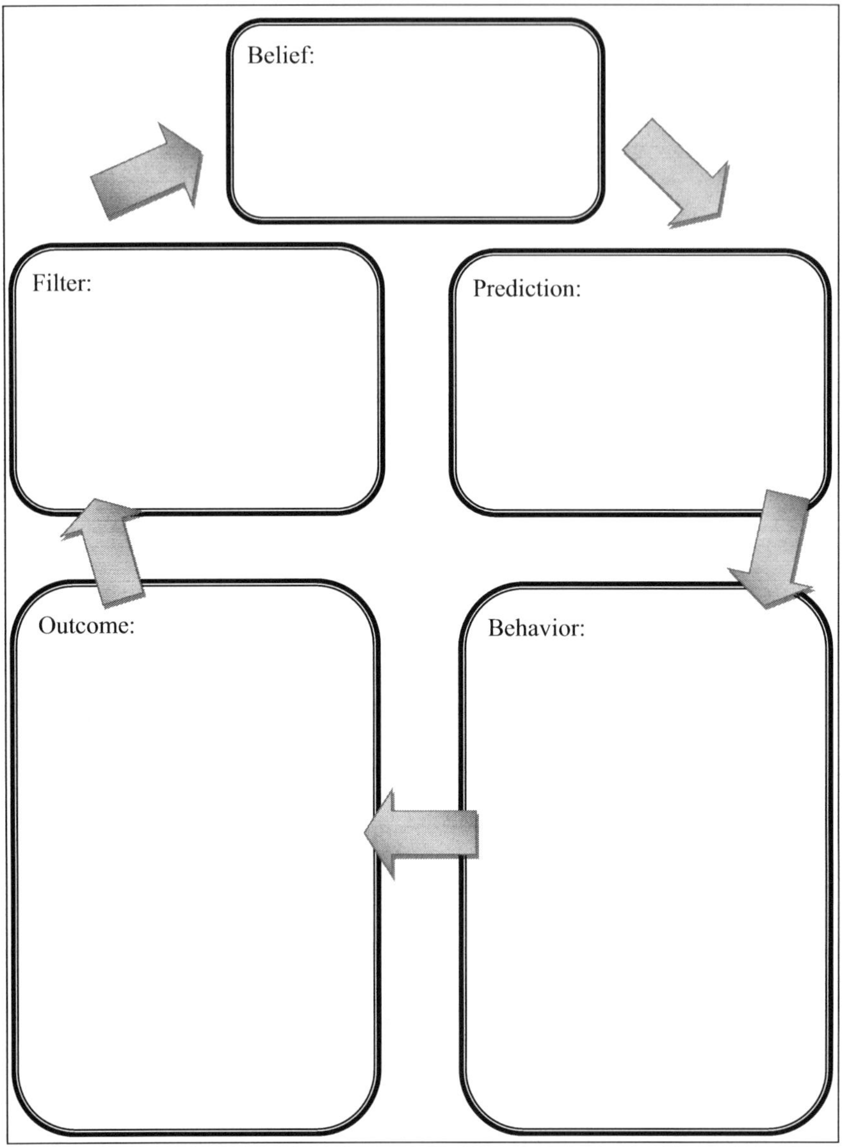

Figure 7.5 Simplified Functional Belief Conceptualization Diagram

can be used to gather new evidence or test out new assumptions. A later chapter (Chapter 10) will go into more detail about behavioral experiments. If you identify a substantial unknown that might either weaken the case for the belief you are evaluating or strengthen the case for an alternate belief, then you want to highlight this, and perhaps suggest that understanding the full truth will be informed by gathering the new evidence:

> So, we've been evaluating this idea that you won't be able to tolerate the anxiety related to speaking in front of your class. But, as we talk more about this, you're explaining that you often call in sick on days you are supposed to give a presentation, so you actually haven't given a presentation in quite a while. So, we don't actually know that you wouldn't be able to tolerate it. We do know that you often think you won't be able to tolerate it and that you often avoid going, but we don't have good evidence that it is unbearable. It sounds like we need to test out your ability to tolerate anxiety-provoking situations. It might be that you are more capable than you think you are.

Evidence for Alternate Explanations and Indirect Proof

The concept of indirect proof is that sometimes the best way to prove something is by proving the falsity of its opposite; a similar example would be disproving something by proving its opposite (Polya, 1973). We want to ask ourselves: "Is there a plausible alternate explanation?" and "If that alternate explanation was true, how would we know?" You can plug this strategy into the hypothesis-A/hypothesis-B strategy above and sort the available evidence to determine whether the alternate explanation is perhaps a better explanation.

Reductio ad absurdum

Reductio ad absurdum is a similar concept; although, clinically it can be difficult to pull off as it involves extending a statement to an extreme to make it sound absurd (Polya, 1973). This is a more extreme version of the general counseling skill, the amplified reflection, where you reflect back what the client said in a more strongly stated manner. An example of reductio ad absurdum would be if you had a client who was upset when a friend did not respond to their text message, you might ask then them if everyone must always respond immediately to their messages. Or, if you have a client who is worried about making a mistake on a task, then you might ask them if making a single mistake would make them into a complete failure. As you move into more emotionally laden content, this strategy is risky and generally not recommended as a frontline strategy, as it has a huge invalidation risk (Linehan, 1997), especially if you did not first lead with validation. The trouble with this strategy is that you are not actually evaluating the target belief, but are distorting the thought and then demonstrating that the distortion is distorted. This strategy is often used in political debates as a way of oversimplifying an issue. It can be hard to achieve lasting change or a deep conviction from this strategy.

List of Questions

There are a number of questions that therapists can ask themselves to guide this collaborative curiosity process, including:

- Can we add context to the supporting evidence to mitigate its effect or that would lead to a new conclusion?

- If we had been in that situation what would we have expected to happen?
- Are there exceptions or discrepancies that we can help them remember?
- What are the facts?
- What would they tell a friend?
- What might a friend tell them?
- Has it always been this way?
- How has believing this thought affected their behavior and the available evidence to draw from?
- Can we go and gather new evidence?

Extended Example

Below is an extended example of the collaborative curiosity phase of the framework. The case of Nicole that was presented in the previous chapter is continued here. If you are reading this book sequentially, you might pause to consider how you are thinking about her case. As a reminder, she is a young mother in dual recovery from substance abuse and PTSD. She has large amounts of shame related to her belief that she is a bad mother. Her main reason for thinking she is a bad mother is the fact that her children were taken out of her custody by the state due to her illegal drug use. She has made some progress in her treatment, but her shame is overwhelming. Additionally, the therapist knows that shame can be a predictor of relapse for people who are in recovery for chemical dependency (see Luoma, Kohlenberg, Hayes, & Fletcher, 2012). The therapist has already engaged in the phenomenological understanding step to gain a better understanding of the situation from Nicole's point of view. That point of view will be expanded below by using a collaborative curiosity that is consistent with the Beckian principle of collaborative empiricism.

Therapist: Nicole, let me restate my understanding of why you think you are a bad mother, based on the evidence we gathered and the notes I took while you were talking.

You strongly believe that you are a bad mother, and this causes you to feel great shame. Some of the main pieces of evidence for your being a bad mother are you were legally declared an unfit mother and you have this mental image of your children suffering in foster care. There is this idea that they are unhappy, and it is your fault. Also, a number of people have told you that you screwed up. Do I have that right?

Client: Yeah, that sounds about right.

Therapist: Is there anything I'm missing?

Client: Well, I mean … my kids were taken away for a reason, my drug use was causing me to be neglectful. I wasn't there for them.

Therapist: Let me add that to my list, the effects of your drug use were that you were neglectful and not there for your kids, while you were using drugs. Is our summary complete now?

Client: Yes, that the bulk of it.

[*sighing*]

Therapist: This is heavy stuff to look at and you're doing a great job looking at all of this with me. Now that we have taken a really good look at why this idea that you are a bad mother might make sense, I want to look at the other side of the coin with you. Can we look at reasons why this thought of you being a bad mother might not make sense?

Client: I guess so. I'd like to think I'm not as bad as I feel right now.

Therapist: In my mind, I have that image you shared of your children crying in foster care, is that what you're thinking about right now?

Client: Yes, I just keep thinking about that.

Therapist: It's a painful image, and I want to see if we can't find or make for a more balanced image. First, let's take a moment and just breathe.

[*pausing*]

First, I want to evaluate some of this evidence put forth as evidence that you are a bad mother. Often our mind can sort of twist an unclear situation to make it look like how we expected it to look. So, if you think you are a bad mother, you might be twisting some of this evidence to be worse than it actually is. Does that make sense?

Client: I guess so.

Therapist: We tend to see what we expect to see, so if we look together, we might be able to help each see things more objectively. So, let's go over this list. A main piece of evidence is that you were declared unfit by the judge, that was an objective fact. The next piece we have is this image of your children being sorely unhappy in the foster system and it being your fault. Can we take a look at that?

Client: Sure.

Therapist: You have this painful image in your mind, but how do you know that this image is true?

Client: Well, it feels true. I feel terrible about it.

Therapist: I know you feel really bad about it. You really don't want your children to suffer especially because of something you did. Do we know for a fact that they are miserable? Has anyone told you they are completely miserable?

Client: No, no one has said that. I just worry about them, and I think this is all pretty hard on them.

Therapist: I'm sure it has been hard on them, but I don't know if this image you have in your mind is completely true.

Client: I guess, I don't know that they are completely miserable or all alone. I just miss them and don't want this to come down on them. I don't want them to be punished for what I did.

Therapist: It feels unfair that they would get punished for what you did and there is probably at least a kernel of truth to the idea that they are unhappy with the situation and it is not their fault. We sort of stumbled on another piece of evidence here. I'm struck by how badly you feel and how much you don't want them to suffer.

Client: Of course, I don't want them to suffer. They are my kids I want them to be happy and I don't want them to suffer.

Therapist: So, this genuinely caring for your children and wanting good things for them and not wanting bad things for them, is this evidence of you being a bad mother or evidence of something else?

Client: Loving your kids is what parents are supposed to do, the problem is I didn't always love them, or I didn't always put them first like I should have.

Therapist: We'll get there, but first, is your love for your children evidence of you being a bad mother?

Client: No, it's evidence of being a good mom. Or at least a decent mom.

Therapist: Let me write that down, we have some evidence against you being a bad mom. Next, let's get to this idea that your children were unhappy and it was your fault.

Client: That was I was talking about. It was my fault.

Therapist: I think there might be some context that we were missing. Was this a deliberate thing you did to them? Did you set out to make them unhappy?

Client: No, obviously not.

Therapist: Right, I wrote down what you said, you said something about being in a fog and trying to deal with your PTSD.

Client: Yeah, I was a real mess for a while there.

Therapist: And, did you choose to have PTSD? Was that something you sought out?

Client: No, that was something that their father did to me, over and over again. I have more perspective on it now. The PTSD wasn't my fault, but it was my fault that I turned to drugs instead. I should have just come in here and dealt with all of this before my life fell apart.

Therapist: Well, how does it make sense that you didn't come in and see someone like me back then?

Client: Well, I've never been in therapy, I also didn't know I needed it or how it worked, or even to that it was an option. Growing up we just never talked about things.

Therapist: So, that's context, you're not happy with how you responded to this traumatic event, but I have a hard time seeing how things could have gone differently knowing what you knew and how you were raised.

Client: I don't want to say that none of it was my fault and I'm a victim. I made some choices that got me right here.

Therapist: Is there a space between it being all your fault and it being none your fault that allows you to have more flexibility but not feel like you are getting away with it?

Client: I guess it is my fault that this happened, but not all my fault, and I didn't get here all on my own.

Therapist: Does that change your emotional experience?

Client: It feels less heavy.

Therapist: But, do you believe that statement?

Client: I do, it is at least partly my fault, but like you said there is some context that it is not all my fault.

Therapist: So, the next piece of evidence we're looking at is that some people told you that you had screwed up. Can we take a look at that?

Client: Yeah, we can talk about that.

Therapist: What do you think their motivation was in telling you those things?

Client: ??

Therapist: Was their goal to make you feel bad? Or was their goal to motivate you to turn the situation around?

Client: Huh, I guess I didn't think about that.

Therapist: So, what do you think now?

Client: It didn't seem mean.

Therapist: Well, your ex sounded like they said it sort of maliciously, but not the correction officer or case worker?

Client: No, they talked with me about how I needed to get it together and get things right so I could get my kids back and not turn into a statistic.

Therapist: So, what does that mean if they told you that you had screwed up, but they wanted you to turn your life around?

Client: I guess, maybe they hadn't given up on me yet.

Therapist: What makes someone not give up on you?

Client: I guess, they believe I can get back on track.

Therapist: Do you believe that is true?

Client: I hope it is.

Therapist: Have you given up hope on yourself?

Client: No, not yet.

Therapist: Why not?

Client: [*tearing up*]
Because I have to get my kids back and make it right.

Therapist: I think we found our new image. Can you take a minute and picture what that is going to look like, when you get your children back?
[*pausing*]

Client: [*tearing but smiling*]

Therapist: [*pausing*]
Can you describe it to me?

Client: [*tearing*]
I see my kids, and I get to run to them and pick them up, and I hug them so tight. They hug me back and it feels like I can breathe again.

Therapist: [*tearing*]
That's a powerful image. That you, the you who did all the hard work to get her kids back. Is she a bad mother?

Client: [*crying*]
No, she's a very good mother, or least she's trying to be.

Therapist: Let's stay with this image and feeling for a moment
[*pausing*]
Is this future mother not you?

Client: She is, or she will be, but not yet.

Therapist: You got to work to get there, but you haven't given up hope yet.

Client: Exactly

Therapist: Is there anything we're missing? Is there any other evidence that you are a good mother?

Client: I don't know, it's hard to think of that.

Therapist: Well, you are here in my office doing some very hard work to help you get your kids back, is this evidence of you being a good mother.

Client: Yeah, I never thought I'd be here, but I have to do whatever it takes.

Therapist: So, you're dedicated to getting your kids back, that sounds like more evidence of being a good mother.

Client: Yeah it is.

Therapist: How about before all this happened, are there things from the past that show that you are a good mother?

Client: When I was in a better place, I used to read them stories and spend time with them. It got harder when my ex became abusive because I was mostly trying to keep him away from the kids, I didn't want them to get hurt too.

Therapist: That sounds pretty big. So, you tried to protect your kids from your abusive ex?

Client: Yeah, he would get really mad about it too. I just knew that was the one thing I'd never be OK with. I would have killed him if he would have tried something.

Therapist: And he got mad when you tried to protect them from him?

Client: Yeah, he would scream at me and hit me when I kept the kids away from him, but that only made me keep them away more.

Therapist: Sounds like a terrifying situation.

Client: It was really bad for a long time.

Therapist: How does this trying to protect your kids from your abusive ex line up with this idea of you being a bad mother?

Client: I guess it wasn't a bad mother thing to do, but maybe I should have left him sooner.

Therapist: Hold on, let's not get into beating yourself up over that. I'll make a note and we can evaluate that later if that is an ongoing concern for you.

In essence the situation was worse for you because you tried to make it better for them. Is that something a bad mother would do?

Client: No, I kind of forgot about how much fighting for my kids that I've done over the years.

Therapist: So, you have a track record of fighting for your kids and trying to protect them, even to your own detriment.

Client: Yeah, life has not been easy.

Therapist: No, life has not been easy for you, but you haven't given up. When you look at this story about someone who survived a domestic violence situation and somehow protected her kids in the process. Only to go on to develop PTSD from that abuse and had their children removed from their custody due to addiction problems that were related to the PTSD. If this was someone else, how would you read the situation?

Client: I think I'd have a lot more compassion for the woman, knowing everything she had been through.

Therapist: Would you think she's a bad mother?

Client: No, I mean she needs to get her kids back and can't give up, but when I look at the story she's a survivor and she really cares about her kids.

Therapist: Are you a survivor and do you really care about your kids?

Client: Definitely

Therapist: I also want to look at how helpful this belief about being a bad mother is. We have this goal in mind, remember that image of getting your kids back, running to them and holding them tight, and they hug you back and you can finally breathe?

Client: [*tearing up a little bit*]
I do

Therapist: Does this belief of being a bad mother make it easier or harder to accomplish your goal?

Client: It makes it harder. I get discouraged and feel like giving up when I think about being a bad mother.

Therapist: So, pulling it together, other people haven't given up on you yet, and neither have you. You have a long history of enduring hardship for your children and you really care about them. You did engage in behaviors that led to your children being taken away, but there is some important context about the domestic violence and PTSD that make it less clear cut than we originally thought. You decided that the situation was partially your fault, but not all the way your fault. You have an image of the type of mom you want to be, and we are going to work together to help you get there. Does that sound about right?

Client: [*sighing and a little tearful*]
Yeah, I guess I forget all that sometimes

Debrief

The therapist is now well set up to assist the client in summarizing and synthesizing this information as they move into the next step of the framework. Before moving to identify disconfirming evidence, the therapist first sought to evaluate the case that had been made for the thought to be true. Some of the evidence, such as Nicole being found to be an unfit mother, were clear-cut pieces of evidence; however, the therapist was able to pull from that process some important context that helped mitigate some of that evidence. The therapist used the loose thread method to test how Nicole knew that her children were completely miserable in order to help soften the image she had in her mind. As Nicole seemed to respond strongly to the painful image of her children suffering, a more adaptive image was developed to help facilitate motivation and action on the part of the client. The therapist drew out alternate explanations for the motivations and folded the construct of being a mother out across time to help her focus on her goal of improving and getting her children back. The therapist attended to her emotional response and used that as evidence against the target thought being completely true, and finally new evidence was obtained to further mitigate the supporting evidence and enhance the disconfirming evidence.

Undoubtedly, this process was enhanced by a thorough understanding of why the client thought the original belief was true and by focusing on the most distressing elements. From here, the therapist would likely be looking to develop further the motivating image that was created. In the next step, the therapist would work on summarizing and synthesizing the information in a fair and balanced manner to create a new believable thought that decreased shame and facilitated her goal.

Summary

While this step is technically the disconfirming evidence step, there is much work that can be done before this point to help set you up for success. First, choosing an ideal treatment target in the focusing section can make a big difference, and coming to have a good understanding of the context and why the client believes that thought will give you a better understanding of how to help them attend to the information they might be missing. It is often easier to expand the client's point of view if you first focus on seeing things from their perspective. We can jointly expand their point of view in the following ways: (1) evaluating the previously presented evidence to see if anything has been skewed, twisted or overstated; (2) attending to disconfirming evidence; and (3) seeking out new evidence with behavioral experiments. The impact of these strategies can be enhanced and solidified with summary and synthesis strategies, which will be discussed in the next chapter.

References

Beck, A. T. (1979). *Cognitive therapy and the emotional disorders.* New York: Meridian.

Beck, J. S. (2011). *Cognitive behavior therapy: Basics and beyond* (2nd ed.). New York: Guilford Press.

Codd III, R. T. (Ed.). (2018). *Practice-based research: A guide for clinicians.* New York: Routledge.

Dryden, W. (2013). On rational beliefs in rational emotive behavior therapy: A theoretical perspective. *Journal of Rational-Emotive and Cognitive-Behavior Therapy, 31*(1), 39–48.

Garber, J., Frankel, S. A., & Herrington, C. G. (2016). Developmental demands of cognitive behavioral therapy for depression in children and adolescents: Cognitive, social, and emotional processes. *Annual Review of Clinical Psychology, 12*(1), 181–216. doi:10.1146/annurev-clinpsy-032814-12836

Hintikka, J. (2007). *Socratic epistemology: Explorations of knowledge-seeking by questioning.* New York: Cambridge University Press.

Kazantzis, N., Beck, J. S., Clark, D. A., Dobson, K. S., Hofmann, S. G., Leahy, R. L., & Wong, C. W. (2018). Socratic dialogue and guided discovery in cognitive behavioral therapy: A modified Delphi panel. *International Journal of Cognitive Therapy, 11*(2), 140–157.

Kazantzis, N., Fairburn, C. G., Padesky, C. A., Reinecke, M., & Teesson, M. (2014). Unresolved issues regarding the research and practice of cognitive behavior therapy: The case of guided discovery using Socratic questioning. *Behaviour Change, 31*(01), 1–17. doi:10.1017/bec.2013.29

Kuhn, D. (2002). What is scientific thinking, and how does it develop? In U. Goswami (Ed.), *Blackwell handbook of childhood cognitive development* (pp. 371–393). Malden, MA: Blackwell.

Linehan, M. M. (1997). Validation and psychotherapy. Empathy reconsidered: New directions in psychotherapy. In A. C. Bohart & L. S. Greenberg (Eds.), *Empathy reconsidered: New directions in psychotherapy* (pp. 353–392). Washington, DC: American Psychological Association.

Luoma, J. B., Kohlenberg, B. S., Hayes, S. C., & Fletcher, L. (2012). Slow and steady wins the race: A randomized clinical trial of acceptance and commitment therapy targeting shame in substance use disorders. *Journal of Consulting and Clinical Psychology, 80*(1), 43–53.

Overholser, J. C. (1994). Elements of the Socratic method: III. Universal definitions. *Psychotherapy: Theory, Research, Practice, Training, 31*(2), 286.

Overholser, J. C. (2010). Psychotherapy according to the Socratic method: Integrating ancient philosophy with contemporary cognitive therapy. *Journal of Cognitive Psychotherapy, 24*(4), 354–363.

Overholser, J. C. (2011). Collaborative empiricism, guided discovery, and the Socratic method: Core processes for effective cognitive therapy. *Clinical Psychology: Science and Practice, 18*(1), 62–66.

Overholser, J. C. (2018). *The Socratic Method of Psychotherapy.* New York: Columbia University Press.

Polya, G. (1973). *How to solve it* (2nd ed.). Princeton, NJ: Princeton University Press.

Salkovskis, P. M., & Bass, C. (1997). Hypochondria-sis. In D. M. Clark & C. G. Fairburn (Eds.), *Science and practice of cognitive behaviour therapy* (pp. 313–340). Oxford: Oxford University Press.

Sandberg, E. H., & McCullough, M. B. (2010). The development of reasoning skills. In E. H. Sandberg & B. L. Spritz (Eds.), *A clinician's guide to normal cognitive development in childhood* (pp. 179–198). New York: Routledge/Taylor & Francis.

Schein, E. H. (2013). *Humble inquiry: The gentle art of asking instead of telling.* San Francisco, CA: Berrett-Koehler.

Tee, J., & Kazantzis, N. (2011). Collaborative empiricism in cognitive therapy: A definition and theory for the relationship construct. *Clinical Psychology: Science and Practice, 18*(1), 47–61.

Trachtman, J. P. (2013). *The tools of argument: How the best lawyers think, argue, and win.* Lexington, KY: Trachtman.

Waltman, S. H., & Palermo, A. (2019). Theoretical overlap and distinction between rational emotive behavior therapy's awfulizing and cognitive therapy's catastrophizing. *Mental Health Review Journal, 24*(1), 44–50.

Chapter 8

Summary and Synthesis

Scott H. Waltman

❖ CONTENTS

The final step of the framework is to help the client summarize and synthesize the inquiry. As Padesky (1993) aptly points out, these are two separate steps. The acts of summarizing and synthesizing are straightforward, but they are key steps in this process.

Rationale for Summary and Synthesis

Sometimes, therapists will make the mistake of prematurely concluding this process after covering some reasons that the target belief might not be true. This is unfortunate because they did all this work to get there and they left before they were really able to get the most out of it. This would be like taking all the time and effort to reach the summit of a great peak and then turning around before you got to the top or reaching

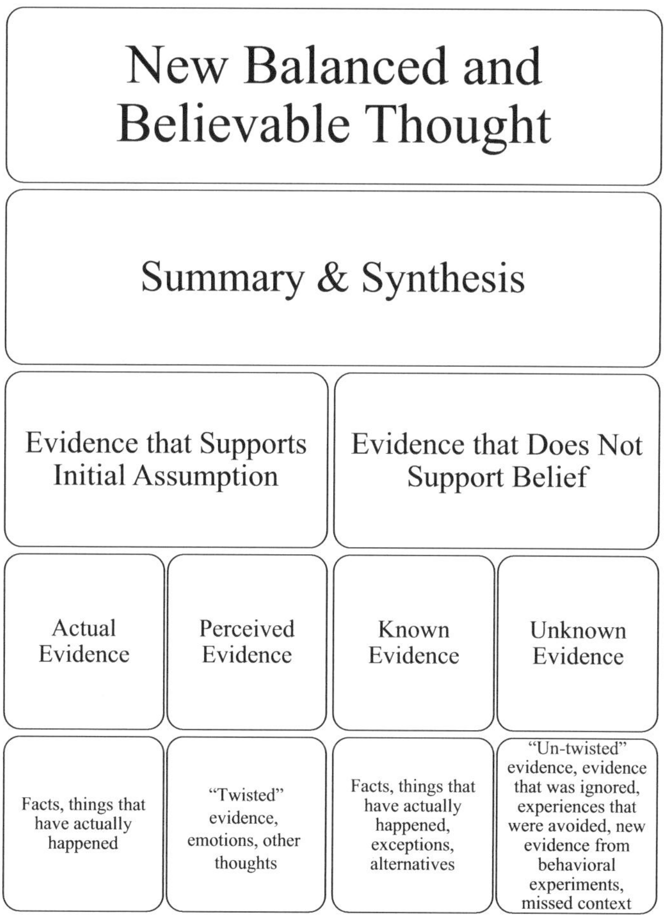

Figure 8.1 Conceptual Overview of Socratic Questioning Model

the top and turning back before taking a good look around. Do not forget to take the time to make the most of the view for which you have worked so hard.

There are a number of reasons why summarizing and synthesizing are important steps in the process. A few of these will be briefly reviewed below. Some of the main reasons are accounting for the emotional toll of the process, counteracting attentional filters, verifying understanding, memory reconsolidation, schematic accommodation, drawing out behavioral implications, and reinforcing skill use.

Accounting for the Emotional Toll of the Process

If we have been doing our job correctly, we have had the client emotionally engaged in evaluating a cognition that is deeply meaningful to them. This likely has involved reviewing various painful memories, difficult situations, and worries about the future. We have also been coaching our clients to stay with their emotional experience as we have evaluated the facts of the situation. While this process might end in catharsis, it can be difficult for our clients to fully attend to what has been discussed if we do not help them pause and reflect on the exercise. Reflective observation is a core step in Kolb's (1984) experiential learning model. They initially might recognize that they "feel better after talking about it," and we want to help them reflect in order to facilitate a deeper consolidation of learning.

Counteracting Attentional Filters

The thing to remember is that the attentional filters that contributed to the development and maintenance of the maladaptive belief we have been evaluating are likely to be at least partially still in play (Beck & Haigh, 2014). Additionally, it is likely that your attention filters are different from your clients, so you will see things that they do not see. This means that it will be easier for you to see that the target belief was not true, and it will be easier for you to generalize from this new belief. This is why we go through the summary and synthesis phase; we need to make the new learning explicit (Beck, 2011).

Verifying Understanding

Similarly to how a cognitive therapist seeks feedback on the client's understanding at the end of the session, we want to seek feedback regarding the client's understanding at the end of a psychotherapeutic intervention (Young & Beck, 1980). We want to check and make sure our understandings are compatible. An ideal way to do this is to have the client provide a summary of the evidence and synthesize that summary with the original statement and their overall belief system.

Memory Reconsolidation

Memory reconsolidation refers to the notion that our memories can be changed based upon how they are recalled and then re-encoded (Alberini & LeDoux, 2013; Schiller,

Monfils, Raio, Johnson, LeDoux, & Phelps, 2010; Schiller & Phelps, 2011). The science of memory reconsolidation is still being worked out, and there is much pseudoscience of which to be wary. However, the finding that the human mind functions differently from a computer hard drive, and memories change over time depending on how they are retrieved and re-encoded, is well established (Randall, 2007). There are a number of strategies a therapist can use to help facilitate corrective learning or consolidation of learning that would be consistent with the principles of memory reconsolidation. A key element in the process is that we need to activate painful negative elements and synthesize the corrective information to bring about the reconsolidation of memories (Alberini & LeDoux, 2013; Schiller et al., 2010; Schiller & Phelps, 2011). This is similar to the emotion-focused therapy notion that, in order to bring about change in emotion, we first need to activate the painful emotion and then induce a new emotion to bring about change (see Greenberg, 2004). A thorough summary and synthesis is an ideal way to bring about this change.

Schematic Accommodation

The basics of schematic modification was explained by Piaget (1976). A schema is a cognitive structure. When a person encounters a new piece of information, it can either be consistent or inconsistent with their schema. If that information is consistent with the underlying belief structure, the information will be assimilated into their schema. If the information is inconsistent, the schema will be modified to accommodate the new information (i.e., accommodation). Judy Beck (2011) explains with her information processing model that it is not quite this simple; in that, a person can twist, distort, or discard information that is schema incompatible. Therefore, to facilitate effective schematic accommodation we need to help the client attend to this new information in a way in which they are not twisting, distorting, or discarding the evidence. Helping them to summarize the evidence and synthesize it with their schema accomplishes this task.

Drawing Out Behavioral Implications

We can gain a larger impact from the Socratic dialogue if we can obtain a commitment from the client to engage in behaviors that are compatible with the new perspective. This will help to shape their environment in order to reinforce the new belief. Additionally, this will help them to have new experiences and new evidence in order to further bolster the belief with additional Socratic strategies.

Reinforcing Skill Use

We are trying to facilitate new learning on a few levels. We are directly facilitating cognitive modification through curious and empathic evaluation of their beliefs. We are also engaged in a skills training process, because we want them to learn to be their own therapist (Beck, 2011).

How to Do It

We have reviewed why this is an important process; now we will review how this process works. There are few questions that can guide this process. Of course, a therapist would not need to ask all (or any) of these questions. These questions are meant to be illustrative of the process.

Here are some questions to ask:

- "So, how does this all fit together?"
- "Can you summarize all the facts for me?"
- "What would be a summary statement that could capture both sides?"
- "How much do you believe that?"
    - ("Do we need to shape this to make it more believable?")
- "How do you reconcile our new statement with the thought we were evaluating?"
    - (Or with the core belief we're targeting?)
- "What is our new way of looking at the situation?"
- "How should we apply our new statement to your upcoming week? "How can we test this out?"
- "What did we learn about your thought processes from this exercise?"

The example of Nicole from the previous two chapter will be used to demonstrate this process. The therapist's summary of the evidence can be found below in an excerpt pulled from the previous chapter.

Therapist: Nicole, let me restate my understanding of why you think you are a bad mother, based on the evidence we gathered and the notes I took while you were talking.

You strongly believe that you are a bad mother, and this causes you to feel great shame. Some of the main pieces of evidence for your being a bad mother are you were legally declared an unfit mother and you have this mental image of your children suffering in foster care. There is this idea that they are unhappy, and it is your fault. Also, a number of people have told you that you screwed up. Do I have that right?

Client: Yeah, that sounds about right.

Therapist: Is there anything I'm missing?

Client: Well, I mean … my kids were taken away for a reason, my drug use was causing me to be neglectful. I wasn't there for them.

… [*Dialogue consisting of the collaborative curiosity step*]

Therapist: So, pulling it together, other people haven't given up on you yet, and neither have you. You have a long history of enduring hardship for your children and you really care about them. You did engage in behaviors that led to your children being taken away, but there is some important context about the domestic violence and PTSD that make it less clear cut than we originally thought. You decided that the situation was partially your fault, but not all the way your fault. You have an image of the type of mom you want to be, and we are going to work together to help you get there. Does that sound about right?

Summary

In order to create a new belief that is balanced and durable, we want to create a summary of the evidence that we have reviewed. Ideally, we will get the client to create that summary, though they might need some help. Some therapists pull for purely positive alternate thoughts and this is a mistake because it does not match the reality of the client's life. For example, if Nicole were to walk away from this process with the alternate thought that she was actually a very good mom, she would be at risk for that belief being shattered when she is reminded that her children were removed from her care due to her negligence and drug use. The drop from an elevated mood connected with a purely positive mood, and the crash associated with the potential shattering of that belief, could also put her at an increased risk for relapse or demoralization. A more durable alternate belief will be reflective of the whole picture, which is why we first make a balanced summary of the big picture.

So, How Does This All Fit Together?

A good first question is to ask your client is how they fit it all together. Possible questions include the following: "So how does this all fit together?" "Can you summarize all the facts for me?" "What's a summary statement that captures both sides?"

Initially, they may tell you that they are not sure or do not know how to fit it all together. This will create a pull for you just to do it for them. Resist that urge, as they will get more out of this if we can help them to get there on their own. You might start by first helping them summarize the supporting evidence and then the disconfirming evidence, and then help them put it all together.

Therapist: Nicole, we just finished talking about all the reasons why the belief that you are a bad mother might be true and then we looked at reasons why it might not be true. We talked about a lot of stuff. Can you create a summary for us that captures both sides?

Client: I'm not sure, it was a lot of stuff.

Therapist: It was, and you did a good job curiously looking at everything with me. Let's start by making a summary of the evidence for you being a bad mother.

Client: Well, my kids were taken away and are now enduring foster care because of what I did, because of my drug use.

Therapist: OK, now let's add a summary of the evidence or mitigating factors that suggest your being a bad mother is not true.

Client: That's harder.

Therapist: Well, what did we talk about?

Client: We talked about how much I love my kids and how hard I've been working to get them back.

Therapist: Yes, excellent! What else?

Client: We talked about how I used to try and protect them.

Therapist: Good, anything else?

Client: I'm not sure.

Therapist: We also talked about how there was some context to what led to your PTSD and resulting addiction that might make the situation not completely your fault.

Client: Yeah, that's right.

Therapist: So, how can we summarize everything together?

Client: Well, I have a history of being a good mother. I got off track and really blew it. My children suffered because of it, but I'm going to do my best to get them back and make it right. I have to make it right.

How Much Do You Believe That? Do We Need to Shape This to Make It More Believable?

This is a good place to remind yourself that just because they said something does not mean they believe it. You want to be aware that there is a big trap here of a client telling you what they think the right answer is or what they think you want to hear. Here we want to check if they believe what they just told us, and we might need to help them restate it in a way that is more believable. Depending on how entrenched the belief that we are evaluating is, we might be targeting incremental shifts in the intensity of belief.

Therapist: So, how much do you believe that statement to be true?

Client: I sort of believe it, I don't know, it sounds right, I'm just not sure if it is true.

Therapist: What are the parts you believe more and less?

Client: Well, I definitely believe I screwed up.

Therapist: Do you believe what you said? that you have a history of being a good mother?

Client: Yeah, I mean not my whole history, but a lot of it.

Therapist: And, what about the part about getting your kids back?

Client: I need to, I have to, but, I'm afraid I won't.

Therapist: We don't actually know what is going to happen, but are you motivated? and do you have what it takes to put in the work to get them back?

Client: 100%

Therapist: So, how can we adjust what you said to be more believable to you?

Client: Maybe, I used to be a good mom, then for a while I was a bad mom, but I'm determined to be a good mom again.

Therapist: Do you believe that statement?

Client: Yes, that works better for me.

Therapist: How much do you believe it?

Client: 90%

Therapist: We can work with that. Let me write that down.

At this point, the therapist has helped the client create a useful summary of the entire dialogue. This can take some work to achieve, but it is useful, and it helps the client consolidate the conversation. Next, we need to help them synthesis this new statement with their prior beliefs.

Synthesis

Analysis is the process of breaking something down and synthesis is the process of creating something new. Socratic dialogue includes both components: we break a situation down to better understand it and then we synthesize to create a new perspective. We can further synthesize that new perspective with the overall schema. Typically, the more important aspects involve helping the client synthesize discrepant statements or findings. This can be done by presenting the previous belief and the new conclusion together to help the client synthesize a new overall belief.

How Do You Reconcile Our New Statement With the Thought We Were Evaluating? (Or With the Core Belief We Are Targeting?)

This step basically involves asking the client how they fit together two ideas that seem to contradict. You can use this to target the cognition you were initially evaluating or a more central core belief. Initially, your client might not be sure how to respond. Depending on how the prior steps went, a client will typically respond with a statement that perhaps the initial belief is not as true as they thought it was. Schematic accommodation through synthesis can be an incremental process that is informed across sessions, following several sessions of Socratic strategies on a single theme or target core belief. A later chapter will discuss working with core beliefs and the following chapter will discuss troubleshooting this process.

Therapist: So, Nicole, I wrote down what you said. You said, "Maybe, I used to be a good mom, then for a while I was a bad mom, but I'm determined to be a good mom again." How do you fit that together with the original statement that you are a bad mother?

Client: Um, I guess I'm not a completely bad mother.

Therapist: Tell me more about that.

Client: Well, sometimes I feel like the absolute worst mom because of the mistakes I made, but that isn't the whole story.

Therapist: If the statement that you are a bad mother isn't completely accurate, is there a new statement we could make that would be more balanced and accurate?

Client: I'm not sure …

Therapist: I like notion of the whole story you said. So, if your life was a book, how could you describe the whole story?

Client: I guess, I've had chapters where I was a good mother, somewhere really bad things happened and I tried to be good, and some chapters where I really messed up.

Therapist: What chapter are you currently in?

Client: My redemption chapter

Therapist: That's powerful, what's the main message from this chapter?

Client: Fighting my way to being a good mother again.

What Is Our New Way of Looking at the Situation?

This is the step where you identify a new belief or the alternate belief. You might have some good candidates already identified from the summary or the earlier synthesis steps. It can be helpful to discuss this after they have created a balanced summary and synthesized the summary with their beliefs. Essentially, we are asking if that original statement is not true, what would be true? You will get a more durable alternate belief if you link it to the balanced summary and synthesis with their pre-existing beliefs.

Therapist: So, Nicole, if this statement that you are a bad mother is not completely true, and if your life is like a book, with you currently being in your redemption story, what is an alternate belief can we cultivate that would be balanced and believable?
Client: I guess, I've made serious mistakes as a mother, but my mistakes don't define me or my future.
Therapist: Do you believe that?
Client: I do.
Therapist: It's a powerful statement, let me take a moment to write it down.

If they don't believe the alternate belief, you can either loop above to refine it or use behavioral experiments to gather evidence to test out whether it is true.

How Should We Apply Our New Statement to Your Upcoming Week? How Can We Test This Out?

We are seeking to bring about cognitive modification, but we don't want to only increase insight without a corresponding change in behavior. Ideally, we want to connect the new cognition with an action plan do something different this week to align behaviors with their new perspective, help the client engage in goal-directed behavior, or gather evidence to test out the new belief.

Therapist: Nicole, you said, "I guess, I've made serious mistakes as a mother, but my mistakes don't define me or my future." I love this thought, and I want to spend a moment with you talking about how we can apply this new thought to what you do in the coming week.
Client: Yeah, that makes sense.
Therapist: So, if this thought that your mistakes don't define you or your future was true, what behaviors do you need to do this week?
Client: I need to keep working towards my goals of getting my kids back, I need to go to my meetings, and I need to look into employment opportunities.
Therapist: Sounds good, and this part of your mistakes not defining you, are there parts during the week where you typically tell yourself that your mistakes define you or your future?
Client: Yeah, I guess, typically at night, when it is quiet, I'll think about how I screwed up and I'll feel terrible and just keeping thinking about what I did wrong.
Therapist: It sounds like we might need to target those times.
Client: That could be good, that is when I typically get lost in my thoughts.

Therapist: It seems like the core issue here is you worrying about your future, and I'm wondering if that imagery we discussed earlier may be helpful at nighttime. How would you feel about engaging in some imagery strategies at night to picture that image we created earlier? I wrote it down. You said, "I see my kids, and I get to run to them and pick them up, and I hug them so tight. They hug me back and it feels like I can breathe again." In addition to going to your meetings and looking into employment during the day, could you use this imagery at night to stay focused on this vision you are working towards?

Client: I can do that.

Therapist: I might even be helpful to further develop this image into something like a drawing, or story, or mantra to help you hold onto it.

Now, the ideal action plan will depend on the client and their situation. You want to ask yourself if the new perspective is helpful and, if it is, then you want to ask yourself how they can put it into practice.

What Did We Learn About Your Thought Processes from This Exercise?

After consolidating learning related to the content of the client's belief, we want to consolidate learning related to the skills we are teaching or the shared conceptualization of the problem.

Therapist: Nicole, we just engaged in a process of evaluating your belief of being a bad mother and we came up with this new idea that your past mistakes don't define you or your future. What did you learn about yourself and your thought processes from this exercise?

Client: I guess, my situation is so bad, I've had a hard time seeing the big picture and remembering that this is just one part of my story.

Therapist: So, when things are bad, it is hard for you to remember and think about when things are not bad?

Client: Yes.

Therapist: That's important to know about yourself.

Let me write that down, as it might be useful for us to review that in future sessions when similar thoughts come up for you. How about this exercise of breaking the situation down and evaluating your thoughts, what did you learn from that process?

Client: I guess, sometimes something can seem true, but if I break it down, it might be more complicated than I initially thought it was.

Therapist: Would you want to do more of this in the future?

Client: Yes, it's helpful to have you help me break it down.

Therapist: I'm not magic, I can teach you how to do what I'm doing.

[*pulls out thought record, see appendix*]

This step can be a place where you gather some useful statements that you can reference with the client in later sessions. For example, this therapist could say in a later session: "OK, this seems like a pretty bad situation, but remember what you said before. You said that when things get bad you have a hard time remembering when things were less bad and seeing how things don't have to be bad in the future." This could make it easier to evaluate future thoughts with the client, as we would be building on past successes.

Imagery

It can be helpful to incorporate imagery into this process. There are a number of ways you can do this. You can have them picture the new thought as being true. You can have them picture someone they trust telling them the thought. You can have them picture themselves being skillful or successful. Imagery is powerful, because it is a good way to invoke a strong emotional response. Josefowitz (2017) previously published an excellent guide on the topic of incorporating imagery into Socratic strategies and thought records.

Chapter Summary

The final step in the framework is summary and synthesis. Here we help the client summarize both sides and synthesize that summary with their pre-existing belief and schema. This is a straightforward step, but it is an important step in consolidating learning and helping the client to take actions that will create change in their life. The following chapter will discuss how to troubleshoot this process.

References

Alberini, C. M., & LeDoux, J. E. (2013). Memory reconsolidation. *Current Biology, 23*(17), R746–R750.

Beck, A. T., & Haigh, E. A. P. (2014). Advances in cognitive theory and therapy: The Generic Cognitive Model. *Annual Review of Clinical Psychology, 10*, 1–24. doi:10.1146/annurev-clinpsy-032813-153734

Beck, J. S. (2011). *Cognitive behavior therapy: Basics and beyond* (2nd ed.). New York: Guilford Press.

Greenberg, L. S. (2004). Emotion-focused therapy. *Clinical Psychology and Psychotherapy: An International Journal of Theory and Practice, 11*(1), 3–16.

Josefowitz, N. (2017). Incorporating imagery into thought records: Increasing engagement in balanced thoughts. *Cognitive and Behavioral Practice, 24*(1), 90–100.

Kolb, D. A. (1984). *Experiential learning: Experience as the source of learning and development.* Englewood Cliffs: Prentice-Hall.

Padesky, C. A. (1993). Socratic questioning: Changing minds or guiding discovery. Paper presented at the A keynote address delivered at the European Congress of Behavioural and Cognitive Therapies, London. Retrieved from: http://padesky.com/newpad/wpcontent/uploads/2012/11/socquest.pdf

Piaget, J. (1976). Piaget's theory. In B. Inhelder, H. H. Chipman, & C. Zwingmann (Eds.), *Piaget and his school* (pp. 11–23). Berlin: Springer.

Randall, W. L. (2007). From computer to compost: Rethinking our metaphors for memory. *Theory and Psychology, 17*(5), 611–633.

Schiller, D., Monfils, M. H., Raio, C. M., Johnson, D. C., LeDoux, J. E., & Phelps, E. A. (2010). Preventing the return of fear in humans using reconsolidation update mechanisms. *Nature, 463*(7277), 49.

Schiller, D., & Phelps, E. A. (2011). Does reconsolidation occur in humans? *Frontiers in Behavioral Neuroscience, 5*, 24.

Young, J. E., & Beck, A. T. (1980). *Cognitive Therapy Scale: Rating manual.* Unpublished manuscript, Center for Cognitive Therapy, University of Pennsylvania, Philadelphia, PA.

Chapter 9

Troubleshooting Socratic Strategies

R. Trent Codd, III

❖ CONTENTS

Socratic methods of clinical dialogue are complex and among the most difficult skills for clinicians to master. A qualitative investigation involving the survey of advanced CBT trainers involved in substantial training initiatives inquired about trainee challenges in learning CBT. The trainers surveyed were unanimous in identifying guided discovery as a significant problem area for many trainees with some describing it as the most difficult skill to master, even among experienced clinicians (Waltman, Hall, McFarr, Beck, & Creed, 2017). This finding resonates with our own experiences training and supervising hundreds of clinicians in CBT as well as those of our training colleagues. When troubleshooting Socratic processes in psychotherapy, the first thing to consider is whether your client is ready to engage in cognitive restructuring. Standard prerequisites to this are whether you have already established a working alliance, oriented the patient to the cognitive model, and whether they accept that how they think

---

Socratic Method Troubleshooting Checklist

Pitfall 1: Not focusing on central cognitive content
Did we take time to understand and assess the situation before selecting a target?
Recommendation: Review chapter on Focusing; Try Focusing Worksheet

Pitfall 2: Engaging in "provided discovery" rather than guided discovery
Was I focused on a preconceived notion about what the right answer was?
Recommendation: Review chapters on Understanding and Curiosity

Pitfall 3: Operating from a positive thinking model rather than realistic thinking one
Was I focused on trying to make the patient see things more positively?
Recommendation: Review chapters on Understanding and Summary & Synthesis

Pitfall 4: Progressing to summarizing and synthesizing prematurely
Did it seem too easy?
Recommendation: Reassess target belief; Review chapter on Understanding and Curiosity

Pitfall 5: Shallow exploration of context
Did we take time to understand the context of the situation and the context of the evidence?
Recommendation: Review chapter on Curiosity

Pitfall 6: Failing to summarize
Did we take the time to pull the whole dialogue together into a coherent summary? Or did I only focus on the elements of the evaluation that supported my case?
Recommendation: Review chapter on Summary & Synthesis

Pitfall 7: Inadequate attention to post-inquiry strategies
Did we create meaningful takeaway messages and action plans based on the evaluation?
Recommendation: Review chapter on Core Beliefs

Do we have a good working alliance? Is the patient able to identify thoughts feelings and behaviors? Do they see a connection between the three?
Recommendation: Review chapter on getting started

Conceptually, what are the behaviors, experiences, and attentional filters which strengthen the belief we are targeting?
What are my hypotheses about why the Socratic dialogue did not (yet) bring about change?
What is the action plan?
What are short-term and long-term strategies for working on this belief?

Figure 9.1 Troubleshooting Checklist

is affecting what they do and how they feel. The steps are covered well earlier in this book, in Chapter 3, "Getting Started." In the current chapter, we describe seven common pitfalls and offer solutions to each. We also present a checklist that clinicians can use when debriefing a session to aid in the troubleshooting process.

Pitfall 1: Not Focusing on Central Cognitive Content

Cognitive content varies in importance. For example, some cognitions have greater association with emotional distress, are more deeply believed, and have greater representation across problem areas than others. Because clients often report a range of thoughts related to problematic situations that may, on their surface, seem to be distorted or otherwise important to examine, many clinicians are too quick to assume a thought is significant and to intervene. A more skillful approach is to take the time to identify which thoughts are most central before proceeding with evaluation. Essentially, each session we are on a time budget and we only have enough time to really evaluate one (maybe two) thoughts really well; therefore, we want to really explore our options to make sure we are spending our limited time wisely. Developing this sort of patient strategic approach increases the odds that the cognition targeted for examination will result in meaningful change and that the therapy will be more efficient overall.

A metaphor may be helpful. Imagine a large solid concrete wall. Further, consider that you have been told that your task is to knock this wall down and that you are given a hammer and chisel for this effort. You are informed that there is a weak spot in this wall that if struck with the chisel will lead to a quick collapse of the wall, but you are not told where that spot is located. You approach the task by chiseling away in many different locations. You only strike the chisel a few times in each location before moving on to the next spot because as you hammer you capture, out of the corner of your eye, a spot that looks like it might be the weak spot. Each time you relocate, thinking you have discovered the weak area, it never turns out to be the case, as the wall remains unchanged. You continue with this approach for some time, but the wall isn't showing any signs of collapsing and you are tired from all the hammering. Eventually you realize that it would be better to put the hammer and chisel down and take your time to systematically inspect the wall for the weak area. You follow this approach and eventually locate it. Then you hammer the chisel twice in this sweet spot and the wall immediately collapses. While intervening upon central cognition will not always lead to rapid collapse of existing belief systems, it is more likely to lead to consequential cognitive change. Knowing where to hammer matters.

The solution to this pitfall, then, is to refrain from chasing every shiny cognitive object the client displays, and to give oneself permission to allow sufficient time to identify the cognition of importance.[1] It also entails remaining focused once central cognition is identified. Distracting cognitive objects sometimes continue to be displayed by clients even after a clinician has put in the hard, patient work of selecting a worthy candidate for examination. Avoiding this pitfall involves the initial target selection as well as maintaining focus.

Pitfall 2: Engaging in "Provided Discovery" Rather than Guided Discovery

As detailed in Chapter 7 of this volume, "Collaborative Curiosity," skillful implementation of Socratic methods involves aligning with the client to jointly discover information. A visual metaphor that captures the ideal posture is the clinician and client sitting next to one another, shoulder to shoulder, facing the same direction, rather than sitting across from each other. From this orientation they can more effectively explore information as a team and from similar perspectives.

Many clinicians, however, fall into the trap of engaging in what can be labeled "provided discovery," which can come in many forms, including lecturing, advice giving, disputing, telling clients what they should think, or otherwise attempting to persuade a client to adopt a different view. Unfortunately, this problem may be worsened by consulting older cognitive behavior therapy texts and forms that suggest one should "challenge" a client's thoughts. The way the word "challenge" functions for most people is not congruent with the spirit of guided discovery and we recommend dropping that form of language from your clinical vocabulary.

Some forms of provided discovery are less obvious and can be difficult for clinicians to identify such as when a clinician offers a statement in the form of a question, but rather than truly functioning as a question it functions as a persuasion attempt. For example, a clinician who asks a client "Don't you think you are blowing this out of proportion?" is posing a question, but rather than pulling for curiosity and reflection is likely transmitting a suggested perspective to the client.

Our experience suggests clinicians fall into this trap for at least two reasons. The first reason pertains to inadequate Socratic skills, which we hope our four-step model assists in remediating. The second, and perhaps less obvious reason, is related to self-imposed pressure to produce cognitive change quickly. When this latter factor is present, clinicians would benefit from an examination of their own related automatic thoughts, as didactic instruction is unlikely to be sufficiently helpful. Some examples of trainee cognitions that we have encountered include:

- "My client will drop out of treatment if I don't help them change their distorted thinking quickly"
- "If I can't modify my client's unhelpful thoughts, I'm not a competent cognitive behavior therapist"
- "I won't achieve a passing score on the CTRS if I don't promptly try to evaluate my client's thoughts"
- "I'll lose client buy-in to the cognitive model if I don't show them their thinking can be changed"

Pitfall 3: Operating From a Positive Thinking Model Rather than a Realistic Thinking One

A prevalent myth about cognitive behavior therapy is that the goal is to produce positive thinking. The notion of thinking positively as a remedy to emotional problems is prevalent in society, perhaps originating with the publication of the famous book by Norman Vincent Peale, *The Power of Positive Thinking*, first published in 1952. Positive thinking doesn't work. If it did, there would be very few people with emotional disturbance because this idea is widely disseminated, and most people will arrive at it as a potential solution naturally (i.e., without explicit instruction). Research has demonstrated that we can teach people to be more optimistic, but that it does not make them less depressed (Miranda, Weierich, Khait, Jurska, & Andersen, 2017). Overly positive (i.e., toxic positivity) thinking can be just as dysfunctional as negative distorted thinking, because it similarly obscures reality. It also might reduce resilience, as it is essentially the opposite of what stress inoculation training is. In order to solve life's problems effectively, one needs a clear and accurate perspective on problem situations. Furthermore, positive thinking may involve client's lying to themselves, and thus may not be deeply believed—this can create a reactance effect, where the corresponding negative belief is strengthened by the disproving of the unrealistically positive belief.

The goal of cognitive behavior therapy is realistic thinking or seeing situations the way they are. Much of the time when a client experiences negative affect they will experience thinking that is distorted in some way. However, this is not always the case. They may, in fact, be seeing the distressing situation accurately. Given the prevalence of distorted thinking coinciding with distressing emotion, and the positive emotional impact of modifying such thinking, it is useful to begin intervention with an examination of appraisal accuracy. If the Socratic process reveals accurate perception, then the client can be more confident that they are able to engage in problem-solving activity on the basis of clear information.

There are two primary ways to avoid this pitfall. The first is to ensure the client comprehends that the goal is accurate thinking and that they can differentiate this from positive thinking. It is useful to address this first when orientating clients to the cognitive model. Many clients will capture the importance of the thought–emotion relationship, but given the prevalence of the positive thinking strategy in society, they will assume this is the approach being suggested. In addition to the problems engendered by the client misunderstanding the model, the clinician might additionally lose rapport with the client because it is likely they have made unsuccessful attempts at positive thinking previously. This may, in fact, be one of the primary reasons that they have presented for therapy (i.e., they couldn't solve their problem by trying to think positively). Our advice is to clarify the goal with respect to cognitive change as early as the first treatment session. Even when clarified early, it is likely the client will "relapse" into thinking that positive thinking is the goal one or more times across sessions and thus this may need to be revisited. The second remedy for this pitfall is for the clinician to keep the goal of realistic thinking salient for themselves; otherwise, they may inadvertently guide the client to superficial and potentially harmful perspectives.

Pitfall 4: Progressing to Summarizing and Synthesizing Prematurely

Another pitfall, perhaps related to a sense of urgency that many neophyte clinicians report, is either progressing to the final step of our four-step process too quickly or not at all. Essentially, the strategy of reframing is skipping from the beginning to the end of the framework; the clinician provides a solution that is of an unknown accuracy and has not been jointly discovered to be believable. Before summarizing and synthesizing, which should always occur, a clinician experienced in Socratic strategies might want to be able to say to themselves something along the lines of "Okay, I think we've explored this fully and the client has enough information to draw a conclusion." Although experience is an important element of knowing when one can accurately say this to themselves, we can recommend some questions that can assist in this determination:

- Could the average person draw a conclusion based on the information available?
- Can I identify areas that we have not explored that might be useful to investigate?
- Am I feeling any sense of urgency to proceed to this final step? If so, what thoughts am I experiencing that are related to this urgency?
- What am I signaling to the client about the desired depth of exploration? Would they conclude that it should involve patience and curiosity or a more rapid and superficial pace?

Pitfall 5: Shallow Exploration of Context

Failing to explore context at depth is another pitfall that can capture the Socratic-oriented clinician. Many clients, at baseline, attempt to solve their emotional concerns quickly. This may be due to a failure to recognize that solving problems frequently takes time and persistence. One goal is to teach clients that all problems cannot be resolved quickly and that quick solutions, even if they appear to work over the short term, may not work over longer time horizons. When a clinician engages in quick and superficial Socratic dialogue, they risk reinforcing a client's existing unhelpful problem-solving posture, which may in fact be part of what has kept them stuck. In contrast, consistent Socratic dialogue that is adequately paced and involves exploration at adequate depth models for the client the vigor and extent of exploration that is often required. Sometimes the learning that occurs in Socratic exchanges is not explicit.

Context impacts the meaning of events. Therefore, for clients to draw accurate interpretations of events they must be assisted in sufficiently exploring the context of their cognition. As is the case for other pitfalls that we have discussed, this error may arise when clinicians are feeling a sense of urgency that they should be progressing the dialogue more quickly than they are, and the remedy is the same. Clinicians should investigate their automatic thoughts related to their sense of pressure with curiosity.

Pitfall 6: Failing to Summarize

The amount of information uncovered during Socratic exchanges can be substantial. Because short-term memory is of limited capacity, clients (and clinicians) can lose track of important data because of the volume available. In addition, the information most salient for clients may not be the most important or useful information. Summarizing is a means for selecting and tying together the key pieces of data from the vast array revealed during the discovery process, in order to make them prominent and usable for clients during the synthesizing process. Summarizing is also a mechanism for the clinician to check their understanding of their dialogue with their client.[2]

Pitfall 7: Inadequate Attention to Post-Inquiry Strategies

Socratic strategies are effective at producing important cognitive change, the impacts of which are often felt inside a session. Many ideas, especially those that had been maintained by clients over long periods of time and that were deeply believed, will likely require follow-up intervention if the changes are to endure. Many clinicians mistakenly assume that, because they observed an in-session change, this will persist over time and in other contexts. It is imperative, therefore, that the clinician attend to post-inquiry strategies as a matter of routine. The key consideration here is to determine jointly how to build on success to create momentum towards lasting change. For example, the clinician should ask themselves, in collaboration with the client, the following questions:

- Can we design another behavioral experiment for further learning?
- What homework exercises can we design that will increase generalization of their learning?
- How can the client continue to explore this idea?
- Can we anticipate when the distressing cognition might emerge outside of session and plan further practice activities?
- Should the client continue to monitor the frequency and believability of this idea over the coming week?

Two Shrewd Practical Strategies

Pragmatically, there are some strategies you might try if you find yourself getting stuck in session. These strategies are most optimally used in situations where you find yourself wondering if the negative belief is true.

Is It True and Is It Helpful?

Cognition can be examined on the basis of accuracy, as well as on the basis of utility. If Socratic dialogue reveals that a distressing appraisal is valid or likely valid, it can frequently be helpful to shift the conversation to an evaluation of the usefulness of the idea. This exploration may be facilitated with these types of questions:

- "Is it helpful to say this to yourself?"
- "What are the consequences of your holding this view (emotional and behavioral)?"
- "Does this idea get in the way of your achieving any of your important goals?"
- "What are the pros and cons of your continuing to maintain this belief?"

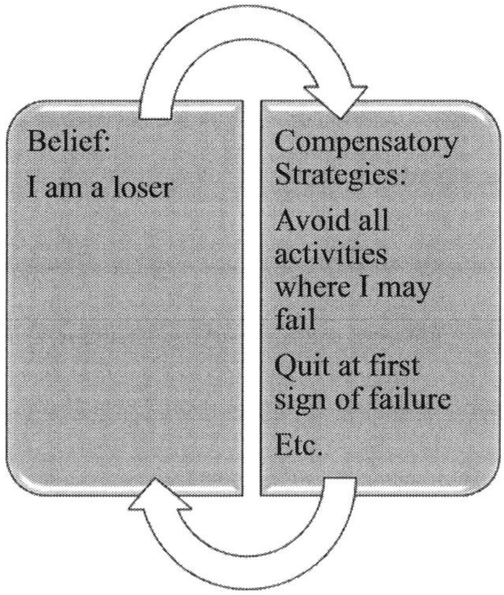

Figure 9.2 Is It True and Is It Helpful?

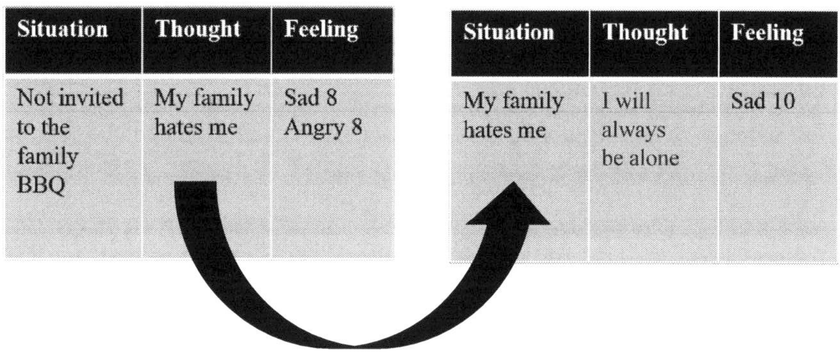

Figure 9.3 Dealing with Debatably True Thoughts

Even though the results of Socratic inquiry may reveal that a negative belief is valid, it is important to reinforce the client's efforts at examination before shifting the focus to a discussion of the belief's utility. Failing to do so may result in some clients' exploration efforts being punished because of the results and thus less likely to occur in the future. Because the results of inquiry cannot be known ahead of time and because the probability of distortion is high when distress is present, clients should always begin their examination on the basis of a thought's validity.

The standard for the new conclusions we draw with Socratic dialogue is that we want to jointly discover thoughts that are true and thoughts that are helpful. This idea was discussed in Chapter 7, "Collaborative Curiosity." This is also a strategy for when you have a negative belief that is not effective but possibly true, based on the evidence. Of course, these are usually negative thoughts that are based on a skewed data set. In pitfall 5, we discussed contextualizing the evidence and the negative thought. Another strategy is to focus less on the truthfulness of the thought and more on the impact of the thought. The basic idea here is that you are asking the client what belief would help them have the type of reaction they want to have. If you consider the A-B-C model of Antecedent-Belief-Consequence, the antecedent of this situation has already been determined, and so we ask the client: "What type of emotional and behavioral consequence do you want to have?" "And, what plausible belief would you need to help you get there?" Of course, the key here is that the alternate belief needs to be realistic and believable. It is recommended that the Hypothesis A/Hypothesis B strategy from Chapter 7, "Collaborative Curiosity," be used to evaluate the new, more helpful, thought. If the situation seems like more of "both-and" situation, then the use of the more dialectical strategies covered in Chapter 12, "Socratic Dialectical Method," can be used.

Dealing with Debatably True Thoughts

There is another strategy that can be used with thoughts that seem false, but are debatably true. This was learned from Greg Brown (though there might be origins beyond him). The basic strategy is simple. If you have a negative thought that is debatably true, you can sidestep that debate, by treating the questionably true thought as a potential situation and focusing on the emotional meaning of the thought. If you look at the example of where you have a client who was not invited to a family function and determines that their family hates them, then this can be hard to evaluate, as we don't empirically know what the family thinks or feels, and also sometimes people hate people. So, instead of focusing on evaluating whether their family hates them, the therapist can instead look at the emotional meaning of the family potentially hating them. In this case, focusing on the underlying vulnerability of, "I'll always be alone," allows for the evaluation of something we can work with that could be productive.

There exists another strategy for the nimble Socratic therapist. Cognition can be roughly categorized in two ways, namely, inferential and evaluative. *Inferential cognition*, as the name implies, involve inferences clients make about events. Consider a client who reports walking down a street and seeing someone they know but haven't seen in a while walking on the other side of the street and in the opposite direction. As they near each other, the client says, "Hello, Jack!" Jack does not respond and continues walking on his path. If the client reports thinking, "He didn't say anything back because he doesn't like me," they are making an inference as to why Jack did not return the greeting. Examining the inference might involve wondering whether there were alternative explanations for Jack's behavior (e.g., he was in a hurry). Inferential cognitions typically receive greater emphasis in the Beckian approach.

If the clinician and client discover that perhaps Jack did continue walking without saying anything because he doesn't like the client, then they might find the elicitation and examination of *evaluative cognitions* to be a useful strategy. Evaluative cognitions, which typically receive greater emphasis in rational emotive behavior therapy, come in four primary categories: demandingness, human worth ratings, awfulizing, and intolerance of frustration (Dryden, 2013; Ellis & Harper, 1961).

Demands occur when one insists that the world differ from the way that it is. In the case involving Jack, this might entail the following idea: "People should always be polite and return greetings!" Human worth ratings involve black-and-white evaluations of self or others as exemplified by "I'm an unlovable person because Jack ignored me" and "Jack is a real inconsiderate person!" When a client awfulizes, they elevate events that are undesirable to the level of catastrophe. For example, if our client thought, "It's absolutely horrible that Jack ignored me!" almost as if they'd lost a limb, they would be engaging in awfulizing thinking. Frustration intolerance involves extreme evaluations of distress that by objective standards is moderate in nature. Thinking "I can't stand it when people disrespect me!" is an example of cognitions of this kind. Even though Jack might not like our client, assisting them with their demands, worth ratings, awfulizing, and frustration intolerance may reduce their distress and positively impact their problem-solving ability.

Conclusion

In this chapter we described seven pitfalls frequently observed in clinicians learning Socratic strategies. The solutions generally fell into two categories: (1) Socratic skill refinement as described in this chapter and other sections of the book; and (2) personal application of cognitive restructuring strategies to Socratic strategy-interfering cognitions. Finally, although we have an overall framework, it is important to remember that ultimately this is a Socratic dialogue and a guided discovery process. As you focus on the key content, earnestly striving to understand the patient and the patient's perspective, jointly applying curiosity and collaborative empiricism to expand that perspective, and pulling it all together with summaries and syntheses to drive meaningful change, you will find that Socratic strategies are both a way of thinking and a way of being. True collaboration and true curiosity will take you far in this practice.

Notes

1 Specific strategies are detailed in Chapter 5, "Focusing on Key Content."
2 The mechanics of this step are detailed in Chapter 8, "Summary and Synthesis."

References

Dryden, W. (2013). On rational beliefs in rational emotive behavior therapy: A theoretical perspective. *Journal of Rational-Emotive and Cognitive-Behavior Therapy, 31*(1), 39–48.

Ellis, A., & Harper, R. A. (1961). *A guide to rational living.* Englewood Cliffs, NJ: Prentice-Hall.

Miranda, R., Weierich, M., Khait, V., Jurska, J., & Andersen, S. M. (2017). Induced optimism as mental rehearsal to decrease depressive predictive certainty. *Behaviour Research and Therapy, 90*, 1–8.

Peale, V. N. (1952). *The Power of Positive Thinking.* New York: Fawcett Crest.

Waltman, S. H., Hall, B. C., McFarr, L. M., Beck, A. T., & Creed, T. A. (2017). In-session stuck points and pitfalls of community clinicians learning CBT: Qualitative investigation. *Cognitive and Behavioral Practice, 24*, 256–267. doi:10.1016/j.cbpra.2016.04.002

Webster, P., Stacey, D., Jones, D. (Producers), & Harris, T. (Director). (1991). *Rubin and Ed.* [Motion Picture]. United States: Working Title Films.

Chapter 10

Thought Records, Behavioral Experiments, and Socratic Questioning

R. Trent Codd, III and Scott H. Waltman

❖ CONTENTS

The goal of Socratic strategies in cognitive behavior therapy (CBT) is to bring about cognitive, behavioral, and emotional change through collaborative empiricism (Kazantzis et al., 2018). As described in previous chapters, collaborative empiricism involves joining with someone to cooperatively discover the truth. This guided discovery process is aided by a skills training approach to therapy (Beck, 2011); to enhance collaboration, the therapist teaches the client the core skills of cognitive modification. In this chapter, we discuss the augmentation of two key approaches to cognitive intervention with Socratic methods: thought records (Beck, Rush, Shaw, & Emery, 1979) and behavioral experiments (Bennet-Levy et al., 2004). We accomplish this by first briefly introducing these interventions, including their core elements, and then providing clinical illustrations of their implementation.

First, it can be helpful to develop a better understanding of how thought records and behavioral experiments can work together to bring about schematic change. A review of Chapter 11 which discusses working with core beliefs is an additional resource for understanding how within-session and across-session strategies can work together to bring about major changes in beliefs and behaviors, ultimately resulting in major changes in emotional functioning. A good understanding of this process is what separates an eclectic therapist from a strategic therapist. If you look at Figure 10.1, you will see that the new beliefs we are trying to foster are built on a balanced evidence base. Cognitively, we can use thought records to evaluate the evidence that they already have (and are aware of); behaviorally, we can use behavioral experiments to gather a new base of evidence to counteract a lack of experience due to avoidance.

In Chapter 2, "Why Doesn't Corrective Learning Happen Automatically," we reviewed how people's behavioral responses are limited by their expectation and how, in turn, that can limit the experiences they have from which to draw when determining whether their thoughts are true. Consider, the example of a person who is afraid of being romantically rejected (due to beliefs of being unlovable) and so they never fully commit to a single relationship. This behavior likely leads to relationship failures, which they may interpret as further evidence of their being unlovable. Conceptualizing how the belief, prediction, behavior, outcome, and interpretation of the outcome fit together can help you and the client understand where the optimal intervention point is.

It can also be helpful to understand how thought records and behavioral experiments can work together to bring about across-session change. A successfully implemented thought record will bring about an incremental shift in perspective. This new perspective can be used as a rationale for trying a new behavioral response to test out the new perspective or to gather more evidence to further evaluate the perspective. New behaviors can lead to new experiences, which can be used to more comprehensively evaluate key cognitive targets (i.e., core beliefs). Through incrementally changing thoughts and behaviors, we can build up a new schematic system that will work better for the client.

Thought Records

Thought records (Beck et al., 1979) represent a central intervention strategy in CBT and are primarily used to teach the cognitive model as well as to facilitate cognitive change. The format, components, and complexity of thought records have evolved

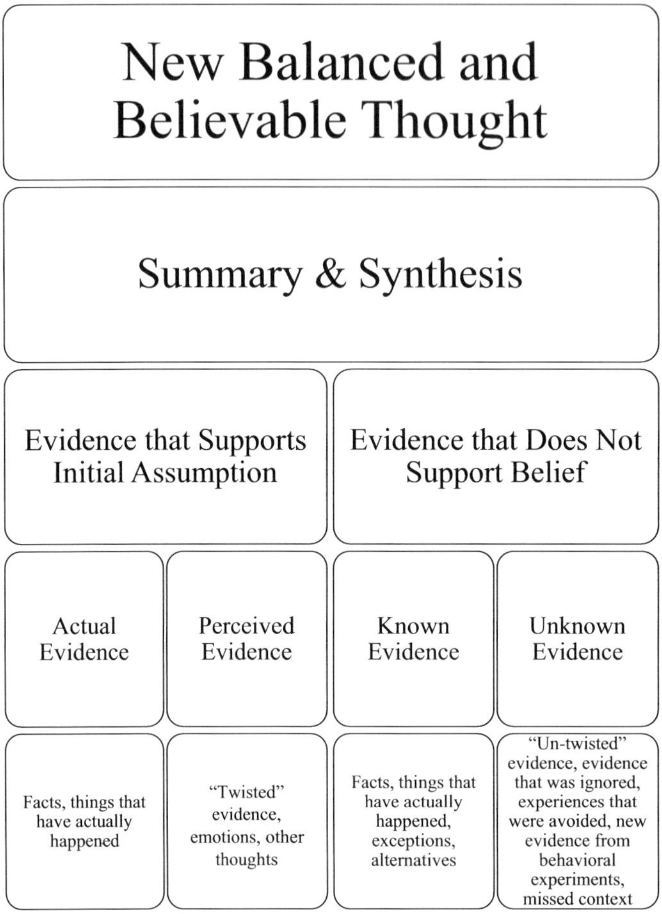

Figure 10.1 Overview of Beckian Socratic Dialogue

substantially since their inception, resulting in numerous published and unpublished versions. For example, Waltman, Frankel, Hall, Williston, and Jager-Hyman (2019) identified 110 non-identical thought records which they coded into 55 unique component combinations. The basic categories for their thought record coding system related to the basic function of the thought record and how that function was accomplished. A thought record can be used early in treatment to demonstrate and teach the cognitive model using the three-column thought record and later cognitive change can be brought about by using other versions of the thought records such as the five-column thought record, the seven-column thought record, or the A-B-C worksheet (see Waltman et al., 2019); this will be elaborated on below.

The names for thought records have also varied across versions and over time. Many names include the word "dysfunctional," as in a dysfunctional thought record or a daily record of dysfunctional thoughts. For the most part, from a clinical perspective,

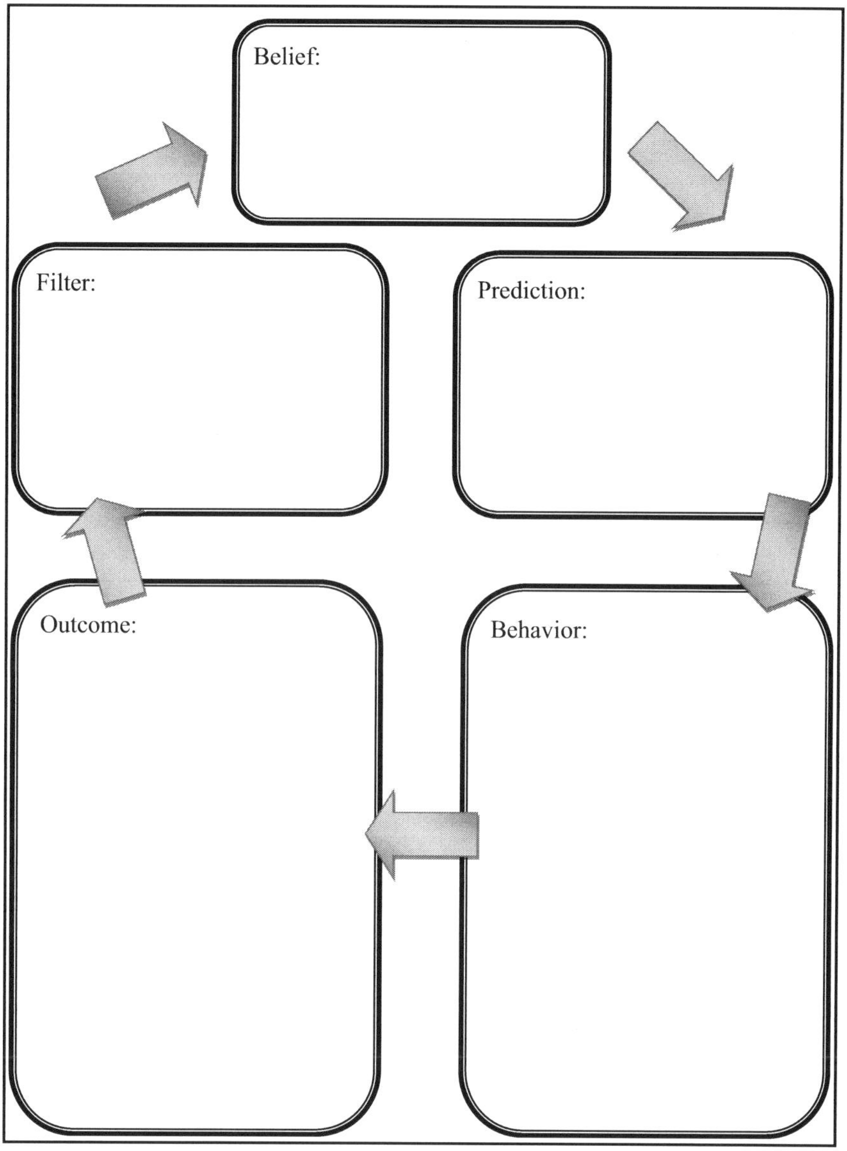

Figure 10.2 Simplified Functional Belief Conceptualization Diagram

the name used with clients matters little as long as the selected name is used consistently with the same client. However, we recommend dropping "dysfunctional" from the title, especially if it is included on a worksheet provided to a client. We make this recommendation for two reasons. First, its presence presumes that the result of inquiry will be the identification of thinking that is dysfunctional. Operating from this assumption violates a central posture of Socratic dialogue: openness to new information and

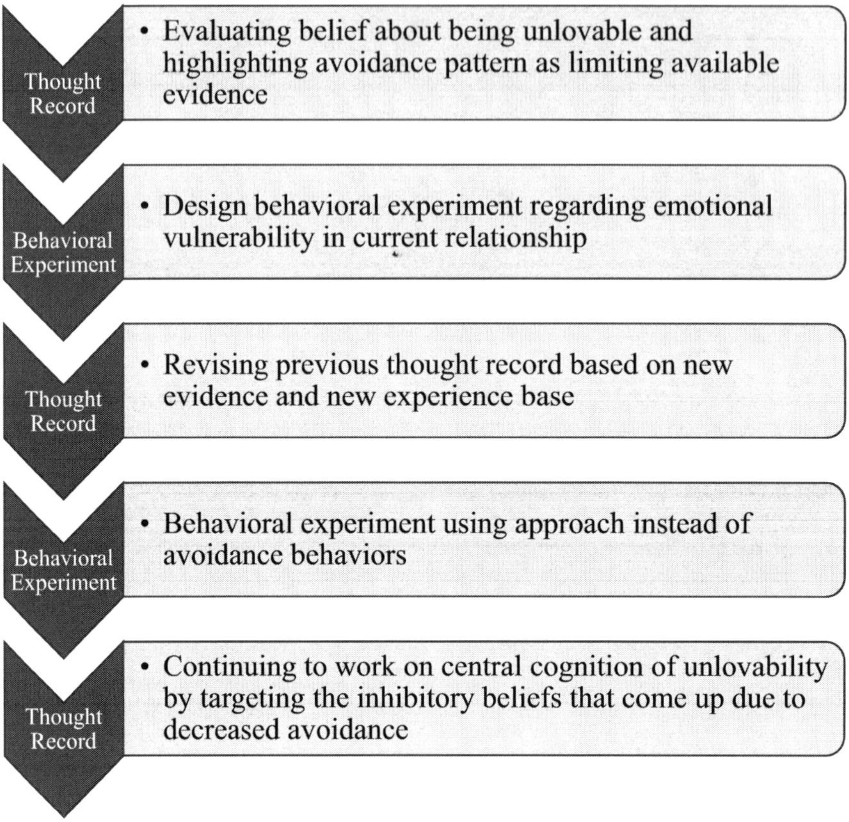

Figure 10.3 Example of Layering Thought Records and Behavioral Experiments

where the inquiry will lead (i.e., Socratic ignorance). The second reason involves the potential for some clients to receive this language as invalidating (see Chapter 12 of this volume on incorporating Socratic strategies into the use of dialectical behavior therapy). We will simply refer to these tools as thought records in this chapter.

Thought records are useful because they externalize the cognitive restructuring process. That is, they provide a written road map that includes prompts for each step in the sequence and a mechanism for future review of key points of learning. Padesky argued that using thought records helps the client learn how to engage in Socratic processes (see Kazantzis, Fairburn, Padesky, Reinecke, & Teesson, 2014). This is aided by the use of a framework to help them learn the main steps. Over time their implementation of the framework can become more flexible, but following a general routine helps them learn the skill. Having this skill on a worksheet they take with them to practice helps transport the skill from the session to their "real lives." Thought records also provide a physicalized way of distancing from thoughts and require active ways of practicing the skill (e.g., writing rather than doing it "in their head"). In this way, we are teaching the client to be their own therapist (see Beck, 2011).

Thought Records: Teaching the Cognitive Model

A core use of thought records is to teach clients the cognitive model. If you are having trouble bringing about cognitive change, you might first wonder how well the client understands and accepts the cognitive model. Another chapter in this book focuses on troubleshooting strategies. The first thing to keep in mind is that clients are more engaged in Socratic strategies when they see how their beliefs are affecting what they do and how they think. So, we first explain the cognitive model and then we demonstrate it for them using the three-column or similar thought record. Chapter 3, "Getting Started," earlier in this volume goes over the details of how to orient the client to the cognitive model and how to pull examples from their life to demonstrate the model. The Focusing Worksheet in this chapter was created to accomplish the tasks of the three-column thought record. We discussed how to use the Focusing Worksheet in great detail in Chapter 5, "Focusing on Key Content." In this chapter, we focus on the use of the more general three-column thought records.

There are a few ways to go about teaching the cognitive model. Some therapists draw out a triangle with thoughts, feelings, and behaviors labeled at the corners. There is a thought record developed specifically for this task called the three-column thought record. The central elements necessary for this task are columns representing the context where the emotional distress occurs, emotion-related thoughts, and the nature of the emotional response. Different versions of the three-column thought record exist, typically the columns are labeled "Situation," "Automatic Thoughts," and "Emotions" respectively—the order differs sometimes. However, columns dedicated to physiological and behavioral responding may also be included, if one of the goals is to help clients discover the relationships between their automatic thoughts and either of these two variables. The implementation involves an interaction between Socratic dialogue and transcribing key items onto the thought record.

The situation, simply put, is the context that gave rise to the distress. Using imagery or acting out the situation can help increase the salience of the important elements of the situation which can lead to a richer memory related to thoughts and emotions later on. Questions for assessing the situation are as follows:

- What event seemed to trigger your distress?
- What was occurring around the time you noticed a shift in your distress?

The context isn't always exclusively external to the person. It may include internal variables that are antecedent to distressing automatic thoughts. In these cases, it can be useful to ask:

- Did you experience anything internally that seemed to prompt your distress (e.g., physical sensations, thoughts, images)?

Depending on the form you are using, automatic thoughts might be next in the sequence. If this is the case, it can be helpful to skip to the emotion column next because this can heighten the saliency of emotion, which can, in turn, serve as a useful retrieval cue for important thoughts. If you follow this strategy it can be helpful to say: "We're going to skip the automatic thought column for just a moment and instead

Situation Description:	
What are the different upsetting things that happened?	
1.	
2.	
3.	
4.	
5.	
6.	
7.	
What was the most upsetting part?	
What thoughts were going through your mind?	What was the corresponding feeling?
Which thought was the most upsetting?	
What's the emotional meaning of that thought?	

Worksheet 10.1 Focusing Worksheet

focus on the emotion column next. We'll discuss why shortly." Useful questions for assessing emotion include the following:

- What distressing emotion(s) were you experiencing?
- What emotional label(s) best captures how you were feeling in this situation?
- How were you feeling emotionally?
- From 0 to 100, how [Depressed/Anxious/Angry/etc.] were you feeling?

After assessing and noting emotional responding we return to the automatic thought column to assess and record the client's stream of consciousness. Here are some example questions:

- What were you saying to yourself right before you noticed that change in [depression/anxiety/anger/etc.]?
- What was running through your mind then?
- Did any pictures or images occur to you?
- What other thoughts or images did you experience?
- If I could observe thought bubbles above your head in that situation, what would I see in those bubbles?
- What ideas were occurring to you at that moment?

After these three elements have been disentangled (i.e., the situation, automatic thoughts, emotions) and recorded on a thought record the next step is to assist the client with understanding their relationship and the usefulness of their disrupting automaticity and separating them from one another. Here are some key questions:

- How do these (pointing to the writing on the thought record) seem to go together?
- When you look at what we have pulled apart here, what do you make of this?
- Is there anything for you to learn from this exercise?
- I wonder if there is any sort of relationship between your thoughts and emotions?
- What is the difference between [situations and thoughts; thoughts and emotions]?
- Do you typically experience situations, thoughts, and emotions separately or all at once? How might separating them be useful?
- Do you think it was useful to write this out? How do you think it would have gone if we just did this in our heads?
- Are you typically aware of your thoughts in these situations or are you more aware of your distressing emotions? Any idea how increasing your awareness of your thoughts might be helpful?

Thought Records: Facilitating Cognitive Change

Based on the analysis of extant thought records and the coding system developed by Waltman and colleagues (2019), there are three different ways a thought record might go about promoting cognitive change. The first method is something called *rational responding* (Beck et al., 1979; Layden, Newman, Freeman, & Morse, 1993). This involves straightaway asking the client to pick an alternate thought that seems more rational. The first five-column thought record was this style of thought record (Beck et al., 1979). The second method a thought record might use to promote cognitive change is by focusing on understanding why the original thought is distorted, such as by identifying cognitive distortions. Burns (1989) was the first to incorporate targeting cognitive distortions with the thought records. Padesky developed and pioneered the third type of thought record, which is typified by her seven-column thought record (Greenberger & Padesky, 2015; Padesky, 1983). The seven-column thought record was developed when she found that her clients were able to use thought records well with her in session, but that they struggled to complete it on their own; she examined what they were doing in session together with what the clients weren't doing on their own and she found that the missing piece was examining the evidence (see Waltman et al., 2019). Therefore, she developed the seven-column thought record with dedicated space for evaluating the evidence of the thought in question in order to help her clients do on their own what she was doing with them.

Our Socratic Thought Record (presented in Worksheet 10.2) was developed to help facilitate our four-step framework for Socratic dialogue. Each of the four steps of the framework have a dedicated chapter in this text and there is also a chapter that pulls the whole process together. Clinicians are free to use whatever thought records they prefer. Currently, the state of the science is that we do not know if there are differences in clinical outcomes for the different thought records. Very few studies have made head-to-head comparisons of the various thought records (Waltman et al., 2019)—although there are some early indications to suggest it might matter or that different populations might respond to different thought records differently (see Waltman et al., 2019). Functionally, there is a difference between asking a client to look at a situation differently, asking them if their views are distorted, and asking them to evaluate the situation in order to come up with a more balanced and accurate thought. The latter strategy is more consistent with collaborative empiricism and is a more Socratic strategy.

The ultimate goal for a clinician using thought records is cognitive change resulting in improved emotional responding. An important prerequisite to the client successfully using the remaining elements of thought records is an adequate understanding of the cognitive model (the first three columns of the thought record just described). Some clients grasp the model quickly, whereas others require many practice trials before they develop this prerequisite skill. Importantly, intellectual understanding of the model is insufficient. Clients must be able to discriminate when they experience affective shifts and use them as cues to search for important cognitive content. Furthermore, they must be able to successfully identify their automatic thoughts.

If you are using a five- or seven-column thought record, then once the first three columns have been completed, the clinician must collaborate with the client to develop a focus for the Socratic dialogue. This process is elaborated on in Chapter 5, "Focusing on Key Content," earlier in the book. Alternatively, the Focusing Worksheet in this chapter highlights how to break a situation down to identify the most distressing elements of the situation, how to identify the various thoughts related to the most distressing part, and then how to focus on either the most distressing thought or the emotional meaning of the most distressing thought. Successful and impactful cognitive intervention is dependent on successful focusing strategies. Picking a thought just because it

Focusing: What are we targeting?

What are the different parts of the problem?

Which part is most upsetting?

What's the meaning I'm attributing to this situation? What am I telling myself?

How are we defining our target?

Understanding: How does it make sense that I think this?

Where did I learn this?

Is this something people have told me before?

What are the facts that tell me this is true?

How does this thought make me behave?

Curiosity: What are we missing?

Is there important context missing from the above statements?

Do my behaviors influence my experiences?

What do we not know?

What are the facts that tell me this might not be true?

Are there any exceptions we're forgetting about?

Summary: How can we summarize the whole story?

Synthesis: How does this summary fit with my original statement?
How does it fit with what I typically tell myself?
Take-Away Message: What's a more balanced and believable statement?

How can I apply that statement to my upcoming week?

Worksheet 10.2 Socratic Thought Record

sounds like a distortion or sounds painful is a gamble that might not pay off, whereas taking the time to understand the situation and weigh your options can help you collaboratively choose the optimal target for your thought record. In addition, doing this together with the client helps them learn how to focus on the key thoughts. Here are some questions that are facilitative of this task:

- What are the different parts of the problem?
- Which part is most upsetting?
- What is the meaning you are attributing to this situation?
- What are you telling yourself?
- If we made a change in just one thought today that would make all the difference in the world for you, which one would it be?
- Which thought upsets you the most?

The next step in this process will depend on what thought record you are using. Ideally, you want the steps you follow in-session to be consistent with the flow or prompts from the thought record you are using so the client can learn these steps for themselves. If you are using our Socratic Thought Record, you will first seek to gain a better understanding of the thought. Here are some questions you can ask them that are consistent with the prompts on the Socratic Thought Record:

- What experiences are this thought based on?
- What are the facts that support this?
- If this was true, what do you think would be the strongest evidence to support it?
- Is this something people have directly said to you in the past?
- What is it like to believe this thought?
- How long have you believed this?
- When do you tend to believe this more and less?
- What do you typically do when thoughts like this come up for you?

After you have developed a good understanding of the thought you are targeting, you will seek to expand that understanding with collaborative (joint) curiosity. Here are some questions you might ask the client that are consistent with the prompts on the Socratic Thought Record.

- Is there important context missing from the above statements?
- Did your previous behaviors influence your experiences?
- What do we not know?
- What are the facts that tell you this might not be true?
- Are there any exceptions we are forgetting about?
- What would you tell a friend?
- What might a friend tell you?
- Has it always been this way?
- How has believing this thought affected your behavior and the available evidence to draw from?
- Can we go and gather new evidence?

The classic steps of Socratic questioning are analysis and synthesis—breaking it apart and putting it back together. A Socratic dialogue using a thought record as a tool is incomplete without a Summary and Synthesis step. Here is where we help the client fit it all together in a way that will produce a durable and balanced belief that can be used to bring about lasting and meaningful change. We can think about summarizing as fitting together the different elements we covered in the evaluation portion of our thought record. The synthesis part is where we fit that summary together with the bigger picture. This is where we make the new learning explicit. Here are some helpful questions that are consistent with the prompts from the Socratic Thought Record.

- So how does this all fit together?
- Can you summarize all the facts for me?
- What is a summary statement that captures both sides?
- How do you reconcile our new statement with the thought we were evaluating? (Or with the core belief we are targeting?)

A final step is to assess the impact of the inquiry. Did the examination reduce believability in the targeted thoughts? Did emotional distress become more proportional to the event? Finally, we want to connect the new perspective to a planned change in behavior, by asking: "How can you apply this new perspective during the coming week?" This sets the stage well for a behavioral experiment that can reinforce the new perspective, either by directly testing it out or gathering new evidence to inform a future thought record.

Behavioral Experiments

Behavioral experiments are a potent cognitive change strategy that are commonly used in CBT (Clark, 1989; Greenberger & Padesky, 2015; Wells, 1997). Behavioral experiments have roots in behavioral therapy and (after being modified) are now widely used in a broad range of cognitive and behavioral therapies (see Bennett-Levy et al., 2004; Greenberger & Padesky, 2015; Waltman, 2020). A core component of CBT is creating cognitive change, and behavioral experiments allow for using behavioral means to bring about cognitive change (i.e., changing thoughts through changing behaviors; see Beck et al., 1979). The heart of Beckian Socratic processes is collaborative empiricism, and behavioral experiments typify this process when they are designed and implemented in a collaborative manner. Additionally, there are traditional cognitive strategies that can be used to enhance behavioral experiments, all of which is discussed below.

In Beck's (1979) seminal text on the theoretical aspects of cognitive therapy, he describes applying the scientific method to experiment on a client's belief. This is essentially, what a behavioral experiment is, the application of scientific inquiry and curiosity to a prediction. Beck went on to explain that an individual's perception of a situation is limited by their perception of reality, and that their engagement with reality is limited by their world view. Conceptually, we can fit this together to understand that a person has a belief based on their experience of reality. That belief can shape their reality and create a feedback loop that strengthens the belief. For example, the person's predictions and behaviors are typically predicated on their belief system, thus limiting their experiences from which to draw in shaping their world views—avoidance prevents the opportunity for corrective learning (Beck, 1979).

It is thought, though not empirically proven, that behavioral experiments are more impactful than thought records. It has been suggested that

> Generating an alternative interpretation (insight) is usually not sufficient to generate a large emotional shift. A crucial, but sometimes neglected, step in therapy is therefore to test the patient's appraisals in behavioral experiments, which create experiential new evidence against the patient's threatening interpretation.
>
> (Ehlers & Wild, 2015, p. 166)

The differential effects of behavioral experiments and thoughts records have been investigated. Bennett-Levy (2003) conducted a seminal mixed methods study comparing behavioral experiments and thought records as part of an experiential CBT training program of therapists and therapists-in-training. He found that behavioral experiments were perceived by the group as being more powerful and compelling than thought records in their self-practice. McManus et al. (2012) extended this line of research and compared the effects of thought records and behavioral experiments in a single-session intervention targeting subclinical obsessive-compulsive disorder-related thoughts. The participants found both approaches to be beneficial and reported evidence of a small advantage of behavioral experiments over thought records, as the targeted thought changed more quickly and there was greater generalization of new learning. Notably, both of these studies were conducted with nonclinical populations, and therefore further research on the topic is needed. Clinically, we recommend using both strategies as they can be used in a complementary manner, as demonstrated at the beginning of the current chapter.

Behavioral experiments (Bennet-Levy et al., 2004; Waltman, 2020) are a commonly used approach to cognitive restructuring that teach clients to use the scientific process to test their beliefs systematically. Like thought records, different versions of behavioral experiments have been developed over the years, though with considerably less variability. Broadly, we can categorize the types of behavioral experiments into three categories:

- *Testing a specific prediction.* Testing a specific prediction is the most common type of behavioral experiment. This can be used to test out whether an alternative thought that was developed using a thought record or rational responding is actually true. You do not actually have to do a thought record to find a prediction to test, though it is a good way to reinforce and build momentum on a successful thought record. The general idea is that we are trying to target the predictions that are preventing skillful behavior to foster more adaptive and more accurate predictions.
- *Gathering new evidence.* Gathering new evidence falls under the umbrella of a behavioral experiment, though it is perhaps not a true experiment. This can be an ideal strategy if there is a lack of disconfirmatory evidence due to avoidance or lack of exposure. These can be done in session or out of session.

- *Doing something different.* This is not actually a behavioral experiment. Sometimes a therapist might say "Why don't we try this and see what happens?" or perhaps assign the client to not engage in the unskillful behavior. These can at times be helpful suggestions, but they are underpowered interventions that could be better if turned into a true behavioral experiment. We are interested in more than getting the client to do something different in their lives; we want to be clever and set them up for success.

Behavioral experiments are the application of the scientific method to thoughts and behaviors. Crawford and Stucki (1990) outline the scientific method as follows: (1) define a question; (2) gather information and resources; (3) form an explanatory hypothesis; (4) test the hypothesis by performing an experiment and collecting data in a reproducible manner; (5) analyze the data; (6) interpret the data and draw conclusions that serve as a starting point for new hypothesis; (7) publish results; and (8) retest. We previously expanded this model to address some of the common stuck points and pitfalls to conducting research in real-world practice-based settings (see Codd, 2018).

Step 1. Have a question
Step 2. Consult the literature/subject matter experts
Step 3. Define the research question
Step 4. Design the study
Step 5. Seek consultation feedback
Step 6. Pilot/proof of concept

Behavioral Experiment Plan

What is a fear or negative prediction that I have which prevents me from having the life I want to have?

What specifically does that fear make me predict will happen? How strongly do I believe this will happen (1-100%)?

Is there a plausible alternative prediction of what could happen? How strongly do I believe this will happen (1-100%)?

Specifically, what am I testing? & Can it be proven?

What's the plan? Who, what, when, where, and how will I test my prediction?
How will I know if it comes true?

What problems might come up and what can I do to plan for success?

Did I conduct the experiment as planned? Do I need to rework the plan?

What actually happened?

What does the outcome of the experiment mean about my prediction and my alternate prediction?
Am I missing anything?

How has my belief in my predictions changed? What would I rate each at (1-100%)?

What did I learn?
How can I build on this new learning in the coming week?

Figure 10.4 Behavioral Experiment Form

Behavioral Experiment Plan

What is a fear or negative prediction that I have which prevents me from having the life I want to have?

Nobody likes me

What specifically does that fear make me predict will happen? How strongly do I believe this will happen (1-100%)? *Prediction no one will return a hello or other greeting, nor will they engage me in any level of conversation (95).*

Is there a plausible alternative prediction of what could happen? How strongly do I believe this will happen (1-100%)?

The way I socially signal impacts how others behave toward me, and if I signal more effectively, I can positively influence the interactions I receive. It's not me, but my social skills (45)

Specifically, what am I testing? & Can it be proven?

Whether I get a different social response depending on my behavior. Will skillful interactions produce a different outcome than unskillful interactions? Yes, if my behavior has an influence, I can track what I do and what impact it has.

What's the plan? Who, what, when, where, and how will I test my prediction?

Over the next week I will pay attention to my social signals when I cross paths with co-workers. Specifically, for half of the work week I will make it a point to look at each co-worker I pass by while smiling, using eyebrow wags and taking a slow breath. The other half of the work week I will look at each co-worker I pass by but will show a flat face. A flat face is expressionless and does not involve smiles, eyebrow wags or change in breathing pace.

How will I know if it comes true?

After each interaction I will rate how positive I believe the interaction to be from 0-10, taking into consideration whether they returned my greeting, attempted to engage me in conversation or said anything complimentary. I will note which days were associated with more positive interactions.

What problems might come up and what can I do to plan for success?

Potential obstacles – a) I might not come across enough people over the work week to draw any conclusions. If this happens, I'll keep the experiment going for an additional work week.; b) Co-workers might not engage me in conversation because they are in a hurry or concerned about something unrelated to me. If this seems to happen, I'll remind myself of these alternative possibilities.

Did I conduct the experiment as planned? Do I need to rework the plan? *Experiment conducted for a week.*

What actually happened?

Of 15 interactions on flat face days – 3 co-workers greeted me, 2 with a smile (I rated these three with an 8 or higher). The other interactions can be characterized by no or very little engagement with me and I rated all of those interactions below a 5 ... On pro-social signal days, I had 12 interactions with 9 of them engaging with me positively (I rated it 8 or higher).

What does the outcome of the experiment mean about my prediction and my alternate prediction?

How I socially signal to others has a positive impact on how they behave toward me, which makes me feel more liked. This may be one reason I've concluded no one likes me. I will continue this for another week to gather more confidence in this.

Am I missing anything?

It might be that my history of poor social signaling has impacted how people see me and perhaps it can change for the better over time too.

How has my belief in my predictions changed? What would I rate each at (1–100%)?

Nobody likes me = 60; My social signaling impacts how others relate to me = 75

What did I learn?

I learned that the social signals I send other people affects how they respond to me.

How can I build on this new learning in the coming week? *I want to keep practicing my skills and tracking responses to gather more data and get more practice*

Figure 10.5 Example of a Behavioral Experiment Form

Step 7. Evaluate and refine
Step 8. Conduct study to scale
Step 9. Clean data and analyze results
Step 10. Interpret results in light of extant literature
Step 11. Disseminate your findings

In the current chapter, we have modified our practice-based research method (see Codd, 2018) and synthesized it with existing behavioral experiment frameworks (Bennett-Levy et al., 2004; Ehlers & Wild, 2015; Leahy, 2017) to create a framework for behavioral experiments that enhances both collaboration and empiricism with an emphasis on clinical utility.

Step 1. Identify a prediction that is getting in your way
Step 2. Identify alternative predictions
Step 3. Define the behavioral experiment question
Step 4. Design the experiment
Step 5. List any obstacles to the successful execution of the experiment or anything that might go wrong (Note strategies for overcoming obstacles)
Step 6. Conduct the experiment
Step 7. Analyze results of the experiment
Step 8. Note what can be concluded from the experiment
Step 9. Re-rate the degree of belief in targeted and alternative beliefs
Step 10. Define an action plan based on the study's conclusions

This model for behavioral experiment will be elaborated on and demonstrated below.

Step 1. Identify a Prediction That Is Getting in Your Way

In a similar way to other Socratic strategies, we want to be strategic as to what we target with behavioral experiments. Keep in mind that the goal of behavioral experiments is to change thoughts by changing behaviors. So, we want to test predictions that are facilitative of the new behaviors we want to encourage or are the negative predictions which prevent more skillful behavior. The questions we teach our clients to ask themselves are as follows: "What is a fear or negative prediction that I have which prevents me from having the life I want to have?" "What specifically does that fear make me predict will happen?" "How strongly do I believe this will happen (1–100%)?"

See the sample behavioral experiment above. There are some key considerations specific to each step in the process. With respect to the first step, identifying cognitions to test, it is important to specify the cognition in a falsifiable form (you can't prove a negative). This can frequently be accomplished by asking oneself what predictions can be derived from the stated belief. There may be one or several implications to any particular belief. In the example provided in the completed behavioral experiment form, the belief "No one likes me" is difficult to test. However, one prediction derived from this idea is that no one will return simple pleasant greetings nor engage the client in chit-chat or deeper conversations. It is much less challenging to arrange an experiment testing the notion "My social signaling impacts whether someone will return my greeting."

Step 2. Identify Alternative Predictions

The questions we teach our clients to ask themselves are as follows: "Is there a plausible alternative prediction of what could happen?" "How strongly do I believe this will happen (1–100%)?"

The second component in which a possible alternative view is specified involves at least two considerations. First, it is important to identify what the client needs to learn in order to solve their problem. The answer to this question points to the type of belief that would be helpful to formulate and test via the experiment. In the example provided above, we determined that one of the things the client needs to learn is that she has some control over how people relate to her and that therefore her "likeableness" is not a fixed quality of hers that leads to these upsetting interactions. Second, given the biasing effects of the client's core beliefs, it is useful to identify aspects of the experimental situation to which they might have trouble attending. Specifying an alternative belief helps navigate their attention to features of the situation to which they might not have otherwise paid attention, therefore interfering with important learning.

Step 3. Define the Behavioral Experiment Question

The questions we teach our clients to ask themselves are as follows: "Specifically, what am I testing?" "Can it be proven?"

This is functionally a place to check and make sure that everyone is on the same page and to talk through the feasibility of testing the idea. In cases where everyone is on the same page, this might seem redundant, but it is failsafe and a place to flesh out the target prediction so you can plan for success.

Step 4. Design the Experiment

The questions we teach our clients to ask themselves are as follows: "What's the plan?" "Who, what, when, where, and how will I test my prediction?" "How will I know if it comes true?"

Designing an experiment is the next component. In addition to ensuring the exercise has the potential to produce new learning in relation to the tested cognition(s), it is very important to describe the experiment in specific detail. For example, how long will the experiment last? How will outcomes be measured? What will the client say/do precisely? How many times will they implement the procedure over the duration of the experiment?

We also want to clearly define what we are testing; otherwise people will twist what happens to fit their expectations. For example, someone with anxiety might complete a difficult task and then erroneously conclude it was a failure because they became anxious during the task. This is why it is important to clearly define the success criteria. In this anxiety example, we can clearly discuss how they likely will be anxious because they are doing something they are afraid of doing, but that we are testing whether they can feel anxious and do it anyway. Notably, you will likely need to review this again during the debrief.

Step 5. List Any Obstacles to the Successful Execution of the Experiment or Anything That Might Go Wrong (Note Strategies for Overcoming Obstacles)

The question we teach our clients to ask themselves is "What problems might come up and what can I do to plan for success?"

Next is an important and frequently overlooked component: anticipating obstacles and problems that might arise. This is a crucial step because typically the first time you do something it does not go as smoothly as you would hope. Clinicians should ask themselves whether the client has the necessary repertoire to conduct the experiment legitimately. In the example case presented above, the client was using a basic skill from Radically Open Dialectical Behavior Therapy (Lynch, 2018) called the Big 3 + 1. First, the client had to be trained on that skill until they could emit it in a competent manner. One can imagine a client raising their eyebrows and smiling in such a way that would be aversive to people rather than welcoming. If they don't have the existing skillset then the clinician should either come up with a different experiment or train the skill before they run the experiment. In addition, it is important to identify what might go wrong or what problems might arise to the degree that these can be anticipated. For example, if there is an out-of-session exposure-type experiment other people might notice the client's behavior. Is this likely? If so, will it present a problem? If a clinician is accompanying them out of the office might someone approach the client and clinician to ask what they are doing? What would you, as the clinician, say that wouldn't violate the client's confidentiality?

We are troubleshooting related to the implementation of the actual experiment and we can also target treatment compliance here. Are there barriers that might come up and get in the way of the client completing the experiment? Are they prone to forgetting? Have we scheduled when they will do it? Do we need to make reminders? Do we need to make coping cards about why it is worth it? Have we planned an optimal time to do the experiment?

Step 6. Conduct the Experiment

The questions we teach our clients to ask themselves are as follows: "Did I conduct the experiment as planned?" "Do I need to rework the plan?"

This step is straightforward. We want them to track whether they did the experiment as planned. There is also a question about whether the plan needs to be reworked. This is because sometimes unanticipated barriers come up. We want to keep the focus on needing to retool the plan as opposed to its being a failure experience for the client. All data is valuable. If we discover a new unanticipated barrier, we might need to rethink the experiment together in session.

Step 7. Analyze Results of the Experiment

The question we teach our client to ask themselves is "What actually happened?"

After conducting the experiment, it is important for the client to record all the relevant data. You will obtain the most accurate data if they track what happens on the same day instead of filling the form out in the waiting room of your office. The most important consideration with this step is for the client to list only the facts and not their interpretation of those facts. Interpretation occurs in the next step. Notice in the example behavioral experiment earlier in this chapter how listing data objectively and interpreting those data are two distinct steps.

Step 8. Note What Can Be Concluded from the Experiment

The questions we teach our clients to ask themselves are as follows: "What does the outcome of the experiment mean about my prediction and my alternate prediction?" "Am I missing anything?"

The goal of this step is to draw out a clear conclusion from the experiment. Early in treatment, this is something you will shape together with them. Remember their conclusions will be filtered through their expectations, and so this is a chance for you to help detangle their perceptions and help draw out a more constructive view. The question about whether they are missing anything is a place to address any negative events that happened in the experiment. There might be important context missing that helps to mitigate negative findings.

Step 9. Re-rate the Degree of Belief in Targeted and Alternative Beliefs

The questions we teach our clients to ask themselves are as follows: "How has my belief in my predictions changed?" "What would I rate each at (1–100%)?"

An important behavioral experiment component is to assess and note the impact of the experiment by re-rating degrees of belief in the two tested ideas (i.e., the target cognition and the alternative).

Step 10. Define an Action Plan Based on the Study's Conclusions

The questions we teach our clients to ask themselves are as follows "What did I learn?" "How can I build on this new learning in the coming week?"

A guiding principle to our approach is an interweaving of cognitive and behavioral strategies to change. Here we see how, after a behavioral experiment, cognitive strategies are used to draw out a new conclusion. Next, we want to build on that conclusion by making plans to do something behaviorally that is based on that conclusion. This will continue to foster new experiences, which will provide a broader base of experiences for our cognitive strategies.

Summary

Thought records and behavioral experiments are two central cognitive restructuring interventions. To optimize effective implementation of these procedures, they should be accompanied by sound Socratic strategies. Further, cognitive and behavioral means of bringing about change can be interlayered to enhance clinical effects. All of this can work together to build momentum and change in our clients' lives.

References

Beck, A. T. (1979). *Cognitive therapy and the emotional disorders.* New York: Meridian.

Beck, A. T., Rush, A. J., Shaw, B. F., & Emery, G. (1979). *Cognitive therapy of depression.* New York: Guilford Press.

Beck, J. S. (2011). *Cognitive behavior therapy: Basics and beyond* (2nd ed.). New York: Guilford Press.

Bennett-Levy, J. (2003). Mechanisms of change in cognitive therapy: The case of automatic thought records and behavioural experiments. *Behavioural and Cognitive Psychotherapy, 31*(3), 261–277. doi:10.1017/s1352465803003035

Bennett-Levy, J. E., Butler, G. E., Fennell, M. E., Hackman, A. E., Mueller, M. E., & Westbrook, D. E. (2004). *Oxford guide to behavioural experiments in cognitive therapy.* New York: Oxford University Press.

Burns, D. D. (1989). *The feeling good handbook.* New York: William Morrow.

Clark, D. M. (1989). Anxiety states: panic and general anxiety. In K. Hawton, P. M. Salkovskis, J. Kirk, & D. M. Clark (Eds.), *Cognitive behaviour therapy for psychiatric problems* (pp. 52–96). Oxford: Oxford Medical Publications.

Codd III, R. T. (Ed.). (2018). *Practice-based research: A guide for clinicians.* New York: Routledge.

Crawford, S., & Stucki, L. (1990). Peer review and the changing research record. *Journal of the American Society for Information Science, 41*, 223–228.

Ehlers, A., & Wild, J. (2015). Cognitive therapy for PTSD: Updating memories and meanings of trauma. In U. Schnyder and M. Cloitre (Eds.), *Evidence based treatments for trauma-related psychological disorders* (pp. 161–187). Cham, Switzerland: Springer.

Greenberger, D., & Padesky, C. A. (2015). *Mind over mood: Change how you feel by changing the way you think.* Guilford Press.

Kazantzis, N., Beck, J. S., Clark, D. A., Dobson, K. S., Hofmann, S. G., Leahy, R. L., & Wong, C. W. (2018). Socratic dialogue and guided discovery in cognitive behavioral therapy: A modified Delphi panel. *International Journal of Cognitive Therapy, 11*(2), 140–157.

Kazantzis, N., Fairburn, C. G., Padesky, C. A., Reinecke, M., & Teesson, M. (2014). Unresolved issues regarding the research and practice of cognitive behavior therapy: The case of guided discovery using Socratic questioning. *Behaviour Change, 31*(01), 1–17. doi:10.1017/bec.2013.29

Layden, M. A., Newman, C. F., Freeman, A., & Morse, S. B. (1993). *Cognitive therapy of borderline personality disorder.* Needham Heights, MA: Allyn & Bacon.

Leahy, R. L. (2017). *Cognitive therapy techniques: A practitioner's guide.* New York: Guilford Press.

Lynch, T. R. (2018). *Radically open dialectical behavior therapy: Theory and practice for treating disorders of overcontrol.* Oakland, CA: Harbinger Publications.

McManus, F., Doorn, K. V., & Yiend, J. (2012). Examining the effects of thought records and behavioral experiments in instigating belief change. *Journal of Behavior Therapy and Experimental Psychiatry, 43*(1), 540–547. doi:10.1016/j.jbtep.2011.07.003

Padesky, C. A. (1983). *Seven column thought record.* Huntington Beach, CA: Center for Cognitive Therapy.

Waltman, S. H. (2020). Targeting trauma-related beliefs in PTSD with behavioral experiments: Illustrative case study. *Journal of Rational-Emotive and Cognitive-Behavior Therapy*, 38, 209–224. https://doi.org/10.1007/s10942-020-00338-3

Waltman, S. H., Frankel, S. A., Hall, B. C., Williston, M. A., Jager-Hyman, S. (2019). Review and analysis of thought records: Creating a coding system. *Current Psychiatry Research and Reviews, 15*, 11–19.

Wells, A. (1997). *Cognitive therapy of anxiety disorders.* Chichester, UK: Wiley.

Chapter 11

Working with Core Beliefs and Schema Work

Scott H. Waltman

❖ CONTENTS

Overview

Some cognitions are harder to change than others. Aaron Beck (1979) explained that core beliefs were rigid absolutistic beliefs. Clinically, when you encounter a core belief, you will find it to be well entrenched and your client will intermittently treat it as being completely true or "feeling" completely true. Working with core beliefs is complicated by the often-lacking training in how to work with core beliefs (James & Barton, 2004). This may be exacerbated by the fact that psychotherapy trainees often receive the bulk of their supervised clinical training on how to start a course of therapy, with some training on the middle phases of treatment, and little training on the end phases of treatment (Waltman, Rex, & Williams, 2011; Waltman, Williams, & Christiansen, 2013). Core belief work is challenging yet rewarding. You will get the most out of this chapter if you first read and put into practice the preceding chapters; this being similar to how we typically do not start with core belief work, but build our way up to it (so we can utilize the skills we previously taught the client).

Review of Core Beliefs and Schema

A more thorough review of the cognitive behavioral model can be found in the early chapters of this book. A review of the key points is given below (see Beck, 1979; Beck & Haigh, 2014; Padesky, 1994; Padesky & Mooney, 2012; Young, 1999; Waltman & Sokol, 2017):

- Core beliefs are the deepest levels of beliefs.
- The term "schema" is used to mean either a belief, a belief structure, or a way of thinking; the term "schema" can be used to refer to a core belief, intermediate belief, assumption, attitude, and so forth.
- These beliefs affect how we think, how we feel, and what we do.
- People have both positive and negative core beliefs.
- A core belief can be inactive until it is triggered or activated by a situational or environmental stressor.
- A more adaptive core belief may already exist, it might just be dormant in the current situation and contingencies.
- When a core belief is activated, it can result in an overall modal activation, which will be elaborated on below.

Modal Activation

One of the main updates to the Generic Cognitive Model (see Beck & Haigh, 2014) is the inclusion of modes. This concept was born out of the development of cognitive behavior therapy (CBT) for personality disorders and schema therapy. A mode represents a constellation of activation of a belief, a feeling, a behavioral response, and an attentional style (Waltman & Sokol, 2017). Various diagnosis-specific modes have been defined by researchers such as Young (1999), who was the developer of schema therapy.

Alternatively, you can seek to identify your client's idiosyncratic (individual) modal response for when their core belief is activated. The advantages of this approach are based on a Gestalt psychology understanding that, in this case, the whole is greater than the sum of its parts; that is, the different modal components work together to reinforce the other elements. For example, the typical modal behavior can be schema-consistent, schema-avoidant, or overcompensatory (Young, 1999); each of these responses can lead to a maintenance of the belief that is driving the schema. Therefore, to adequately target a core belief, you may need to target the entire modal response, or create an individualized treatment plan that targets each component of the mode.

When to Target Core Beliefs and Schema

Typically, a therapist will first focus on creating conditions that will make it easier to successfully target core beliefs and schema. This includes the following:

- Successfully building a relationship of trust
- Creating a shared understanding of their conceptualization

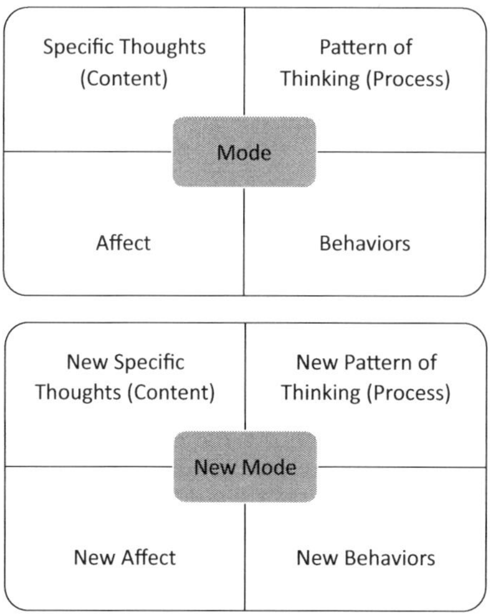

Figure 11.1 Modal Change

- Teaching the client skills to help them tolerate the distress of working on core issues
- Teaching the client cognitive restructuring skills
- Collaboratively using those skills to bring about some change in their life or a reduction in their distress
- Cultivating new patterns of behavior based on new beliefs

Not every client wants or needs to work on their core beliefs or schema. Many clients find they are quite satisfied with the above steps and you might instead move towards termination. It is important to note that core belief work is often emotionally deeper, and it typically involves working through situations that have historically been avoided and can entail a relatively longer course of treatment.

Typical Change Trajectories

Typically, core belief work represents a liminal point (or the threshold between two states). When someone is working towards a goal, there is a point where their focus shifts from the gains they have made to the gains they still need to make (Bonezzi, Brendl, & Angelis, 2011). This point is a risk for discouragement, as sometimes the journey ahead seems further than someone thinks they can go (Bonezzi et al., 2011). At early stages of core belief work, the client will be acting in new ways, intellectually knowing the target core belief is probably not as true as they have been treating it, and yet they still often feel wary.

Typically, the behavior patterns and thought patterns need to be changed before the feelings catch up. Your client might express some dismay that the things you are asking them to do are emotionally difficult. This process involves asking our clients to take emotional risks, which can result in both a fear and excitement. The fear is often more salient, and we want to help them learn to recognize and hold onto both emotional experiences. In this process, your client might say something like: "In a way it is terrifying, but I'm feeling a lot better." In considering this emotionally difficult work, it can be helpful to remember that the only way out is through. As Robert Frost (1915) wrote, "The best way out is always through. And I agree to that, or in so far as that I can see no way out but through." It can be helpful to tell your clients that if there were an easier way, you would have already tried it with them.

In-Session and Across-Session Strategies

In order to bring about change in a well-entrenched belief, there are strategies that you can use in a single session with your client (i.e., in-session strategies). There are also interventions or strategies we use across sessions to bring about change (across-session strategies). These strategies will be discussed below. A case example will be utilized as necessary to help illustrate the process.

Case Example: Aiden

Aiden (pseudonym) was a salesman in his late thirties. He was charming and handsome, but he often felt empty and unwanted. He initially entered therapy following a suicidal crisis where he had interpreted his then-fiancé as wanting to back out of marrying him after she expressed some dissatisfactions with the wedding plans. His condition stabilized following some cognitive behavioral skills training, though his core beliefs remained a pronounced part of his clinical presentation. He was most triggered in situations where he "felt" that he was losing face. In these situations, he would be quick to perceive rejection and feel a resulting panic, making frantic efforts to maintain his image. Although he had an underlying core belief of being worthless, his problem could be understood more clearly by looking at the modal activation associated with this belief. He would behave impulsively, by making promises that were too big to keep or pestering his partner with elaborate and intense reassurance-seeking behaviors. He would become fixated on what others must be thinking about him. He would feel intense anxiety and panic. All of this together made for abrupt shifts in his life and functioning.

Collaboratively Setting the Cognitive Target

The first thing you need to do is collaboratively designate a core belief as a target that you will work on across a number of sessions. Previous chapters have identified how to break down a situation, identify the hot thought, and then use the downward arrow strategy to find the emotional meaning of the hot thought. Evaluating the theme across the emotional meaning of their hot thoughts will give you a good idea about what a potential core belief might be.

You can also use a thematic analysis to identify potential core beliefs; where you ask your client what types of situations tend to be difficult for them. Then, discuss what comes up for them in those situations: How do they think? How do they feel? What do they do (mentally and behaviorally)? If you can map out the mode, you can make that a treatment target.

Usually, you will want to start with the most prominent element as it will be the easiest to identify. For example, with Aiden, the most prominent element was the panicky feeling he would get. From here, the therapist could say: "Let's study where these feelings come up for you." From there, you can talk about those situations. You can directly inquire about the emotional meaning of his thoughts by asking your clients the following questions: "In these situations, what does it feel like is happening?" or "What are you afraid is happening?" or "What about this situation is so upsetting to you?" You might need to use the downward arrow strategy: "If that was happening, why would that be so bad for you?" or "If that was true, emotionally what would that mean to you?" This will give us a good idea of a core belief or something in the neighborhood of a core belief.

From there, you need to draw out the resulting emotions and behaviors. You can then put together their modal response. Finally, you need to create a non-pathologizing shared label, so you can target and talk about the mode in a way that will not be shaming with the client: "So, what should we call this mode that you get into sometimes?" In Aiden's case: "What should we call this mode where you feel panicky, have thoughts that your value is dropping, act impulsively and frantically, and fixate on what other people are thinking about you?" After we have created a label for this mode, we can discuss making this an overall target for therapy.

In-Session Strategies

Traditional Socratic Strategies

Our four-step framework for Beckian Socratic Dialogue (i.e., Focusing on Key Cognitions, Phenomenological Understanding, Collaborative Curiosity, and Summary and Synthesis) can be used to directly evaluate the core belief. It is unlikely that a single encounter will be enough to completely restructure a strongly held, emotionally laden belief that has been held for years (if not decades). Initially, the therapist will try to evaluate the overall belief. The goal of this encounter is to foster ambivalence that the core belief is not 100% true and to identify the different elements that cause the person to believe that the belief is true. Subsequently, the therapist will target the smaller elements of evidence. They will focus on evaluating the evidence and experiences that the client subjectively holds as the strongest evidence for their belief. The therapist will also track current situations where the modal activation is occurring to help facilitate new discrepant experiences and perceptions.

Drawing Out a Continuum

The continuum technique (see James & Barton, 2004) is a strategy for reducing the rigidity and extremity of core beliefs. We typically see much all-or-nothing thinking with core beliefs, which is partly the reason that the emotional response is so strong. This is also part of what reinforces the belief; almost nothing is purely good, and so something that is partially bad is interpreted as being all bad, reinforcing the negative core belief.

In the case of Aiden, his absolutistic belief about being worthless led to his engaging in unsustainable efforts to prove his value. The overreach would eventually fail, and he would interpret this as having proved that he really is worthless. Drawing out a continuum of value, as opposed to seeing people as either being worthwhile or worthless helped Aiden to see that even if some people did, in fact, not see his value, this did not mean he had no value. These Beckian strategies were supplemented with rational emotive behavior therapy strategies, which are well suited to evaluating extremity of thought. Ellis' notion of inherent human value (Ellis & Harper, 1961) also helped to soften the false dichotomy between worthless and worthwhile.

Imagery

Not all clients respond well to imagery work. It can be helpful to discuss why we use it from a cognitive-behavioral perspective. Imagery strategies are powerful because they can induce a change in affect. We want to use them to counter the modal activation process. Creating a vision or image that is consistent with their goals or the alternate belief you are building up can help them shift their modal activation, making it easier to behave in an effective manner, and creating more discrepant experiences.

In the case of Aiden, we wanted to identify some imagery that countered his feeling frantic. As we delved into understanding that feeling, we pulled out a notion of feeling like he might disappear, and so we chose an image of permanence. He responded well to the imagery of the constancy of a mountain. He was taught the mountain meditation from a mindfulness-based treatment protocol (see Bowen, Chawla, & Marlatt, 2011), and he was provided with an audio-recording to practice the imagery. He responded well to this imagery and he took on a self-instructional strategy (see Meichenbaum & Goodman, 1971), whereby he could remind himself to be like the mountain whenever he felt his panicky mode activating, which was quite effective at modulating his resulting behavior.

Creating a Less Vicious Cycle

In a previous chapter, we reviewed how a belief can influence what you expect, what you do, and how you perceive the outcome of your behavior; all of this can create a vicious cycle in which a belief becomes self-perpetuating. We want to assist our clients in creating a new way of being in order to reinforce the new belief we are cultivating. We want both to increase behaviors that are compatible with the new belief we are building up and to decrease behaviors that are incompatible with the new belief. If you are cultivating a new mode, you will want to define the behaviors that will be consistent with the new modal response. You will want to discuss behaviors to practice in general. When there are breakdowns in implementing new skillful behaviors, this can be a great opportunity to use cognitive strategies to identify and evaluate the inhibitory cognitions that prevented the behavior. All learning is valuable.

In addition, you will want to teach them how to recognize when the old modal response is being triggered, so they can engage in the new behavior in order to foster the new modal response. In Aiden's case, this involved developing a behavioral response that was more balanced than his over-reaching or frantic reassurance seeking behaviors. This involved developing a skillset that did not reinforce the paradigm of his value being dependent on how he felt other people were treating him. We drew out the behaviors of someone whose value was not contingent on other people liking them and we used behavioral strategies to increase those behaviors. As he learned to be more measured and to focus more on the behaviors that he was doing for himself, his mood improved and so did his relationships.

Distress Tolerance Work

Often behaviors and thoughts need to change before feelings catch up. Core belief work involves confronting fears, takings risks, tolerating discomfort, and inhibiting safety behaviors. All of this can be difficult work that can be aided by the use of various skills. The goal is to find skills that facilitate skillful behavior. Across the broad umbrella of cognitive and behavioral therapy, there are a number of helpful skills to draw from. The idea is to use whatever skills you are good at teaching and that work well for your clients. Our chapter on getting started covered the basics of skills training.

Pros and Cons

A classic strategy for working with core beliefs is to weigh the pros and cons of the belief (Leahy, 2017). This strategy can be done in a few ways. You can directly evaluate the advantages and disadvantages of the core belief. You can also evaluate the

Target strongly held belief that we are evaluating:

How does this help me?	How does this hurt me?
Are there additional benefits that come from believing this belief?	Are there additional costs that come from believing this belief?
Are there additional benefits that come from behaving as if this belief was true?	Are there additional costs that come from behaving as if this belief was true?

Consider rating the items by importance (1–10, with 10 being top importance) or by duration (short-term and long-term)

What are the short-term and long-term trends for the effect this belief has on my life?

Does this belief help me move towards my goals and ambitions?

Does believing this belief me cause me to behave in a manner that ends up supporting the belief? (self-fulfilling prophecy)

What is the lesson from this exercise? & What do I want to do about it?

Consider doing a second form with the new balanced belief you have been trying to build up

Figure 11.2 Pros and Cons of Core Beliefs

believing of the belief (defusion) or the acting in accordance with the belief (schema-dependent behavior). You can also extend the exercise to weigh the pros and cons of the new alternate belief, believing the new alternate belief, and of the behaviors that would line up with the new belief.

Two-Chair Work

Two-chair work, also called empty chair work, is a classic strategy for emotion-focused therapy or schema therapy. It is also commonly used in other therapeutic approaches such as Gestalt therapy. As there are a number of different theoretical orientations that utilize two-chair work, there is a diversity of thought regarding how it works. Broadly, when targeting core beliefs, the various explanations can be collapsed under the concept of a corrective emotional experience (Yalom, 1995). That is to say that modifications to early schema are being made via experiential methods that are well suited to increasing emotional activation and engagement (see Padesky, 1994).

There are a number of ways to do chair work. When a therapist is targeting change in core beliefs or schemas, they are typically working with a client who has more awareness and a more balanced perspective (i.e., insight) of their early adversity than their younger self did. The chair work will typically involve a conversation between the current version of themselves and younger version of themselves, where the current version of themselves explains context or elements to their younger self that would have improved the situation then (e.g., context about why something they internalized early on as being their fault was not actually their fault).

The key question to address is "What is it that you think you needed at that time but did not get?" The chair work can be targeted at emotionally processing that unmet need and then meeting that need now; this is the corrective emotional experience. Sometimes, this can expand to a three chair work, where the older self coaches the younger self to be more effective, skillful, or assertive in a difficult interaction; also creating a corrective emotional experience. See Pugh (2018) for a more comprehensive guide to cognitive behavioral chair work.

Letters

Letters can be an alternative to chair work. This is often less emotionally intense than chair work (possibly making it less impactful). People can write letters to their younger self, people who are deceased, or even their future self. This can also be used as a way to collect someone's thoughts before they later engage in chair work. With Aiden's case, this strategy was used to help him convey to a much younger version of himself ideas related to a healthier masculinity, his imagery of being the mountain, and some of the non-conditional love he had not experienced at that age. Keep in mind the goal of a corrective emotional experience. We want to evoke the emotion associated with the early maladaptive schema, activate that early schema, and then activate and induce corrective experiences, information, and emotions, to bring about cognitive and emotional change. Therefore, this cannot be done as a purely rational task; emotional activation and engagement are the reason this works at the deep level in which it does.

Imagery Rescripting

Rescripting strategies are somewhat controversial, in that clinicians can see them as being counter to accepting reality; however, there is good evidence that they work (Reimer & Moscovitch, 2015). It is useful for a therapist to know what their options are. Rescripting strategies are often used to target painful or distressing memories of formative moments. It is important to make a distinction between traumas and adversity. There are a number of events that people will describe as being "traumatic," that are not actually traumas. Those are good targets for rescripting strategies. When the memories are of actual traumas, you might first consider using a dose of a trauma-focused therapy.

Imagery rescripting (see Holmes, Arntz, & Smucker, 2007) can comprise either trying to alter a previous memory to soften the memory or by creating new images altogether. The Imagery Rehearsal Therapy (IRT; Krakow & Zadra, 2006; Waltman, Shearer, & Moore, 2018) model can be a useful method for rescripting. First, you have the client write out a narrative of what happened. Then you modify that narrative in a way that is mutually acceptable. This can involve larger changes such as having the client respond in a more effective manner (i.e., changing what they did), having them have had a more effective interpretation or internal response at the time (i.e., changing how they felt), or extending the story to a later point where the bad thing had happened but they were still doing well in the big picture (i.e., changing the subjective ending to emphasize it is now over and did not define them). The IRT model is where you construct both narratives together and then you have the client review the rescripted narrative daily to help with the uptake of the new image.

Across-Session Strategies

There are also larger across-therapy strategies that we use across sessions to facilitate schematic modification. Most of these strategies are elaborations or extensions of strategies previously covered in this book.

Evidence Logging

This strategy targets someone's attentional filter. We teach them to attend to the elements of evidence they have been missing. If your client has had a tendency to discount the positives, we will have them track and log what they have been missing. If they have a tendency to catastrophize, we will have them track and log all the times they were afraid something terrible would happen and it did not happen.

The ideal type of evidence of which to keep a running log is the evidence that supports the new belief you are building up (Padesky, 1994). Typically, you will first need to teach a client to notice these elements. Often, this is first done with you pointing out discrepant or new experiences in session. After you have done this a few times, you can demonstrate the types of evidence the client has typically missed or not held onto. From there, you can have them start tracking these (and similar) elements in a log that they use in an ongoing manner. You can review the log at the beginning of your sessions and suggest items to be added when you find things that were missed during your therapy sessions. Across time, they develop a preponderance of evidence to support the new belief. This can also be a useful tool to have them review when they do not "feel" like the new belief is true. Impactful items on the list can be good candidates for the imagery strategies outlined above.

Core Belief-A/Core Belief-B

Core Belief-A/Core Belief-B is a strategy that is similar to the Hypothesis-A/Hypothesis-B strategy discussed in an earlier chapter. This is also similar to the evidence logging strategy above. The idea is you sort what happens and what they do into the categories of either supporting the previous core belief or the new core belief and you have them keep this log in an ongoing manner. This strategy is ideal when there is a mix of evidence where the previous belief is partially supported but the new belief is a better explanation of the overall evidence.

Reinforcing Skill Use

The strategy of selective reinforcement is an important part of this process. Each session you should be verbally reviewing their skillful behavior and providing reinforcement. Sometimes, increased connection with the therapist can be one of the strongest reinforcers we have. We want to teach them to self-reinforce. We also want to draw

Sort the evidence according to the belief it supports

Core Belief A	Core Belief B
What belief are we evaluating?	What alternative belief have we been considering?
Evidence that supports Core Belief A	Evidence that supports Core Belief B
Summary of Hypothesis A Evidence	Summary of Hypothesis B Evidence
Overall Summary	

Figure 11.3 Core Belief-A/Core Belief-B

out the natural reinforcers that accompany skillful behavior and help them see that connection.

Making Changes to the Environment

Earlier in treatment, we sought to influence the environment by increasing behaviors that were compatible with the belief (or new modal activation) we are building up. After the client has found some success at smaller changes, they often consider larger changes such as leaving unhealthy relationships, setting firmer interpersonal boundaries, going back to school, seeking promotions, seeking new jobs, or other lifestyle changes. Environmental changes can help reinforce the new belief, and as the saying goes, "Wherever you go, there you are" (Kabat-Zinn, 2006). This means that a change of circumstances might not be the complete solution they hope it to be—people tend to overestimate the impact that a change will have on how they feel (i.e., impact bias). Therefore, we want to reinforce autonomy and help our clients think through big decisions before they make them. We also want to keep up the other interventions we have been doing with them.

Fostering the More Adaptive Mode

In the later phases of core belief work or schema therapy, we focus on fostering a lifestyle consistent with the new mode we have developed. This includes the new belief, new pattern of thinking, new behavioral response, and the corresponding affect. As stressors and triggers come up, we teach the clients to disengage from the old mode and switch to the new modal response. This is often accomplished well through the use of imagery strategies, such as focusing on the image of a more successful self who has well developed the modal pattern of response. The imagery can also be focused on new discrepant experiences or other elements that help induce the mood state and activate the mode we are building up. As your clients continue to act in accordance with this mode, they will reinforce this belief and new way of being.

Objectives, Goals, Values, and Visions

As your clients increase their skillful behavior and let go of previous beliefs and assumptions, there is a space to clarify the objectives, goals, values, and visions they have for their future. Often as people begin to get in touch with a more authentic self and start to live a life that is less guided by fear, there is an opportunity to revisit what they want to make important in life and what they want out of life. Committed action and valued living (Hayes, 2005) are a great way to enrich their lives and strengthen the new belief system you have collaboratively built.

Summary

Core belief work or schema work is not inherently different from working with other cognitions; however, it can be a longer process. Effectively targeting core beliefs and schema can be approached as a multi-intervention process that involves cognitive, behavioral, experiential, and emotion-focused strategies to bring about change. Fostering the constellation of belief, behavior, emotion, and thought pattern (i.e., modal response) can make for a more impactful change of core beliefs or schema.

References

Beck, A. T. (1979). *Cognitive therapy and the emotional disorders.* New York: Meridian.
Beck, A. T., & Haigh, E. A. P. (2014). Advances in cognitive theory and therapy: The Generic Cognitive Model. *Annual Review of Clinical Psychology, 10,* 1–24. doi:10.1146/annurev-clinpsy-032813-153734
Bonezzi, A., Brendl, C. M., & Angelis, M. D. (2011) Stuck in the middle: The psychophysics of goal pursuit. *Psychological Science 22*(5), 607–612.
Bowen, S., Chawla, N., & Marlatt, G. A. (2011). *Mindfulness-based relapse prevention for addictive behaviors: A clinician's guide.* New York: Guilford Press.
Ellis, A., & Harper, R. A. (1961). *A guide to rational living.* Englewood Cliffs, NJ: Prentice-Hall.
Frost, R. (1915). A servant to servants. *North of Boston*. New York: Henry Holt.
Hayes, S. C. (2005). *Get out of your mind and into your life: The new acceptance and commitment therapy* (2nd ed.). Oakland, CA: New Harbinger Publications.
Holmes, E. A., Arntz, A., & Smucker, M. R. (2007). Imagery rescripting in cognitive behaviour therapy: Images, treatment techniques and outcomes. *Journal of Behavior Therapy and Experimental Psychiatry, 38*(4), 297–305.
James, I. A., & Barton, S. (2004). Changing core beliefs with the continuum technique. *Behavioural and Cognitive Psychotherapy, 32*(4), 431–442.
Kabat-Zinn, J. (2006). *Mindfulness for beginners.* Louisville, CO: Sounds True.
Krakow, B., & Zadra, A. (2006). Clinical management of chronic nightmares: imagery rehearsal therapy. *Behavioral Sleep Medicine,* 4(1), 45–70.
Leahy, R. L. (2017). *Cognitive therapy techniques: A practitioner's guide.* New York: Guilford Press.
Meichenbaum, D. H., & Goodman, J. (1971). Training impulsive children to talk to themselves: A means of developing self-control. *Journal of Abnormal Psychology, 77*(2), 115.
Padesky, C. A. (1994). Schema change processes in cognitive therapy. *Clinical Psychology & Psychotherapy, 1*(5), 267–278.
Padesky, C. A., & Mooney, K. A. (2012). Strengths-based cognitive-behavioural therapy: A four-step model to build resilience. *Clinical Psychology & Psychotherapy, 19*(4), 283–290.
Pugh, M. (2018). Cognitive behavioural chairwork. *International Journal of Cognitive Therapy, 11*(1), 100–116.
Reimer, S. G., & Moscovitch, D. A. (2015). The impact of imagery rescripting on memory appraisals and core beliefs in social anxiety disorder. *Behaviour Research and Therapy, 75,* 48–59.
Waltman, S. H., Rex, K. H., & Williams, A. (2011). Naturalistic examination of a training clinic: Is there a relationship between therapist perception and client self-report of treatment outcomes? *Graduate Student Journal of Psychology, 13,* 17–24.
Waltman, S. H., Shearer, D., & Moore, B. A. (2018). Management of post-traumatic nightmares: A review of pharmacologic and nonpharmacologic treatments since 2013. *Current Psychiatry Reports, 20*(12), 108.

Waltman, S., & Sokol, L. (2017). The Generic Cognitive Model of cognitive behavioral therapy: A case conceptualization-driven approach. In S. Hofmann & G. Asmundson (Eds.), *The science of cognitive behavioral therapy* (pp. 3–18). London: Academic Press.

Waltman, S. H., Williams, A., & Christiansen, L. R. (2013). Comparing student clinician and licensed psychologist clinical judgment. *Training and Education in Professional Psychology, 7*(1), 33.

Yalom, I. D. (1995). *The theory and practice of group psychotherapy.* New York: Basic Books.

Young, J. E. (1999). *Cognitive therapy for personality disorders: A schema-focused approach.* Sarasota, FL: Professional Resource Press.

Chapter 12

Socratic Dialectical Method

Using Cognitive and Socratic Strategies in Dialectical Behavior Therapy for Borderline Personality Disorder

Lynn M. McFarr and Scott H. Waltman

❖ CONTENTS

History of Dialectical Behavior Therapy and Cognitive Strategies

Although, Dr Linehan has insisted that dialectical behavior therapy (DBT) is a form of cognitive behavior therapy (CBT), she has also emphasized that it is not a traditional cognitive therapy in that there is not a focus on evaluating beliefs and it is not conceptualized from the cognitive model. From the perspective of DBT, the primary problem in borderline personality disorder (BPD) is in the emotion regulation system, and the treatment is conceptualized through a behavior therapy, Zen practice, and dialectical philosophy lens—not a cognitive model. Therefore, Socratic questioning would not routinely be considered a key intervention, in part because of the radical behavior therapy stance towards thoughts (i.e., just another behavior). An additional reason is the belief that cognitive restructuring could be perceived as being invalidating, and perhaps most importantly, the process seemed outside the capabilities of emotionally dysregulated people with BPD.

It is important to understand the historical relationship between cognitive strategies and DBT. The first DBT manual was published under the name of cognitive behavioral treatment for BPD (Linehan, 1993); however, this was likely a use of the *Effectively* skill, as in 1993, CBT was dominant and fewer people knew what DBT was. This title (and good science) helped Linehan reach the masses. DBT is more of a behavior therapy than is CBT. From the perspective of radical behavioral therapy, cognitions are viewed as behaviors (Linehan, 1993), and behaviors are best targeted by addressing the contingencies, which does not include cognitive restructuring. Additionally, in keeping with the DBT model for BPD developing out of a combination of a biological vulnerability and an invalidating environment, thoughts are not seen as causative for BPD but more epiphenomenal (i.e., people do not have BPD because they have extreme thinking, rather they have extreme thinking because they have BPD)—this being another reason for the historical lack of focus on cognitive modification in DBT.

The second pillar of DBT, Zen practice, is focused on accepting and being mindful of thoughts rather than evaluating or changing them. However, the third pillar, dialectics, is a philosophical stance that, as most philosophies are, is a method of problem solving and debate, and essentially a world view. The practice of dialectics is analogous to "thinking in shades of grey" from CBT, with a major conceptual difference. In DBT this practice is called *walking the middle path* and it focuses on dialectics to acknowledge the truth in both sides (i.e., truth in the black and truth in the white). Dialectical thinking is focused on coming up with a synthesis that honors opposing truths—a very cognitive process.

Although the most obvious dialectic in DBT is the balance between acceptance (Zen practice) and change (behavioral science), There is also a dialectical tension between acceptance (mindfulness of thoughts) and change strategies (check the facts) regarding targeting cognitions and their role in emotion dysregulation. Without resolving this, the practice of cognitive strategies (which have always been part of DBT) have been an uneasy fit and any additions (beyond the ones on the original text) are highly debated. In this chapter, we illustrate how cognitive strategies, particularly the use of Socratic questioning, can strengthen and enhance DBT, in a manner that is model-consistent.

Potential Barrier to Using "C" in DBT

Philosophical and theoretical assumptions aside, there are very good practical reasons why DBT was designed as a radically behavioral therapy and thoughts were not historically considered a primary avenue of intervention. Using cognitive change strategies with a population that has problems with emotional dysregulation and a history of invalidation can be challenging, as we will review below.

Potential Barriers: Dysregulation

van Elst and colleagues (2003) found frontolimbic brain abnormalities in patients with borderline personality disorder in a volumetric magnetic resonance imaging study. This would be suggestive of a possible correlate of impulsivity and aggressive behavior. People with BPD have been found to have problems with emotion regulation secondary to hyper-activation of the amygdala in response to emotional stimuli (Paret et al., 2016). Functional magnetic resonance imaging studies have demonstrated this hyper-activation in real-time (Paret et al., 2016).

A recent study demonstrated this more rapid increase in distress and longer episodes of aversive tension (Stiglmayr, Grathwol, Linehan, Ihorst, Fahrenberg, & Bohus, 2005). The study provides support for the theory that patients with BPD experience more frequent, stronger, and longer-lasting states of aversive tension, with perceptions of rejection, being alone, and failure being the three most common pathways to dysregulation.

It is important to understand how emotional dysregulation affects the Socratic process. Practitioners of CBT will commonly draw out a simple triangle to demonstrate the interaction between thoughts, feelings, and behaviors. The basic idea is that how you are thinking affects how you are feeling, but the arrows actually go both ways and how we are feeling also affects how we are thinking. So, extreme emotional dysregulation leads to extreme thinking, where it is difficult to consider alternatives. In addition, when people are emotionally flooded, often new learning is not occurring.

Potential Barriers: Invalidation

There is a risk of invalidation when employing Socratic strategies with this population. Change strategies, by their very nature is invalidating of the client's current condition. Since clients with BPD are exquisitely sensitive to invalidation, even the most well-meaning therapist attempting Socratic questioning may be countered with hostility, shutting down, or other avoidance behaviors.

An important context to keep in mind is the likely historical wounds of growing up in an invalidating environment. Your client has likely had their views and beliefs harshly and punitively invalidated by other people, prior to their coming in for therapy. This can lead to an increased sensitivity to being invalidated. Or, they may have internalized this invalidation and they might shift to a harsh self-stance when you initially start evaluating a thought. It is likely that they have received repeated communication that *they* are the problem; their thoughts, their emotions, or their behaviors are too much. Therefore, an examination of beliefs, even if gentle, can be experienced in the following way: "Oh great, one more person telling me it's me, it's all in my head." Or, they might harshly self-invalidate: "I know this isn't true, what's wrong with me that I can't do this?" This leads to shame spiraling and possible in-session disassociation.

Additionally, when the rigid, judgmental beliefs that clients with BPD hold about themselves and their environments are elucidated through the process of Socratic questioning, this may trigger a significant shame response. They may feel judged by the very questions, judge themselves, and engage in self-invalidation. The primary emotion of shame can quickly turn to a secondary emotion of anger towards the impetus of the shame, which might be you as the clinician. As one can imagine, this would interfere with any clinician's ability to utilize Socratic questioning in session. Additionally, this can shape the clinician's behavior and make them less likely to attempt Socratic strategies in the future.

Potential Barriers: Oversimplification of Problem Solving

Another barrier to this practice is a phenomenon known as oversimplification of problem solving (Linehan, 1987). In DBT, clients can engage in behavioral strategies known as "apparent competence," in which they truly believe that they have a grasp on situations and can handle the intervention, the homework, the exploration of thoughts. However, the task actually outstrips their capabilities, which can lead to shame and avoidance. This can happen in the Socratic process by clients expressing understanding and insight about the cognitive content, and any homework that may result from it. But later they are incapable of producing the results both therapist and client agreed upon and can become angry and self-loathing.

Another way in which self-invalidation may take form in session around Socratic questioning is that the client may engage in what is referred to as the oversimplification of problem solving. That is, the client (and clinician) may come up with explanations or solutions that are superficial and unlikely to solve the problem. This can happen in the process of Socratic questioning where both clinician and client can prematurely agree that they have "gotten to the bottom of it" when they have only just scratched the surface. Other times, the new alternate thought sounds nice, but it is not actually believable or reflective of the facts. Overly positive or implausibly positive beliefs set the client up for failure as they do not match the realities of life. This results in emotional crashing, when the brittle belief falls apart outside of session.

Exchange between Linehan and Beck at ABCT

Circa 2004, at the annual meeting of the Association for Behavioral and Cognitive Therapies (ABCT), then called the Association for the Advancement of Behavioral Therapies (AABT), the originator of cognitive therapy, Dr Aaron T. Beck, and the originator of DBT, Dr Marsha Linehan, had an exchange where they discussed the use of Socratic questioning with people who have persistent emotional dysregulation. Marsha asked Tim point blank, "How can you do Socratic questioning with a high dysregulated person?" He said, "You can't. At that point just tell them what to do." This suggesting a consensus among key experts that tradition Socratic strategies vis-à-vis cognitive therapy strategies do not work with people who are acutely highly emotionally dysregulated. Therefore, attempting to use unmodified traditional cognitive therapy strategies with this population is not advised. The purpose of this chapter is to demonstrate what strategies will work with this population and how to use them in practical terms.

But Isn't "C" Already in DBT?

Absolutely, standard DBT incorporates cognitive strategies. There is a whole subsection on cognitive modification procedures in the change procedures chapters in the original DBT text (Linehan, 1993); though, the cognitive strategies found in the core strategies chapters are the cognitive validation strategies (Linehan, 1993). The new skills manual has an entire worksheet and handout devoted to checking the facts, suggesting an increased openness to using cognitive change strategies in DBT. In the first edition of the DBT text, Linehan acknowledges the use of cognitive strategies, "Many of the DBT strategies require the therapist (*implicitly*, if not explicitly) to identify, challenge, and confront problematic beliefs, assumptions, theories, judgmental evaluations, and tendencies to think rigidly and in absolute and extreme terms (i.e., non-dialectical thinking)" (Linehan, 1993; p. 366; emphasis added).

The key here is that the emphasis was on implicitly undermining beliefs over time through a change in the relationship to thoughts. There are number of proven cognitive elements already found in DBT, including teaching cognitive self-observation, checking the facts, targeting myths about emotions, and dialectical thinking.

Teaching Cognitive Self-Observation

As we discussed in an earlier chapter, the first step in learning to use cognitive Socratic change strategies effectively is learning to be more aware of your thought processes. This self-monitoring process is essential to good cognitive work. In DBT, this skill is embedded in the mindfulness skills, so that clients learn to observe and describe their thoughts. In DBT, there are also some cognitive defusion strategies that go with observing thoughts, but not becoming entangled by them. Another chapter in this text will more directly target the use of defusion strategies from a Socratic framework.

Check the Facts

Checking the facts is the most obvious cognitive change strategies. In DBT, checking the facts is part of the emotion regulation module; however, it is used in a different way than traditional cognitive therapists would use it. Traditional cognitive therapists would state that emotion dysregulation is a product of extreme thinking (e.g., the use of all-or-nothing thinking), and the cognitive therapist would target that thinking to bring about emotional change. In DBT, checking the facts is used to see whether the emotional experience fits the facts of the situation, in order to then determine the best behavioral strategy (opposite action or problem solving) to improve the situation and bring about emotional regulation through behavior change.

Myths about Emotions

DBT includes some cognitive type interventions that target people's beliefs about emotions. This is similar to what a cognitive therapist might do if they were using a framework such as emotional schema therapy (see Leahy, 2018). Although the format for addressing myths about emotion in DBT is mostly didactic, it does target beliefs about emotions, which can bring about cognitive change.

Dialectical Thinking

Thesis, antithesis, and synthesis are the three common elements that are considered in dialectical philosophy; however, there is some controversy in the field of philosophy regarding the best way to use and understand dialectics (Mueller, 1958). A common criticism is that there is a pitfall of deliberately focusing on counterpropositions that are seemingly the opposite of the proposition in order to create a paradox to be resolved. Although dialectics can be used to resolve paradoxical situations, its purpose is to find the truth by synthesizing that which is found in different perspectives (Mueller, 1958).

Therapists, patients, and sometimes family members are taught to walk the middle path and to hold onto dialectical thinking as a world view and means of resolving disputes and distressing thoughts. Learning to use these strategies is a cognitive change strategy, even if one of the core dialectics consists of change and acceptance. Many would argue that acceptance is a cognitive change strategy in itself.

Limits to Current Socratic Strategies in Standard DBT

The thought record is perhaps the most commonly used cognitive change strategy in CBT (see Waltman, Frankel, Hall, Williston, & Jager-Hyman, 2019). In DBT, instead of thought records, there are chain analyses, which functionally are a series of thought records. A traditional thought record focused on evaluating a single automatic thought is one link in the chain; a chain analysis involves looking at a chain of links. This focus on the overall chain analysis instead of the individual links made sense for a number of reasons. First, knowing which link to focus on without first doing a chain analysis can be difficult when working with people who have BPD. Context is important here. Remember the biological findings related to more rapid increases in distress and longer episodes of aversive tension (Stiglmayr et al., 2005). Patients with BPD experience more frequent, stronger, and longer-lasting states of aversive tension. This can result in smaller difficulties leading to larger problems, as lingering and building aversive tension makes patterns of thinking and behavior more extreme, which often results in major emotional or behavioral problems. The strategy of the chain analysis is to look at how that process builds and culminates, with the goal being to learn to intervene early in the chain with a different behavior derived from the solution analysis. Additionally, the focus on chain analyses over thought records made sense in light of the thinking that people with BPD would not be able to do cognitive restructuring when they were highly dysregulated (see above).

Do We Need "C" in DBT?

So, given all of the potential barriers, why would anyone even consider enhancing DBT with additional cognitive interventions? Particularly with the most difficult CBT strategy to learn? Guided discovery and Socratic questioning have been found to be possibly the most difficult CBT strategy to learn (see overview of framework chapter & Waltman, Hall, McFarr, Beck, & Creed, 2017).

One reason for considering bolstering the cognitive strategies in DBT relates to suicidal ideation. DBT has been shown to be effective at reducing problem behaviors such as suicide attempts (Cristea, Gentili, Cotet, Palomba, Barbui, & Cuijpers, 2017). Also, DBT outperforms treatment as usual in decreasing suicidal behaviors and non-suicidal self-injury (Panos, Jackson, Hasan, & Panos, 2014). Further, standard DBT with DBT skills training appears to be more effective than DBT-informed therapy without skills training (Linehan et al., 2015). At the same time, a recent meta-analysis has demonstrated that while DBT is effective for reducing suicidal behaviors, a corresponding reduction in suicidal ideation has not been observed (DeCou, Comtois, & Landes, 2019). The researchers speculated that this might be due to the emphasis on changing behaviors over changing thoughts in DBT; similarly, they pointed out that fewer researchers focus on reporting suicidal ideation, so future research is certainly needed on the topic (DeCou et al., 2019).

This is a good reason to consider pulling in more cognitive strategies to target chronic risk factors such as suicidal ideation. If we have effective interventions from other treatments (i.e. Socratic questioning in CBT), shouldn't we be using those to help reduce suicide risk in clients with BPD? CBT is effective for reducing suicidal ideation. (e.g. Alavi, Sharifi, Ghanizadeh, & Dehbozorgi, 2013). Given what is at stake and the mission of DBT, we should be willing to use any and all effective strategies to strengthen the effect of the treatment, as long it does not violate the basic tenants of the treatment. One cannot simply change a well-studied therapy and assume that the added component does not make a difference when assessing the scientific base for the treatment. Fortunately, adding Socratic questioning to DBT would not violate the radical behavior theoretical base given that thoughts should be just as amenable to assessment as any other behavior.

Other Treatments for Borderline Personality Disorder that Include Cognitive Components

Reviewing the cognitive components from other treatment packages can help demonstrate the need and potential feasibility of using cognitive strategies with populations that have high levels of emotional dysregulation.

Traditional Cognitive Therapy

Clinicians have applied traditional cognitive therapy to BPD (see Layden, Newman, Freeman, & Morse, 1993); notably, the clinical trial of cognitive therapy for BPD used a protocol that had an uncanny resemblance to a DBT skills manual (see Brown,

Newman, Charlesworth, Crits-Christoph, & Beck, 2004). Early cognitive therapy for BPD texts had a main cognitive intervention called rational responding where you ask your client to come up with a more rational response as a way to cognitively restructure. The trouble with this approach is that folks with BPD can often think of a more logical response, they just don't believe it because it does not match their emotional experience. Other cognitive therapy strategies might include imagery to increase the emotional salience of the rational response (Layden et al., 1993), which can be a helpful strategy.

Schema Therapy

Schema therapy (ST) was initially developed due to a need to better explain and address problems such as those seen in patients with BPD. The concept of modes was first introduced in the ST literature to account for rapid changes in the presentation of clients with BPD. Schema therapists noted that when these patients became dysregulated, they would have extreme thinking patterns, high emotional activation, and engage in impulsive behaviors (see Fassbinder, Schweiger, Martius, Brand-de Wilde, & Arntz, 2016). Alternatively, when these people were regulated, their thinking would not be extreme, their emotions would not be elevated, and their behavior would not be impulsive (these different presentations representing different modal states; see Fassbinder et al., 2016).

In ST, the therapist works to bring about emotion regulation and change by providing a corrective experience via the therapeutic relationship, cognitive change via a distancing strategy (i.e., defusion via a perspective taking task), and then focusing on changing the behavioral response (Fassbinder et al., 2016). A schema therapist works to help the client disengage from the ineffective mode and build up the more effective alternative mode; however, the method of doing this is quite different in ST as opposed to DBT: "A core difference between the two approaches is that DBT directly focuses on the acquisition of emotion regulation skills, whereas ST does seldom address emotion regulation directly" (Fassbinder et al., 2016, p. 1).

A schema therapist may use a number of cognitive strategies that are similar to those used by a traditional cognitive therapist. Additionally, a schema therapist will conduct a functional analysis of the historical function of the schema/mode, draw out the likely outcome of not changing, and focus on building up a more adaptive modal response. Imagery and experiential strategies can also be an important part of this work (Jacob & Arntz, 2013). The chapter on working with core beliefs in this text will also touch on other ST strategies.

Mode Deactivation Therapy

Another cognitive therapy used in the treatment of people with emotional regulation problems is mode deactivation therapy (MDT), which was born out of CBT and has elements of DBT (i.e., validation) integrated into it. Functionally, it is an eclectic therapy (Apsche, 2010). MDT is most often used with youths who have conduct problems or legal involvements. The main intervention from MDT is a modified cognitive restructuring process call Validation–Clarification–Redirection (VCR; Apsche, 2010). The developer of the treatment found that they had difficulty applying traditional cognitive therapy to populations with emotional lability and behavioral impulsivity. Notably, their description of CBT is a straw man's argument of CBT being overly rigid, purely rational, and confrontational—to apply their model to their description of CBT, a clarification to this perception is that perhaps "bad CBT" did not work well with people who have emotional lability and behavioral impulsivity.

The general flow of the VCR method is largely therapist led. First, the therapist provides validation regarding the possible elements of truth in the statement being evaluated. Next, the therapist provides clarification that there are other possible explanations that could be true, and there is a pull towards softening or decreasing the extremity of the perception. Finally, the therapist redirects the client to a functional alternative belief (FAB) that is in keeping with a behavioral response that is consistent with the treatment goals or client's life goals.

Common Elements of Cognitive Strategies across Treatments for BPD

While there is a good diversity among cognitive change strategies, there are common elements that increase the likelihood of the effective use of cognitive strategies with this population:

- Emphasis on validation
- Emphasis on relationship
- Use of the relationship to bring about cognitive change
- Use of imagery
- Focus on cognitive shifts that will produce effective behavior
- Experiential work
- Two-chair work
- Distancing and defusion strategies

How Can We Improve the "C" in DBT?

While previous research has demonstrated frontolimbic brain abnormalities in patients with borderline personality disorder—this being associated with emotional dysregulation and behavioral disinhibition (van Elst et al., 2003). Imaging studies have also demonstrated that if we can teach people with BPD to downregulate their dysregulation (with DBT skills training; see Bohus & Wolf-Arehult, 2012 as cited in Paret et al., 2016), amygdala activation decreases in-the-moment and that amygdala-lateral-prefrontal cortex connections can change over time (Paret et al., 2016).

This is important to the ordering of interventions with this population. Traditional cognitive therapists working with a neurotypical population would use cognitive restructuring to achieve emotional regulation; whereas, traditional DBT therapists use fact checking in order to determine which behavioral strategy will lead to emotional regulation. We are suggesting a third option for therapists who want to target cognitive change in session. The challenge we face is that we need to get the client regulated prior to cognitive strategies. Therefore, there are new methods for both practitioners of CBT and DBT when using these strategies. We will look at how to use the skills that already exist in DBT in different configurations to bring about cognitive change with Socratic methods. To be consistent to the DBT model that cognitive change is then connected to the ultimate goal of behavior change.

New Strategy: Capitalizing on a Key Strategy

Behavioral Chain Analysis

Functional analysis, sometimes called behavioral analysis or chain analysis, is a tool for understanding a behavior (Waltman, 2015); it is also the principal skill used in individual DBT sessions. The goals of chain analysis are to identify what stimuli are prompting a behavior and what contingencies are reinforcing that behavior (Ferster, 1972; Lewon & Hayes, 2014; Skinner, 1957). Functional analysis is typically considered to be an assessment tool; however, it can also be used as a clinical intervention (Linehan, 1993). In other words, chain analysis is used to hypothesize the function of a behavior. The results of a functional analysis produce a "functional diagnosis" (Yoman, 2008, p. 331), which informs the treatment targets—clinicians strategically target the mechanisms that are thought to be maintaining the problem.

Skinner (1983) once argued that psychology needed functional analysis. The chain analysis predates behavior therapy (Yoman, 2008) and occupies a central role in the behavioral therapies. Functional analysis is typically considered to be an assessment tool and has been shown to be effective in inpatient, outpatient, home, and school-based treatment settings; however, it can also be used as a clinical intervention (Linehan, 1993), and it is assumed that every individual (1:1) DBT session will include a chain analysis.

What does this have to do with Socratic questioning? Functional analysis is typically concerned with behavior and Socratic questioning is typically concerned with thoughts. Practitioners of both methods are interested in developing a deeper understanding of the contingencies that cause problems to maintain. The process of chain analysis is similar to Socratic methods in that in both instances, the therapist is encouraged to take the stance of a "Naïve Observer." That is, the therapist should not assume that they understand how the client gets from one link in the chain to the next, much in same the way a therapist engaging in guided discovery does not assume the final destination of the exploration of the thought. This process also typifies collaborative empiricism (Tee & Kazantzis, 2011) in that the dyad is jointly discovering.

Cognitive Chain Analysis

The skills required to complete a cognitive chain analysis are very similar to those required to complete a chain analysis, and this makes for an ideal strategy from the perspective of both the therapist and the client.

How to Do It: Cognitive Chain Analysis

Step 1: Do a Regular Behavioral Chain Analysis

This step is covered well in several other texts and the assumption is that DBT therapists will have a good handle on this step. See Rizvi and Ritschel (2014) for a more elaborate review on how to conduct a chain analysis.

Step 2: Watch for Themes in Thoughts that Lead to Target Behaviors

It is recommended with this population that the use of Socratic questioning be anchored to a specific behavior rather than extrapolating the thought and looking at it as an abstract construct. This is prudent given how the mantra of "follow the affect" is often not advised with this population. Therefore, instead of finding which thought is associated with the most intense emotion, we want to see which thought is leading to our target behavior (or preventing more skillful behavior). This is, in part, to keep the intervention anchored to the target behavior, which helps maintain the focus of the treatment on eliminating problematic behaviors. In the following example, we see how the therapist uses Socratic strategies as part of a chain analysis to identify a potential thought on which to focus and then establishes a connection between that thought and the problem behavior.

Therapist: So, when you ended up yelling at your friend on Thursday sounds like the prompting event was her getting off the phone with you quickly. You called her back and yelled.

Client: Yes

Therapist: And what was the consequence?

Client: She hung up and hasn't talked to me since,

Therapist: Okay take me through this. When she got off the phone quickly what went through your head?

Client: She doesn't want to talk to me

Therapist: And if that were true, that would mean what?

Client: That she isn't my friend

Therapist: And if that were true, what?

Client: That I have no friends

Therapist: And why would that be?

Client: Because I am unlovable

Therapist: So, you were having lots of negative, judgmental thoughts
Okay so how do you get from there to calling her back and yelling?

Client: Because it is unfair that she got off the phone when I needed her.

Therapist: So, you told yourself what?

Client: I've got to tell her it's unfair.

Therapist: And you were hoping if you told her it was unfair what would happen?

Client: I don't know, I felt like I had to.

Therapist: Or what would happen?

Client: I would explode.
Therapist: Because the emotion was?
Client: Anger
Therapist: And right under the anger?
Client: So, so much hurt
Therapist: So, it seems like the function of the behavior was to communicate your hurt and anger in the hopes that communicating would do what for you?
Client: She'd hear how hurt I was.
Therapist: How did that go?
Client: She didn't. She hung up.
Therapist: Right. Were you communicating "hurt?"
Client: No. I was just being angry.
Therapist: Here's the thing. By communicating anger and people hanging up on you, do you think you feel more lovable?
Client: Oh, God no
Therapist: Alright
Client: But I am never going to feel loveable.
Therapist: I think holding on to that belief will sure have an impact on how you act.

Step 3: Collaboratively Test If There Is a Connection between the Target Thought and the Problem Behavior

The question to address here is whether they see a connection between this thought and the behavior. Socratic questioning then can be used to enhance the understanding of the internal contingencies that reinforce or perpetuate the behavior. Standard questions and elements of a typical chain analysis would involve looking at what someone was thinking and feeling before the target behavior occurred. Thoughts related to perceptions of threat often include mental images or predictions of what someone thinks will happen. One of the best ways to collaboratively test whether there is a connection between the target thought and the problem behavior is to review previous chain analyses. If a common pattern is observed, then a rationale for targeting the thought can be easily made.

Step 4: Evaluate the Thought in the Solution Analysis Using Traditional Socratic and Dialectical Strategies

As people with persistent emotion dysregulation are given to failures in dialectical thinking, you might choose to use the Socratic Dialectical Method Thought Record presented later in this chapter or other strategies found elsewhere in this book. Clinicians will want to look for missing context and to highlight gaps in knowledge. Another chapter will focus on Socratic strategies for therapists who are using Acceptance and Commitment Therapy and those may be useful for targeting cognitions related to nonacceptance or willfulness. A guiding principle in the evaluation of a thought is "Is it true and is it helpful?" Evaluating the impact of a belief is a way to evaluate the helpfulness of the thought: "How does believing this thought make you feel? "And then what do you do?" "Will believing this thought make it easier to accomplish your goal?" "What are the short-term and long-term consequences of believing this thought?"

The basic idea here is that you are asking the client what *believable* belief would help them have the type of reaction that would be skillful. Notably, this might need to be a perspective of radical acceptance. If you consider the A-B-C model of Antecedent-Belief-Consequence. The antecedent of the situation has already been determined and so we ask the client: "What type of emotional and behavioral consequence do you want to have?" "And what plausible belief would you need to help you get there?" A Socratic practitioner using DBT will be focused on developing perspectives that facilitate skillful behavior. Increases in skillful behavior will lead to improvements in their life, resulting in new experiences which can be used to reinforce previous Socratic evaluations.

Step 5: Foster Behaviors and Skills that Are Consistent with the More Adaptive Thought

We are aiming to bring about cognitive modification, but we don't want only to increase insight without a corresponding change in behavior; DBT is a behavioral therapy. Ideally, we want to connect the new cognition with an action plan to do something different this week as part of a solution analysis to (1) align behaviors with their new perspective, (2) help the client engage in goal-directed behavior, or (3) gather evidence to test out the new belief.

Longer Example of a Cognitive Chain Analysis

Another typical DBT interaction around suicide ideation is to say directly "There's no evidence that people who are dead have better lives than people who are alive." This is a fair enough statement that usually does function to give the patient a new perspective. You can see an example of a variation of this statement in a later clinical example in this chapter. This statement delivered in an irreverent manner serves two functions in DBT: (1) to jar the patient and get them off their current emotional track; and (2) to provide an alternative, unorthodox view of death. As you will see in the later example, the therapist can build on this statement with Socratic methods to target directly a reduction in suicidal ideation and change in behavior.

Socratic questioning is thought to lead to a deeper level of cognitive change (Beck, 2011), and has been found to be predictive of reductions in depression (Braun, Strunk, Sasso, & Cooper, 2015). Empirically, there is a question of whether using Socratic strategies to help the client take a new perspective on the situation would be more impactful than providing the irreverent statement. It may be that directly providing the balanced thought without a guided discovery or Socratic process is not as effective with patients with BPD, which may contribute to the lack of movement on suicidal ideation in patients receiving DBT (see DeCou et al., 2019).

Below is an example of how a therapist could use Socratic methods and the cognitive chain analysis to target a reduction in suicidal ideation and increase in skillful behavior. This strategy would be used after basic safety planning, making the environment safe, and a good dose of DBT. This strategy is recommended for use with thoughts connected with suicidal ideation or self-harm behaviors that did not shape with standard behavioral chain analyses.

Therapist: So, I notice the thought that keeps coming on this chain is that if you kill yourself, your pain will be over. Like it did Friday.

Client: Yes, of course

Therapist: Well, I don't know of course. It seems when you have this thought and believe it, you are way more likely to engage in suicidal behavior.

Client: Well, yes, it's an out. I would love a do over on this life. The one I am in sucks.

Therapist: And when you thought it Friday, what happened? Did your urge to die raise or lower?

Client: Raised

Therapist: OK, so, when you had that thought, your urge to die increased. And you are telling me you think that dying would solve your problem. What problem would it solve?

Client: All of them. I'd be dead.

Therapist: How do you know it would solve your problem?

Client: I'd be dead.

Therapist: How do you know being dead will solve your problems?

Client: Well, death is the end of your life so the problems in your life would definitely be over.

Therapist: How do you know? Seriously what's the evidence?

Client: Well science has something to say.

Therapist: Okay let's take science. Does science have anything definitive to say about what happens after death? Has it ever been published in a journal or even The NY Times?

Client: No

Therapist: Seems also that you believe in some kind of afterlife since you were talking about a "do-over."

Client: Yeah, maybe I believe a little bit in reincarnation.

Therapist: OK, so, let's go with that. The thought is, If I die, I will be reincarnated and I won't have these problems." What do you know about reincarnation?

Client: Not that much

Therapist: OK, so depending on your belief system, you kind of have to learn the same lessons over and over. Or you go down on the ladder of enlightenment. Like you come back as a snake or centipede.

Client: Oh, I wouldn't want that.

Therapist: And, you wouldn't have me to help you with it! So, the thought that underlies your suicidal ideation and keeps it going is the belief that your problems would be solved by dying, right?

Client: Yes

Therapist: Yes, and what are you taking from this piece of work?

Client: That it rests on the idea that death means the end of problems, but if we really think about it we don't know for sure that it's true.

Therapist: OK, how much do you believe that on a scale of 0–100?

Client: About 85%
Therapist: What does the other 15% say?
Client: Maybe I am willing to take her chance that we are wrong
Therapist: Because you do still kind of believe it will work?
Client: Yeah
Therapist: And when you were dysregulated on Friday, how much did you believe it?
Client: Oh, like 100
Therapist: OK, so, I don't want to pretend this is an easy fix. And I kind of think that's the problem.
What's the thought that's right under "if I die it will solve my problems" the world should work that way because …
Client: My problems should be solvable.
Therapist: Why should they be?
Client: I deserve to have an easy fix.
Therapist: Right. Why?
Client: Because, I am a good person and shitty things have happened to me and I deserve a break.
Therapist: OK, so, see the problem? It's not just that you think suicide will solve the problems. You also think that you should have an easy fix for the problems you have. Makes sense that a solution like suicide might be appealing then?
Client: Yeah, hadn't thought of it like that.
Therapist: And, if I had an easy answer, I would give it to you. I promise.
Client: Thanks
Therapist: I don't know though, have you ever run into easy answers for difficult problems?
Client: No, it is so unfair.
Therapist: Well we have that to talk about too.
But let's get back to this chain. You are having thoughts like, "Doing this will solve my problems." "My problems should be easy to solve." And, "If they aren't easy to solve, it's unfair." "I have had bad things happen and I deserve a break." Does that sum it up?
Client: Yes, pretty well
Therapist: And when you think all that, what are you steered towards doing?
Client: Suicide.
Therapist: Right. Is that what happened Friday?
Client: Yes, totally
Therapist: OK, so, if you are carrying around those thoughts, how motivated are you going be to solve the very hard problems of your life?
Client: Not very, obviously.
Therapist: And, that's where I think we keep getting stuck on the chain, we can come up with all sorts of great solutions but if you are holding onto the idea that you shouldn't be the one to solve them, then we are really not going far. Who do you think should be solving those problems for you?
Client: Well my dad to start with. And then probably Kyle.
Therapist: OK, so, do they agree they are responsible for solving your problems?

[*Undermining active passivity*]

Client: No, that's the problem.

Therapist: Are they ever going to agree?

Client: Probably not

Therapist: Seems like that might be undermining the whole thing. If you are sitting around waiting for them to agree to solve your problems the. How long will you be waiting?

Client: Forever

Therapist: Okay, so what do you want to do with this?

Client: I guess I will have to solve them, but I am not happy about it.

Therapist: Understood.

So, let's tie this back to Friday. How can you use this there?

Client: Well if I go down the rabbit hole of, "This is unfair and I shouldn't have to do this," I need to remind myself to not be so willful.

Therapist: Yes, I can see how this is getting at willfulness. Okay so what skills you could use there? [*Ensuing discussion of skills and solution analysis*]

Debrief

The therapist could have stuck with the straightforward behavioral problem solving and been directive about the "people who are dead don't have better lives" approach, but in this case, it wasn't just that, it was also that her problems should be easily solved and solved by someone else. In DBT terms, this is "active passivity"—the idea that clients will work actively to get the world to regulate them and solve their problems. This often stems from clients having little success trying to solve their own problems due to low frustration tolerance and a belief in the "should" related to oversimplified problem solving.

This Socratic questioning and cognitive chain analysis can be seen as part of the trouble shooting of the previous solution analyses that have not stopped the client from entertaining suicide as a solution. Socratic questioning was used in this case to elucidate the beliefs that kept the client from engaging and committing to the active problem solving. The importance of this is that troubleshooting the solution analysis is a neglected area of DBT and perhaps could bear the most fruit in terms of shaping behaviors. If we understand the beliefs that interfere with enacting behavioral solutions and target them, then we can increase the success of our solution analyses and improve the lives of our clients. The hope is that using dialectical and Socratic strategies to target these inhibitory beliefs will lead to lasting cognitive and behavioral change. The key step not to lose sight of is linking the strategies back to explicit behavioral plans as part of the solution analysis.

Socratic Dialectical Method Thought Record

A reading of the preceding chapters in this book will give you a better understanding of our framework for Socratic dialogue.

Step 1: Regulations Check

The first step in this process is to check and see how regulated your client is. In the DBT emotion regulation module, we use a 0–100 scale where 100 represents maximum emotionality and 0 represents an absence of emotion. Either extreme will not be effective. If they are dissociated, you might need to use some grounding skills to get them present and in the room with you (and themselves). If they are highly emotionally activated/dysregulated, you will want to coach them to use some in-session regulation skills with you. This typically consists of more than a few deep breaths and you could expect to spend around 15 minutes doing this if the emotions are intense. Something to watch for is a catastrophizing of the emotions not quickly coming down on their own. The optimal skill to use depends on the client and what you do well. Common strategies include diaphragmatic breathing, imagery, progressive muscle relaxation,

Regulation check: *On a scale from 0–100, how intense is your current emotional state? Consider using some of your regulation skills to bring the intensity down to a moderate level.*		
Proposition: (*What thought are we evaluating?*)		
Counterproposition(s): (*What is an alternate point of view we want to consider or evaluate?*) (*There might be a few counterpropositions to consider*)		
Check the Facts: *List out the facts below and check (✓) the columns the facts fit best with. A single fact could support multiple conclusions, so we want to list all the facts and see which conclusion has the most support.*	Proposition (✓)	Counter proposition(s) (✓)
Curiosity: *What are we missing? What do we not know? Is there important context missing from the above statements? Are there any exceptions we're forgetting about?*		
Summary: *How can we summarize the whole story?*		
Synthesis: *Connect together the different truthful elements with the term "AND"*		
Take-Away Message: *What's a more effective and believable statement?* *How can I apply that statement to my upcoming week?*		

Figure 12.1 Socratic Dialectical Method Thought Record

grounding, soothing with five senses, or mindfully sitting with the emotions. Some clients do well with a combination of strategies, and you will want them to practice what works outside of session as well.

Step 2: Define the Proposition

The next step is to identify what statement you are looking to evaluate. In dialectics, this term can be called the thesis or proposition (with the alternative perspective being the antithesis or counterproposition). Picking the right thought to pursue is important and an earlier chapter in this book will cover in detail how to identify the optimal cognitive targets.

In working with this population, there are at least three strategic targets: (1) thoughts that commonly show up on the chain analyses you do together in session; (2) predictions that prevent skillful behavior or self-defeatist predictions that prevent behaviors necessary for building a life worth living; and (3) thoughts connected to suicidal ideation (e.g., the emotional meaning of the main reason they want to die or assumptions related to main reason they think life cannot get better). A common belief related to suicidal ideation that frequently occurs on chains is that suicide will solve the problem of their pain.

Step 3: Identify Counterpropositions

This is an important step in the process, and as a therapist this is not a place to sit back and go with whatever comes up. We want to be considering strategic alternative perspectives. You do not want to suggest overly positive or purely positive alternatives because those can be rejected out of hand by the client. This is a place to use your level 4, 5, and 6 validation skills and conceptualize the situation to try and see what they might be missing. It can be helpful to look at how you might view the situation if you were in it. Or how they might view the situation on a day where they are more regulated or a day with less adversity. Here is where we can draw from the mode deactivation therapy FAB described above, in that we can look to soften the proposition. The counterproposition does not need to be a polar opposite of the proposition, though usually it is in the direction of effective behavior.

Sometimes metaphor can be helpful. We have included a worksheet that introduces the concept of propositions and counterpropositions using the metaphor of a 3-D camera. A 3-D camera is able to create 3-D images by integrating the image from multiple vantage points. Similarly, we can create a more "3-D" understanding of the situation by synthesizing the truth found in multiple points of view.

A strategic counterpoint can help the process and you might need to access your own wise mind to help the client find it. Conceptually, you want to think about what perspective would help create a more nuanced and accurate understanding of the situation. Alternatively, you can focus on the believable alternative they are missing. Sometimes, the fact that there might be more to the story that we still do not know can be a suitable counterproposition. Other times, a focus on what behavior is needed in the situation can be the counterproposition.

DBT therapists are great at being flexible and focusing on doing whatever works. When working with suicidal ideation, it can be helpful to draw from the Collaborative Assessment and Management of Suicidality (CAMS; Jobes & Drozd, 2004) framework.

Taking a 3-D Perspective with Dialectics

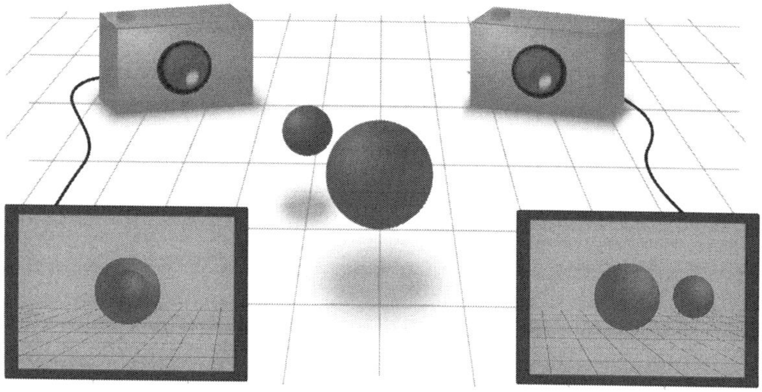

A multi-lensed camera is able to create a 3-D image by synthesizing multiple perspectives. By using dialectical thinking we can create a 3-D view of the situation by synthesizing the truth that is found from different perspectives. First, we need to identify the different perspectives we want to evaluate.

Describe the situation:

Target proposition:
(What is your interpretation of the situation or expected outcome?)

What are our counter-propositions?:
(What are the alternative explanations that are plausible and helpful?)
(Consider how you might view the situation from a different view, on a different day, with the help of your therapist, or from your wise mind.)

Next Steps: Check the Facts and Move Towards Synthesis

Figure 12.2 3-D View and Dialectics

In CAMS, the clinician assesses both the client's desire to live and desire to die, and then they assess the main reason for wanting to live and the main reason for wanting to die. They also look at what it would take to improve the situation. A clinician could target the main reason for wanting to live and the feasibility of that happening as two potential counterpropositions. Alternatively, you could target the feasibility of the situation's improving as a counterproposition. Taking it a step further, you could assess whether practicing acceptance would improve their experience.

If your client is especially without hope, you might need to use imagery to cultivate a good counterproposition. If you can help them develop a mental image of their life as worth living, then we can have some good potential counterpropositions. If you do this, targeting whether this is something worth fighting for as a counterproposition can be a way to sidestep initial predictions that it will never happen. Or if they are "sure" this is something they won't be able to do, you can use imagery strategies to imagine a future version of themselves who has learned and developed their DBT skills and evaluate whether that version of their self could have the kind of life they want to build. There are many good counterpropositions to consider.

Step 4: Check the Facts

There are different ways to go about checking the facts. The current method in the DBT manual is focused on checking to see if your thinking is distorted (e.g., whether you are perceiving a threat or catastrophizing). Other methods for checking the facts include weighing the evidence or using a more inductive approach. A systematic review of thought records found that they tend to attempt cognitive change in three different ways: (1) directly asking for a different thought; (2) demonstrating the need for a different thought by showing how the thought is distorted; (3) developing a new thought by evaluating the situation and the evidence (Waltman et al., 2019). The current DBT skills manual focuses more on the second method and we will focus more on the third method; this is in keeping with the focus on collaborative empiricism.

It is one thing to show that your thinking is distorted and another to help someone find a more balanced and believable thought. Both methods have value and you can think of this as being like a chain analysis and a solution analysis—one is focused on evaluating how a problem happened and the other is focused on looking at how to keep the problem from happening again.

In order to check the facts, you first need to lay out the facts. If you wanted to look at the confirmatory and disconfirmatory evidence, you should consider using the standard thought record found in this book and described in detail in the preceding chapters. We found that this tends to be a difficult process. Instead, we suggest a strategy that integrates both the checking-the-facts skill and the middle-path skill. As you can see in our Socratic Dialectical Method Thought Record, we are using an approach that is consistent with a popular method for treating health anxiety called Hypothesis A/Hypothesis B (Salkovskis, & Bass, 1997). Integrating these components results in a process where we list out the proposition and counterproposition that we are evaluating, list out the facts about the situation, and then check which statement is supported by which fact. The same fact could support multiple conclusions, and this gives the therapist a chance to fold in some validation, highlighting, "Well, I can see how you got there."

Things to be careful of are other thoughts, interpretations, judgments, as well as emotions, being used as facts. It is a fact that they had that thought and a fact that they felt that way, and we are focusing on a more stringent definition of facts. Our facts should be evidence that either conclusion (the proposition or counterproposition) is true.

Step 5: Curiosity

The main goal of this step is to attempt to account for outside factors or missing pieces of the puzzle. Are there gaps in our knowledge? Are there things we don't know? Is there important context to explain evidence that supports the proposition? Are there other relevant elements to fold into the process?

If the check-the-facts step is the confirmatory evidence step, then this is also the disconfirmatory evidence step. This would involve being curious about any signs that the proposition was not true. If we have done a good job of supporting the counterproposition, we might not need to solicit evidence directly that the proposition is not true; instead, we can focus on bolstering support for the counterproposition. Chapter 7, "Collaborative Curiosity," earlier in this volume, has a wealth of strategies to help in this step.

Step 6: Summary

Often this can be an emotionally taxing process for our clients and so we want to spend some time helping them fit it all together. The summary and synthesis steps are important and easy for novice therapists to skip. This is where we work to make new learning explicit. Because we typically do not have the same schema and belief structures as our clients it is often easier for us to see a new perspective before clients do. There can also be a pull for the therapist to try and pick a purely positive thought because they might feel better. Unrealistically and blindly positive thoughts are not consistent with radical acceptance.

Further, fantasy can be a type of disassociation that keeps people from making hard decisions and taking difficult steps in their lives. Therefore, we are looking to develop new thoughts that are balanced and adaptive. This process involves summarizing the different aspects of the dialectical tension and the current observed support for the different components: "How can we fit together all the different pieces of truth that we found?" Accordingly, a summary statement is not simply a statement of whichever component has more support.

Step 7: Synthesis

Synthesis is the traditional final step of the philosophical dialectical process. Here is where we work to reconcile the truth that we found from different perspectives to create that "3-D" view which was described earlier. Often this is done by sewing together seemingly incompatible elements with the term "and." For example:

> There is evidence that my mother never loved me like I needed her to AND this does not mean that I am unlovable as a person. It is painful to not be loved by someone like my mother AND I think it was more about her than about me. I have met some people that loved me AND I'm learning to love myself.

There are two levels on which we are working to synthesize: (1) directly synthesizing the elements of the dialectics (dialectical synthesis), and (2) synthesizing the dialectical synthesis with their overall cognitive schema (schematic accommodation). Once we have a dialectical synthesis, we want to help them synthesize that with their initial propositions and their overall life assumptions. How does the new conclusion compare to the initial assumption? And their underlying beliefs? How do they reconcile their previous assumptions and this new complex perspective?

It can be helpful to incorporate imagery into this process. There are a number of ways you can do this. You can have them picture the new thought as being true. You can have them picture someone they trust telling them the thought. You can have them picture themselves as being skillful or successful. Imagery is powerful, because it is a good way to invoke a strong emotional response. Josefowitz (2017) previously published an excellent guide on the topic of incorporating imagery into Socratic strategies and thought records.

Step 8: Consolidation of Learning and Connecting to Behavioral Goals

We also want to help solidify these gains by helping the client translate the cognitive shift into behavior change. So, we ask them how they want to put the new perspective into practice in the coming week or how they want to test it out in the coming week. If this had been the emotion regulation module in DBT, checking the facts would be a step in determining if the best behavior plan was to use opposite action or problem solving. To be model consistent, we recommend you anchor the exercise in these conclusions. If the initial proposition turned out the not an accurate or effective perspective, then opposite action to that initial perspective might be indicated. Notably, opposite action to the initial proposition might be the same behavior as acting in accordance with the new dialectical synthesis perspective, which can fall under the umbrella of problems solving. The question to consider is "What specific behavior will be effective and skillful?"

Example of Socratic Dialectical Method Thought Record

What follows is an example of how the Socratic Dialectical Method Thought Record is used in session. In this example, Patricia, a lesbian, Afro-Caribbean American woman with BPD, who is in her thirties, is using this method in session with her therapist to target a reduction in her ongoing suicidal ideation. Some background to understanding about Patricia is that the invalidating environment that her BPD developed in was one where she as a child was often placed in the role of caretaker for her mother, who likely had alcohol dependence. Patricia was taught to invalidate and hide her emotional experience and to be overly passive and accommodating, which would eventually lead to periods of uncontrol and verbal aggression. She later learned to take this emotion out on herself. Over time, her environment was shaped to reinforce her behaviors further, as the people who tended to stick around in her life were those who were abusive and exploitative towards her. She entered therapy after her third serious suicide attempt and her life worth living involves having mutually supportive relationships in her life. She then had a few months of DBT skills training, and the concepts were starting to click; accordingly, her therapist began to focus on evaluating and targeting the persisting cognitions that are associated with her suicidal ideation and self-harm behaviors.

In this session, the therapist used the above framework to target thoughts related to suicidal ideation using a Socratic Dialectical Method. The therapist noted from the diary card review that suicidal ideation came up in the week. They started a chain analysis on the ideation and found that the same thoughts came up in this chain as in previous chains that ended in suicidal ideation or self-harm. So, the therapist decided to move into evaluating those thoughts as part of the solution analysis.

Therapist: Patricia, this thought has come up in a few of the chains we've done together. Is this something you think about often?

Client: Not constantly

Therapist: So, you're not constantly having this thought. I'm glad to hear that, because it sounds like a painful thought. Is this a thought that commonly comes up on your road to self-harm or self-harm thoughts?

Client: Yes

Therapist: Let me map out my understanding of what you've told me in our chain analysis, so we can see if I'm on the right track.

So, you got home from work and your partner was sitting on the couch on their phone. The house was a mess, there were dishes in the sink, dinner hadn't been started. It looked like nothing had been done since you left. You told yourself that you have to do everything and got angry. You started cleaning loudly hoping that she would get up and help but she just turned the TV volume up. You got into an argument where hurtful things were said. Afterwards, you cried to yourself as you made dinner. Then, you spent most of the night thinking about how this always happens, and you'll always be a servant for other people and how you wished you were dead. That's the chain we wrote out, right?

Client: Yeah, that sounds familiar.

Therapist: And, these thoughts towards the end, that this always happens, and you'll always be a servant for other people are similar to other thoughts we've seen in previous chains.

Client: Right, so, yes, I often have those thoughts when I feel that way.

Therapist: And, do those thoughts tend to make you more or less suicidal?

Client: More!

Therapist: I think a key question for us to look at is why those thoughts result in you feeling suicidal

Client: I think it is because I realize that I'll never have the type of relationship that I want, that I'll always be trapped in this situation

Therapist: [*Irreverently*] Well, I can assure you that the only way to make sure that you never have the relationship you want is to kill yourself.

Client: Huh, I guess that's right. Like things can't get better if I kill myself

Therapist: Exactly

Client: But I still don't believe I'll ever have the relationship I want.

Therapist: I know that is an important part of your life worth living. What if we apply some of our DBT skills to evaluate these thoughts, are you willing to do that?

Client: If you think it will help

Therapist: OK, so the first step is to check and see how regulated we are.

What emotions are you currently feeling and how intense are they?

Client: Currently sad, not as sad as I was when we first started

Therapist: 0–100, with 100 being maximum sadness, how sad are you currently?

Client: Maybe 80, 85, maybe more. I'm pretty sad about this.

Therapist: Great job naming your emotions and putting a number with it. Let's take a moment and apply some of our skills to your sadness. Let's use what worked last week. Let's sit up in our chairs, open palms, and practice our diaphragmatic breathing.

Client: [following along]

Therapist: I think today I'll add a mantra to my practice.

Breathing in, just this moment. Breathing out, just this breath.

[continuing in the practice]

Client: [following along]

Therapist: [after a period of sustained practice]

How intense are your emotions now?

Client: My sadness is about a 60. Also, I feel more connected with you

Therapist: Let's plan to remember this was useful for you.

OK, the next step in this process is to define the different elements of the dialectic. First, what is the thought that we are evaluating?

Client: That I'll never have the kind of relationship I want to have.

Therapist: To make it clearer, how are we defining the kind of relationship that you want to have?

Client: One where we both help out and I don't have to do everything

Therapist: Are we focusing on division of labor?

Client: Yes, that's a totally foreign concept to my relationship!

Therapist: And is it more about you not doing everything or about them doing more?

Client: Both!

Therapist: OK, so the proposition we're looking at is the prediction that you'll never have a relationship where you don't do all the work. Does that sound right?

Client: That's exactly what I'm afraid of.

Therapist: Next, we want to draw out some counterpropositions or alternate points of view to consider. So, what are some other ways of looking at the situation that might have some truth to them?

Client: Well, you told me that a life where I have different relationships with other people and myself is possible and I'm just trusting you.

Therapist: And what would be the necessary conditions for that to happen, for you to have different relationships?

Client: I'd need to be better at standing up for myself and I might also need better people in my life.

Therapist: I like the idea that being assertive will help you get what you want and how are we defining this idea of better people?

Client: People who don't take advantage of me and who carry their own weight.

Therapist: So, people that don't expect you do everything or people who do more work?

Client: Again, both!

Therapist: It sounds like we have three counterpropositions to look at.

1. That you can have better relationships by learning to be more assertive
2. That you might need to address the division of labor expectations that people have or meet new people with different expectations
3. That you might need to meet people who do more work or get the people in your life to do more with your assertiveness skills

We can do this a few different ways, we can pick one of these to evaluate with standard CBT methods. The dialectical method is to look for the truth in each perspective and try to fit those pieces together to get a better understanding of the truth.

So, we have the initial proposition that you'll never have the type of relationships you want (meaning a relationship where there is more equity in the division of labor). Then we have these counterpropositions that we came up with: that by learning to be more assertive you could have better relationships, that by either addressing people's expectations of division or labor or meeting people with different expectations you could have better relationships, and finally that either by getting the people you are in relationships with to do more work with your assertiveness skills or by meeting new people who are more productive you can have better relationships.

I'm writing these down on this form so we can track what we're looking at.

Next, let's use our check the facts skill and write out the facts of the situation.

Client: So, like what are the facts?

Therapist: Yes, what are the facts relevant to the proposition and counterpropositions of your ability to have the type of relationships that you want?

Client: Well, I don't have the relationship I want. My partner never listens to me and I do all the work!

Therapist: So, the fact that you are currently unhappy with the relationship is well demonstrated and we don't need to evaluate that part further. Are there facts that show that this will always be the case?

Client: Every relationship I've ever had has been like this

Therapist: Meaning, every relationship you've had has involved you doing most the work?

Client: Yes, that's right.

Therapist: Well, that's some evidence, let's write that down as another fact.

Now, when you say every, you mean all of them?

Client: Yes

Therapist: Were there ever any that were worse than the others?

Client: Yes, some didn't just take me for granted, some were abusive and extra bad.

Therapist: I'm glad you're out of those situations now

Client: Me too

Therapist: So, in general you've tended to do most the work, and sometimes it has been worse than others. I'm curious then if there are times that it has been slightly less bad than usual. What was the least bad division of labor you've had in a relationship?

Client: I had a roommate Jill, who wasn't too bad, she would do some stuff, eventually, but would leave dishes in the sink or clothes on the floor that I would typically end up cleaning up.

Therapist: And, this was the agreement the two of you had about the division of labor?

Client: Agreement?

Therapist: It sounds like expectations were more intuited than defined and agreed upon?

Client: Yeah, you mean some people talk out loud with other people about who does what?

Therapist: Yes, it sounds like we've found a few more facts for our 'check the facts' list.

Jill was less bad than the others and there typically isn't an agreement or discussion about expectations or division or labor.

Are there other facts for our list?

Client: Well, my mother always expected and still expects me to take care of her.

Therapist: So, that's another fact to include on our list. Anything else?

Client: I'm not sure.

Therapist: What about facts related to this idea of you becoming more skillful, are there facts relating to that which we want to consider?

Client: I am learning DEARMAN, I'm not great at it yet, but I am learning new skills.

Therapist: Yes, excellent, what else?

Client: People in group have talked about how they have had some success using DEARMAN with family and friends.

Therapist: So, maybe the skill works, at least some of the time. What about this idea of addressing other people's expectations for division of labor or meeting other people with different expectations?

Client: Well, I guess I could learn to have an actual conversation with people about who does what and about how I don't want to do everything.

Therapist: I love that idea, let's write that down.

And we've established with the example of Jill that some people are different than others. Is it possible that there are some people out there who might be receptive to an assertive you, who might accept your limits related to division of labor, and who might be more productive around the house?

Client: I guess so, I mean there must be, right?

Therapist: Yes, definitely

Client: OK, good

Therapist: So, let's go through and check which column the facts support. Do the facts support the idea that you'll never have the type of relationship you want to have AND/OR do they support one of our counter propositions about your ability to learn to be more skillful, to use those skills to bring change into the relationship, or to meet new people.

First let's start with the idea that you currently aren't happy with your relationships and that most of your relationships have involved you doing most the work, which conclusions does that support?

Client: The proposition?

Therapist: Good, yes, I think so too

We have this example of Jill and her doing a little more than everyone else, where does this fit?

Client: Maybe both, I wasn't happy with how it was split up, but it gives me hope that some people are better at this than others

Therapist: What about this piece that expectations for division of labor have typically gone unsaid?

Client: So, that is sort of evidence that maybe things can get better if I can learn to do that, and I haven't been able to do that yet, and maybe also evidence that things won't get better

Therapist: So, both again, what about this idea of learning new skills and the DEAR MAN skills?

Client: That's the counterpropositions all the way. Also, the idea that I could have some of the success that the other people in group have had. But, do you think that I can do it?

Therapist: Yes, I wouldn't be teaching you this skill if I didn't think that it worked and if I didn't think you could do it

Finally, we have this piece about there being other people out there who might be better fits related to expectations and workload. Where should we put that?

Client: Maybe, the things can get better column? I never thought I deserved better than what I have, but maybe I do.

Therapist: That sounds like maybe another thought for us to work on a different day.

Client: Yeah, that would probably be good.

Therapist: So, now we want to take a moment and apply some curiosity to what we just did to see if maybe we missed anything or if there are any other important factors to consider.

I wonder if there might be some outside variables at play, are there any common characteristics in people that you tend be in relationships with?

Client: What do you mean?

Therapist: Well, we're looking at the idea of division of labor at home are there any commonalities across the people you tend to be in relationships with in regards to domestic skills?

Client: I guess none of them are really good at domestic stuff. I tend to date younger and most of them don't seem to know how to cook or clean. I guess their mom did that for them.

Therapist: And, for you it was kind of the opposite, you tended to do those things for your mom.

Client: You're right, we have very different backgrounds.

Therapist: And possibly different expectations too.

Client: Yes, very much so.

Therapist: Is there any other context we might be missing? Or other important things to consider?

Client: I don't think so

Therapist: If I was to imagine them trying to help out, I imagine they probably wouldn't be as good at cooking or cleaning as you are.

Client: Chuckling, yeah, you're right. I never eat anything they cook, because they don't understand how to season.
Therapist: Is this something you've told them in the past?
Client: Yeah, we've had some fights over it.
Therapist: Oh?
Client: Yeah, they told me that if I was going to insult their cooking that they weren't going to cook.
Therapist: So that is maybe some context to consider, we'll have to fold that into future problem solving.
OK, the next step is to summarize the big picture and all the points of truth that we've covered. How would you summarize the truths we've discussed?
Client: I'm unhappy and I've always been unhappy, but maybe things can get better
Therapist: What are the elements of truth relating to things getting better?
Client: Good skills exist
Therapist: And?
Client: They've worked for people I know
Therapist: And?
Client: ??
Therapist: And you can learn to use them too
Client: Oh, right!
Therapist: And, what about other people?
Client: I can either use DEARMAN to address the expectation of my partner or I can find someone else
Therapist: Wow! OK, so let's fit all that together using the word "and."
Client: I'm current unhappy because I do most the work and I typically have done most the work and that doesn't mean things can't get better and I can learn to use skills like DEARMAN and I know people who it has worked for and I can learn it too and I can use that to try and change my relationship or find a new relationship.
Therapist: Do you believe that?
Client: I do
Therapist: So, what is the takeaway message from this?
Client: Things will only get better if I use my skills
Therapist: And how do you want to apply that to the coming week?
Client: I think I need to beef up my DEARMAN skills
Therapist: Perfect, let's review the skill and plan some practice for the week.

Debrief

The therapist decided to target the belief about relationships not getting better after it continued to come up as an antecedent to problem behaviors and was not shaped by previous solution analyses. The therapist took the time to understand the assumption better before moving into defining counterpropositions, which then allowed the therapist to have some ideas about what the effective counterpropositions would be. A few alternatives were selected, and they were close enough that they were evaluated together. The client appeared to be exhibiting some all-or-nothing thinking (i.e., "this always happens") and the therapist chose to take the Socratic route of evaluating the overgeneralization instead of immediately discounting the statement as distorted. A key strategy for demonstrating a statement that is overgeneralized is by demonstrating variability, the therapist chose to first look at "Is it ever worse?" so they could later counterbalance to "Well if it is sometimes worse, then it is sometimes better." This helps build a case for the possibility of change.

The therapist also used the counterpropositions as anchor points, directly asking for facts that supported the counterpropositions. After developing some good facts and checking them, there is a curiosity place which is important because it is easy for either party to get tunnel vision. Here the therapist wondered what might have happened in the past if the partners would have tried to help out, and we learned that the client might have previously punished those attempts. The therapist chose to sidestep focusing on this for the time being, as there was a perceived pitfall of the client perceiving this as blame for the situation, and there was not enough time in the session to address a potential "shame spiral." The therapist would certainly address that ineffective behavior later when setting up new DEARMAN plans. Finally, they drew it all together and connected it with a solid behavior plan of focusing on developing her DEARMAN skill, and skills were demonstrated as being her road out of the situation that had resulted in her previously being suicidal.

All the steps in this process are DBT components configured in a Socratic manner consistent with collaborative empiricism to maximize the potential for successful cognitive restructuring with a BPD population. Further, from a behavioral perspective, the end point of the task is the same place at which you would end if you were doing traditional emotion regulation work. Therefore, it is DBT compatible and will not interrupt the flow of treatment.

Summary

This chapter summarized Socratic strategies for working with a population that has BPD from a DBT framework. Skills and strategies that have been presented are consistent with the DBT model and are configured in a manner to maximize the potential for successful Socratic strategies. All Socratic strategies presented are grounded in behavioral therapy and focus on fostering behavior change. New skills such as the Cognitive Chain Analysis and Socratic Dialectical Method Thought Record use DBT components and are demonstrated with clinical examples. Key elements for working with this population include using regulation strategies prior to cognitive strategies, and then connecting the outcome of the Socratic evaluation to behavior change.

References

Alavi, A., Sharifi, B., Ghanizadeh, A., & Dehbozorgi, G. (2013). Effectiveness of cognitive-behavioral therapy in decreasing suicidal ideation and hopelessness of the adolescents with previous suicidal attempts. *Iranian Journal of Pediatrics, 23*(4), 467–472.

Apsche, J. A. (2010). A literature review and analysis of mode deactivation therapy. *International Journal of Behavioral Consultation and Therapy, 6*(4), 296.

Beck, J. S. (2011). *Cognitive behavior therapy: Basics and beyond* (2nd ed.). New York: Guilford Press.

Braun, J. D., Strunk, D. R., Sasso, K. E., & Cooper, A. A. (2015). Therapist use of Socratic questioning predicts session-to-session symptom change in cognitive therapy for depression. *Behaviour Research and Therapy, 70*, 32–37.

Brown, G. K., Newman, C. F., Charlesworth, S. E., Crits-Christoph, P., & Beck, A. T. (2004). An open clinical trial of cognitive therapy for borderline personality disorder. *Journal of Personality Disorders, 18*(3), 257–271.

Cristea, I. A., Gentili, C., Cotet, C. D., Palomba, D., Barbui, C., & Cuijpers, P. (2017). Efficacy of psychotherapies for borderline personality disorder: A systematic review and meta-analysis. *JAMA Psychiatry, 74*(4), 319–328.

DeCou, C. R., Comtois, K. A., & Landes, S. J. (2019). Dialectical behavior therapy is effective for the treatment of suicidal behavior: A meta-analysis. *Behavior Therapy, 50*(1), 60–72.

Fassbinder, E., Schweiger, U., Martius, D., Brand-de Wilde, O., & Arntz, A. (2016). Emotion regulation in schema therapy and dialectical behavior therapy. *Frontiers in Psychology, 7*, 1–19.

Ferster, C. B. (1972). The experimental analysis of clinical phenomena. *Psychological Record, 22*, 1–16.

Jacob, G. A., & Arntz, A. (2013). Schema therapy for personality disorders—A review. *International Journal of Cognitive Therapy, 6*(2), 171–185.

Jobes, D. A., & Drozd, J. F. (2004). The CAMS approach to working with suicidal patients. *Journal of Contemporary Psychotherapy, 34*(1), 73–85.

Josefowitz, N. (2017). Incorporating imagery into thought records: Increasing engagement in balanced thoughts. *Cognitive and Behavioral Practice, 24*(1), 90–100.

Layden, M. A., Newman, C. F., Freeman, A., & Morse, S. B. (1993). *Cognitive therapy of borderline personality disorder.* Needham Heights, MA: Allyn & Bacon.

Leahy, R. L. (2018). *Emotional schema therapy: Distinctive features.* New York: Routledge.

Lewon, M., & Hayes, L. J. (2014). Toward an analysis of emotions as products of motivating operations. *The Psychological Record, 64*, 813–825.

Linehan, M. M. (1987). Dialectical behavior therapy for borderline personality disorder: Theory and method. *Bulletin of the Menninger Clinic, 51*(3), 261.

Linehan, M. (1993). *Cognitive-behavioral treatment of borderline personality disorder.* New York: Guilford Press.

Linehan, M. M., Korslund, K. E., Harned, M. S., Gallop, R. J., Lungu, A., Neacsiu, A. D., ... & Murray-Gregory, A. M. (2015). Dialectical behavior therapy for high suicide risk in individuals with borderline personality disorder: A randomized clinical trial and component analysis. *JAMA Psychiatry, 72*(5), 475–482.

Mueller, G. E. (1958). The Hegel legend of "thesis-antithesis-synthesis." *Journal of the History of Ideas, 19*(3), 411–414.

Panos, P. T., Jackson, J. W., Hasan, O., & Panos, A. (2014). Meta-analysis and systematic review assessing the efficacy of dialectical behavior therapy (DBT). *Research on Social Work Practice, 24*(2), 213–223.

Paret, C., Kluetsch, R., Zaehringer, J., Ruf, M., Demirakca, T., Bohus, M., ... & Schmahl, C. (2016). Alterations of amygdala-prefrontal connectivity with real-time fMRI neurofeedback in BPD patients. *Social Cognitive and Affective Neuroscience, 11*(6), 952–960.

Rizvi, S. L., & Ritschel, L. A. (2014). Mastering the art of chain analysis in dialectical behavior therapy. *Cognitive and Behavioral Practice, 21*(3), 335–349.

Salkovskis, P. M., & Bass, C. (1997). Hypochondria-sis. In D. M. Clark & C. G. Fairburn (Eds.), *Science and practice of cognitive behaviour therapy* (pp. 313–340). Oxford: Oxford University Press.

Skinner, B. F. (1957). *Verbal behavior.* New York: Appleton Century-Crofts.

Skinner, B. F. (1983). Can the experimental analysis of behavior rescue psychology? *The Behavior Analyst, 6*, 9–17..

Stiglmayr, C. E., Grathwol, T., Linehan, M. M., Ihorst, G., Fahrenberg, J., & Bohus, M. (2005). Aversive tension in patients with borderline personality disorder: A computer-based controlled field study. *Acta Psychiatrica Scandinavica, 111*(5), 372–379.

Tee, J., & Kazantzis, N. (2011). Collaborative empiricism in cognitive therapy: A definition and theory for the relationship construct. *Clinical Psychology: Science and Practice, 18*(1), 47–61.

van Elst, L. T., Hesslinger, B., Thiel, T., Geiger, E., Haegele, K., Lemieux, L., ... & Ebert, D. (2003). Frontolimbic brain abnormalities in patients with borderline personality disorder: A volumetric magnetic resonance imaging study. *Biological Psychiatry, 54*(2), 163–171.

Waltman, S. H. (2015). Functional analysis in differential diagnosis: Using cognitive processing therapy to treat PTSD. *Clinical Case Studies, 14*(6), 422–433.

Waltman, S. H., Frankel, S. A., Hall, B. C., Williston, M. A., & Jager-Hyman, S. (2019). Review and analysis of thought records: Creating a coding system. *Current Psychiatry Research and Reviews, 15*, 11–19.

Waltman, S. H., Hall, B. C., McFarr, L. M., Beck, A. T., & Creed, T. A. (2017). In-session stuck points and pitfalls of community clinicians learning CBT: Qualitative investigation. *Cognitive and Behavioral Practice, 24*, 256–267. doi:10.1016/j.cbpra.2016.04.002

Yoman, J. (2008). A primer on functional analysis. *Cognitive and Behavioral Practice, 15*, 325–340.

Chapter 13

Socratic Strategies and Acceptance and Commitment Therapy

R. Trent Codd, III

❖ CONTENTS

Strategies that would now be called mindfulness-based strategies were an early component of cognitive therapy (Beck, 1979), although they weren't heavily emphasized until recently—after being popularized by the contextual behavioral therapies. Beck initially used the terms *distancing* and *decentering*. These refer to a metacognitive process. That is, having the ability to take a step back mentally and recognize thoughts as thoughts, or even recognizing that your thoughts may not be accurate, represents a mental distancing. Of course, the practice of the mindfulness-based cognitive behavior therapies is much more complex and elaborate than simply taking a mental step back.

One of the most common clinical mistakes of clinicians who practice acceptance and commitment therapy (ACT; Hayes, Strosahl, & Wilson, 2016) is to get lost in talking about ACT instead of actually doing ACT with their patient (Brock, Batten, Walser, & Robb, 2015). The use of Socratic strategies from an ACT perspective focuses on asking questions and having a dialogue that facilitates the practice of ACT. To be consistent with the ACT model, this chapter will focus on using Socratic strategies to facilitate psychological flexibility as opposed to traditional cognitive modification.

Socratic Strategies and ACT

ACT is a third-wave cognitive behavior therapy based on Relational Frame Theory (RFT; Hayes, Barnes-Holmes & Roche, 2001), a behavioral theory of language and cognition. ACT is built upon a set of philosophical assumptions that differ from those underpinning second-wave cognitive behavior therapies, such as Beck's cognitive therapy. RFT and the philosophical assumptions underlying ACT have clinical implications, including what the goals of therapy should and should not be and what interventions are suitable in the pursuit of these goals. These implications have been interpreted by many to mean that Socratic strategies are an absolute contraindication when working from the ACT model.

We believe this interpretation is mistaken and that Socratic strategies can be a valuable addition to an ACT clinician's armamentarium. In this chapter, we discuss the incorporation of Socratic strategies that are consistent with an ACT/RFT perspective. First, we will talk about considerations related to ACT/RFT in general; later, we will talk about how to use Socratic questions to facilitate doing ACT.

Understanding ACT and RFT

The assimilation of Socratic strategies in an ACT/RFT congruent manner requires comprehension of several core concepts. Similar to the DBT chapter in this book, this is not a comprehensive guide to ACT. Several good texts on ACT already exist (see Hayes, Strosahl, & Wilson, 2016 and Luoma, Hayes, & Walser, 2017). In this section we provide an overview of the key ideas, with a special focus on how Socratic strategies can be used to enhance your ACT practice.

Relational Frame Theory[1]

Humans actively engage in relating. This means that they arbitrarily relate objects to one another across a wide range of dimensions. For example, they relate objects in terms of relative size, importance, similarity, distance, perspective, and temporality among many other dimensions. In brief, the RFT perspective is that relational thinking is the core feature of complex human cognition.

Humans readily think in a relational way. A classic exercise frequently presented in ACT workshops and books (e.g., Hayes, 2005) demonstrates how easy it is to relate two things in virtually any possible way. The exercise asks participants for two separate nouns (randomly chosen) followed by a series of relational questions. Regardless of the nouns selected, relations across the assessed dimensions can always be found. For example, we randomly chose "dog" and "boat" as nouns for illustration purposes. We now apply the following relational questions: How are a dog and boat *similar* to one another? Some similarities are that both can travel, hurt you, and require regular care and maintenance. How is a dog *better than* a boat? A dog can provide companionship and doesn't require mechanical parts. How is a dog the *opposite* of a boat? A dog is a living thing, whereas a boat is not. We could continue to ask relational questions about these two nouns while always being able to answer with identifiable relationships.

Because of the ease with which humans engage in relating (i.e., language) they develop increasingly vast relational networks over time and those networks can come to dominate their direct experience (Hayes, Brownstein, Haas, & Greenway, 1986). Getting stuck in the trap of doing "what's right" rather than what works provides an example of this difficulty. For example, if one feels that the morally correct thing to do is tell inconsiderate people off even though they have experienced a range of painful social consequences (e.g., job loss) when they have done so, their behavior is likely under the control of language-based processes rather than direct experience. Useful questions to ask clients to consider whether their rules have become overextended or insensitive to changes in the environment.

Relational frames have three core features: mutual entailment, combinatorial entailment, and transformation of stimulus function. Mutual entailment involves the learning of bi-directional relations when only one relation has been taught. For example, if one is taught that A is the same as B, one will derive that B is the same as A without any explicit training. Mutually entailed relations can link with one another— a process known as combinatorial entailment. Having already learned that A is equal to B, one might separately learn that B is equal to C. Even though there wasn't any explicit training in terms of how A and C are related one will combine these two relations (i.e., A = B & B = C) and derive that A is equal to C and that C is equal to A. That is, there were two trained relations which produced four derived relationships for a total of six. Finally, if A, B, or C becomes associated with an emotion, like fear, then the other events in the relational network will likely elicit fear too.

Consider a more concrete example involving a child who is introduced to a person named Jack. The child first learns through explicit training that the word "Jack" is the same as a Caucasian male in his thirties who has brown hair. Although not explicitly trained, she derives that the man she sees is equated with the word "Jack." Jack has a loud, deep voice which elicits fear in the child on a subsequent occasion when he speaks to her. Jack (the person, not the word) acquires various stimulus functions involving fear (e.g., rapid heartbeat, sweating). Because of the bi-directionality of language the child derives a sameness relationship between these physical sensations and Jack the person. These four relations (two trained and two derived) combine so that the child derives that the word "Jack" is in a bi-directional relationship with fear. Furthermore, the word "Jack" now acquires the same stimulus functions as Jack the person, eliciting fear in her when the word is spoken. Because the word "Jack" has acquired aversive functions the child may now start to avoid thinking the word "Jack" or other thoughts, emotions or events that it has become associated with via its participation in additional relational networks.

Learned relations cannot be unlearned. They can only be elaborated. Consequently, when working from an ACT/RFT model one should be cautious with using Socratic strategies that might add to an expansion of the relational frames with which troublesome thoughts participate. Sometimes broadening of networks is useful and sometimes it is not. From an ACT/RFT perspective the primary consideration is whether expanding the relational network will increase psychological flexibility. Psychoeducation is an example of when teaching new relations can be helpful. For instance, a panic disorder patient with heart palpitations in an equivalence relation with "heart attack," might benefit from learning that heart palpitations may also equal "fight-flight response," with different stimulus functions (e.g., "unpleasant, but not dangerous"). Another example of when elaborating relational networks is indicated from an ACT/RFT model is when doing so frames events in new ways that are appetitive rather than aversive. For example, consider a scientist who finds flying highly aversive to the point of avoiding air travel altogether, even though this is necessary for her to attend conferences. If she values the dissemination of her scientific work product, we might ask questions that help her frame air travel with this important value. This may transform the previously aversive functions of air travel with the appetitive functions of her value.

One means of avoiding unhelpful elaboration of relational networks is to ask clients questions that pull for observation of their thinking processes without judgment and with curiosity. The goal with this type of questioning is to facilitate a client's ability to watch their thoughts come and go without attempting to alter the relational networks. This instead alters the function of their networks. Some questions might include the following:

> Can you notice that you are having the thought X?
> I wonder what it would be like to sit back and watch your thoughts unfold?
> What is your mind giving you now?

Rule-Governed Behavior

Behavior can be either rule or contingency governed. Rule-governed behavior (Skinner, 1969) refers to behavior under the control of contingency-specifying stimuli (i.e., thoughts about the contingency) rather than direct interaction with those contingencies. As noted previously, rule-governed behavior can be problematic because rules are typically insensitive to changes in the environment. This can result in clients persisting with behavior that is unhelpful despite repeated direct experiential feedback from the environment that their behavior is ineffective.

There are three categories of rule following (Hayes, Zettle, & Rosenfarb, 1989): pliance, tracking, and augmenting. Pliance (derived from compliance) is a type of rule following that is based on social consequences, such as pleasing others. For example, a client might have learned early in life that when asked how they are doing they should always say they are well, even if they are not well. They might have been socialized to see this as the socially appropriate thing to do. However, this may block their ability to receive support and connection from important others.

Tracking is rule following based on the correspondence between the rule and direct contingencies. Cognitive restructuring is likely to be most helpful with problem behavior maintained by inaccurate tracks. Augmenting is rule following that alters how events function as consequences by either creating new consequences or altering the value of existing consequences. Augmentals can be useful in helping behavior come under the control of delayed reinforcement. For example, a client who is pursuing doctoral study can be helped to persist in their program, even though the payoff is years away, by relating the doctoral pursuit to important values.

Thought Suppression

Thought suppression has been shown to lead to an increase in the occurrences of the suppressed thought (Wenzlaff & Wegner, 2000) and a range of undesirable emotional outcomes (e.g., Feldner, Zvolensky, Eifert, & Spira, 2003; Harvey, 2003; Koster, Rassin, Crombez, & Näring, 2003). Consequently, Socratic strategies should not pull for client responses that function to suppress thoughts. We believe a mistaken perception exists that this is the intended function of Socratic dialogue in Beck's cognitive therapy and hope that our elaborated four-step model makes clear that this is not the goal.

Socratic Questioning and the Psychological Flexibility Model

While traditional Beckian cognitive change strategies are not necessarily consistent with ACT, if we use a broader way of defining Socratic strategies, we can discuss how to use these questions to enhance your ACT practice. Traditional Socratic questioning is a process of deconstruction (analysis) and reconstruction (synthesis). Over the years, people have started to use the term "Socratic questioning" to mean any questioning designed to make someone reflect on or experience an internal process. A recent paper expanded on this concept and divides the types of Socratic questions a therapist might ask into three categories (see Okamoto, Dattilio, Dobson, & Kazantzis, 2019): *exploratory* (understanding the concern), *perspective-shifting* (explore alternatives), and *synthesizing* (facilitating discovery). For the remainder of this chapter, we will review questions and types of questions from these three categories that can be used to help you do ACT. Of course, it should be noted that another common clinical mistake in ACT is doing too much talking (or too much listening; Brock et al., 2015); Socratic strategies are a dialogue and listening is an important part of that process (Padesky, 1993). Further, as we have emphasized in this text, a pace that allows for the experience of emotions is advised, when using Socratic strategies while doing ACT, the metric is always what is going to help facilitate the process of fostering psychological flexibility.

ACT theorists articulate six psychological processes as treatment targets. These processes are acceptance, defusion, present moment awareness, self-as-context, values and committed action. Socratic strategies tied to these six core processes in ways that are congruent with relational frame theory as previously discussed are ACT/RFT congruent. Example questions are provided below, though these are not intended to be used as a therapy script, and certainly not a list of rapid-fire questions. ACT is a flexible therapy that requires a pace that allows for emotional expression and experience in the present moment. The optimal questions and processes will depend on your conceptualization of your client's experiential avoidance.

Acceptance

Reducing experiential avoidance is a primary goal in ACT. Acceptance involves the disruption of escape and avoidance behavior and can be characterized as approach behavior with respect to private aversive experiences (e.g., painful thoughts, emotions). Complete acceptance of psychological experiences is encouraged including the notion that emotional pain is a regular part of life and will never be eliminated. Acceptance is not sought for the sake of acceptance alone, but rather because it facilitates valued living.

Acceptance is frequently misunderstood because of the colloquial uses of the term and it is useful to clarify what it does not mean. It does not mean resignation, tolerating, or convincing oneself that feeling emotional pain is acceptable. Rather it involves opening up and fully embracing all of one's psychological experiences. Willingness is a term that is frequently used in place of acceptance because conceptually it comes closer to what is meant by acceptance in this context. However, conceptual understanding of acceptance, and indeed many other ACT concepts, is insufficient for a full grasp of the construct. Acceptance is primarily learned through experiential means.

Here are some example questions that may be used to target this process and categorized in accordance with Okamoto et al. (2019):

I wonder whether you are trying not to have pain in your life? [exploratory]
How have your attempts to remove or reduce this pain worked? [synthesizing]
What would happen if you just sat with that (thought/emotion/memory/etc.) for a few moments? [perspective-shifting]
Can you sit still and allow yourself to experience this fully? [perspective-shifting]
I wonder whether this thought/emotion/etc. needs to be your enemy? Do you really need to run from it? [perspective-shifting]
Have you considered the possibility that feeling/thinking these things are a natural part of living life? [synthesizing]
What do you hope will happen if you are successful at getting rid of this depression/anxiety/etc.? [synthesizing]
When you try to get rid of your thoughts/emotions/etc. does your life get bigger or smaller? [synthesizing]
What have you been struggling with and what has that been like? [exploratory]

Defusion

Defusion involves the process of learning that thoughts are just thoughts and not the things to which they literally refer—a strategy that alters the behavioral impact of troublesome thoughts. Stated another way, defusion strips words of their literal functions so that they can be experienced as arbitrary symbols rather than facts. Returning to our earlier example of the child and Jack, when the word "Jack" elicited fear responding in the child—she was fused with the word. That is, she responded with fear when only the word Jack appeared, as if he were physically present, which he was not. Defusion interventions would help this child see that Jack the person isn't literally there and that all she is truly experiencing in the moment are the four letters J-A-C-K. When a client can see words for what they are, they are less inclined to try to escape or avoid them.

There are several ways to execute defusion. In general, questions that facilitate distancing from thoughts and observing the process of thinking facilitates defusion. The process of executing behavioral experiments and thought records can facilitate defusion because they both require distancing from one's thoughts by physically writing one's thoughts down (e.g., on a thought record handout). Indeed, the notion that cognitive reappraisal can promote defusion has been demonstrated empirically (Kobayashi, Shigematsu, Miyatani, & Nakao, 2020).

Sometimes, it can be helpful to demonstrate that it is possible to think something that is not true. You might ask your patient to say to themselves that they are a banana (see Robb, 2005). Ask them to say it sincerely. You might say it with them, "I am a banana." Next, explore their internal experience saying something they know is not true. Ask whether they can recognize that this is just noise? The next step is to apply this to their more troublesome thoughts.

Some examples of Socratic questions that can be used in the service of defusion are as follows:

Can you experience these thoughts as just a string of letters?
What is your sense of the difference between a description and an evaluation? Is that thought you are struggling with a description or an evaluation? [synthesizing]
Do you find in these moments of struggle that you see the world *from* your thoughts? Or do you have a different perspective? [exploratory]

Defusion is best learned through experiential exercises rather than pure intellectual discourse. Thus, a useful strategy is to implement a defusion exercise and then debrief it with Socratic questions. For example,

I wonder what the impact of saying that thought over and over very rapidly would be? [exploratory] I know it's silly, but would you be willing to give a try?

Execute exercise. After the exercise:

What did you experience? [synthesizing]
What happened to that word's meaning? [synthesizing]

Present Moment Awareness

Attention is frequently allocated to past and future events and rarely, without conscious intention, focused on what is occurring in the present moment. Present moment awareness occurs when attentional processes are focused on immediate experience with the qualities of curiosity and non-judgment. Present moment awareness is important because it can increase sensitivity to moment-to-moment changes in the environment, helping to bypass unhelpful rules that pull us away from our direct experience. In addition, refocusing attention to the present moment competes with rumination and brooding.

Like other ACT processes, present moment awareness is best learned through experiential practice. Socratic questions can be used to facilitate deeper learning from such exercises as well as prompt their use. Examples of questions that can be used to facilitate present moment awareness are as follows:

Where is your mind right now? Past, future or present? [exploratory]
Is this like you? That is, when you get stuck does your mind tend to be in the (past/future)? [synthesizing]
I wonder if it would be useful to get present for a moment (said when client is caught up in her thoughts)? [perspective-shifting] Then prompt present moment skills.
Can you notice the sensations of the air against your nostrils as you breathe in and out? [perspective shifting]
Describe the sensations of your feet as they rest on the floor. [perspective-shifting]
Would it be helpful for us to find a cue indicating you are no longer present? What might serve as a useful cue? [synthesizing]
How can you get present in these moments? [synthesizing]

Self-as-Context

ACT therapists seek to assist clients with building a sense of self characterized by the location from which they observe their private experiences. This contrasts with the sense of self many clients possess in which they equate their private experiences with themselves (known as self-as-content). Developing self-as-context confers many advantages including a safe vantage point from which to observe challenging thoughts and emotions. It also facilitates distancing and observation of language-based processes.

Socratic questions that may be used include the following:

What part of you is noticing that you are having that thought? [synthesizing]
Can you notice that you are noticing that you are having that thought? [perspective-shifting]
When you capture that part of yourself that is aware of your thoughts/emotions, what impact does that have? [synthesizing]
How can experiencing the part of you that is watching your thoughts/emotions help you move forward? [synthesizing]

Values

Values are verbally articulated life directions that matter to a client. They describe how they would like to behave in the world in terms of a class of behavior. Values are not the same as goals in that the former do not have end points, whereas the latter do. For example, a client might indicate they value being a loving parent. This has no concrete end point so long as one is a parent because one can always be more loving. In contrast, goals such as spending the evening solely focused on one's child or telling the child that you love them have fixed ends, though they can be repeated. Values and goals relate to one another in that goals signify that one is moving along (or not) their valued direction(s).

Common difficulties associated with values are clients confusing values with goals and their selecting values based on what they think they should value. Assisting clients with values clarification should include assisting them with identifying the function of the values they articulate so that they only settle on valued directions that are truly appetitive.

Socratic strategies for use with values and goal clarification include the following:

How effective have you been over the last week (or other time frame) at living in accordance with your values (0–10)? [exploratory]
How effective have you been over the last week (or other time frame) at living in according of your value X (specific value)? [exploratory]
If you could make a change in how you are living out your values in a way that would make all the difference in the world, what would that change be? [perspective shifting]
If no one could ever know that you effectively lived out value X, would you still want to live in accordance with that value? Why do you think I asked you that? [exploratory]
If you lived out value X effectively and it didn't lead to positive feelings, perhaps even lead to painful feelings, would you still want to live in accordance with value X? Why do you think I asked that? [exploratory]
When you are on your deathbed, how will you have wanted to live in terms of (marriage, career, parenting, etc.)? [exploratory]
If I observed you over the last week, would I see your behavior lining up with value X? [synthesizing]

Committed Action

Committed Action is where behavioral patterns start to build momentum. This process involves setting goals, delineating discrete behavior specific to those goals and making commitments to these behavioral outcomes. It also involves the continual re-orienting, as needed, to the desired behavioral trajectory described by the value. Finally, internal barriers likely to emerge as the client makes behavioral changes is anticipated and ACT-consistent interventions are encouraged.

Questions facilitative of committed action include the following:

Moving forward this week (or other time frame), if you were to increase the effectiveness of living in accordance with your values by 1 or 2 points, what would you do differently? What would I observe you doing? [perspective shifting]

Can you have the troublesome thought/emotion X and still move in this important direction? [perspective shifting]
Must you resolve these painful thoughts/emotions before you move forward in your life? How has this strategy worked for you previously? [synthesizing]

Conclusion

Despite the perception that Socratic strategies are contraindicated from an ACT/RFT perspective, they can indeed be useful to clinicians working from within this model, if they are used in a manner that is consistent with the model. However, model congruent application of these strategies requires an understanding of core concepts related to rule following and arbitrarily applicable relational responding. This understanding is essential because it speaks to how, why, and when these strategies should and should not be applied. In general, ACT/RFT-consistent strategies only elaborate on relational networks when this will lead to an increase in psychological flexibility, emphasize an examination of the function rather than form of thoughts, be delivered in a manner that doesn't have thought-suppressing functions, and transform previously aversive functions to appetitive ones. We reviewed the hexaflex model of psychological flexibility and demonstrated how Socratic questioning can be used to help facilitate the practice of ACT.

Note

1 A comprehensive treatment of Relational Frame Theory is beyond the scope of this chapter. The interested reader is referred to N. Törneke (2010). *Learning RFT: An Introduction to Relational Frame Theory and Its Clinical Application.* Oakland, CA: New Harbinger Publications.

References

Beck, A. T. (1979). *Cognitive therapy and the emotional disorders.* New York: Meridian.
Brock, M. J., Batten, S. V., Walser, R. D., & Robb, H. B. (2015). Recognizing common clinical mistakes in ACT: A quick analysis and call to awareness. *Journal of Contextual Behavioral Science, 4*, 139–143.
Feldner, M. T., Zvolensky, M. J., Eifert, G. H., & Spira, A. P. (2003). Emotional avoidance: An experimental test of individual differences and response suppression using biological challenge. *Behaviour Research and Therapy, 41*(4), 403–411.
Harvey, A. G. (2003). The attempted suppression of presleep cognitive activity in insomnia. *Cognitive Therapy and Research, 27*(6), 593–602.
Hayes, S. C. (2005). *Get out of your mind and into your life: The new acceptance and commitment therapy.* Oakland, CA: New Harbinger Publications.
Hayes, S. C., Barnes-Holmes, D., & Roche, B. (2001). *Relational frame theory: A post-Skinnerian account of human language and cognition.* New York: Springer Science & Business Media.
Hayes, S. C., Brownstein, A. J., Haas, J. R., & Greenway, D. E. (1986). Instructions, multiple schedules, and extinction: Distinguishing rule-governed from

schedule-controlled behavior. *Journal of the Experimental Analysis of Behavior, 46*(2), 137–147.

Hayes, S. C., Strosahl, K. D., & Wilson, K. G. (2016). *Acceptance and commitment therapy: The process and practice of mindful change.* New York: Guilford Press.

Hayes, S. C., Zettle, R. D., & Rosenfarb, I. (1989). Rule-following. In *Rule-governed behavior* (pp. 191–220). Boston, MA: Springer.

Kobayashi, R., Shigematsu, J., Miyatani, M., & Nakao, T. (2020). Cognitive reappraisal facilitates decentering: A longitudinal cross-lagged analysis study. *Frontiers in Psychology,* 11, 103. https://doi.org/10.3389/fpsyg.2020.00103

Koster, E. H., Rassin, E., Crombez, G., & Näring, G. W. (2003). The paradoxical effects of suppressing anxious thoughts during imminent threat. *Behaviour Research and Therapy, 41*(9), 1113–1120.

Luoma, J. B., Hayes, S. C., & Walser, R. D. (2017). *Learning ACT: An acceptance and commitment therapy skills-training manual for therapists* (2nd ed.). Oakland, CA: New Harbinger Publications.

Okamoto, A., Dattilio, F. M., Dobson, K. S., & Kazantzis, N. (2019). The therapeutic relationship in cognitive-behavioral therapy: Essential features and common challenges. *Practice Innovations, 4*(2), 112–123.

Padesky, C. A. (1993). Socratic questioning: Changing minds or guiding discovery. Paper presented at the keynote address delivered at the European Congress of Behavioural and Cognitive Therapies, London. Retrieved from: http://padesky.com/newpad/wpcontent/uploads/2012/11/socquest.pdf

Robb, H. R. (2005). I am NOT a banana. *SMART Recovery News & Views, 11*(4), 7. Retrieved from: www.smartrecovery.org/wp-content/uploads/2017/10/fall2005newsviews.pdf?highlight=online

Skinner, B. F. (1969). *Contingencies of reinforcement: A theoretical analysis.* Englewood Cliffs, NJ: Prentice-Hall.

Wenzlaff, R. M., & Wegner, D. M. (2000). Thought suppression. *Annual Review of Psychology, 51*(1), 59–91.

Chapter 14

Socratic Strategies for Physicians and Prescribers

R. Trent Codd, III and Scott H. Waltman

❖ CONTENTS

The implementation of Socratic strategies from the perspective of a prescribing provider involves several considerations. Although the entirety of this book contains strategies that are helpful to psychiatric prescribers, the current chapter focuses on issues more solely relevant to this group of clinicians. A primary concern for prescribers involves patient adherence to medication. However, briefer and less frequent contact which necessitates, among other things, the ability to determine which beliefs can be targeted in brief interactions and which require a longer course of psychotherapy are additional considerations. Finally, we discuss strategies for recruiting gains produced by medication to further optimize patient outcomes.

Targeting Medication Adherence

The rates of medication adherence for psychiatrically ill patients are sub-optimal (Julius, Novitsky, & Dubin, 2009; Pampallona, Bollini, Tibaldi, Kupelnick, & Munizza, 2002), with Basco and Rush (1995) finding the probability of compliance across studies and mood disorders to be between .53 and .63. Furthermore, nonadherence is associated with a range of problematic outcomes including elevated hospitalization and suicide rates (e.g., Gilmer et al., 2004; Haddad, Brain, & Scott, 2014). Thus, enhancing outcomes for patients prescribed psychiatric medication requires the targeting of variables related to nonadherence.

The spirit of Socratic strategies in psychotherapy is one of collaborative empiricism, involving a clinician and client jointly applying curiosity and scientific principles to thought and behavior patterns (see Kazantzis et al., 2018). Although collaborative empiricism is a central element of Socratic strategies, it is not necessarily characteristic of many prescriber–patient relationships. Somewhat reflective of this is the frequently used language of "compliance" and "non-compliance" with medication, which suggests a non-collaborative view of these relationships. A therapeutic alliance characterized by collaboration seems to be an important factor in patient adherence to medication (e.g., Cruz & Pincus, 2002; Dearing, 2004).

There are some important differences in the way Socratic concepts are adopted in a medication adherence context relative to the psychotherapy process. For instance, Socratic ignorance does not really mean true ignorance (Overholser, 2010, 2011, 2018). It would be irresponsible and medically dangerous to disregard evidence-based medicine and Food and Drug Administration (FDA) recommendations. Further, Socratic questioning cannot be used to get your patient to determine what the optimal medication or dose will be; however, Socratic strategies can be used to target the beliefs and behaviors that impede medication adherence (which we discuss below).

Several factors are related to patient medication nonadherence including socioeconomic, patient, disease-related, healthcare system and therapy-related factors (Costa et al., 2015). Therapy and patient-related factors are the most amenable to Socratic strategies. Several such factors (Basco & Rush, 2005), together with sample Socratic questions related to each, are as follows.

Forgetting to Take One's Medication

In the past what's been helpful in reminding you to take your medication?

Where do you think we can find some useful reminder strategies?
What have you successfully used to help you remember other important activities? Might that be useful here?
I have some ideas regarding strategies that might be helpful. Would you be interested in hearing some of these? [If so, describe then suggest a behavioral experiment testing out their effectiveness]

Running Out of Medication

What has made it difficult for you to keep your appointments? [if missing appointment(s) is reason for running out]
I wonder whether it would be helpful to specify when you should pursue a refill? How far in advance would make sense?
What makes refilling your medication a challenge?
Do you have any ideas about what it means to take this medication that might be getting in the way?
Do you know anyone who regularly remembers to refill their medicine? What do they do? Would it be helpful to ask them?

Busy or Chaotic Personal Schedules

Taking medication can certainly be a challenge with a schedule as busy as yours. Have there been times when you have been more successful despite your schedule?
Do you try to remember to take your medication on the fly or do you have a concrete plan? Any sense of the pros and cons of each approach?
When you can take your medication despite these challenges, what impact do you notice on your mood [or other relevant symptoms]?

Turbulent Life Periods

You were successful in regularly taking your medication before things got so rough. I wonder whether it would be useful to come up with a different strategy during this challenging period of time.

Thoughts about Side Effects

Do you have any ideas that are interfering with your willingness to take your medication?
Is it possible you are catastrophizing?
Have you noticed any relationship between the way you think about your side effects and how uncomfortable they are?
Would it be useful to examine the pros and cons of continuing your medication given the side effects?
Have you also noticed positive effects from taking your medication?
What is the most important reason to you to take this medication? When considering this, does it make the side effect price tag seem more tolerable?

Misinformation

Where did you learn that information? How confident do you feel in the accuracy of that source?

What would be a good way to determine whether a [website/friend/etc.] is a reliable source of information?

I have some information that I would like to share with you about your medication. Would you be interested in hearing this?

After Improvement, Believing Medication Is No Longer Necessary

In the past when you felt better, did you also feel you didn't need your medication then? If so, what happened after you stopped taking your medication?

Sometimes visuals are helpful. Would you consider mapping out the course of your illness with me? [Map out periods of medication discontinuation to see whether they correlate with hospitalization or other negative outcomes]

When graphing the course of illness: What did other people notice when you stopped your medicine? What was the build up like? What was happening in your life right before the change in symptoms?

What were your symptoms like before you started medication?

Is it possible that you have lost track of how much you were suffering before you started taking medicine? I wonder whether it would be helpful to gather some information about how you were doing then?

Motivational Interviewing

Motivational interviewing (MI; Miller & Rollnick, 2009, 2012) combined with Cognitive Therapy has demonstrated efficacy in facilitating adherence in some psychiatric populations (e.g., Daley, Salloum, Zuckoff, Kirisci, & Thase, 1998; Kemp, Kirov, Everitt, Hayward, & David, 1998; Swanson, Pantalon, & Cohen, 1999). MI has several overlapping components with collaborative empiricism though there are some key differences between the two approaches. Socratic strategies primarily intersect with MI in similarly emphasizing a nonconfrontational and cooperative approach to care and underscoring the importance of increasing change talk to assist the patient in putting their conclusions into action.

Data are supportive of MI's impact on behavior change even when it is delivered with low intensity. For example, Monti et al. (2007) found that one, 30–45-minute MI intervention in an emergency room setting, followed by two brief phone contacts at one and three months, led to significant reductions in alcohol consumption and alcohol-related consequences among young adults. These impressive outcomes survived when assessed one year later. These data should be comforting to prescribers who frequently have less clinical contact time with patients relative to psychotherapists yet must still seek to change behavior within their allotted time.

Some examples of MI-consistent questions include:

If you decided to take your medication regularly, do you think you could do it?
How would your symptoms improve if you took your medication?
Tell me about a time when your irritability caused problems in your relationship.
What is the difference between Joe Smith on medication and the Joe Smith of today? [after discontinuing medicine]
In what ways were things better when you were taking your medication regularly?
How does taking your medicine relate to your important goal of X?
On a scale of 1–10, how important is overcoming this depression to you with 10 = most important? Ask why a lower number was not selected. For example, if they say 7 you ask why not a 5 or a 6?
How has taking your medication been helpful?
Did you notice anything different on days you didn't take your medicine?

Troubleshooting Nonadherence From the Beginning

Given the nonadherence rates among those taking psychotropic medication (see previous citations), it may be wise for clinicians to presume adherence promoting strategies will be necessary with every patient. Making such a presumption ensures adequate attention will be afforded to factors related to adherence.

General questions that assess for common adherence interfering beliefs can be useful. For example, one might ask: "Do you have any beliefs about what it would mean for you to take this medication?" "Is there anything that would get in the way of taking this medication consistently?" or "What have you heard or read about this medication?" These questions may reveal that a patient equates taking medicine with personal weakness, that they believe the prescribed medication is habit forming (when it isn't) or that the recommended medication is dangerous in ways that are not substantiated by research. They may also uncover the anxious patient's tendency to "convince" themselves they have, or will have, the many side effects they read about online. Finally, they might reveal unrealistically optimistic ideas regarding the medication's effects. This is problematic when patients fail to experience symptom relief at the level they anticipated, and this causes them to abandon their commitment to the medication. Eliciting these cognitive obstacles early in treatment allows them to be targeted for intervention before they can produce large patterns of nonadherence.

A prerequisite for Socratic questions to be effective is the availability of relevant information to the patient (Padesky, 1993). If a patient is unfamiliar with the effects of a medication the necessary conditions for Socratic questioning are not satisfied. In these circumstances, therefore, it is necessary to provide them with evidence for why medication in general or a specific medication is recommended. Questions can follow information giving in order to strengthen comprehension and to check for understanding.

Adherence Should Be an Ongoing Concern

Adherence should not be conceptualized in all-or-nothing terms as studies have found that most people periodically skip, miss, or alter dosing (see Basco & Rush, 2005). Routine assessment of adherence throughout treatment is important. The "nagging parent" role should be avoided when questioning around medication adherence. Instead, as previously emphasized these interactions should be characterized by a curious and collaborative approach which sets the stage for an honest discussion with the patient about these issues.

With an established prescriber–patient relationship conducive to forthright discussions of adherence challenges we can work with the patient to identify and overcome obstacles. Useful assessment questions include: "Has anything come up since we met last that made it more difficult to take your medication?" and "How successful have you been at taking your medication? What is getting in the way?"

If challenges with compliance are endorsed, the general intervention formula is to ask the patient to describe a specific instance and to elicit cognition related to those nonadherent occasions. Once important cognitive targets are identified, the full range of Socratic strategies can be employed.

Adherence Following a Relapse

When a patient relapses, it is important to assist them in learning from the experience in a manner that reduces the likelihood of future relapses based on adherence challenges. Although they are undesirable, both lapses and relapses are useful learning experiences when they are approached as laboratories rather than events for which the patient should engage in self-punishment. Here are some sample questions facilitative of this goal:

"All learning is valuable. What can we learn from this experience?
"What was the build up like?"
"What belief will facilitate compliance and how can we build that up?"

Briefer and Less Frequent Interactions

Typically, providers of medication management see their patients less often and with briefer encounters than providers who are solely providing psychotherapy. This can present the prescriber with some challenges when attempting to intervene on adherence-interfering beliefs. We offer some suggestions related to this difficulty.

First, if you are the prescriber and the patient is engaged in psychotherapy with another provider whom they are meeting with more frequently, you can coordinate with that provider to learn which skills the patient is being taught so that you can cue them to use their skills in the medication adherence context. You can also request certain skills be taught or that the psychotherapist engage in more sustained work on problematic cognitions that you have uncovered. Second, it is important to know how to triage cognitive targets effectively. There are many thoughts and beliefs that are amenable to brief Socratic methods implemented by a prescriber. However, beliefs that are deeply held, recur across many episodes of non-adherence and are non-responsive to brief intervention may benefit from a referral for a fuller dose of psychotherapy. Finally, providing patients with written materials directly or by referral that addresses medication-interfering cognition and related skills is often an effective adjunct to in-session Socratic strategies.

Reinforcing Gains

Improvements in mood produce positive changes in the overall cognitive behavioral system. Thus, when medication results in an enhanced mood the prescriber should take advantage of those gains to further facilitate desired changes in cognition and behavior. These improvements, in turn, can be targeted toward the adherence concerns discussed in this chapter, but the learning need not be confined to this difficulty. Learning can and should ultimately be consolidated in a way that supports the patient's self-efficacy, because this creates an opportunity to use those new resources to help the patient enlarge their life.

Building Self-Efficacy

Medication often does the heavy clinical lifting. However, not everyone given a prescription gets better. So, the questions we want to explore with the patient include "What are the things they did that helped them get better?" There is a further question of what it means about them that they were able to do these things.

As a prescriber you want the patient to see a connection between medication usage and feeling better. You also want them to attribute feeling better to taking the medication as prescribed; however, you do not want them to attribute feeling better solely to the medication. If the medication is the tool that helped them feel better, they were the ones who learned how to use the tool to get there—a tool is only as good as its wielder. The thing to keep in mind here is that many of our patients have core beliefs and schema of incompetence, which means that they are likely to filter events in a way that is schema-consistent—downplaying their successes. So, you in turn want to slow down, so that you can highlight their successes and capabilities. For example, you might say:

> Yes, medication helped you feel better, but medication is only a tool and you are the user of the tool. Not everyone I prescribe this to has the same results, so let's look at what you have been doing to achieve these results.

Collaboratively Enlarging the Client's Life

The absence of bad isn't necessarily the presence of good. As medication might help reduce symptoms, we want to help our patients make positive changes in their lives to foster resilience and recovery. A psychotherapist might approach this much earlier in treatment by asking something like the following: "How much time and energy do you spend being angry and thinking about all the things you are angry about?" "How exhausting is that?" "How fun is that?" "Is this the kind of life you want?" "Where would you rather invest that time and energy?" "Is there a place in your life where we could spend that time and energy in a way that would make your life better?" This would set the stage for behavioral goals. A behaviorally oriented therapist would work with the patient to reduce time spent behaving under aversive control and increase time and energy in goal- and value-directed behaviors—this is the behavioral route for symptom improvement. Prescribers have more options. You can directly work with how a patient is feeling through psychopharmacology, but the principle remains. What are you going to do with the hole in the patient's life that the symptoms used to fill? How much time and energy did they use to spend being depressed, angry, anxious, and so forth, and is there potential to use that time and energy to facilitate behavior change that will help maintain their gains and lead to a better life? Consider the following interaction.

Provider Frank, I'm glad to hear you're feeling better, it sounds like the medication is helping. Does that sound correct?

Patient It does, it's hard to believe this is what everyone else feels like. I feel so not angry all the time.

Provider That makes me happy. I'm glad to hear you have some relief.

Patient Me too!

Provider Frank, now that you are feeling a little better, I was wondering if we could have a conversation about how to build on these gains to perhaps get you more benefit, would that be OK?

Patient Yeah, that sounds fine.

Provider So, before when you were feeling really angry and unhappy, how were you spending your free time?

Patient Being unhappy.

Provider Yes, that sounds right, what were you doing during these times?

Patient I guess just thinking about things that were making be angry. I would spend hours thinking about my boss, my job, my life, all the things I hated.

Provider That sounds pretty miserable, how did that affect your overall mood?

Patient I guess it made me angrier.

Provider I can see that. So, if spending your time thinking about all the things you are unhappy about made you more unhappy, let's spend some time thinking about things that might help improve your mood and your life. So, how much time and energy would you say you used to spend being angry and thinking about things that made you angry?

Patient Oh, I was angry all the time, and I was always thinking about things that made me angry.

Provider So, we all have a limited amount of time and energy, so, if a lot of your time and energy was going into being angry, what were you missing out on?

Patient I was missing out on being with my family, having fun, and doing things I used to enjoy doing.

Provider I would love for you to have those things again. If there is a hole in your life from where the anger used to be, what do you want to fill your life with?

Patient That's a good question, I was so focused on being angry and not wanting to be angry anymore that I hadn't really thought about what I actually wanted.

Provider This is an exciting conversation to be having; let's think about how you would rather spend your time and energy.

Patient Well, my anger made me so disconnected from other people, so I guess I want to focus on improving relationships and being around people that I care about.

Provider Are you enjoying being around the people you care about more now that you are less angry?

Patient I am, it's kind of weird, but I think I like my family, at least more than I thought I did.

Provider That's a pleasant surprise to find. And how are they responding to you being less angry?

Patient They also seem weirded out by it.

Provider You were so angry for so long. Which version of you do they prefer?

Patient Definitely, the less angry me.

Provider Awesome, so, how do you want to invest your reallocated time and energy in a way that will help foster your relationship with your family?

Patient I think I want to spend more time with them.

Provider I like that idea; it can help to be more specific and to set reasonable goals to work towards. Specifically, how do you want to spend more time with your family? What do you want to do more of? What do you want to do less of?

Patient Well, I need to spend less time in the garage or backyard by myself. I want to start going to my son's games. I think that really matters to him. I want to start having more alone time, like dates, with my wife. And, I need to find some ways to connect more with my younger son that I don't really understand at all. I think I just need to start getting to know him better, he's been hanging around me more now that I'm less angry.

Provider These sound like good places to start. I like the idea of building on the momentum you gained from the medication.

Patient Me too, I guess I didn't realize that things could actually get better. I feel optimistic about the future.

Provider Let's both write down what you are planning to do, and we can talk about it next time we meet.

In the preceding example, we can see the prescriber having an exchange that is quite like what a therapist might do earlier in treatment. Here we see the prescriber build on the medication gains to create a behavior plan for creating sustained change in the patient's life. It might be that unanticipated barriers to goal achievement come up, and perhaps the patient may benefit from a referral for a course of brief goal-directed psychotherapy to help overcome those barriers. The goal of this step is to collaboratively build on gains and to focus on behavior change to facilitate new experiences and new learning.

Summary

Socratic strategies may be useful to prescribers in addressing patient adherence with medication. However, prescribers are at a disadvantage when their therapeutic interactions are confined in terms of time and frequency. We offered a range of strategies for working within these constraints including collaborating with a psychotherapist the patient is concomitantly engaged with and referring the patient out for psychotherapy. Proactive strategies for the prevention of nonadherence were also offered. Finally, we discussed using Socratic strategies to build on medication gains to create further behavioral change in the patient's life.

References

Basco, M. R., & Rush, A. J. (2005). *Cognitive-behavioral therapy for bipolar disorder.* New York: Guilford Press.

Basco, M. R., & Rush, A. J. (1995). Compliance with pharmacotherapy in mood disorders. *Psychiatric Annals, 25*(5), 269–279.

Costa, E., Giardini, A., Savin, M., Menditto, E., Lehane, E., Laosa, O., ... & Marengoni, A. (2015). Interventional tools to improve medication adherence: Review of literature. *Patient Preference and Adherence, 9*, 1303–1314.

Cruz, M., & Pincus, H. A. (2002). Research on the influence that communication in psychiatric encounters has on treatment. *Psychiatric Services, 53*(10), 1253–1265.

Daley, D. C., Salloum, I. M., Zuckoff, A., Kirisci, L., & Thase, M. E. (1998). Increasing treatment adherence among outpatients with depression and cocaine dependence: Results of a pilot study. *American Journal of Psychiatry, 155*(11), 1611–1613.

Dearing, K. S. (2004). Getting it, together: How the nurse patient relationship influences treatment compliance for patients with schizophrenia. *Archives of Psychiatric Nursing, 18*(5), 155–163.

Gilmer, T. P., Dolder, C. R., Lacro, J. P., Folsom, D. P., Lindamer, L., Garcia, P., & Jeste, D. V. (2004). Adherence to treatment with antipsychotic medication and health care costs among Medicaid beneficiaries with schizophrenia. *American Journal of Psychiatry, 161*(4), 692–699.

Haddad, P. M., Brain, C., & Scott, J. (2014). Nonadherence with antipsychotic medication in schizophrenia: Challenges and management strategies. *Patient Related Outcome Measures, 5*, 43–62.

Julius, R. J., Novitsky Jr, M. A., & Dubin, W. R. (2009). Medication adherence: A review of the literature and implications for clinical practice. *Journal of Psychiatric Practice, 15*(1), 34–44.

Kazantzis, N., Beck, J. S., Clark, D. A., Dobson, K. S., Hofmann, S. G., Leahy, R. L., & Wong, C. W. (2018). Socratic dialogue and guided discovery in cognitive behavioral therapy: A modified Delphi panel. *International Journal of Cognitive Therapy, 11*(2), 140–157.

Kemp, R., Kirov, G., Everitt, B., Hayward, P., & David, A. (1998). Randomised controlled trial of compliance therapy: 18-month follow-up. *The British Journal of Psychiatry, 172*(5), 413–419.

Miller, W. R., & Rollnick, S. (2009). Ten things that motivational interviewing is not. *Behavioural and Cognitive Psychotherapy,* 37(2), 129–140.

Miller, W. R., & Rollnick, S. (2012). *Motivational interviewing: Helping people change*. New York: Guilford Press.

Monti, P. M., Barnett, N. P., Colby, S. M., Gwaltney, C. J., Spirito, A., Rohsenow, D. J., & Woolard, R. (2007). Motivational interviewing versus feedback only in emergency care for young adult problem drinking. *Addiction, 102*(8), 1234–1243.

Overholser, J. C. (2010). Psychotherapy according to the Socratic method: Integrating ancient philosophy with contemporary cognitive therapy. *Journal of Cognitive Psychotherapy, 24*(4), 354–363.

Overholser, J. C. (2011). Collaborative empiricism, guided discovery, and the Socratic method: Core processes for effective cognitive therapy. *Clinical Psychology: Science and Practice, 18*(1), 62–66.

Overholser, J. C. (2018). *The Socratic method of psychotherapy.* New York: Columbia University Press.

Padesky, C. A. (1993). Socratic questioning: Changing minds or guiding discovery. Paper presented at the A keynote address delivered at the European Congress of Behavioural and Cognitive Therapies, London. Retrieved from: http://padesky.com/newpad/wpcontent/uploads/2012/11/socquest.pdf

Pampallona, S., Bollini, P., Tibaldi, G., Kupelnick, B., & Munizza, C. (2002). Patient adherence in the treatment of depression. *The British Journal of Psychiatry, 180*(2), 104–109.

Swanson, A. J., Pantalon, M. V., & Cohen, K. R. (1999). Motivational interviewing and treatment adherence among psychiatric and dually diagnosed patients. *The Journal of Nervous and Mental Disease, 187*(10), 630–635.

Chapter 15

Socratic Strategies for Teaching Socratic Strategies

R. Trent Codd, III and Scott H. Waltman

❖ CONTENTS

Model-Consistent Supervision and Training

It has been noted that, "Cognitive therapy supervision parallels the therapy itself" (Padesky, 1996; p. 289). Incorporating experiential and demonstrative components of a therapy into supervision is called model-consistent supervision (Beck, Sarnat, & Barenstein, 2008; Padesky, 1996; Sudak & Codd, 2019; Waltman, 2016). This framework is based on the idea of experiential learning, noting that many people learn best by doing. As Socratic strategies are among the hardest for trainees to learn (Waltman, Hall, McFarr, Beck, & Creed, 2017), there are advantages to having training experiences rich with Socratic dialogue. For example, a preliminary examination found that trainers who used more Socratic strategies in clinical consultation with their trainees had their trainees demonstrate a higher level of clinical competency when compared to their trainers who used less Socratic strategies (Waltman, Naman, Morgan, Wickremasinghe, Nehme, & McFarr, 2014). There are many other important elements to CBT supervision and training and the interested reader is directed to the excellent text by Sudak and colleagues (2016) on the topic. The current chapter focuses on supervision and training strategies as they relate to Socratic dialogue.

Skills Training Approach

In Chapter 5, "Getting Started," we discussed experiential learning. In general, skills training is accomplished as follows: first, introducing a skill and explaining how it works; second, demonstrating the skill and then using the skill together; third, debriefing the skill and how it went; fourth, capitalizing on new learning and discrepant experiences to facilitate overall learning and cognitive change; and, finally, practicing the skill in real-world and in-the-moment settings. People learn well through experiential methods—learning through doing (Wenzel, 2019). These elements of skills training

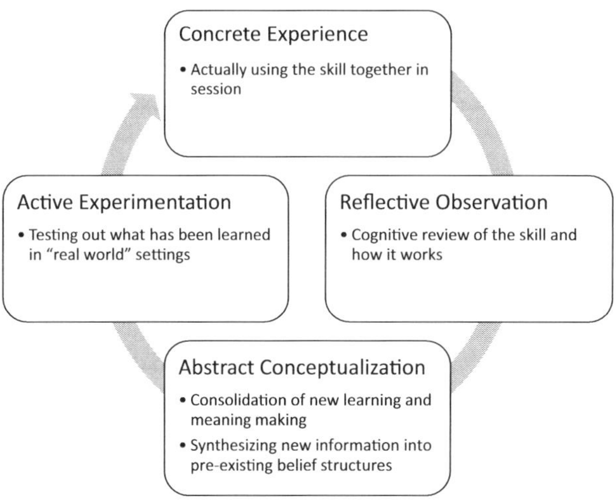

Figure 15.1 Kolb's Model of Experiential Learning

can be incorporated into Kolb's (1984) four phases of experiential learning: concrete experience, reflective observation, abstract conceptualization, and active experimentation (see Edmunds et al., 2013; Waltman, Hall, McFarr, & Creed, 2018), which are elaborated on below.

Concrete Experience

The first step in skills training is concrete experience with the skill to be trained. Thus, if we want our supervisees or trainees to learn how to use Socratic strategies, we need to arrange learning experiences for them that involve many practice opportunities. Ideally, their first exposure to the skill isn't with a patient, but rather in the safe confines of a supervisory relationship or training event. The first component of this step is a description of the skill and the rationale for its use, which can be accomplished in a few ways. Video clips of Socratic strategies can be shown. Role-plays are another useful vehicle. Initially, the supervisee/trainee can play the part of a client while the supervisor/trainer plays the clinician delivering Socratic strategies. As the Socratic trainee's skill develops the direction of the role-play can be reversed with the trainee now playing the part of the clinician and the supervisor/trainer playing the client. Role-plays may also be varied in terms of patient complexity and area of focus.

Another type of useful training exercise involves trainee practice in generating Socratic questions (see James, Morse, & Howarth, 2010). Practice opportunities can be contrived in several ways. First, supervisor–supervisee role-plays can be stopped at various points in time with the trainee then prompted to provide as many Socratic questions as possible given the content of the dialogue. This alternation of role-play, pause and generate questions, resume role-play, can continue for as long as it seems useful. Second, supervisee session recordings can be paused at key times (e.g., where more skillful Socratic strategies can be developed) with the supervisee similarly prompted to generate alternative questions. A final example is, in a group supervision context, providing group supervisees with a client statement and then having them each generate Socratic responses one or more times. Regardless of which of these approaches is used, it is helpful for the supervisor/trainer to shape responses. For example, they might say "What I really liked about that question was X" or "You might be able to make that more succinct by saying X, Y, Z" or "The portion where you said X was strong. I would only recommend nuancing the question with X, Y, and Z." Shaping responses publicly benefits fellow supervisees/trainees in addition to the individual whose receiving feedback on their response.

Reflective Observation

Many supervisors and trainers omit this step. After they teach the skill, they assume that the clinician in training understood everything as well as they did. It is important this is a collaborative process because this ensures the supervisee/trainee leaves the training interaction with the intended learning points. Otherwise, they might dogmatically hold onto inconsequential elements or miss key elements entirely. Here is an example of how this might look in practice:

"We just did a lot and I want to check in with you to see how you are doing and what you make of this whole evaluating your thoughts strategy we are using"
"How are you feeling after the exercise we did together?"
"What are your views on this exercise?"
"Does this seem like it will be helpful to you?" "Is this something you want to spend some more time practicing and learning how to do?"
"Do you have any questions about the process?"

Carving out time to clarify any misconceptions and answer questions they might have is essential.

When the training complexity evolves to the point of the trainee taking the role of clinician in role-plays, you want to lead with providing positive feedback (Bellack, Mueser, Gingerich, & Agresta, 2013). Reinforce what they did well and reinforce their willingness to engage in the process. Remember, what gets reinforced increases in probability and failing to provide reinforcement for skillful behavior, including approximations, effectively fails to provide the reinforcement needed for it to recur. Constructive feedback is also important when responses can be further developed (Bellack et al., 2013).

Revisiting skills training is frequently necessary, especially in the first session following exposure to the skill. Typically, shaping is required after they start using the skills as homework; normalizing this beforehand can make it easier to do later. "OK, it sounds like we have a general idea how the skill works. The next step is to put it into practice, so you can bring back your experiences. We can talk about how it went and smooth out the skill for you."

Abstract Conceptualization

This is the consolidation-of-learning step. The intent is to assist them with making sense of what they learned from skill practice sessions. Even when not directly targeting their belief system, a link between what you are doing and their beliefs about themselves can be made.

Capitalize on any opportunity to highlight competent clinical behavior. For example, if they were able to use progressive muscle relaxation to decrease their client's overall distress, there is a lesson here about their having some control over how they are feeling. If they implemented a skill despite not liking it or finding it aversive to deliver, there is a lesson about their ability to persist in doing things that are not fun by exercising their ability to choose to do it regardless. If they apply a skill that does not work as intended, there is a lesson about their willingness to try and having an open mind.

When you target cognitive change, either directly through Socratic strategies or indirectly through changing behavioral patterns, there will be new experiences and new information to draw out and reinforce. Work to integrate this new information into their overall belief system. Key questions to ask include asking how this new experience or information fits with their previous assumptions, and if necessary, how they explain the discrepancy.

Active Experimentation

Experiential learning is an ongoing process, the fourth link in Kolb's experiential learning cycle (1984) is active experimentation; this is where the trainee practices the skills in the world outside supervision and consultation. This can be framed in a way that validates the in-supervision findings, such as "Let's see if this skill works in the real world." However, it can be good to temper expectations.

"Real world" skill practice is ideally done as homework (or outside skills practice). However, supervisors miss important opportunities if they treat skills as things that the supervisee is only supposed to use outside of session—they also will not really know about their mastery or fluidity with the skill. In-the-moment skills practice is very valuable.

Key Competencies Related to the Four Component Model of Socratic Dialogue

The trainer can think of these four components as four different sets of competencies that the trainee needs to master. This whole text is devoted to teaching this model, and a review of it in its entirety is recommended for anyone looking to develop a solid grasp of Socratic strategies. Below we review key competencies on which trainers and supervisors may wish to focus in their training and supervision efforts.

Step 1: Focusing

The first step in applying Socratic strategies is to identify the targets for these strategies. In a practical sense, there is insufficient time to address every thought that seems important. Consequently, the discipline to focus on thoughts that are central to problems and related to core difficulties and underlying beliefs must be developed. Frequently, these are called the *hot thought* (Greenberger & Padesky, 2015), so therapists are taught to follow the affect or "find the heat."

The key competencies for this skill are as follows:

- The ability to collaboratively break down a situation to its components
- The ability to guide a patient through identifying their thoughts, feelings, and behaviors
- The ability to evaluate which thoughts are the most distressing or most central in the case conceptualization
- The ability to use the downward arrow
- The ability to shape a thought into a form that can be evaluated
- The ability to create a shared or universal definition for a target cognition

Step 2: Phenomenological Understanding

This step is one of validation. In dialectical behavior therapy (DBT) terms, this is an opportunity for level 4, 5, and 6 validation (see Linehan, 1997). We provide specific recommendations for the integration of Socratic strategies and DBT in a separate chapter. The primary goal of this step is to understand the client and the target cognition. The guiding principle is that people come by their beliefs honestly, so we want to come to understand how it makes complete sense that they came to think that way. This early emphasis on validation is also strategic in that it is relationship enhancing and can be regulating for the client. In our experience, people are more willing to have an open mind to alternatives when they feel like they are being truly and sincerely listened to.

The key competencies for this skill are as follows:

- The ability to attend to the emotional meaning of the thought and provide validation
- The ability to gather information about the context in which the thought developed
- The ability to inquire about the evidence that supports the thought
- The ability to conceptualize how believing this thought might shape behavior, and in turn how that might shape experiences

Step 3: Collaborative Curiosity

While this is functionally the disconfirming evidence step, curiosity is key to this process. In the seminal math logic book *How to Solve It*, Polya (1973) describes determining the unknown as a key problem-solving step. Once we can see from a client or supervisee's point of view, we can work to expand that view together. We ask ourselves: "What are they missing?" Functionally, there are two kinds of blind spots: things you don't see and things you don't know. The clinician/supervisor needs to determine what the client/supervisee is not attending to because of attentional filters as well as the gaps in their experiences that developed as a result of their avoidance pattern.

Many great questions and lines of inquiry are frequently found from evaluating elements contained in the previous steps. People often twist information to fit into their pre-existing assumptions and beliefs. Therefore, we frequently assist with their mentally taking a step back in order to examine the context as well as the big picture. We ask ourselves: "If the thought wasn't true, what would the indicators of that be, and can we search for that evidence?" Drawing on time orientation can be useful, such as by asking: "Has it always been this way?" or "Does it always have to be this way"?

The key competencies for this skill are as follows:

- The ability to restate the case for why the thought is true
- The ability to re-evaluate that case in objective terms
- The ability to look for missing context
- The ability to look for exceptions and overgeneralizations
- The ability to hypothesize what discrepant evidence might exist and how to find it
- The ability to design behavioral experiments to gather new evidence

Step 4: Summary and Synthesis

The summary and synthesis steps are important and easy for novice therapists to skip. New learning is made explicit in this step. Because we typically do not have the same schema and belief structures as our clients or supervisees, it is often easier for us to see a new perspective before they do. Also, the therapist can feel pulled to try and pick a purely positive thought because they might feel better. This is problematic because purely positive thoughts or thoughts that are only based on the disconfirming evidence can be brittle if they do not fit the reality of the client's life. Therefore, the focus should be the development of new thoughts that are balanced and adaptive. This process involves summarizing both sides of the story, and helping the client develop a new more balanced thought that captures both sides. It is important to assess whether the new thought is believable.

Once we have a summary statement, synthesizing it with their previous statements and assumptions is a crucial next step. This is accomplished by asking the clinician/supervisee: "How does the new conclusion compare to the initial assumption?" "And their underlying beliefs?" "How do they reconcile their previous assumptions and this new evidence?" Assistance with the solidification of these gains is important and can be realized by helping them translate the cognitive shift into behavior change. For instance, we ask them how they want to put the new thought into practice in the coming week or how they want to test it out in the coming week.

The key competencies for this skill are as follows:

- The ability to collaboratively summarize the entire dialogue
- The ability to aid the patient in drawing a balanced conclusion based on the summary statement
- The ability to collaboratively test the believability of the new conclusion
- The ability to collaboratively synthesize the new conclusion with the original statement
- The ability to collaboratively synthesize the new conclusion with the target underlying belief
- The ability to create a behavioral plan to put the new conclusion into practice

Competency-Based Assessment: Socratic Dialogue Rating Matrix

When we teach our trainees to effectively use Socratic strategies in supervision, we are hoping that they will learn to effectively make use of these strategies with their clients.

Table 15.1 Collaborative Empiricism Matrix

	Low Collaboration	**High Collaboration**
Low Empiricism	Low Collaborative Empiricism	Supportive Therapy
High Empiricism	Provided Discovery Disputing by labeling thinking as distorted or irrational	Collaborative Empiricism Jointly Discovering Fosters client motivation Brings about change

Based on Tee & Kazantzis (2011).

Therapist Name:	Rater Name:	
Session Being Rated:	Date of Rating:	
Instructions: *Review the Collaborative Empiricism Matrix then determine where the skills from the session being rated fit. Include a rationale for the rating and suggestions for skill development below your ratings.*		
Focusing	*Low Collaboration*	*High Collaboration*
Low Empiricism	Therapist did not focus on any single thought or belief to evaluate	Therapist and client discussed one topic client cared about without moving towards evaluation
High Empiricism	Therapist selected a thought to focus on based on their intuition or interpretation of the situation	Therapist and client cooperatively chose an optimal intervention target after weighing alternatives and creating a shared definition of the target
Determination:		
Notes:		
Understanding	*Low Collaboration*	*High Collaboration*
Low Empiricism	No efforts to understand how the target thought makes sense/ no validation	Providing validation and possibly erroneously validating the accuracy of the thought before it has been evaluated – tacit agreement
High Empiricism	Therapist attends to evidence supporting thought with an absence of emotional validation	Therapist provides emotional validation by exploring the context and evidence supporting the thought; balanced validation with Socratic ignorance
Determination:		
Notes:		
Curiosity	*Low Collaboration*	*High Collaboration*
Low Empiricism	No attempt to explore why thought might not be true	Warm exchange, focused on staying positive or offering unsubstantiated reframes
High Empiricism	Telling why the thought is not true. Focus on disputing and challenging thought – focus on cognitive distortions	Collaboratively re-examining the case for why the thought is true, evaluating discrepant evidence, and looking for missing evidence. Therapist must display sincere curiosity.
Determination:		
Notes:		
Summary & Synthesis	*Low Collaboration*	*High Collaboration*
Low Empiricism	No attempt to pull it all together	Asking for an alternative thought without summarizing evidence. Accepting an overly positive thought without testing the believability of the thought. Failing to recognize that a lack of disconfirmatory evidence might be due to behavioral avoidance.
High Empiricism	Telling the client what conclusions should be made	Cooperatively summarizing the dialogue. Helping the client draw a new conclusion based on that summary. Testing the believability of that conclusion. Reconciling that conclusion with the initial statement. Making plans to put the conclusion into action.
Determination:		
Notes:		
Overall Area of Strength:		
Overall Area to Improve:		
Main Feedback (be specific):		

Worksheet 15.1 Socratic Dialogue Rating Matrix

To help foster growth in Socratic strategies, we developed the Socratic Dialogue Rating Matrix to be used for training purposes. This scale can be used to rate a therapy session or roleplay on the use of collaborative empiricism across the four-component model of Socratic dialogue.

Summary

Socratic strategies are among the most difficult skills for trainees/supervisees to master (Waltman et al., 2017). In this chapter, we discussed strategies for optimizing training and supervision of individuals in the use of these strategies. The key elements included the frequent use of Socratic strategies on the part of the trainer/supervisor and the implementation of an instructional strategy based on Kolb's (1984) experiential learning model. Finally, we offered an assessment tool that trainers, supervisors and their students can use to rate their Socratic dialogue performance objectively.

References

Beck. J., Sarnat, J. E., & Barenstein, V. (2008). Psychotherapy-based approaches to supervision. In C. Falendar & E. Shafranske (Eds.), *Casebook for clinical supervision: A competency-based approach.* Washington, DC: American Psychological Association.

Bellack, A. S., Mueser, K. T., Gingerich, S., & Agresta, J. (2013). *Social skills training for schizophrenia: A step-by-step guide.* New York: Guilford Press.

Edmunds, J. M., Beidas, R. S., & Kendall, P. C. (2013). Dissemination and implementation of evidence-based practices: Training and consultation as implementation strategies. *Clinical Psychology: Science and Practice, 20*(2), 152–165.

Greenberger, D., & Padesky, C. A. (2015). *Mind over mood: Change how you feel by changing the way you think.* New York: Guilford Press.

James, I. A., Morse, R., & Howarth, A. (2010). The science and art of asking questions in cognitive therapy. *Behavioural and Cognitive Psychotherapy, 38*(1), 83–93.

Kolb, D. A. (1984). *Experiential learning: Experience as the source of learning and development.* Englewood Cliffs, NJ: Prentice-Hall.

Linehan, M. M. (1997). Validation and psychotherapy. Empathy reconsidered: New directions in psychotherapy. In A. C. Bohart & L. S. Greenberg (Eds.), *Empathy reconsidered: New directions in psychotherapy* (pp. 353–392). Washington, DC: American Psychological Association.

Padesky, C. A. (1996). Developing cognitive therapist competency: Teaching and supervision models. In P. Salkovskis (Ed.), *Frontiers of cognitive therapy* (pp 266–292). New York: Guilford Press.

Polya, G. (1973). *How to solve it* (2nd ed.). Princeton, NJ: Princeton University Press.

Sudak, D. M., & Codd III, R. T. (2019). Training evidence-based practitioners. In S. D. (Ed.), *Evidence-based practice in action: Bridging clinical science and intervention* (409–424). New York: Guilford Press.

Sudak, D. M., Codd, R. T., Ludgate, J. W., Sokol, L., Fox, M. G., Reiser, R. P., & Milne, D. L. (2016). *Teaching and supervising cognitive behavioral therapy.* Hoboken, NJ: Wiley.

Tee, J., & Kazantzis, N. (2011). Collaborative empiricism in cognitive therapy: A definition and theory for the relationship construct. *Clinical Psychology: Science and Practice, 18*(1), 47–61.
Waltman, S. H. (2016). Model-consistent CBT supervision: A case-study of a psychotherapy-based approach. *Journal of Cognitive Psychotherapy, 30*(2), 120–130.
Waltman, S. H., Hall, B. C., McFarr, L. M., Beck, A. T., & Creed, T. A. (2017). In-session stuck points and pitfalls of community clinicians learning CBT: Qualitative investigation. *Cognitive and Behavioral Practice, 24,* 256–267. doi:10.1016/j.cbpra.2016.04.002
Waltman, S. H., Hall, B. C., McFarr, L. M., & Creed, T. A. (2018). Clinical case consultation and experiential learning in CBT implementation: Brief qualitative investigation. *Journal of Cognitive Psychotherapy, 32*(2), 112–126.
Waltman, S., Naman, K., Morgan, W., Wickremasinghe, N., Nehme, J., & McFarr, L. (2014). *Learning to think like a cognitive behavioral therapist: The use of guided discovery in CBT supervision and fidelity of CBT in clinical practice.* Poster presented at the Cognitive Therapy SIG Happy Hour at the Annual Conference for the Association for Behavioral and Cognitive Therapies, Philadelphia, PA.
Wenzel, A. (2019). *Cognitive behavioral therapy for beginners: An experiential learning approach.* New York: Routledge.

Chapter 16

The Self-Socratic Method

Scott H. Waltman

❖ CONTENTS

Socrates used questioning and confrontation to help people arrive at what he regarded as universal truths. The basic process is a straightforward combination of analysis (breaking things down) and synthesis (putting things back together). This process allows for transformation, discovery, and cognitive change. In the cognitive and behavioral sciences, we work to use Socratic strategies to apply scientific principles to our thinking. This involves evaluating how we think and what we believe in order to see whether this is actually true and helpful. Often, the most painful beliefs that we have learned from various life lessons are a mixture of truth and assumption. These distortions of the truth can cause unnecessary suffering and cause us to behave in ways that are not helpful. Working with a therapist who is trained in Socratic methods can help to facilitate this process of change.

Our revised model for Socratic questioning consists of first *focusing* on the key beliefs to target. After a suitable or strategic target has been identified, we then work to develop an *understanding* of the thought. That is, to understand how it makes perfect sense that we came to think in this way. Once we have understood how we developed this point of view, we then work to expand that view through the process of *curiosity*. In order to create a new belief that is durable, we will use *summary and synthesis* strategies to reconcile our initial assumptions with the newly developed, more balanced perspective.

Focusing: What are we targeting? *What are the different parts of the problem?* *Which part is most upsetting?* *What's the meaning I'm attributing to this situation? / What am I telling myself?* *How are we defining our target?*
Understanding: How does it make sense that I think this? *Where did I learn this?* *Is this something people have told me before?* *What are the facts that tell me this is true?* *How does this thought make me behave?*
Curiosity: What are we missing? *Is there important context missing from the above statements?* *Do my behaviors influence my experiences?* *What do we not know?* *What are the facts that tell me this might not be true?* *Are there any exceptions we're forgetting about?*
Summary: How can we summarize the whole story? **Synthesis:** How does this summary fit with my original statement? *How does it fit with what I typically tell myself?* **Take-Away Message:** What's a more balanced and believable statement? How can I apply that statement to my upcoming week?

Figure 16.1 Socratic Thought Record

Step 1: Focusing

The first step in applying Socratic strategies is to identify the targets for these strategies. Some estimates suggest that humans have 10,000–15,000 different thoughts in any given day. In a practical sense, we simply do not have enough time to address every thought that we think might be distorted. We want to target the thoughts that are central to our problems and related to our core difficulties. Research has found that how we think affects how we feel and what we do, and so we can use our feelings and behaviors as signals for where the strategic points of intervention might be located.

First, you might want to ask yourself why you would want to learn this Self-Socratic Method. What are you hoping to accomplish? Are you trying to reduce feelings of depression or anxiety? Are you trying to change self-defeating thinking that prevents you from living the life you want to live? Are you trying to stop or reduce a behavior that does not serve you well? If you can figure out what it is that you want and what thoughts are getting in your way, you can target those thoughts to bring about strategic and transformative change in your life.

Everyone is different and so this process can require some reflection and sometimes the logging of your thought processes. There are common types of thoughts we see that relate to different emotional states. For example, people with depression tend to have negative beliefs about themselves, other people, and the future. These often have themes of hopelessness, futility, defectiveness, and self-defeating predictions (e.g., "Why bother—it won't work out anyway?"). People with depression are also prone to overgeneralizing, that is to say, seeing things that are partially bad as being completely bad. This is possibly due to phenomena such as mood-dependent memory, in which, when one is feeling depressed, it is harder to remember events associated with not being depressed—so the world will seem to be worse than it actually is.

Depression isn't the only emotional state that has its own set of typical thoughts and thinking processes. Anxiety often accompanies catastrophic thinking. That is to say, people see bad outcomes as being more likely to happen than they actually are. They also see these possible bad outcomes as being worse than they would actually be, and they see themselves as being less likely to be able to handle or cope with the adversity than they actually would be. So, people with anxiety often benefit from learning to make more accurate predictions about the possibility of something bad happening, the severity of that possibility, and their ability to endure difficult things.

Anger is a self-defense emotion. We tend to get angry when we perceive a threat, and so asking yourself what is so physically or emotionally dangerous about a situation can help you get an idea of what types of thoughts to evaluate. We also see anger deriving from perceptions of unfairness and assumptions that the world should be fair. This goes along with the idea of *shoulds* or *musts*—people often have unwritten rules and expectations for themselves, other people, and the world in general. You have ideas about how others should act, and we can get angry when we see people as not doing the things that we think they *should* be doing. "Shoulds" are tricky, because people often have good reasons for their shoulds being "right," but as we have all observed the world does not run on reason. Rigidly demanding that other people and the world follow our shoulds is a recipe for misery. Some people can benefit from evaluating their shoulds directly, while others prefer to evaluate whether holding to the "should" is beneficial.

Guilt and shame tend to go together. Guilt is feeling bad about your behavior: "I did something wrong." Shame is feeling like there is something wrong with you. Guilt is a judgement of the behavior and shame is a judgment of yourself. Shame tends to be toxic, and typically, we work with people to assess if the guilt or shame is warranted or helpful. Helpful focusing questions include: "Is what I did actually wrong?" "Are my feelings proportionate to the situation?" "Does this behavior define the totality of who I am and who I will always be?" "Can I make amends?"

Alternatively, you can track situations that bring up the emotion or behavior that we are targeting to identify suitable thoughts on which to focus. In these cases, you might want to ask yourself: "What was I thinking that led me to feel or act in that way?"

There are a number of questions people can ask themselves to facilitate this step, including:

- What is so upsetting or difficult about the situation?
- What is the most upsetting part?
- How are you making sense of it?
- How does this relate back to your underlying beliefs?
- What is the most distressing thought?
- Can we break that thought down into different components?
- What does that thought mean to you?

A useful strategy that Socrates would use in his Socratic method was to first look at how the main idea was being defined. Our distortions in thinking are often influenced by distortions in our expectations and assumptions. For example, if someone was evaluating worries that they have about whether they are a good parent, we would first look at whether their definition of a good parent is fair. It can be helpful to look at universal definitions or standards, as many of us are our harshest critics. So, what is a reasonable standard or definition that could apply to everyone? And, how do my thoughts and beliefs measure up against that universal standard?

Step 2: Understanding

This step can be thought of as a practice of self-validation. The task of this step is to understand yourself and the target thought. The guiding principle is that people come by their beliefs honestly and we want to come to understand how it makes complete sense that you came to think that way.

There are several questions people can ask themselves in order to guide this process:

- What experiences are this thought based on?
- What are the facts that support this?
- If this was true, what do you think would be the strongest evidence to support it?
- What are the reasons I think this is true?
- Is this something people have directly said to me in the past?
- How much do I believe this?
- How long have I believed this?

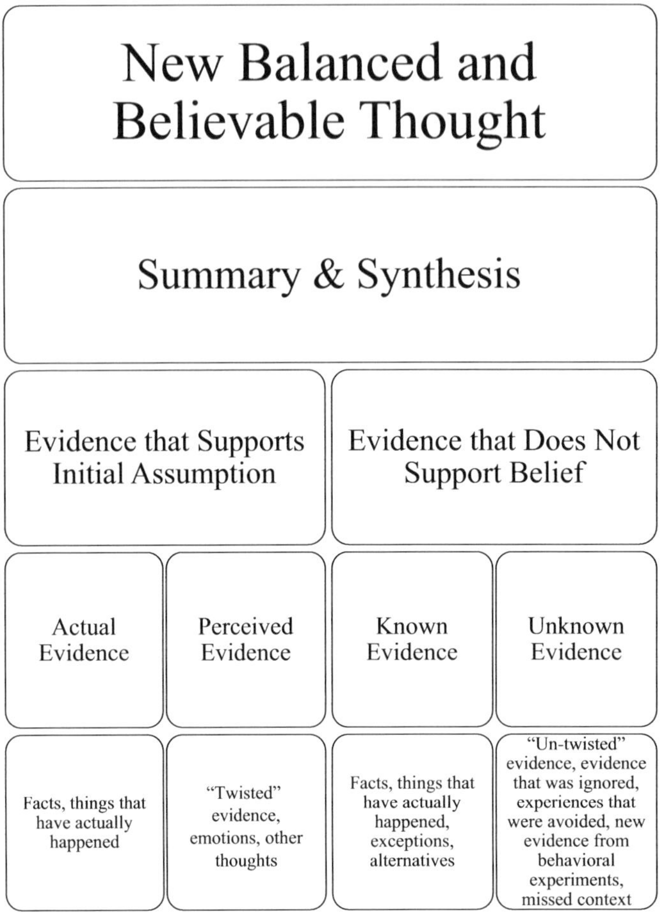

Figure 16.2 Overview of Self-Socratic Process

- When do I tend to believe this more and less?
- What do I typically do when thoughts like this come up for me?

Step 3: Curiosity

Now that we have a good understanding of why we believe the thought we are evaluating, we then want to expand that understanding with curiosity. Functionally, there are three types of evidence we want to look for and attend to as we seek to develop more balanced and helpful thinking: perceived evidence, known evidence, and unknown evidence.

Perceived Evidence is evidence that we have used to support our belief that might not actually support this thought. Sometimes, we use one thought as evidence to support another thought and we end up building a mental house of cards that we can

Table 16.1 Commonalities Across Distortions and Irrational Beliefs

Thought Processes	Descriptions
Errors in Prediction	Examples: Catastrophizing, Fortune-Telling or Impact Bias Description: Errors in prediction of outcomes that cannot be known or of an unlikelihood negative valence. Alternatively, this can manifest as seeing potential event as having an unrealistically large impact on one's life or the situation (i.e., seeing something as the solution all your problems or seeing something as the absolute worst thing that could happen).
Errors in Overgeneralizing	Examples: All-or-Nothing Thinking, Overgeneralizing, and Magnification (Minimizing) Description: Creating a false dichotomy and failing to attend to dimensional (continuum) elements of the appraisal. This can also be an error of permanence where something is seen as permanent or unchangeable when it is not.
Errors in Perceptions	Examples: Selective Abstraction, Negative Filter, Mind Reading, Emotional Reasoning, and Personalizing Description: Attentional filtering errors where people tend to emphasize or solely attend to information that is consistent with their expectations.
Illusions of Control	Examples: Magical Thinking, Illusion of Control, and Hindsight Bias Description: Illusions where an individual sees themselves as having power over things they do not, as having known things they could not have known, or other superstitious thinking.
Core Irrational Beliefs	Demandingness: Absolutistic musts; Demands of the universe and other people Awfulizing: Judging something as absolutely terrible or worse than bad. Frustration Intolerance: Refusal to tolerate distress and seeing self as being unable to tolerate distress Person Rating: Judging or labeling yourself or someone else in absolute terms

realize is flimsy reasoning if we take a closer look. Other times, we use our emotions as evidence—we call this emotional reasoning and it is a circular logic. For example, people should feel anxious in the presence of danger, but people with anxiety disorders tend to use the feeling of anxiety as evidence that something is unsafe. So, a first step in our Self-Socratic Method is to evaluate whether the evidence you are using to support your belief does, in fact, support your belief. Ask yourself, is this a fact? Is this a feeling? Is this an assumption? It might be that you need to break the situation down more and evaluate the different building blocks that are supporting the thought.

Some people find it is useful to evaluate their perceived evidence by looking to see if there are any distortions or pitfalls to their thinking. There are a number of different lists out there that people use to evaluate patterns of problematic thinking. People typically have a "go-to" distortion pattern into which they fall. For example, some people are given to catastrophizing patterns of thinking; whereas others are given to seeing things in terms of all-or-nothing, instead of seeing the nuance. If you can learn what your common thinking pattern is, you can learn to watch for it, and perhaps correct for it. Knowing that you are using a cognitive distortion, does not tell you what a more balanced perspective would be, but it can help you understand that perhaps the situation is not severe as it feels. By breaking the situation down with our Self-Socratic Method, you can come to take a perspective that is balanced and free from distorted thinking patterns.

Known Evidence is evidence we already know about that does not support the thought that we are evaluating. People tend to twist information to fit into their pre-existing assumptions and beliefs. So, we want to take a step back mentally to look at both the context and the big picture. We ask ourselves: "If the thought wasn't true, what would be the indicators of that, and can we look for that evidence?" We may need to draw on time orientation. "Has it always been this way?" "Does it always have to be this way?"

In the previous step, we asked ourselves, "What is the evidence that this thought is true?" In the current step, we are asking ourselves: "Is there any evidence that this thought is not true?" It can be helpful to remind ourselves that we are looking to develop a perspective of balanced truth, and so we want to be able to see both sides clearly. Question to ask ourselves include: "Are there times something different happened?" "Is it always this way?" "What am I missing?" A good strategy is to look from a different vantage point. We started out looking from the vantage point of the particular behavior or emotion we were seeking to address. If you can think of times when you are feeling better or acting better, and then look at the situation from those points of view, at this point we can ask ourselves: "What is the evidence against this thought that I'm evaluating?" or "What are the facts about the thought that I sometimes forget?" It can be helpful to list this evidence out.

Unknown Evidence is evidence that would pertain to our evaluation, but is out of our awareness or experience base. Conceptually, it can be useful to think about how our assumptions guide our predictions and behaviors, which in turn impacts what we do and what we experience. All of this can limit the evidence from which we have to draw in evaluating our belief. For example, if you have fears of being a failure, there are probably chances you have not taken for fear of failing. Consistently avoiding taking risks can limit the amount of success you have in your life, so when you start to evaluate whether or not you are a failure, you might find that you don't have as much to show for your life as you would have liked. You could erroneously conclude from this that you are a failure. Although scientific reasoning would dictate that you don't actually know what you are capable of, because the risk has been avoided. In these cases, you need to go out and experiment in life, and gather new evidence to form new beliefs. A therapist can be especially helpful in helping you design experiments where you get out of your comfort zone and enlarge your life. Key principles include incremental progress, setting yourself up for success, and reflecting on the successful aspects of your experiments so you can build on successes.

Step 4: Summary and Synthesis

The summary and synthesis steps are important and easy for people to skip. This is where we work to integrate new learning into our belief structures. There can be a pull for people to try to pick a purely positive thought because they might feel better.

The trouble with purely positive thoughts or thoughts that are only based on the disconfirming evidence is that they can be brittle if they do not fit the reality of the life. Therefore, we are aiming to develop new thoughts that are balanced and adaptive. This process involves summarizing both sides of the story and developing a new, more balanced thought that captures both sides. The question we want to ask is whether the new thought is believable. We also want to hold onto the notion that change in strongly held beliefs and assumptions can be an incremental process. Once we have a summary statement, we want to synthesize that with our previous statements and assumptions. How does the new conclusion compare to the initial assumption? And to our underlying beliefs? How do we reconcile our previous assumptions with this new evidence? We also want to solidify these gains by translating the cognitive shift into behavior change. So, we ask ourselves how we plan to put the new thought into practice in the coming week or how we want to test it out in the coming week.

There are a number of questions we can ask ourselves to help with this question:

- So how does this all fit together?
- Can we summarize all the facts?
- What is a summary statement that captures both sides?
- How much do they believe that?
- Do we need to shape this to make it more believable?
- How do they reconcile our new statement with the thought we were evaluating? Or with the core belief we are targeting?
- How should we apply our new statement to their upcoming week? How can we test this out?
- What did we learn about our thought processes from this exercise?

Conclusions

Meaningful cognitive change is often a process that takes time and effort. The Self-Socratic Method is a good place to start. Once you identify a new belief that you want to build up, the next step is to build up behaviors that would correspond with that belief. Practicing building up these behaviors and beliefs can make for meaningful changes in your life. Change is incremental and often there can be unexpected barriers that come up. A therapist can be useful in helping you overcome these barriers to make sustainable changes in your life.

Index

Note: Page numbers in *italic* denote figures and worksheets, those in **bold** denote tables.

Made in the USA
Columbia, SC
30 June 2025

d44fa9f8-0725-4ff5-92ca-790899e651a0R02